Thesis: pg 73, 74, 75, 79, 91

Engaged Scholarship

Ref: Pg 90

Interesting

Absurd

Irrelevant

~~Obvious~~

Obvious

mbfs - 89

Engaged Scholarship

A Guide for Organizational and Social Research

Andrew H. Van de Ven

OXFORD
UNIVERSITY PRESS

OXFORD

UNIVERSITY PRESS

Great Clarendon Street, Oxford OX2 6DP
United Kingdom

Oxford University Press is a department of the University of Oxford.
It furthers the University's objective of excellence in research, scholarship,
and education by publishing worldwide. Oxford is a registered trade mark of
Oxford University Press in the UK and in certain other countries

© Andrew H. Van de Ven 2007

The moral rights of the author have been asserted

Reprinted 2013

British Library Cataloguing in Publication Data
Data available

Library of Congress Cataloging in Publication Data
Data available

ISBN 978-0-19-922630-6

I am honored to dedicate this book
To my faculty mentor
who introduced me to engaged scholarship
by example and practice

Andre L. Delbecq
Santa Clara University

⬚ ACKNOWLEDGEMENTS

The author and the publishers wish to thank the following for permission to reproduce material.

Fig. 1.3 from Understanding Scientific Reasoning 4th Edition by Giere. 1997. Reprinted with permission of Wadsworth, a division of Thomson Learning: www.thomsonrights.com. Fax 800 730-2215.

Fig. 2.1 reprinted from *Minnesota Studies in the Philosophy of Science Volume IV: Analyses of Theories and Methods of Physics and Psychology*, edited by M. Radner and S. Winokur, published by the University of Minnesota Press. © 1970 by University of Minnesota.

Figs. 2.2 and 2.3 reprinted from *Variations in Organization Science*, edited by Joel A. C. Baum and Bill McKelvey, pp. 344–5, copyright 1999 by Sage Publications, Reprinted by Permission of Sage Publications Inc.

Fig. 3.1 reprinted from 'Heuristic Classification' by W. J. Clancey, in *Artificial Intelligence*, p. 296, Copyright 1985, with permission from Elsevier.

Fig. 3.2 reprinted from *Messing About in Problems* by C. Eden, S. Jones, and D. Sims, p. 42, Copyright 1983, with permission from Elsevier.

Fig. 4.5 reprinted from *The Social Psychology of Organizing*, 2e by Karl E. Weick, published by McGraw-Hill Publishing Co., with permission of The McGraw-Hill Companies.

Figs. 5.2 and 5.3, Howard Aldrich, *Journal of Management Inquiry* (June 2001), pp. 118–9, copyright 2001 SAGE Publications, Reprinted by Permission of SAGE Publications.

Fig. 5.4 reprinted from the *Academy of Management Review* (Copyright © 1999 The Academy of Management). Author: Ann Langley Article Title: Strategies for Theorizing from Process Data.

Fig. 6.4 Suchman, Edward. "Flow Chart." In *Evaluative Research: Principles and Practice in Public Service and Social Action Programs*. © Russel Sage Foundation, 112 East 64th Street, New York, NY 10021. Reprinted with permission.

Fig. 7.2 reprinted by permission, S. R. Barley, 'Images of imaging: Notes on doing longitudinal field work', *Organization Science*, volume 1, number 3, August 1990. Copyright 1990, the Institute for Operations Research and Management Sciences (INFORMS), 7240 Parkway Drive, Suite 310, Hanover, MD 21076 USA.

Fig. 8.3 reprinted by permission, P. R. Carlile, 'Transferring, translating, and transforming: An integrative framework for managing knowledge across boundaries', *Organization Science*, volume 15, number 5, October 2004. Copyright 2004, the Institute for Operations Research and Management Sciences (INFORMS), 7240 Parkway Drive, Suite 310, Hanover, MD 21076 USA.

Fig. 9.2 reprinted from the *Academy of Management Review* (Copyright © 1981 The Academy of Management). Authors: Roger Evered and Merly Reis Louis; Article title: Alternative perspectives in the organizational sciences: 'Inquiry from the inside' and 'Inquiry from the outside'.

⬜ CONTENTS

⬚ PREFACE

This book proposes a method of *engaged scholarship* for studying complex social problems that often exceed our limited individual capabilities to study on our own. *Engaged scholarship* is a participative form of research for obtaining the advice and perspectives of key stakeholders (researchers, users, clients, sponsors, and practitioners) to understand a complex social problem. By exploiting differences in the kinds of knowledge that scholars and other stakeholders can bring forth on a problem, I argue that engaged scholarship produces knowledge that is more penetrating and insightful than when scholars or practitioners work on the problems alone.

This book is written primarily for doctoral students and faculty who wish to know how to engage others to obtain a deeper understanding of their research problem and question. It provides a guide for involving stakeholders in each step of the research process: (1) ground the research problem and question being examined in the real world; (2) develop plausible alternative theories to address the research question; (3) design and conduct research to empirically evaluate the alternative models; and (4) apply the research findings to resolve the research question about the problem. These four inter-related steps are arranged in a diamond model that serves as the organizing framework for the book. Engaged scholarship can be practiced in many different forms, including basic social science with advice of key stakeholders, collaborative co-production of knowledge with stakeholders, design science to evaluate an applied program, and action research to intervene in the problem of a client.

Writing this book has been an engaging labor of love. It represents the culmination of efforts to learn the principles of engaged scholarship over the years with so many people and organizations that it is not possible to remember or recognize them all. It is a product of trial-and-error in attempting to practice engaged scholarship, to read the literature about it across diverse fields of social science, and to teach it in a PhD research methods course over the past thirty years.

Most of my learning experiences in engaged scholarship came from studying organization and management problems. Beginning in 1968 as an MBA student at the University of Wisconsin-Madison, I served as a research assistant on a NASA grant to study matrix organizations for a team of faculty consisting of Andre Delbecq, Alan Filley, Larry Cummings, Fremont Shull, and Andy Grimes. While the subject was interesting, I was fascinated by their engaging and creative discussions. Toward the end of the year Prof. Andre

Delbecq invited me to serve as his research assistant in the Institute for Research on Poverty. Through his example and practice, I gained my first field exposure to principles of engaged scholarship and it is to him that I dedicate this book.

I followed Andre to many neighborhood block meetings to identify the needs of low-income people, and of their reluctance to express their views particularly when city and county officials were present. While conducting these meetings, we also reviewed the literature on individual and group decision making, and experimented with various brainstorming methods that might give people equal opportunities to talk and listen to each other. Through these trial-and-error meetings we developed what became known as the Nominal Group Technique; which subsequently became the most widely used method of group brainstorming. I still recall the rewarding feeling of an elderly person telling us after one neighborhood block meeting that this was the first time in his life where he felt he could speak his mind. This engaged field research experience hooked me.

The stimulating challenges of addressing real problems and advancing new social scientific knowledge have continued to motivate me in subsequent studies throughout my career. During the 1970's they included a study of community organizing and inter-organizational relationships in creating early childhood programs in 14 Texas counties, and an organization assessment study of the designs and contexts of jobs, work groups, and organizations of job service and unemployment compensation programs located throughout Wisconsin and California. In the 1980s I coordinated the Minnesota Innovation Research Program that involved 30 researchers who tracked the development of 14 different innovations in real time from concept to implementation. Since 1994 I have been conducting a longitudinal field study of the processes of organizational change that are unfolding in Minnesota health care organizations and industry.

Each of these studies dealt with research problems and questions that were more complex and required more time than I anticipated and more competence than I had. Trained initially in traditional approaches to conducting social research, I tended to launch my field studies with a specific research question and some general concepts and propositions that were derived from the literature and discussions with others. But as field observations began, in each case I was humbled by the complexity of the research problem, and of the necessity to obtain the perspectives of other colleagues, practitioners, and students to better understand the problem. Involving others took more time and surfaced both consistent and conflicting information about a problem domain that were often difficult to reconcile. But the time and trouble of engaged scholarship paid off. Involving others forced me to alter my initial conceptions of the research problem and to modify the study in ways that I would not have done on my own. While frustrating at times, I can say in retrospect that some of my greatest insights and learning experiences came from engaging others in better understanding complex social problems and ways to study them. I draw upon these and other studies throughout the book to exemplify principles of engaged scholarship.

My initial effort in writing this book began about ten years ago by compiling detailed class notes for a PhD social research methods course that I teach about every year at the Carlson School. Since then, three additional versions of the book were drafted and used in this course. Each time I received rich and diverse feedback from the 15–20 PhD students and faculty taking the course from various social disciplines and professional schools at the University of Minnesota. I am also indebted for countless hallway discussions, brown bags, and meetings about the book with my Minnesota faculty colleagues, especially Professors Phillip Bromiley, John Dickhaut, Daniel Forbes, Paul Johnson, Arik Lifschitz, Alfred Marcus, Harry Sapienza, Roger Schroeder, Pri Shah, Myles Shaver, Kingshuk Sinha, Srilata and Aks Zaheer, Shaker Zahra, Mary Zellmer-Bruhn, and Minyuan Zhao.

Revisions were also significantly influenced by the literature on the philosophy and practice of social science. As discussed in Chapter 2, epistemology is a contested terrain among those adopting a positivist, relativist, realist, or pragmatic philosophy of science. I received wonderful guidance from my philosophy colleagues, Professors Norman Bowie and Ronald Giere, and the collaboration of a doctoral student, John Bechara, in navigating this contested terrain. I also gained a deeper appreciation of the philosophical underpinnings of engaged scholarship in discussions with Mary Jo Hatch, Matthew Kratz, Bill McKelvey, and Mayer Zald, as well as taking a PhD philosophy of science course taught by my marketing colleague, Prof. Akshay Rao.

A number of colleagues worldwide also used an earlier version of this book in research methodology courses they were teaching at their schools. They included Paul Adler (University of Southern California), Joe Banas (Washington University), Kevin Dooley (Arizona State University), Yves Doz (INSEAD), Sanjay Gosain (University of Maryland), Pertti Järvinen (University of Tampere, Finland), Seija Kulkki (Helsinki School of Economics), Tor Larsen (Norwegian School of Management), Darius Mahdjoubi (University of Texas), Michael O'Leary (Boston College), Johan Roos (Ecole Polytechnique, Lausanne), Majken Schultz (Copenhagen Business School), and Xi Zhu (East China University of Science and Technology). Their feedback and that of their students was most helpful in preparing the final draft.

While writing the book I received much helpful feedback from participants in many invited seminars and workshops conducted in the USA, Canada, Europe, Southeast Asia, and Mexico. I must also recognize a number of wonderful colleagues who carefully read and provided useful comments on chapters of the book. They include Jean Bartunek, Tom Cummings, Raghu Garud, Karen Golden-Biddle, Trisha Greenhalgh, Mary Jo Hatch, Anne Huff,

Gerard Hodgkinson, Ann Langley, Ed Lawler, Henry Mintzberg, Andrew Pettigrew, Scott Poole, Joe Porac, Georges Romme, Denise Rousseau, Sara Rynes, David Transfield, Michael Tushman, Joan van Aken, Connie Wanberg, Karl Weick, David Whetten, and Edward Zlotkowski. Their feedback was critical, constructive, and immensely helpful.

In the final analysis, my indebtedness to Julie Trupke, my assistant, rises to the top of the list. Her copy editing of each version of this book has been priceless!

In conclusion, I wish to express deep appreciation for support from two very special individuals who have tremendously influenced my scholarship. One individual is Mr. Vernon H. Heath, former founder and chairman of Rosemont Company. He is not only the benefactor of my endowed professorship that provides the resources supporting my work, but he has also exemplified principles of engaged management and empathy with his colleagues and employees throughout his career. The second individual is Mr. Herbert J. Addison, retired senior editor of Oxford University Press. He is my Dean of publishing editors. Through his wise and skilled editorial role, Herb has made significant contributions to advancing knowledge of organization and management. I was privileged to be guided and mentored by Herb in authoring and editing four previous books. I am delighted to continue this relationship in Herb's honor with Oxford University Press, and to be working with his gifted and wonderful colleagues, Senior Editor David Musson and his associate, Matthew Derbyshire.

Last, but certainly not least, I am indebted to my wife, Martha, and our sons, Jim and John, and daughter-in-law, Deborah. They have engaged me most in this undertaking, and made it an exciting, growing, and enjoyable experience. Thank you!!!

Andrew H. Van de Ven

Minneapolis, Minnesota

1 Engaged Scholarship in a Professional School

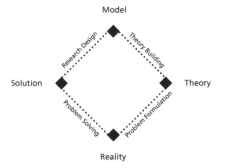

[Academics] appear to have entered a period of non-engagement, cherishing their autonomy over engagement and retreating into the ivory tower.

(Patrick Saveau quoted in Cushman 1999: 328)

Scholarship means something more than research, and engagement is the means for scholarship to flourish.

(Chapter 1, this volume, p. 9)

Understanding how research can advance scientific and practical knowledge is an ongoing challenge for scholars who work in professional schools, such as business, engineering, social work, medicine, agriculture, education, public administration, journalism, and law. A central mission of scholars in professional schools is to conduct research that both advances a scientific discipline and enlightens practice in a professional domain (Simon 1976). Professional schools typically build their raison d'être on the mission of conducting research knowledge that advances both science and practice (Simon 1976; Kondrat 1992; Tranfield and Starkey 1998). But this mission remains an elusive ideal.

Studies show that practitioners often fail to adopt the findings of research in fields such as medicine (Denis and Langley 2002; Dopson et al. 2002), human resources (Anderson et al. 2001; Rynes et al. 2002), social work (Kondrat 1992) and management (Tranfield et al. 2003; Rousseau 2006).

Many top journals[1] have highlighted growing concerns that academic research has become less useful for solving practical problems and that the gulf between science and practice in a profession such as management is widening. There are also growing criticisms that findings from academic as well as consulting studies are not useful to practitioners and do not get implemented (Beer 2001; Gibbons et al. 1994). Management scholars, for example, are being criticized for not adequately putting their abstract knowledge into practice (Beyer and Trice 1982; Lawler et al. 1985; Hodgkinson et al. 2001). Practicing managers, as well, are criticized for not being aware of relevant research and not doing enough to put their practice into theory (Weick 2001; Van de Ven 2002). As a result, organizations are not learning fast enough to keep up with the changing times.

Academic researchers sometimes respond to these criticisms by claiming that the purpose of their research is not to make immediate contributions to practice; instead it is to make fundamental advances to scientific knowledge that may eventually enlighten practice. However, there is evidence that academic research is also not adequately advancing scientific knowledge. One important indicator of the impact and use of published research by the scientific community is the number of times this research is cited as informing subsequent scientific articles. Based on his citation analysis, Starbuck (2005) reports that papers published in management journals were cited on average only .82 times per article per year. Hence, much current academic research is not contributing in intended ways to either science or practice.

Ways of Addressing the Theory–Practice Gap

This book focuses on the relationship between theory and practice primarily in organization and management studies, which is my field of study. I do not attempt a comprehensive review of the debate, either in general or with respect to the management and organization literature. Rather, I review three ways in which the gap between theory and practice has been framed (as discussed by Van de Ven and Johnson 2006), and then focus on one approach that motivates proposing a method of engaged scholarship. A perusal of literature and discussions with scholars in other professional domains suggest that the principles below for addressing the gap between theory and practice apply equally well in many other professional fields.

---

[1] The relationship between management science and practice has received much attention in special issues of the *Academy of Management Journal* (Rynes et al. 2001) and *Executive* (Bailey 2002), *Administrative Science Quarterly* (Hinings and Greenwood 2002), *British Journal of Management* (Hodgkinson 2001), and several other more specialized management journals.

A KNOWLEDGE TRANSFER PROBLEM

The limited use of research knowledge for science and practice is typically framed as a knowledge transfer problem. This approach assumes that practical knowledge (knowledge of how to do things) in many professional domains derives at least in part from scientific knowledge. Hence, the problem is one of translating and diffusing research knowledge into practice. I discuss this knowledge transfer problem in Chapter 8. Research knowledge is not often communicated in a form that facilitates its transfer, interpretation, and use by an audience as intended. I argue that a deeper understanding of communicating knowledge across boundaries and a more engaged relationship between the researcher and his/her audience are needed if research findings are to have an impact in advancing science and practice.

SCIENCE AND PRACTICE ARE DISTINCT FORMS OF KNOWLEDGE

A second approach to the theory–practice gap views scientific knowledge and practical knowledge as distinct kinds of knowing. Recognition that science and practice produce distinct forms of knowledge has been long-standing. It dates back to Aristotle, who in *The Nicomachean Ethics* (1955), distinguished between *techne* (applied technical knowledge of instrumental or mean–ends rationality), *episteme* (basic knowledge in the pursuit of theoretical or analytical questions), and *phronesis* (practical knowledge of how to act prudently and correctly in a given immediate and ambiguous social or political situation). More recently, Polanyi (1962), Habermas (1971), Latour (1986), and Nonaka (1994) have made further distinctions between explicit epistemic scientific knowledge and more tacit practical knowledge, which overlap Aristotle's techne and phronesis distinctions. Each reflects a different ontology (truth claim) and epistemology (method) for addressing different questions. To say that the knowledge of science and practice are different is not to say that they stand in opposition or they substitute for each other; rather, they complement one another.

In her review of the theory–practice gap in social work, Kondrat (1992) points out that what has been missing from the discussion are empirical studies of knowledge from practice. What knowledge does the practitioner of an occupation or profession use, and how does he/she obtain it? So also, Schon (1987) asks what does the competent practitioner know? and how does he/she go about knowing 'in' practice? Rather than regard practical knowledge as a derivative of scientific knowledge, these kinds of questions address the epistemological status of 'practical knowledge' as a distinct mode of knowing in its own right. 'When this status is granted, the practical takes its place alongside the scientific as constitutive elements of professional knowledge' (Kondrat 1992: 239).

Scholarly work and managerial work differ in context, process, and purpose. The context of the practitioner is situated in particular problems encountered in everyday activities (Hutchins 1983; Lave and Wenger 1994). As such, managers develop a deep understanding of the problems and tasks that arise in particular situations and of means–ends activities that comprise their solutions (Wallace, 1983). Knowledge of practice in a professional domain is typically customized, connected to experience, and directed to the structure and dynamics of particular situations (Aram and Salipante 2003: 190). In contrast, science is committed to building generalizations and theories that often take the form of formal logical principles or rules involving causal relationships. 'Scientific knowledge involves the quest for generality in the form of "covering" laws and principles that describe the fundamental nature of things. The more context free, the more general and stronger the theory' (Aram and Salipante 2003: 1900). The purpose of practical knowledge is knowing how to deal with the specific situations encountered in a particular case. The purpose of scientific knowledge is knowing how to see specific situations as instances of a more general case that can be used to explain how what is done works or can be understood.

We may have misunderstood the relationship between knowledge of science and practice, and this has contributed to our limited success in bridging these two forms of knowledge. Exhortations for academics to put their theories into practice and for managers to put their practices into theory may be misdirected because they assume that the relationship between knowledge of theory and knowledge of practice entails a literal transfer or translation of one into the other. Instead, I suggest taking a pluralist view of science and practice as representing distinct kinds of knowledge that can provide complementary insights for understanding reality.

Each kind of knowledge is developed and sustained by its own professional community, consisting of people who share a common body of specialized knowledge or expertise (Van Maanen and Barley 1986). Each community tends to be self-reinforcing and insular, and limited interactions occur between them (Zald 1995; Cook et al. 1999). Each form of knowledge is partial— 'A way of seeing is a way of not seeing' (Poggi 1965). Strengths of one form of knowledge tend to be weaknesses of another. Once different perspectives and kinds of knowledge are recognized as partial, incomplete, and involving inherent bias with respect to any complex problem, then it is easy to see the need for a pluralistic approach to knowledge co-production among scholars and practitioners. This leads to a third view of the theory–practice gap—namely, a knowledge production problem.

A KNOWLEDGE PRODUCTION PROBLEM

There is a growing recognition that the gap between theory and practice may be a knowledge production problem. In part this recognition is stimulated by critical assessments of the status and professional relevance of practice-based social science (Simon 1976; Whitley 1984, 2000; Starkey and Madan, 2001; Hinings and Greenwood 2002). Gibbons et al. (1994) and Huff (2000), among others, question the status quo mode of research typically practiced in business and professional schools.

This status quo approach to social research has many variations, but it tends to reflect an unengaged process of inquiry. Researchers typically go it alone to study a research question without communicating with or being informed by other stakeholders (scholars from different disciplines, practitioners with different functional experiences, and other potential users and sponsors) who can make important contributions to understanding the problem domain being investigated. This status quo form of unengaged research is evident in the following characteristics of a research report: (1) a research problem or question is posed but little or no evidence is presented that grounds the nature and prevalence of the problem, its boundary conditions, and why it merits investigation; (2) a single theoretical model is proposed with little consideration given of plausible alternative models for addressing the research problem or question; (3) the research design relies on statistically analyzing questionnaire or secondary data files (such as PIMs, patent data, Compustat, or census files) without the researcher talking to any informants or respondents in the field; and (4) results are presented on the statistical significance of relationships with little or no discussion of their practical significance and implications. Because such research is not grounded in 'reality,' does not entertain alternative models for representing reality, nor is it informed by key stakeholders, it often results in making trivial advancements to science, and contributes to widening the gap between theory and practice. Anderson et al. (2001) characterize this kind of unengaged scholarship as 'puerile science' that is often low in both relevance and rigor. As a consequence, it joins the large proportion of research papers that are not used to advance either science or practice.

Many suggestions have been made for revising and improving this status quo approach to social science research. Many of these suggestions are institutional in nature, such as modifying academic tenure and reward systems, funding criteria for competitive research grants, editorial policies and review procedures of academic journals, and creating additional outlets for transmitting academic findings to practitioners (Lawler et al. 1985; Dunnette 1990). Structural reforms such as these are important institutional arrangements that enable and constrain research. But discussions of structural reforms like this tend to overlook the choices and actions available to individual scholars undertaking research in a professional domain. In this book I focus on methods and strategies that have more immediate relevance to individual scholars engaged in the knowledge production process.

Engaged Scholarship

At the level of the individual researcher, Pettigrew formulates the problem this way:

If the duty of the intellectual in society is to make a difference, the management research community has a long way to go to realize its potential. . | . The action steps to resolve the old dichotomy of theory and practice were often portrayed with the minimalist request for management researchers to engage with practitioners through more accessible dissemination. But dissemination is too late if the wrong questions have been asked. (Pettigrew 2001: S61, S67)

He goes on to say that a deeper form of research that engages both academics and practitioners is needed to produce knowledge that meets the dual hurdles of relevance and rigor for theory as well as practice in a given domain (see also Hodgkinson et al. 2001).

Pettigrew sketches a vision that is not limited to business school research but reflects a much larger movement of engaged scholarship for transforming higher education (Zlotkowski 1997–2000). To Ernest Boyer (1990), a leading proponent of this movement, engaged scholarship consists of a set of reforms to break down the insular behaviors of academic departments and disciplines that have emerged over the years. Engaged scholarship implies a fundamental shift in how scholars define their relationships with the communities in which they are located, including faculty and students from various disciplines in the university and practitioners in relevant professional domains.

It's about faculty members having a profound respect for those other than themselves, whether they be practitioners or students. . . . There is a profound emphasis on the concept of deep respect and, I might even say, humility vis-à-vis other kinds of knowledge producers. Not because we don't have an important and distinctive role to play in knowledge production, but because we don't have the exclusive right to such production. As we begin to engage in partnerships with both our students and outside communities of practice on the basis of such deep respect, we allow ourselves to become real-world problem solvers in a way that is otherwise not possible. Indeed, I would suggest that unless we learn to develop deeper respect for our nonfaculty colleagues, we run the risk of becoming 'academic ventriloquists'—speaking for our students, speaking for the communities we allegedly serve—but not really listening to them or making them our peers in addressing the vital issues that concern all of us. (Edward Zlotkowski quoted in Kenworthy-U'ren 2005: 360)

Engagement is a relationship that involves negotiation and collaboration between researchers and practitioners in a learning community; such a community jointly produces knowledge that can both advance the scientific enterprise and enlighten a community of practitioners. Instead of viewing organizations and clients as data collection sites and funding sources, an engaged scholar views them as a learning workplace (idea factory) where practitioners and scholars co-produce knowledge on important questions and issues by testing alternative ideas and different views of a common problem. 'Abundant evidence shows that both the civic and academic health of any culture is vitally enriched as scholars and practitioners speak and listen carefully to each other' (Boyer 1996: 15).

Applying these notions of engaged scholarship to the full range of activities of faculty in universities, Boyer (1990) discussed the scholarship of *discovery, teaching, application,* and *integration.* These four dimensions interact to form a rich and unified definition of scholarship. Subsequently, Boyer (1996) further expanded his definition to include the *scholarship of engagement,* which emphasizes how academics relate their teaching, discovery, integration, and application activities with people and places outside the campus and ultimately direct the work of the academy 'toward larger, more humane ends' (Boyer 1996: 20).

For many American public universities, engaged scholarship represents a call to return to their charter mandate of a Land Grant University, as established by the Morrill Land Grant Act of 1862 (Schuh 1984). Three ideas of engagement were central to the founding ideals of a Land Grant University. First, it would provide upper-level education for the masses— a direct response at the time to the elitism and limited relevance of the private universities in the country. Second, the Land Grant University would generate new knowledge by addressing questions and problems of society. Although agriculture was dominant at the time, every area of activity was to be a legitimate subject of intellectual inquiry. Third, the Land Grant University would have a strong outreach mission, which is to provide intellectual leadership by applying the tools of science and technology to address the problems of society. These three ideas gave rise to the familiar tripartite mission of teaching, research, and service. As this brief history indicates, engaged scholarship represents a re-enactment of the founding values and roles of universities as institutions engaged in society and of individual scholars engaging students and community practitioners in their teaching, research, and service.

The engaged scholarship movement has proliferated into numerous university-based initiatives of community outreach, service-learning, clinical teaching, extension services, social emancipation causes, and community-based participatory research. As evident in a Google.com listing of 36,000 entries on 'engaged scholarship,' in November 2006, these initiatives are highly diverse and diffused. Service learning is perhaps the most widely diffused form of engaged teaching, due largely to efforts by national organizations and federal grants (such as Campus Compact, American Association for Higher Education, the National Community Service Trust Act of 1993, and others). Service learning is a credit-bearing educational experience in which students become involved in an organized service activity that augments understanding of topics covered in a university classroom with experiences as volunteers in local sites serving community needs, such as philanthropic agencies, primary and secondary schools, churches, old-age homes, half-way houses, etc. (Bringle and Harcher 1996; DiPadova-Stocks 2005). Professional schools tend to take less of a missionary and more of a training view of service learning through a wide variety of university–industry internships, mentorships, clinical research, and field study projects. An experiment conducted by Markus et al. (1993) found that students in service learning courses had more positive course evaluations, more positive beliefs and values toward service and community, and higher academic achievement. Bringle and Harcher (1996) review other research indicating that service learning has a positive impact on personal, attitudinal, moral, social, and cognitive outcomes for students.

Despite this diffusion and evidence, one of the major barriers to sustained faculty involvement in engaged scholarship is the risk associated with trying to achieve promotion and tenure. A number of national commissions and professions have begun to address these institutional barriers. For example, the 2006 report of the Commission on Community-Engaged Scholarship in the Health Professions focuses on recommendations for recruiting, retaining, and promoting community-engaged faculty members in health professional schools. In addition, the US Department of Education and the W. K. Kellogg Foundation co-sponsored the development of a Community-Engaged Scholarship Toolkit that guides faculty in preparing their career statements and records for faculty promotion and tenure in healthcare and other professional schools (Calleson et al. 2004).

This book applies the principles of engaged scholarship to social research, or what Boyer calls the *scholarship of discovery.*

No tenets in the academy are held in higher regard than the commitment to knowledge for its own sake, to freedom of inquiry and to following, in a disciplined fashion, an investigation wherever it may lead. The *scholarship of discovery,* at its best, contributes not only to the stock of human knowledge but also to the intellectual climate of a college or university. Not just the outcomes, but the process, and especially the passion, give meaning to the effort. The advancement of knowledge can generate an almost palpable excitement in the life of an educational institution. As William Bowen, former president of Princeton University, said, scholarly research 'reflects our pressing, irrepressible need as human beings to confront the unknown and to seek understanding for its own sake. It is tied inextricably to the freedom to think freshly, to see propositions of every kind in ever-changing light. And it celebrates the special exhilaration that comes from a new idea. (Boyer 1990: 17)

In addition to conveying this passion for knowledge discovery, the term *engaged scholarship* reflects an important identity. *Scholarship means something more than research, and engagement is the means for scholarship to flourish.* Boyer resurrected the honorable term *scholarship*, gave it a broader and more capacious meaning that conveyed legitimacy to the full scope of academic work. 'Surely, scholarship means engaging in original research. But the work of the scholar also means stepping back from one's investigation, looking for connections, building bridges between theory and practice, and communicating one's knowledge effectively' (Boyer 1990: 16).

Pettigrew (2005: 973) asks the question, 'How many of us see ourselves as intellectuals, scholars, and/or researchers?' He states:

> An intellectual is a person having a well-developed intellect and a taste for advanced knowledge, while a scholar is a person with great learning in a particular subject. And a researcher is a person who engages in careful study and investigation in order to discover new facts or information. Even from these rather limited definitions, the narrowness of the researcher identity and role becomes very evident.... Scholarship to me implies not just great breadth of learning and appreciation, but also the duty to make these available in dedicated learning, teaching, and professing. An intellectual would be capable of the appreciative system of a scholar but would be harnessing that competence to engage way beyond the boundaries of academic and into the wider reaches of society. I wonder how many of us have made explicit choices of engagement with one or other of the three identities/roles? (Pettigrew 2005: 973)

This poses the important question of how an engaged scholar might formulate a research study of a complex problem in the world that advances both theory and practice? To do this a mode of inquiry is needed that converts the information obtained by scholars in interaction with practitioners (and other stakeholders) into actions that address problems of what to do in a given professional domain. Many research questions and problems exceed the capabilities of individual researchers to study them alone. A methodology is needed that significantly expands researchers' capabilities to address such complex problems and questions.

I propose a method of engaged scholarship for expanding the capabilities of scholars to study complex problems and create the kind of knowledge that advances both science and practice. *Engaged scholarship* is defined as a participative form of research for obtaining the different perspectives of key stakeholders (researchers, users, clients, sponsors, and practitioners) in studying complex problems. By involving others and leveraging their different kinds of knowledge, engaged scholarship can produce knowledge that is more penetrating and insightful than when scholars or practitioners work on the problems alone.

ENGAGED SCHOLARSHIP RESEARCH MODEL

Past arguments for collaborative research have tended to be one-sided and focus on the relevance of academic research *for* practice. I focus more attention in this book on the question of how scholarship that is engaged *with* (rather than *for*) practice can advance basic scientific knowledge? Engaged scholarship emphasizes that research is not a solitary exercise; instead it is a collective achievement. Engagement means that scholars step outside of themselves to obtain and be informed by the interpretations of others in performing each step of the research process: problem formulation, theory building, research design, and problem solving.

Using a diamond model as illustrated in Figure 1.1, I propose that scholars can significantly increase the likelihood of advancing fundamental knowledge of a complex phenomenon by engaging others whose perspectives are relevant in each of these study activities:

- *Problem formulation*—situate, ground, diagnose, and infer the research problem by determining who, what, where, when, why, and how the problem exists up close and from afar. As discussed in Chapter 3, answering these journalist's questions requires meeting and talking with people who experience and know the problem, as well as reviewing the literature on the prevalence and boundary conditions of the problem.
- *Theory building*—create, elaborate, and justify a theory by abductive, deductive, and inductive reasoning (as discussed in Chapter 4). Developing

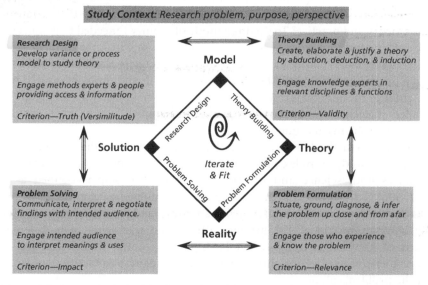

Figure 1.1. Engaged scholarship diamond model

this theory and its plausible alternatives requires conversations with knowledge experts from the relevant disciplines and functions that have addressed the problem, as well as a review of relevant literature.

- *Research design*—develop a variance or process model for empirically examining the alternative theories. As noted in Chapters 5–7, doing this well typically requires getting advice from technical experts in research methodology and the people who can provide access to data, and of course, the respondents or informants of information.
- *Problem solving*—communicate, interpret, and apply the empirical findings on which alternative models better answer the research question about the problem. Chapter 8 argues that increases in the difference, dependence, and novelty of knowledge between people at a boundary require more engaged forms of communication, starting with written reports and presentations for knowledge transfer, then conversations to interpret different meanings of the report, and then pragmatic and political negotiations to reconcile conflicting interests.

These activities can be performed in any sequence. I discuss these research activities in a problem solving sequence beginning with problem formulation, then searching for theories relevant to the problem, testing them, and applying the findings. There are many other possible starting points and sequences. For example, some scholars may start with a theory and then search for a problematic situation that may be appropriate for applying and evaluating the theory. Other scholars may be methodologically inclined, and interested in finding problems and developing theories with their methodological tools (as was the case in early developments of social network analysis). Still others may begin with a solution or program that requires evaluation research in order to determine the particular kinds of problems and context for which it may be appropriate.

These different starting motivations and orientations quickly meld together in the course of a study because the four activities are highly interdependent and are seldom completed in one pass. Multiple iterations and revisions of these research activities are often needed throughout the duration of a study. In the process, many sub-problems emerge in performing each research activity, and all remain simultaneously active and need to be addressed as an interdependent set. It is only when the process is complete that a fairly coherent pattern emerges as reflected in Figure 1.1.

Maintaining balance in performing these tasks repetitively is important. Given finite resources for conducting a study, I recommend that scholars allocate their time and efforts about equally to problem exploration, theory building, research design and conduct, and problem solving activities. Spending too much time or effort on only one or two research activities often results in unbalanced or lop-sided results where some activities are 'over-engineered' while others are incomplete.

This suggestion of paying equal attention to all four research activities is not evident in many research methodology texts in the social sciences. They tend to focus on research design, and pay relatively little attention to the processes of problem formulation, theory building, and problem solving. In addition, while these texts provide good technical treatments of research designs and data analysis, they largely ignore social processes of engaging stakeholders in problem formulation, theory building, research design, and problem solving (as illustrated in Figure 1.1). Social research is an intensely social process. Throughout the book I emphasize that all four research activities are equally important in conducting a study, and that each activity entails a different set of tasks that can be accomplished better by engaging relevant stakeholders rather than going it alone.

The essential steps in performing the four activities of the diamond model are illustrated in Figure 1.1. They can be evaluated in terms of five criteria: relevance, validity, truth, impact, and coherence.[2] The problem should be grounded in a reality that is relevant to an intended research audience in the scholarly and professional communities. The theoretical model should be expressed clearly, it should consist of a logically valid argument. The design and conduct of the research should apply the standards and methods that a scientific community believes will produce a truthful solution. The findings of the research should have an impact in advancing science and enlightening practice in a profession. In addition to relevance, validity, truth, and impact, a fifth criterion—coherence—is equally important for evaluating the engaged scholarship process.

In the PhD seminar I teach on engaged scholarship, the major assignment is for students to develop a good research proposal.[3] A good research proposal is defined as one that adequately describes each of the research activities in terms of the criteria presented in Table 1.1. Students submit different parts of the proposal every few weeks of the semester. As an instructor, I provide students feedback on their in-progress proposals, and they revise their research proposals several times until it is judged to be acceptable. Thus, through several iterations of revising-and-extending their proposals, students develop a research proposal, which they submit for funding and implement either as a research project or as an initial draft of their dissertation proposal.

---

[2] Scholars from different philosophical persuasions often associate different meanings with these criteria. My interpretations of these criteria should become clear in subsequent chapters devoted to each of the research activities in the engaged scholarship model.

[3] The most recent version of this course can be accessed by following the link on *MGMT 8101, Theory Building and Research Design* from my faculty web page at the Carlson School of Management, University of Minnesota (available at: (http://umn.edu/~avandeve). This course web page provides a wealth of additional information, resources, and links that supplement the topics and issues discussed in this book.

Table 1.1. Criteria for evaluating a research proposal

1. Statement of the research problem: _____
   - is situated in terms of perspective, focus, level, and scope;
   - problem symptoms or elements are clearly defined & grounded in reality;
   - a diagnosis is made that analyzes patterns or relationships among elements;
   - based on the diagnosis, an inference (a claim with reasons) is made for the problem.

2. The research question: _____
   - is stated in analytical and researchable terms;
   - permits more than one plausible answer.

3. The research proposition (theory): _____
   - clearly states an expected relationship among concepts or events;
   - is supported with an argument (i.e., claim, reasons, evidence, assumptions, & reservations);
   - directly addresses the research question and problem;
   - is compared with a plausible alternative theory or the status quo answer;
   - travels across levels of abstraction.

4. The research design clearly spells out: _____
   - theoretical unit of analysis and unit of observation;
   - case/survey/experimental design for variance or process theory;
   - sample or replication logic and sample selection;
   - definitions and measurement procedures for variables or events;
   - threats to internal, statistical, external, & construct validities.

5. Research implementation and problem solving for theory and practice: _____
   - the contributions/implications of the research for science *and* practice are clearly stated;
   - methods for communicating and sharing findings with target audiences/users are discussed;
   - statement of how research findings will be used/applied is prudent;
   - relevant stakeholders are engaged in each of the above steps.

Comments: Total Score: _____

Note: Please evaluate this report by using this five-point scale:
1 = not addressed or evident in the report
2 = attempt made but some errors occurred in the analysis/answer.
3 = attempt made but the result needs more work, elaboration, or refinement.
4 = attempt made with good result; issue accomplished; no further work needed.
5 = attempt made with excellent result; issue accomplished with distinction.

Engaged scholarship can be practiced in many different ways for addressing a variety of basic and applied research questions. For example, researchers might engage stakeholders in a study in order to: (1) obtain their perspectives and advice on a basic research question; (2) collaborate and co-produce knowledge; (3) design and evaluate a policy or program; or (4) intervene and implement a change to solve a client's problem. As these alternatives suggest, principles of engaged scholarship apply to many forms of basic or applied social research. They are discussed later in this chapter.

The four research activities in the engaged scholarship model illustrated in Figure 1.1 serve as the organizing framework of this book. Following an overview of the philosophy of science underlying this model of engaged scholarship, I discuss each of the four research activities in the engaged scholarship model. I also indicate how subsequent chapters treat detailed steps and procedures entailed in each research activity.

PHILOSOPHY OF SCIENCE UNDERLYING ENGAGED SCHOLARSHIP

Underlying any form of research is a philosophy of science that informs a scholar's approach to the nature of the phenomenon examined (ontology) and methods for understanding it (epistemology). Philosophers have debated these issues endlessly, and constructed a variety of philosophies for conducting research. Practitioners of science, in turn, are influencing how these philosophies are developed and expressed in their research. Chapter 2 attempts to provide a synthesis of this reciprocal relationship between the philosophy and practice of science with a historical review of four philosophies of science—positivism, relativism, pragmatism, and realism. It provides a discussion of how key ideas from each philosophy inform engaged scholarship, and how the practice of engaged scholarship might influence these philosophies of science.

Since the demise of the received view of positivism and logical empiricism in the philosophy of science, it is now widely recognized that scientific knowledge cannot be known to be true in an absolute sense (Suppe 1977: 649). Rather, from a critical realist perspective that I adopt, there is a real world out there, but our attempts to understand it are severely limited and can only be approximated. This perspective argues that all facts, observations, and data are theory-laden and embedded in language. Moreover, most phenomena in the social world are too rich to be understood adequately by any single person or perspective. Consequently, any given theoretical model is a partial representation of a complex phenomenon that reflects the perspective of the model builder. No form of inquiry is value-free and impartial; instead each model and perspective is value-full. This requires scholars to be far more reflexive and transparent about their roles, interests, and perspectives when conducting a study than they have in the past. For example, instead of assuming an authoritative and objective 'God's Eye view' of social phenomena, I follow Henrickx (1999) in proposing that engaged scholars adopt a participant frame of reference to learn about and understand a subject through discourse with other stakeholders.

Critical realism views science as a process of constructing models that represent or map intended aspects of the world, and comparing them with rival plausible alternative models (Rescher 2000). For example, Giere (1999: 77) states,

Imagine the universe as having a definite structure, but exceedingly complex, so complex that no models humans can devise could ever capture more than limited aspects of the total complexity. Nevertheless, some ways of constructing models of the world do provide resources for capturing some aspects of the world more or less well than others.

Research knowledge of a complex phenomenon advances by comparing the relative contributions of different models. Azevedo (1997) discusses how the coordination of multiple models and perspectives may reveal the robust features of reality by identifying those features that appear invariant (or convergent) across at least two (and preferably more) independent theories. From her perspective, a pluralist approach of comparing multiple plausible models of reality is essential for developing reliable scientific knowledge.

But the engagement of different stakeholders in a study often produces inconsistent and contradictory perspectives of a problem domain being examined. Pluralistic perspectives should not be dismissed as noise, error, or outliers—as they are typically treated in a triangulation research strategy. Chapter 9 discusses how these different outcomes require an expansion of traditional explanations of triangulation that focus on convergent central tendencies to include explanations based on inconsistent findings through arbitrage and contradictory findings with methods for reasoning through paradoxical findings.

It is often easier to construct meaningful explanations in cases where the evidence is convergent. For example, Azevedo (1997) advocates the use of multiple models for mapping a problem being investigated, and argues that knowledge that is reliable is invariant (or converges) across these models. Convergent explanations rely on similarities, consensus, and central tendencies in explaining a problem or issue under investigation. Convergent explanations tend to treat differences and inconsistencies as bias, errors, outliers, or noise.

More difficult (but often more insightful) explanations emerge when different data sources yield inconsistent or contradictory information about a phenomenon. Arbitrage provides a strategy for developing holistic, integrative explanations based on different accounts of the same phenomenon. Friedman (2000: 24) points out that in academe and elsewhere, 'there is a deeply ingrained tendency to think in terms of highly segmented, narrow areas of expertise, which ignores the fact that the real world is not divided up into such neat little bits.' He argues that the way to see, understand, and explain complex problems in the world is to systematically connect the different dots, bits, and pieces of information through arbitrage—'assigning different weights to different perspectives at different times in different situations, but always understanding that it is the interaction of all of them together that is really the defining feature of the [system]' (Friedman 2000: 23–4). Arbitrage is a strategy of explaining differences by seeing the interdependencies and webs of entanglements between different and divergent dimensions of a problem, its boundaries, and context.

Finally, contradictory information from different sources may represent instances of conflicting values and interests among pluralistic stakeholders about the problem or issue being examined. Explanations of a problem domain should obviously reflect these contradictions when observed. In Chapters 8 and 9, I discuss four general methods for reasoning through paradoxes by either: balancing between opposites, shifting levels of analysis, alternating positions over time, and introducing new concepts that dissolve the paradox. Inconsistent and contradictory findings are important, for they represent anomalies that trigger theory creation.

Campbell's (1988: 389) evolutionary perspective of science provides a possible avenue for addressing the simultaneous need to establish valid and reliable representations of a problem domain being examined. He argues that the models that better fit the problems they were intended to solve are selected, and the gradual winnowing down of plausible rival models or hypotheses by the scholarly community produces an evolutionary conception of the growth of scientific knowledge. This evolutionary perspective is based on a pragmatic philosophy of science. Among the plausible alternative models competing to explain a given phenomenon, the model that wins out at a particular moment in time is the one that is judged to best represent the phenomenon. Fortunately, only a finite set of three to five plausible models tend to compete for selection at a given time, as indicated by Collins's (1998) historical review of competing models for explaining a phenomenon.

Explanations based on arbitrage and paradoxical reasoning represent dialectical methods of inquiry where understanding and synthesis of a complex problem evolve from the confrontation of divergent thesis and antithesis. Dialectical reasoning is not a strategy for addressing narrow technical problems where one looks for expert judgments to converge on a correct answer. Instead, it is a strategy for triangulating on complex real-world problems by involving individuals whose perspectives are far from the average (Mitroff and Linstone 1993: 69). In a complex world, different perspectives make different sorts of information accessible. By exploiting multiple perspectives, the robust features of reality become salient and can be distinguished from those features that are merely a function of one particular viewpoint or conceptual model.

Thus, engaged scholarship is essentially a pluralistic methodology. Azevedo (2002) points out that communication across perspectives is a precondition for establishing robust alternative models of a problem. She adds,

Individual theories are not considered true or false. Rather their validity is a function not only of how well they model the aspect of the world in question but of how connected they are, in terms of consistency and coherence, with the greater body of scientific knowledge. These connections can be established a number of ways...but communication across perspectives and willingness to work toward establishing coherence is a precondition. (Azevedo 2002: 730)

Pluralism consists of not only multiple perspectives, but also a degree of openness and equality among them for addressing complex social phenomena. Participants often experience conflict and interpersonal tensions associated with juxtaposing people with different views and approaches to a problem. Managing conflict constructively is not only important but lies at the heart of engaged scholarship. Attempting to avoid tensions between scholars and practitioners, as we have in the past, is a mistake, for it blinds us to very real opportunities that are possible from exploiting the differences underlying these tensions in understanding complex phenomena.

PROBLEM FORMULATION

Problem formulation consists of situating, grounding, and diagnosing a research problem or issue in reality. Of course, different observers will see different 'realities.' In Chapter 3 I take a critical realist perspective and argue that there is a real world out there, but our representation and understanding of it is a social construction; reality does not exist independently of the observer's schemata or conceptual frame of reference (Weick 1989). As a consequence, the formulation of a research problem involves a complex sensemaking process of applying various conceptual templates or theories to determine what to look for in the real world and how to unscramble empirical materials into a recognizable and meaningful research problem.

Problem formulation plays a crucial role in conducting research and potentially affects succeeding phases, including theory building, research design and conduct, and conclusions. Yet problem formulation is often rushed or taken for granted. People tend to be solution-minded, rather than problem-minded. When problem formulation is rushed or taken for granted, in all likelihood important dimensions of the problem go undetected and opportunities are missed (Volkema 1995).

Social science today suffers from elaborating theories that are often based on insufficient grounding in concrete particulars. It also suffers from a lack of relevance as perceived by the intended audiences or users of the research (Beer 2001; Rynes et al. 2001). As a consequence, theories tend to be grounded in myths and superstitions. Those who generalize from experience can answer the questions, 'For example? From whose point of view? What is the point of view?' Lacking answers to these questions often leads to unfounded generalizations. In crime investigation, establishing the case is mandatory for pursuing it. Merton (1987: 21) cautioned that an important first element in the practice of science is *'establishing the phenomenon.'* Evidence and argument should clearly indicate that it is enough of a regularity to require and allow explanation. In this way 'pseudofacts that induce pseudoproblems are avoided' (Hernes 1989: 125).

Grounding the problem or phenomenon in reality is a crucial step in any research study. You might ask, what kind of research problems require engagement of others? I argue that the more complex the problem or the bigger the research question, the greater the level of engagement is required of researchers from different disciplines and practitioners with different functional experiences. Engagement of others is necessary because most real-world problems are too complex to be captured by any one investigator or perspective. Caswill and Shove (2000b: 222) point out that there are many significant questions and problems whose formulation and theoretical development depend on engagement and close interaction between scholars and practitioners.

Big questions have no easy answers, and they seldom provide an immediate pay-off to practitioners or academics (Pettigrew 2001). By definition, big questions often do not have clear solutions until after the research has been conducted and policy questions have been addressed. Big questions also require a process of arbitrage in which researchers and practitioners engage each other to co-produce solutions whose demands exceed the capabilities of either researchers or practitioners (Hodgkinson et al. 2001). Thus, at the time of designing a research project prospective solutions to research questions are secondary in comparison with the importance of the research question that is being addressed. A good indicator of a big question is its self-evident capability to motivate the attention and enthusiasm of scholars and practitioners alike. Indeed, as Caswill and Shove (2000b: 221) state, practitioners are 'often more attracted by new ideas and concepts than by empirical materials.'

Critics have argued that practitioner involvement in formulating research questions may steer the questions in narrow, short-term, or particularistic directions (Brief and Dukerich 1991; Grey 2001; Kilduff and Kelemen 2001). Ironically, this argument seems to assume that academics know better how to formulate researchable questions than practitioners, but when interacting with practitioners, researchers may behave as 'servants of power' (Brief 2000) by cowering to the interests of powerful stakeholders. Like Anderson et al. (2001), I view an engaged scholar as being more humble and also standing in a more egalitarian relationship with practitioners and other stakeholders when trying to understand an important question or phenomenon that requires research. Big research questions tend to reside in a buzzing, blooming, confusing world. Learning about the nature of the question or phenomenon in such ambiguous settings is facilitated by obtaining the divergent perspectives of numerous stakeholders. Heedful accommodation and integration of diverse viewpoints yields a richer gestalt of the question being investigated than the sensemaking of a single stakeholder (Morgan 1983; Weick 1995).

Caswill and Shove (2000a, 2002b) critique the assumption that the advancement of theory requires academic detachment, and that collaborative research merely implements and exploits, but does not advance, social theory.

The trouble is that arguments about independence and interaction, and about theory and application are readily and sometimes deliberately confused. In everyday discussion, it is sometimes asserted, and often implied, that interaction outside the academy is so demanding of time and mental energy that it leaves no room for creative thought. In addition, when distance is equated with purity, and when authority and expertise is exclusively associated with analytic abstraction, it is easy (but wrong) to leap to the conclusion that calls for interaction threaten academic inquiry. (Caswill and Shove 2000b: 221)

Indeed, the belief that interactions between people with different views and approaches advances academic (and practical) inquiry lies at the heart of engaged scholarship.

THEORY BUILDING

Theory building involves the creation, elaboration, and justification of a body of knowledge that is relevant to the research problem. A theory is the mental image or conceptual framework that is brought to bear on the research problem. Theories exist at various levels of abstraction for representing knowledge. A formal classification of the structure of knowledge is the Dewey indexing system found in all libraries. It classifies all knowledge into ten categories with ten subcategories, another ten sub-subcategories, and so on. This classification system packages knowledge by disciplines, paradigms, schools of thought, and theories on various subjects. You may not like such a formal hierarchical structure of knowledge, but you need to know it if you hope to find a book in the library.

This nested hierarchical structure not only indexes bodies of knowledge, it also structures our views of reality by specifying what problems and what aspects of problems are relevant and not relevant. Selecting and building a theory is perhaps the most strategic choice that is made in conducting a study. It significantly influences the research questions to ask, what concepts and events to look for, and what kind of propositions or predictions might be considered in addressing these questions. Because a theory is so influential in directing (or tunneling) a research study, Chapter 4 examines the activities and patterns of reasoning involved in theory building, and the importance of engaging others in the process of theorizing.

Different and opposing views are often expressed about theory building. They range from those who emphasize theory creation and argue that trivial theories are often produced by hemmed-in methodological strictures that favor validation rather than imagination (Weick 1989; Mintzberg 2005), to those who focus on elaborating and justifying a theory by calling for clear definitions, internal logical consistency, and verifiability (Bacharach 1989; Peli and Masuch 1997; Wacker 2004). In part these writers are right in describing one theory building activity, but wrong in ignoring other activities involved in theory building. Many of these oppositions dissolve when theory building is viewed not as a single activity, but as entailing at least three activities—creating, constructing, and justifying a theory.

Chapter 4 discusses how these three activities entail different patterns of reasoning: (1) the creative germ of a promising (but often half-baked) conjecture is typically created through a process of abductive reasoning to resolve an anomaly observed in the world; (2) then a theory is constructed to elaborate the conjecture by using basic principles of logical deductive reasoning to define terms, specify relationships, and conditions when they apply; and (3) if the merits of the theory are to be convincing to others, the theory is justified by crafting persuasive arguments and using inductive reasoning to empirically evaluate a model of the theory in comparison with rival plausible alternative models. In other words, theory creation involves an abductive process of 'disciplined imagination' (Weick 1989), theory construction entails logical deductive reasoning, and theory justification requires inductive reasoning and argumentation. Hence, theorizing entails different patterns of reasoning, and much can be learned about the scientific enterprise by understanding the complementary relations among these different patterns of reasoning.

A key recommendation discussed in Chapter 4 is to develop alternative theories and methods to study a problem. Multiple frames of reference are needed to understand complex reality. As mentioned before, engaged scholarship is a pluralistic methodology. Any given theory is an incomplete abstraction that cannot describe all aspects of a phenomenon. Theories are fallible human constructions that model a partial aspect of reality from a particular point of view and with particular interests in mind. Comparing and contrasting plausible alternative models that reflect different perspectives are essential for discriminating between error, noise, and different dimensions of a complex problem being investigated. Allison (1971) provides a good example of triangulating on the Cuban Missile Crisis with three models—a rational actor, organization behavior, and a political model. Each model is a conceptual lens that "leads one to see, emphasize, and worry about different aspects of an event" (Allison 1971: 5). Combined, complementary models provide richer insights and explanations of a phenomenon that would otherwise remain neglected.

The choice of models and methods varies, of course, with the particular problem and purpose of a study. The more complex the problem or question the greater the need to map this complexity by employing multiple and divergent models. Triangulation of methods and models increases reliability and validity. It also maximizes learning among members of an engaged scholarship team. Presumably different models reflect the unique hunches and interests of different participants in the research project. Sharing approaches and findings enhance learning among co-investigators. Each strategy represents a different thought trial to frame and map the subject matter. As Weick (1989) argues, undertaking multiple independent thought trials facilitates good theory building.

The typical strategy in social science research is to use a single theory to examine a given phenomenon. I argue that you have much greater likelihood of making important knowledge advances to theory and practice if the study is designed so that it juxtaposes and compares competing plausible explanations of the phenomenon being investigated (Kaplan 1964; Stinchcombe 1968a; Singleton and Straits 1999; Poole et al. 2000). Stinchcombe (1968a), for example, advises researchers to develop 'crucial' propositions that 'carve at the joints' (as Plato described) of positions by juxtaposing or comparing competing answers. Examining plausible alternatives promotes a critical research attitude. It also leverages knowledge differences by examining the extent to which evidence for competing alternative models compares with status quo explanations. Knowledge of many topics has advanced beyond the customary practice of rejecting a null hypothesis when a statistical relationship is different from zero. Such a finding is a cheap triumph when previous research has already shown this to be the case. More significant knowledge is produced when rival plausible hypotheses are examined. Such studies are likely to add significant value to theory and practice. Testing rival plausible hypotheses also provides the insurance of a win–win outcome for investigators—no matter what research results are obtained, if properly executed it can make an important contribution.

RESEARCH DESIGN

Building plausible theories that address the research question and problem typically sets the stage for designing operational models to empirically examine key aspects of the theories. Research design activities include developing specific hypotheses and empirical observation procedures (based on the theoretical model) that predict what data should be obtained if the model provides a good fit to the real world. A theory is typically not open to direct inspection, while a model makes operational some specific predictions of a theory, which can be subjected to empirical inspection. The theory and the hypothesis are related by reasoning or calculation, while the real world and the data are related by a physical interaction that involves observation or experimentation. As Giere states,

it is understood that the model fits only in some respects and then only to some specified degree of accuracy. . . . If what is going on in the real world, including the experimental setup, is similar in structure to the model of the world, then the data and the prediction should *agree*. That is, the actual data should be described by the prediction. On the other hand, if the real world and the model are not similar in the relevant respects, then the data and the prediction may *disagree*. (Giere 1997: 30)

This process can be generalized when comparing alternative predictions or hypotheses from plausible alternative models. Empirical evidence can be obtained on alternative predictions and compared to determine which empirically-based prediction offers the better or stronger explanation. When data evaluating the hypotheses from one model offer worse explanations than hypotheses from other models, then presumably the former model is abandoned in favor of the latter models.

A wide variety of research designs can be employed to gather empirical evidence for evaluating the predictions or hypotheses from different models. Research methodology texts typically divide and discuss these research designs in terms of experiments (e.g., Kirk 1995), quasi-experiments (Shadish et al. 2002), comparative case studies (Yin 2003), and various qualitative research methods (Denzin and Lincoln 1994; Miles and Huberman 1994). Before delving into the operational details of these research designs in Chapters 6 and 7, Chapter 5 provides an overview of two basic approaches that are often undertaken to examine process versus variance models. These two models capture basic distinctions between research studies undertaken to investigate either: (1) variance or causal questions of 'what causes what'; or (2) process questions of 'how things develop and change over time.'

Mohr (1982) first distinguished variance and process models in an explanation of organizational behavior. In developing a formalism for the representation of social action, Abell (1987) contrasted variance and narrative approaches, while Abbott (1984, 1990) compared stochastic and narrative explanations in sociology. The common thread running through these works is the difference between scientific explanations cast in terms of statistical associations between independent and dependent variables versus explanations that tell a narrative or story about how a sequence of events unfolds over time to produce a given outcome. Chapter 5 discusses these divergent explanations between variance and narrative explanations. They constitute fundamentally different research approaches for examining variance theories that make causal predictions among variables, as distinct from process theories that examine progressions in the temporal development of how events unfold in a social entity, be it an individual, group, organization, or larger community.

An example from the study of organizational change may be useful to clarify these distinctions between variance theories and process theories. Van de Ven and Huber (1990) point out that studies of organizational change tend to focus on two kinds of questions:

- What are the antecedents or consequences of the change?
- How does a change process emerge, develop, grow or terminate over time?

The 'What' question usually entails a variance theory explanation of the input factors (independent variables) that statistically explain variations in some outcome criteria (dependent variables). The 'How' question requires a process theory explanation of the temporal order and sequence in which a discrete set of events occurred based on a story or historical narrative (Abbott 1988). In terms of causality, the 'What' question requires evidence of co-variation, temporal precedence, and absence of spurious associations between the independent and dependent variables. The 'How' question explains an observed sequence of events in terms of some underlying generative mechanisms that have the power to cause events to happen in the real world and the particular circumstances or contingencies when these mechanisms operate (Tsoukas 1989).

A researcher adopting a variance model is inclined to decompose organizational processes into a series of input–output analyses by viewing each event as a change in a variable (e.g., the number of product innovations), and then examining if changes in this variable are statistically associated with some other independent variable (e.g., R&D investment). From a variance theory perspective, events represent changes in the states of a variable, and these changes are the building blocks of variations among variables in an input–process–output model. But since the process question is not whether, but *how*, a change occurred, one needs to narrate a story of the sequence of events that unfolded as the product innovation emerged. Once the sequence or pattern of events in a developmental process is found, then one can turn to questions about the causes or consequences of the event sequence.

Having distinguished the two questions, it is important to appreciate their complementary relationship. An answer to the 'What' question typically assumes or hypothesizes an answer to the 'How' question. Whether implicit or explicit, the logic underlying an answer to a variance theory is a process story about how a sequence of events unfold to cause an independent (input) variable to exert its influence on a dependent (outcome) variable. For example, to say that R&D investment causes organizational innovativeness is to make important assumptions about the order and sequence in which R&D investment and innovation events unfold in an organization. Thus, one way to significantly improve the robustness of answers to the first (variance theory) question is to explicitly examine the process that is assumed to explain why an independent variable causes a dependent variable.

By the same token, answers to 'How' questions tend to be meaningless without an answer to the corresponding variance theory questions. As Pettigrew (1990) argues, theoretically sound and practically useful research on change should explore the contexts, content, and process of change through time. Just as change is only perceptible relative to a state of constancy, an appreciation of a temporal sequence of events requires understanding the starting (input) conditions and ending (outcome) results.

Given the different but complementary epistemologies of variance and process theories discussed in Chapter 5, I delve into detailed considerations for designing variance and process studies in Chapters 6 and 7. Chapter 6 focuses on experimental, quasi-experimental, and survey designs for empirically evaluating causal models in variance research. Chapter 7 discusses methods for designing and conducting longitudinal cases, historical, and field studies to examine processes of how phenomena develop and change over time.

You might question if this 'theory testing' approach admits to a more exploratory 'grounded theory building approach' to research? My response is that the difference between these two modes of inquiry is a matter of timing and sequence in performing the theory building and research design activities of the diamond model. In exploratory studies, propositions typically develop after data are collected and analyzed. Thus, I recommend that the methods discussed in Chapter 4 for developing theories be applied after or while the data are being collected and analyzed. However, as discussed in Chapter 2, all data, facts, and observations are laden with theories that are tacit or explicit in the minds of the investigators. Any observations presuppose a selective frame of reference of a chosen object and concepts. Before collecting data, the focus of an exploratory study can be significantly clarified by meeting with key study stakeholders to discuss and explain what concepts might be used to observe the phenomenon.

Most studies, of course, include elements of both theory building and theory testing. Numerous iterations in running the paths of the diamond model are typically required in conducting any research project. Seldom, if ever, can a researcher complete a study by running the paths in one linear sequence; much back-tracking and jumping from one base to another is the typical process sequence.

USING RESEARCH FOR PROBLEM SOLVING

The problem solving activity of the engaged scholarship process focuses on linking the research findings back to the problem observed in the practitioner and the scientific communities. Generally, this involves executing the research design to produce empirical evidence for a solution to the research problem and question that initially motivated the research. At a minimum, a research solution entails a report of research findings and a discussion of their implications for theory and practice. Many researchers consider their communication task completed when they publish their report in a scientific journal and make verbal presentations of it at professional conferences as well as to host organizations and practitioners who sponsored the research.

This practice assumes that communicating research findings entails a one-way transfer of knowledge and information from the researcher to an audience. The underlying assumption of this view is that if an idea is good enough, it will be used. But research knowledge based on sound empirical evidence is often not used or adopted as intended by either scientists or practitioners. I argue that a deeper understanding of communicating knowledge across boundaries and a more engaged relationship between the researcher and his/ her audience are needed if research findings are to have an impact in advancing science and practice.

It is one thing to write a research paper, and quite another to transfer, interpret, and implement study findings at the communication boundaries of both scientific and practitioner communities. Estabrooks (1999: 15) points out that 'Many factors get in the way of using research, and empirically, we know very little about what makes research use happen or not happen.' Recently, scholars have begun to reconceptualize knowledge transfer as a learning process in which new knowledge is shaped by the learner's pre-existing knowledge and experience. Individuals are not simply sponges, soaking up new information without filtering or processing. 'Knowledge use is a complex change process in which "getting the research out there" is only the first step' (Nutley et al. 2003: 132). Neither scientists nor practitioners simply apply scientific research, but collaborate in discussions and engage in practices that actively interpret its value to accomplish their tasks.

I anchor Chapter 8 in Carlile's (2004) framework of knowledge transfer, translation, and transformation. It provides useful insights into how researchers might communicate their study findings at the knowledge boundaries with different audiences. The framework emphasizes that communication across boundaries requires common knowledge among people to understand each other's domain-specific knowledge. When the difference, dependence, and novelty of domain-specific knowledge between people at a boundary increase, then progressively more complex processes of knowledge transfer, translation, and transformation are needed to communicate the meanings and potential uses of that knowledge.

When the people at a knowledge boundary share the same common lexicon and syntax for understanding their different and interdependent domain-specific knowledge, then it can be communicated using a conventional information processing view of knowledge transfer from a speaker to listeners through written and verbal reports. The major challenge of knowledge transfer is to craft a sufficiently rich message and medium to convey the novelty of the information from the speaker to the audience. For example, written reports, verbal presentations, and face-to-face interactions between the speaker and listeners represent three increasingly rich media for knowledge transfer. In addition, logos, pathos, and ethos represent three increasingly rich dimensions of a message.

Knowledge transfer, however, even when communicated in the richness of a rhetorical triangle, typically remains a one-way transmission of information from a sender to a receiver. The listener in knowledge transfer remains relatively silent, but is never inactive. Authors of research reports will not

LOGOS
PATHOS
ETHOS

know this unless they engage in conversations with readers or listeners of a report. Then it becomes clear that listeners often have different interpretations and meanings of the novel information than the speaker intended. A research report is not treated as a social fact or as having a 'fixed' meaning. Rather, it is open to multiple and unlimited meanings, interpretations, and actions among participants (speakers and listeners) engaged in the text. Hence, when communicating research findings, a research report should be viewed as a first—not the last—step for researchers to engage in conversations with potential users, and thereby gain a broader and deeper appreciation of the meanings of research findings.

When interpretive differences exist in the meanings of research findings, then a more complex communication boundary of 'knowledge translation' must be crossed. At this boundary, speakers and listeners engage in conversations and discourse to mutually share, interpret, and construct their meanings of research findings. Speakers and listeners become co-authors in mutually constructing and making sense of their interactions. At the knowledge translation boundary, conversation is the essence and the product of research. Engaging in conversation and discourse with an audience requires researchers to adopt a hermeneutic 'participant view' rather than a 'God's Eye view' of research findings.

Communicating across knowledge transfer and translation boundaries may surface conflicting interests among parties that entails an even more complex political boundary where participants negotiate and pragmatically transform their knowledge and interests from their own to a collective domain. As Carlile (2004) states, 'When different interests arise, developing an adequate common knowledge is a political process of negotiating and defining common interests.'

Finally, seldom can knowledge transfer, translation, and transformation be accomplished with only one communication among people across boundaries. Numerous interactions are required to share and interpret knowledge, create new meanings, and negotiate divergent interests. The engaged scholarship process provides a strategy to approximate this by repeated engagements of stakeholders in each activity of the research process: problem formulation, theory building, research design, and problem solving.

FORMS OF ENGAGED SCHOLARSHIP

Engaged scholarship can be practiced in many different ways and for many different purposes. Figure 1.2 illustrates four different forms of engaged scholarship. As discussed in Chapter 9, these different forms of engaged scholarship depend on: (1) whether the purpose of a research study is to examine basic questions of description, explanation, and prediction or on

Research Question/Purpose

	To Describe/Explain	To Design/Control
Extension Detached Outside	Basic Science with Stakeholder Advice 1	Policy/Design Science Evaluation Research for Professional Practice 3
Intension Attached Inside	2 Co-Produce Knowledge with Collaborators	4 Action/Intervention Research for a Client

Research Perspective

Figure 1.2. Alternative forms of engaged scholarship

applied questions of design, evaluation, or action intervention, and (2) the degree to which a researcher examines the problem domain as an external observer or an internal participant.

1. *Informed basic research* is undertaken to describe, explain, or predict a social phenomenon. It resembles a traditional form of basic social science where the researcher is a detached outsider of the social system being examined, but solicits advice and feedback from key stakeholders and inside informants on each of the research activities as listed in Figure 1.1. These inside informants and stakeholders play an advisory role, and the researcher directs and controls all research activities.

2. *Collaborative basic research* entails a greater sharing of power and activities among researchers and stakeholders than informed research. Collaborative research teams are often composed of insiders and outsiders who jointly share the activities listed in Figure 1.1 in order to co-produce basic knowledge about a complex problem or phenomenon. The division of labor is typically negotiated to take advantage of the complementary skills of different research team members, and the balance of power or responsibility shifts back and forth as the tasks demand. Because this collaborative form of research tends to focus on basic questions of mutual interest to the partners, it has much less of an applied orientation than the next two forms of engaged scholarship.

3. *Design and evaluation research* is undertaken to examine normative questions dealing with the design and evaluation of policies, programs, or models for solving practical problems of a profession in question. Variously called 'design or policy science' or 'evaluation research,' this form of research goes beyond describing or explaining a social problem, but also seeks to obtain evidence-based knowledge of the efficacy or relative success of

NORMATIVE –

[handwritten margin notes: COMPARE CSR versus B or Benefit; Basis for CAC; Consulting]

alternative solutions to applied problems. Evaluation researchers typically take a distanced and outside perspective of the designs or policies being evaluated. Inquiry from the outside is necessary because evidence-based evaluations require comparisons of numerous cases, and because distance from any one case is required for evaluation findings to be viewed as impartial and legitimate. But engagement of stakeholders is important so they have opportunities to influence and consent to those evaluation study decisions that may affect them. In terms of the engaged scholarship model, these decisions include the purposes of the evaluation study (problem formulation), the criteria and models used to evaluate the program in question (research design), and how study findings will be analyzed, interpreted, and used (problem solving).

4. *Action/intervention research* takes a clinical intervention approach to diagnose and treat a problem of a specific client. Kurt Lewin, a pioneer of action research, suggested a learning strategy of both engaging with and intervening in the client's social setting. The foundation of this learning process was client participation in problem solving using systematic methods of data collection, feedback, reflection, and action. Since Lewin's time, action research has evolved into a diverse family of clinical research strategies in many professional fields. Action research projects tend to begin by diagnosing the particular problem or needs of an individual client. To the extent possible, a researcher utilizes whatever knowledge is available from basic or design science to understand the client's problem. However, this knowledge may not apply or may require substantial adaptation to fit the ill-structured or context-specific nature of the client's problem. Action research projects often consist of N-of-1 studies, where systematic comparative evidence can only be gained through trial-and-error experiments over time. In this situation action researchers have argued that the only way to understand a social system is to change it through deliberate intervention and diagnosis of responses to the intervention. This interventionist approach typically requires intensive interaction, training, and consulting by the researcher with people in the client's setting.

Sometimes advocates of a particular form of research make disparaging remarks about other forms. This is unfortunate because all four forms of engaged scholarship are legitimate, important, and necessary for addressing different research questions (description, explanation, design, or control of a problematic situation). Which is most appropriate depends on the research question and the perspective taken to examine the question. Pragmatically, the effectiveness of a research approach should be judged in terms of how well it addresses the research question for which it was intended (Dewey 1938).

Although the four forms of engaged scholarship entail different kinds of relationships between the researcher and stakeholders in a study, engagement is the common denominator. The more ambiguous and complex the problem, the greater the need for engaging others who can provide different perspectives for revealing critical dimensions of the nature, context, and implications of the problem domain.

CAVEATS OF ENGAGED SCHOLARSHIP

Several caveats of engagement should be recognized. As discussed in Chapter 9, the practice of engaged scholarship raises a number of issues that are often not salient in traditional approaches to social research. They include: (1) the challenges of engagement; (2) being reflexive about the researcher's role in a study; (3) establishing and building relationships with stakeholders; and (4) spending time in field research sites. Engagement does not necessarily imply that a researcher loses control of his/her study, but it does entail greater accountability to the stakeholders involved in a study. Engagement often raises false expectations that concerns expressed will be addressed. Engagement does not require consensus among stakeholders; much learning occurs through arbitrage by leveraging differences among stakeholders. Negotiating different and sometimes conflicting interests imply that creative conflict management skills are critical for engaged scholars. Without these skills, engagement may produce the ancient Tower of Babel, where intentions to build a tower to reach heaven were thwarted by the noisy and confusing language of the people.

Engaging stakeholders (other researchers, practitioners, sponsors, users, or clients) in problem formulation, theory building, research design, and problem solving represents a more challenging way to conduct social research than the traditional approach of researchers going it alone. But throughout this book I argue that the benefits exceed the costs. By involving stakeholders in key steps of the research process, engaged scholarship provides a deeper understanding of the problem investigated than is obtained by traditional detached research. My argument assumes, of course, that the primary motivation of engaged scholars for undertaking research is to understand this complex world, rather than to get published and promoted. The latter is a by-product of the former.

Discussion

This chapter introduced a research process model of engaged scholarship that serves as the organizing framework for this book. This model incorporates a contemporary philosophy of science and a set of methods for undertaking research with the aim of advancing knowledge in both a scientific discipline and in the practice of a profession. I argued that a research project involves four activities:

1. Problem formulation—ground the research problem and question in the real world;
2. Theory building—develop or select a conceptual model that addresses the problem as it exists in its particular context;
3. Research design and conduct—gather empirical evidence to compare plausible alternative models that address the research question; and
4. Problem solving—communicate and apply the research findings to solve the research question about the problem existing in reality.

Subsequent chapters discuss ways to perform each of these activities in this process model of engaged scholarship. Scholars can cover the four bases of the diamond model in any order they like. But all the bases must be covered to complete a research project.

This engaged scholarship diamond model incorporates to a wide variety of research methods including: basic or applied; theory building or theory testing; variance or process theory; cross-sectional or longitudinal; quantitative or qualitative; and laboratory, simulation, survey, archival, or other observation methods. Depending on the problem or question being investigated, engaged scholarship may involve any of these different categories of research. While engaged scholarship entertains a wide variety of research methods, it directs the research process by specifying the core set of activities of a research project that need to be performed from start to finish. Because the core activities of problem formulation, theory building, research design, and problem solving are highly interdependent, so also are the methods that are selected for doing these activities. Thus, the critical task is to adopt and execute the research models and methods that fit the chosen research problem or question being addressed.

ALTERNATIVE RESEARCH MODELS

A basic proposition of the ES model is to compare and contrast a proposed model with plausible alternative models. To 'walk this talk,' I compare the engaged scholarship model with two other plausible alternative models for conducting social research: a general systems model of problem solving by David Deutsch (1997) and a model of the scientific episode by Ronald Giere (1999).

Deutsch's Problem Solving Model

Several scholars have observed that science can be seen as a problem solving activity (Campbell 1988; Azevedo 1997, 2002; Deutsch 1997). For example, David Deutsch, a quantum physicist at the University of Oxford, describes science in terms of five problem solving stages: (1) the *problem*; (2) a *proposed model* or conjectured solution; (3) *criticism* with experimentation; (4) a *solution* of replacing erroneous theories; and (5) a *new problem* that recycles the process. Deutsch (1997: 62) explains the problem solving stages as beginning when a problem surfaces. A problem starts when a theory is not adequate and a new theory is needed. It is defined not only as an emergency or the root of anxiety, but is more when ideas are not adequate and there may be a better explanation (Deutsch 1997). In other words and as discussed in Chapter 3, research often begins with an anomaly requiring abductive reasoning because the current explanation or theory may be too narrow or not broad enough to explain the anomaly.

Following the discovery of a problem (stage 1), the next stage is *conjecture*. This is 'where new or modified theories are proposed in the hope of solving the problem (stage 2). The conjectures are then *criticized . . .* using scientific methods of experimental testing. This entails examining and comparing them to see what offers the best explanation, according to the criteria inherent in the problem (stage 3)' (Deutsch 1997: 64). A conjectured theory is not adopted when it seems to provide explanations worse than other theories. But, if one of the principle theories is abandoned for a new one (stage 4), then the problem solving exercise is deemed a 'tentative' success. Deutsch says the success is tentative since later problem solving may involve replacing or changing these new theories and in some cases even going back to and revising the ideas that were deemed unsatisfactory. Deutsch states, 'the solution, however good, is not the end of the story: it is a starting point for the next problem solving process (stage 5)' (Deutsch 1997: 64).

Deutsch points out that the objective of science is not to find a theory that is deemed true forever; it is to find the best theory currently available. A scientific argument is intended to persuade us that a given explanation is the best one available. It cannot say anything about how that solution will fare in the future when it is subjected to a new type of criticism and compared with explanations that have yet to be invented. Deutsch says (1997: 64–5), 'A good explanation may make good predictions about the future, but the one thing that no explanation can even begin to predict is the content or quality of its own future rivals.'

As with the engaged scholarship model, Deutsch points out that the stages of specific problem solving are seldom completed in sequence at the first attempt. There is usually repeated backtracking before each stage is completed. Only when the process is finished does a coherent pattern emerge that reflects the five linear stages of problem solving.

While a problem is still in the process of being solved we are dealing with a large heterogeneous set of ideas, theories, and criteria, with many variants of each, all competing for survival. There is a continual turnover of theories as they are altered or replaced by new ones. So all the theories are being subjected to *variation* and *selection*. (Deustch 1997: 68)

Deutsch cites Popper for this evolutionary epistemology. However, he cautions not to overstate the similarities between scientific discovery and biological evolution, for there are important differences. One difference is that biological variations (mutations) are random, blind, and purposeless. In human problem solving, the creation of models or theories is itself a complex, knowledge-laden process driven by human intentions. Perhaps an even more important difference is that there is no biological equivalent of *logical reasoning* and *argument.* The stronger the arguments for problems and theories, the more influential or persuasive they are. Science, like problem solving, justifies an explanation as being better than another currently available explanation.

Giere's Model of a Scientific Episode

Ronald Giere, a philosopher of science at the University of Minnesota, has been influential in introducing a pragmatic realist epistemology of science. This view downplays the idea that there might be universal natural laws encoded in true general statements. Rather, scientists are seen as engaged in constructing models that represent or fit the world in relatively better or worse ways. It is a kind of realism regarding the application of models to the real world, but it is a realism that is perspectival rather than objective or metaphysical (Giere 1999: 60–1). Giere states,

My account of scientific epistemology pits one model, or family of models, against rival models, with no presumption that the whole set of models considered exhausts the logical possibilities. This means that what models are taken best to represent the world at any given time depends on what rival models were considered along the way. And this seems, historically, a contingent matter. So the models of the world held at any given time might have been different if historical contingencies had been different. (Giere 1999: 77)

Based on this perspectival realist epistemology, Giere (1997) proposed a model of the scientific episode (or research project) consisting of four components: (1) a *real-world* object or problem under investigation; (2) a theoretical *model* of the real-world object or process; (3) some operational hypotheses or *predictions* derived from the model including a research design of what the data should be like if the model really does match with the real world; and (4) some *data* (or solutions) that are obtained by observation or experimentation with the real world (Giere 1997). Giere arranges these components as shown in Figure 1.3, which correspond closely to the four research activities in the engaged scholarship diamond model. The figure illustrates four important relations.

1. The relationship between the real world and the model is expressed by a conceptual proposition or analogy asserting that the model fits the real-world problem or phenomenon being examined. It is understood that the

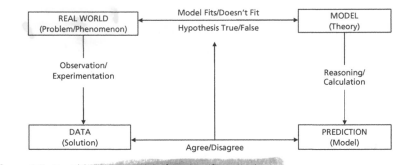

Figure 1.3. Ronald Giere's model of a scientific episode

Note: The activities of ES diamond model inserted into Giere's (1997: 30) figure of the four elements of a scientific episode.

model fits only in some respects and then only to some specified degree of accuracy. If the model does not fit accurately in the intended respects, then the theoretical model is false.

2. The model and the prediction (what we call theory) are related by *reasoning or argumentation.* The real world and the data are related by a *physical interaction* that involves observation or experimentation. 'If what is going on in the real world, including the experimental setup (our research design), is similar in structure to the model of the world then the data (solution) and the prediction or theoretical hypothesis should *agree.* That is, the actual data should be described by the prediction. On the other hand, if the real world and the model are not similar in the relevant respects, then the data and the prediction may *disagree*' (Giere 1997: 30).

3. The top half of the Figure 1.3 pictures the relationship between the real world and the model in question. Are the model and the real world similar in the respects under study and to an appropriate degree of accuracy? This relationship is typically not open to direction inspection. The bottom part of the figure, by contrast, pictures a relationship that can be evaluated by relatively direct inspection. Scientists can examine the data and see whether they agree with the predictions derived from the operational theory or model.

4. The left side of the figure illustrates relationships existing between the problem or phenomenon and data obtained from the real-world observations. The data are generated through physical interactions with bits of the real world. The right side of the figure between model and theory, by contrast, consists of conceptual relationships that are mainly symbolic. The model exists mainly as a description of a possible type of object.

Like the four bases of the engaged scholarship model and Deutsch's stages of problem solving, Giere's figure illustrates a fully developed scientific episode containing all four components of a research project arranged to make possible an evaluation of how well a model fits the real world. Giere points out that many scientific reports do not include all four components, and many do not unfold in the deductive, model-testing manner as outlined here.

It is common for example, to find reports that describe only the part of the real world under investigation together with some new data. There may be no mention of models or predictions. Similarly, we often find discussions of new models of real-world entities or processes with no mention of data or predictions. Occasionally we find accounts of models of real-world things that include predictions but no discussion of data. We can learn a lot from such reports. Unless all four components are present, however, there may be nothing we can subject to an independent evaluation. (Giere 1997: 31)

Conclusion

You may wonder if engaged scholars in professional schools should conduct more applied and less basic research? The answer depends on the research question and perspective taken to study a problem domain. As Figure 1.2 illustrates, engaged scholarship can be practiced to study a variety of basic and applied questions. Engaged scholarship represents a strategy for surpassing the dual hurdles of relevance and rigor in the conduct of fundamental research on complex problems in the world. By exploiting differences in the kinds of knowledge that scholars and practitioners from diverse backgrounds can bring forth on a problem, engaged scholarship produces knowledge that is more penetrating and insightful than when scholars or practitioners work on the problem alone. More specifically, the quality as well as the impact of research can improve substantially when researchers do four things: (1) confront questions and anomalies arising in practice; (2) organize the research project as a collaborative learning community of scholars and practitioners with diverse perspectives; (3) conduct research that systematically examines alternative models pertaining to the question of interest; and (4) frame the research and its findings to contribute knowledge to academic disciplines, as well as one or more domains of practice.

Simon (1976) argues that significant invention in the affairs of the world calls on two kinds of knowledge: practical knowledge about issues and needs from the perspective of a profession and scientific knowledge about new ideas and processes that are potential means for addressing these issues and needs. Historically invention is easier and likely to produce incremental contributions when it operates among like-minded individuals. Thus we find applied researchers who tend to immerse themselves in the problems of the end-users and then apply available knowledge and technology to provide solutions for their clients. We also find pure disciplinary scholars immersed in their disciplines to discover what questions have not been answered and then apply research techniques to address these questions. In either case if researchers cannot answer their initial questions, they modify and simplify them until they can be answered. As this process repeats itself, the research questions and answers become increasingly specific contributions to narrow domains of problems and inquiry. Tranfield and Starkey (1998) point out that researchers may locate themselves in different communities of practice and scholarship at different times,

> but they cannot stay fixed in either the world of practice (without risking epistemic drift driven by politics and funding) or in the world of theory (without retreating to academic fundamentalism). The problems addressed by management research should grow out of the interaction between the world of practice and the world of theory, rather than out of either one alone. (1998: 353)

In the conduct of engaged scholarship, researchers are equally exposed to the social systems of practice and science, and are likely to be confronted with real-life questions that are at the forefront of the kind of knowledge and policies that are used to address problems in the world. This setting increases the chance of significant innovation. As Louis Pasteur stated, 'Chance favors the prepared mind.' Research in this context is also more demanding because scholars do not have the option of substituting simpler questions if they cannot solve real-life problems. Engaged scholarship is difficult because it entails a host of interpersonal tensions and cognitive strains that are associated with juxtaposing investigators with different views and approaches to a single problem. But focusing on the tensions between scholars and practitioners, as has often been the case in the past, may blind us to the very real opportunities that can be gained from exploiting their differences in the co-production of knowledge. As Simon (1976) observed, if research becomes more challenging when it is undertaken to answer questions posed from outside an academic discipline, it also acquires the potential to become more significant and fruitful.

The history of science and technology demonstrates that many extraordinary advancements have often been initiated by problems and questions posed from outside the scientific enterprise (Ruttan 2001). Necessity is indeed the mother of important invention. Scholarship that engages both researchers and practitioners can provide an exceedingly productive and challenging environment; it not only fosters the creation of knowledge for science and practice, but it may dissolve the theory–practice gap.

2 Philosophy of Science Underlying Engaged Scholarship*

John P. Bechara and Andrew H. Van de Ven**

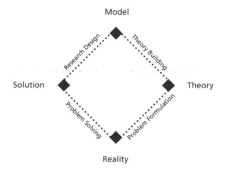

> *It is better to choose a philosophy of science than to inherit one by default.*

(Chapter 2, this volume, p. 37)

Many of us are practitioners—not philosophers—of science. We don't think much about *ontology* and *epistemology* so that we can get on with the craft of doing research instead of talking about it. But underlying any form of research is a philosophy of science that informs us of the nature of the phenomenon examined (ontology) and methods for understanding it (epistemology). Whether explicit or implicit, we rely on a philosophy of science to interpret the meanings, logical relations, and consequences of our observational and theoretical statements. Many of us inherit the philosophy of science that underlies the research practices of our teachers and mentors. Inheriting a philosophy of science is understandable if an orthodox view of the scientific method exists and is simply taken for granted by the scientific community. While such consensus may have existed among social scientists in the 1960s and early 1970s, the past 30 years have witnessed a major deconstruction and revision of traditional views of social science.

---

* There is a glossary to the philosophy of science terms on page 298.

** John Bechara is a doctoral student and Andrew Van de Ven is a professor at the Carlson School of Management at the University of Minnesota.

As discussed in this chapter, critics argue that social science cannot be *MBA's* objective, rational, and cumulative because language, culture, social norms, political ideologies, mental biases, and selective perception constitute the inputs and processes of science. Science is an intensely human social process, and hence subject to all of these factors that limit the capabilities for social science to be objective, rational, and cumulative. Since the demise of the 'Received View' of positivism[1] in the 1960s and 1970s other philosophies of science—such as relativism, pragmatism, and realism—have been developing and are competing for adoption by social scientists. They provide a repertoire of alternative ways to interpret the nature of things we study and the methods for doing so. Practitioners of science, in turn, are influencing how these philosophies are developed and expressed in their research.

This chapter attempts to provide a synthesis of the reciprocal relationship between the philosophy and practice of science by undertaking a brief historical review of four philosophies of science—positivism, relativism, pragmatism, and realism. It provides a discussion of how key ideas from each philosophy inform engaged scholarship, and how the practice of engaged scholarship might influence these philosophies of science. Engaged scholarship requires a comparative understanding of different philosophies of science. An understanding of a complex problem or phenomenon being investigated can be enhanced by engaging the perspectives of diverse scholars and stakeholders. Appreciating these diverse perspectives often requires communicating across different philosophical perspectives. It also requires maintaining the diverse intellectual differences that not only create an opportunity for arbitrage, but also for a productive interplay of perspectives, models, and world views (Alvesson and Sköldberg 2000).

This chapter also emphasizes that the philosophy underlying our scientific practice is a choice, and should not simply be a default inherited without question from our teachers and mentors. Understanding the implications of this choice is important not only for engaged scholarship, but for any reflective and responsible scientific inquiry. We turn to philosophy of science to provide us with the conceptual tools and frameworks to reflect on our practice, and to understand alternative ways to do social science.

Before reviewing four alternative philosophies of positivism, relativism, pragmatism, and realism, it is important to clarify in a reflexive spirit that our own version of engaged scholarship adopts a critical realist perspective. This view takes an objective ontology (i.e., reality exists independent of our cognition) and a subjective epistemology. More specifically, this perspective is based on the following principles.

- There is a real world out there (consisting of material, mental, and emergent products), but our individual understanding of it is limited.

---

[1] Putnam (1962) referred to logical positivism and logical empiricism as the received view.

In general, physical material things are easier to understand than reflexive
and emergent social processes.

- All facts, observations and data are theory-laden implicitly or explicitly.
  Social sciences have no absolute, universal, error-free truths, or laws as any
  scientific knowledge.
- No form of inquiry can be value-free and impartial; each is value-full.
  Some methods are better warranted than others depending on the phe-
  nomenon.
- Knowing a complex reality demands use of multiple perspectives.
- Robust knowledge is a product of theoretical and methodological triangu-
  lation where evidence is not necessarily convergent but might also be
  inconsistent or even contradictory.
- Models that better fit the problems they are intended to solve are selected
  allowing an evolutionary growth of knowledge.

Alternative Philosophies of Science

We turn now to a brief historical review of positivism, relativism, pragmatism, and realism. Table 2.1 summarizes the discriminating characteristics of
these four philosophical schools, and provides an outline of the review
discussed below. In addition, the Appendix to this chapter contains a glossary
of key philosophical terms that may be a useful reference while reading the
chapter. (The Appendix is located at the end of this volume, before the
Bibliography.) The four philosophies of science are featured in this chapter
not only because they influence our view of engaged scholarship, but also
because they reflect many of the current practices and debates among social
scientists.

Johnson and Duberley (2000, 2003) distinguish positivism, relativism,
pragmatism, and realism in terms of their ontological and epistemological
perspectives.[2] Logical positivism is ontologically objective (implicitly assumes
an objective world independent of cognition) due to its construal of an
empirical reality devoid of metaphysical entities and epistemologically objective due to its emphasis on correspondence between statements and reality
using *inductive* verification. In contrast, relativism is ontologically subjective

---

[2] Ontology focuses on the nature of things, while epistemology deals with how we gain knowledge
about these things. Campbell (1988) points to a circularity problem in these definitions because any
ontological description presupposes an epistemological one, and vice versa. 'Ontology has to do with
what exists, independently of whether or not we know it. But to describe what exists I have to use a
language of knowledge claims, and hence contaminate the definition with epistemology' (Campbell
1988: 440).

Table 2.1. Comparison of the characteristics of Logical Positivism, Relativism, Pragmatism and Realism

Dimensions	Logical Positivism	Relativism	Pragmatism	Realism
Definition	Philosophical movement inspired by empiricism, instrumentalism, and positivism (Vienna Circle, Berlin School).	Contemporary intellectual movement characterized by its skepticism about the foundations of Western philosophy (historical relativism, social constructivism, postmodernism, critical theory, hermeneutics).	Philosophical movement characterized by the relation of theory and praxis and specifically in the predetermined outcomes of an inquiry (relativism—Dewey and Rorty; realism—Peirce, James, and Rescher).	Philosophical movement characterized by the existence of a mind-independent reality and the ability of a theory to capture partial aspects of reality (conjecture realism, structural realism, realistic pragmatism, critical realism . . .).
Ontology	Objective: Reality is the empirical world (the world of the senses i.e., the rejection of the metaphysical).	Subjective: Reality is socially constructed.	Subjective: Similar to postmodernism. Objective: Reality places limitations and constraints on our actions.	Objective: Reality exists independent of our cognition. Thus, there is no basis to reject the metaphysical (epistemic fallacy).
Epistemology	Objective: The correspondence between our statements and reality through inductive verification or deductive falsification.	Subjective: There is no privileged epistemology due to the incommensurability of discourses.	Subjective and dependent on practical consequences.	Subjectivist: There is no predefined or predetermined methodology or criteria to judge the veracity our knowledge.
Knower	Positivist: The knower is independent of the empirical world (passive observer). Furthermore, the mind can mirror the empirical reality.	Constructivists: The knower is in the world and cannot stand outside of his/her socio-linguistic constructs to view it objectively.	Consequentialist: The knower has a priori cognitive frameworks which affect his/her perception of the world.	Perspectivalist: The knower has a priori cognitive frameworks which affect his/her perception of the world.
Language	Language is value free and provides a means to mirror and correspond to the empirical world (analytic/synthetic distinction).	Language is self-referential; i.e., it does not refer to any transcendental entity beyond itself. This presupposes its value and interest-laden nature.	Language is not self-referential but actionable and functions to meet the agent's goals and purposes.	Language is not self-referential or theory neutral but describes, albeit partially, the underlying mechanism and structure of a phenomenon.

due to its construal of a socially constructed reality and adopts a subjective epistemology due to its denial of an objective and impartial representation of social reality. Pragmatism includes philosophers, who take either objective or subjective views of ontology, but all adopt a subjective epistemology that emphasizes the relation between knowledge and action—knowledge is 'truthful' to the extent that it is successful in guiding action. Finally, realism adopts an objective ontology (there is a reality out there independent of cognition) and an objective or subjective epistemology. In short, positivism and relativism represent the outer limits of philosophical thought with their contrasting ontology and epistemology, and hence, bracket the discussion of pragmatism and realism, which lie in-between positivism and relativism.

The choice of these four philosophical schools and their labels was based in part on the historical development of the philosophy of science as an academic discipline. According to Boyd (1991) and Suppe (1977) it began with the logical positivists. Subsequent literature largely developed in reaction to it, such as social constructivism, which is placed under the relativist label and scientific realism, which is placed under the realist label. Understanding how these different perspectives developed in reaction to each other provides a useful first step in appreciating, selecting, and possibly synthesizing a philosophy of science that overcomes some of the concerns and criticisms of contemporary skeptics and hopefully initiates a process of reflexivity.

Before beginning, we admit that you may interpret the philosophies of science reviewed here very differently, and may disapprove of the choice of perspectives and the labels used to frame our discussion.[3] We say this in an open and reflexive spirit of choosing and synthesizing the philosophy of science that fits your scholarly practice. We do not presume that this chapter captures the breadth and depth of perspectives needed to make a well-grounded choice or synthesis. However, we do hope to raise awareness that the particular philosophy of science that is practiced is, and ought to be, a critical choice, rather than a default. Further study in the philosophy of science may be needed to make this choice.

---

[3] In previous drafts we received critical feedback on a variety of ways to classify and label the many philosophies of science. We confess to not having found a solution that adequately reflects and is sensitive of the philosophical identities of various scholars. In particular, we appreciate and are sympathetic of the critical feedback from interpretive, postmodern, and hermeneutic scholars who objected to our grouping of their perspectives under the label 'relativism.' One reviewer said she 'felt offended' by the label because of a pejorative 'anything goes' ethical connotation associated with the term 'relativism.' This is not our intent. Following Suppe (1977), Laudan (1984), and McKelvey (2002a), we use relativism as an 'existence concept' of the philosophical perspectives that view reality as socially constructed and that 'deny the existence of any standard or criterion higher than the individual by which claims to truth can be adjudicated' (McKelvey 2002b: 896).

BACKGROUND

Human beings have a unique capacity to represent reality and reflect upon it. This capacity coupled with the desire to control nature prompts scientific inquiry, or what Reichenbach (1963) called 'the art of correct generalization.' The goal of this art is to create knowledge—not mere opinion—that can be generalized across space and time. Philosophy of science examines the conceptual foundations and methods of this process of scientific inquiry.

Like most forms of Western intellectual thought, the history of philosophical thought of science can be traced back to the ancient Greeks. Reichenbach (1948, 1963), for example, begins his historical lineage with the debate between the *rationalists* and the *empiricists*. The rationalists believed that reason was the sole source of reliable knowledge. Reason was able to control empirical observations and order them into a logical system that made the prediction of future observations possible.

One of the first rationalists—also known as an *idealist*—is Plato (427–347 BC). He believed that an 'idea' exhibits the properties of objects in a perfect way, and thus we learn about these objects through their respective ideas not through the objects themselves. The laws of 'ideas' govern and provide reliable knowledge of the physical world. Plato's student, Aristotle (384–322 BC), similarly believed that the mind was the source of those laws. The leading rationalist of the *Enlightenment* period and the founder of modern philosophy, Rene Descartes (1596–1650), argued that the distinctive feature of *rationalism* was a belief that the laws that control the physical world can only be discovered through the reasoning of the mind (Russell 1972). Implicit in this assertion is the distinction between observer and the world, also referred to as *Cartesian dualism*. However, Descartes never denied completely the contributions of empirical observations to our knowledge of the physical world. He relied on logical *deductive rules*, beginning with a set of axioms or premises considered to be true to infer valid conclusions about the world. For example, if all swans are white, and the particular bird that we observe is a swan, then we deduce that the bird is white.

In contrast, empiricists believed that sensory experience was the sole source of reliable knowledge. The most devout empiricist was Francis Bacon (1561–1626), recognized as the pioneer in the logical systematization of the scientific inquiry (Russell 1972). He, as well as the ancient Greek philosopher Democritus (460–370 BC) and eighteenth century philosophers John Locke (1632–1704) and David Hume (1711–76), attempted to replace the rationalist method of *deduction* with *induction* as the proper method for attaining reliable knowledge of the physical world. Induction starts with the enumeration of past and present empirical observations to draw inferences about the physical world. For example, if all the swans we observe are white, then we conclude that all swans are white.

Although rational deduction and empirical induction remain with us today, both forms of inquiry suffer from numerous shortcomings. In particular, Reichenbach (1963) discussed three major shortcomings: (1) the assumption of rationalism that the premises in a deductive argument are true without resorting to sensory observation; (2) the assumption of empiricism that all knowledge is based on sensory experience while it is clear that the method of induction is not a product of sensory experience; and (3) the assumption of empiricism that the limited past and present observations provide a basis to predict future observations. This last shortcoming was one of the major contributions of Hume in specifying the *problem of induction*.

> The rationalist cannot solve the problem of empirical knowledge because he construes such knowledge after the pattern of mathematics, and thus makes reason the legislator of the physical world. The empiricist cannot solve the problem either; his attempt to establish empirical knowledge in its own right as derived from sense perception alone breaks down because empirical knowledge presupposes a non-analytic method, the method of induction, which cannot be regarded as a product or experience. (Reichenbach 1963: 90–1)

Immanuel Kant (1724–1804) attempted to reconcile the rationalist and empiricist views by synthesizing their respective contributions. He contended that there exist *synthetic a priori* principles of the physical world that preclude any sensory experience. This synthetic a priori consists of *axiomatic principles* such as the premises of geometry or causality that are assumed to be 'given' to the human mind. Furthermore, he contended that axiomatic theorizing can be used to derive other synthetic statements about the physical world that act as regulative mechanisms to organize sensory experience and subsequently create knowledge. Thus, with the synthetic a priori, Kant believed he showed that knowledge was a combination of a priori and a posteriori principles, or a combination of rationalism and empiricism.

Kant's contributions occurred during a period of cultural development in the eighteenth century known as the *Age of Enlightenment*. The Enlightenment was characterized by liberation from the theo-centric view and replaced by an anthropocentric view that emphasized human reason as the sole means to understanding the world (Russell 1972; Popkin 1999). It was in this cultural context that Auguste Comte (1798–1857) coined the word *positivism* as a philosophy aimed at showing that human knowledge had reached a stage of development that transcends religious dogma and places hope in the progressive accumulation of knowledge using the empirical sciences and specifically physics as the model of all sciences. Years later logical positivism emerged in Germany as an extension of the Enlightenment, a synthesis of the scientific development of the nineteenth and early twentieth centuries, and a reaction to G. W. Hegel's (1770–1831) metaphysics, which sought to explain reality in terms of abstract metaphysical entities that did not have any empirical manifestation. According to Johnson and Duberley (2000), the three major rationalist tenets used by the positivists were: subject–object dualism (Cartesian dualism—the world is independent of the subject), truth as an agreement of the mind with reality, and truthful knowledge is to correctly represent reality in the mind. In addition, the three empiricist tenets used by the positivists were: induction as the mode of reasoning to gain knowledge of reality, reduction of reality to empirical data, and reduction of causality to Humean[4] constant conjunction.

LOGICAL POSITIVISM[5]

Logical positivism emerged from the Vienna Circle—Moritz Schlick (1882–1936), Rudolf Carnap (1891–1970), and Herbert Feigl (1902–88); and the Berlin School—Hans Reichenbach (1891–1953) and Carl Hempel (1905–97). These pioneering scholars were mainly scientists and mathematicians who became philosophers. Logical positivism rejected Kant's a priori elements in science due to their *analytic* nature/self-referential character, adopted a blend of positivism, empiricism, *instrumentalism,* and benefited from the contributions of Frege, Russell, and Whitehead in mathematics and Wittgenstein in language. It construed the role of philosophy as the analysis of science from a logical perspective using what was known as a language of verifiable propositions (Blumberg and Feigl 1948). According to Suppe (1977), the goal of logical positivism was to eliminate all metaphysical entities from philosophy and science that implied ontological neutrality (i.e., emphasis on epistemology) (Niiniluoto 1999). From August Comte, it adopted the privileging of science (and specifically physics) as a model for all other sciences. From Ernest Mach (1838–1916), logical positivism adopted a radical empiricist attitude whereby the only source of knowledge of the physical world was sense observation. From Henri Poincare (1854–1912) logical positivism adopted instrumentalism, which denied theoretical terms any referential value.[6] From Gottlob Frege (1848–1925) and Bertrand Russell

---

[4] Hume defined causality as a product of habitual experience. The four conditions to ensure causality are: constant conjunction (two events are constantly associated with each other), antecedence (events occur sequentially in time), contiguity (both events are spatially in the same location), and necessity (no alternative observation). The last condition, necessity, was problematic since it was impossible to observe all instances of the phenomenon under investigation and thus any universal law from a finite number of observations can never be certain.

[5] Another form of logical positivism was logical empiricism, which substituted the ontological neutrality of the former with a realist ontology (i.e., that there exist a partial mind-independent reality). One of the most ardent logical empiricists was Herbert Feigl (a member of the Vienna circle) at the University of Minnesota who founded the Center for the Philosophy of Science, and was instrumental in diffusing logical positivism in the United States during the first half of the twentieth century.

[6] Referential value refers to the existence of unobservable entities in the physical world, which are represented using theoretical terms in science.

(1872–1970) logical positivism adopted logic as a means to analyze science and accepted the analytic nature of mathematics. It is this development in mathematics that led to the demise of neo-Kantianism and the synthetic a priori (Ayer 1982) since the latter relied on mathematics as a source for knowledge of the physical world. Finally, from Ludwig Wittgenstein (1889–1951), logical positivism adopted the *verifiability theory of meaning*, which states that understanding the meaning of a proposition consists of understanding the circumstances in which it could be verified or falsified. In the remainder of this section, we will focus on some of the main positivistic tenets followed by some of its earliest critics.

According to Boyd (1991), the verifiability theory of meaning, or *verificationism*, was a doctrine used by logical positivism to address the *demarcation problem* between science and non-science (metaphysics). One implication of verificationism was the distinction between science and mathematics/logic. Science was considered to be the only source of *synthetic knowledge* of the world based on empirically observable terms. Mathematics and logic were considered to be sources of *analytic knowledge.* Giere (1988: 26) illustrates this relationship between theoretical and observational terms in Figure 2.1. He points out that logical positivism distinguished scientific theories from pure axiomatic logic or mathematics by the empirical interpretation of non-logical terms and the use of correspondence rules to explicitly link theoretical terms with observational terms.

The standard doctrine was that the meaning of theoretical terms is totally a function of the meaning of the observational terms together with purely formal relations

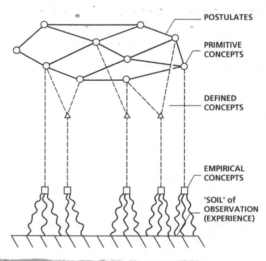

Figure 2.1. A logical empiricist picture of a scientific theory

Source: Reproduced from Feigl (1970) in Giere, R. N. (1988). *Explaining Science: A Cognitive Approach*. Chicago: University of Chicago Press, p. 25.

specified by the axioms of the theory. The result is instrumentalism with regard to the theory part of theories. Theoretical terms do not refer to real entities; they are mere instruments for organizing claims about the things referred to by observational terms. The view of scientific theories was typically pictured as in Figure 2.1. (Giere 1988: 26)

Another implication of verificationism was the separation between the genesis of a theory and its validity. The genesis of a theory was viewed as the context of discovery, which was believed to be the concern of psychology and history. The validity of a scientific theory provided the context of justification, which was believed to be the concern of logic and philosophy. Implicit in this separation is the independence of the social, psychological, and economic factors influencing the scientist and his/her scientific theories. Reichenbach states:

What we wish to point out with our theory of induction is the logical relation of the new theory to the known facts. We do not insist that discovery of the new theory is preformed by a reflection of a kind similar to our expositions; we do not maintain anything about the question of how it is performed—what we maintain is nothing but a relation of a theory to facts, independent of the man who found the theory. (1938: 382)

This led logical positivism to focus attention on theories as finished products waiting to be justified and to ignore factors in the genesis of theories (Suppe 1977: 125). In Weick's (1999) terms, logical positivism was concerned with theory, rather than the process of theorizing as discussed in Chapter 4. Furthermore, logical positivism emphasized induction as a means of developing empirically verifiable generalized propositions from empirically verifiable particular propositions.

Logical positivism formulates research questions and hypotheses in propositional form and necessitates the use of empirical tests to verify these propositions through careful control (manipulation) to avoid confounding conditions and outcomes. The researcher is assumed to be independent of the objects observed in the world, and capable of studying the objects without influencing, or being influenced by, them. When influence in either direction (threats to validity) is recognized or suspected, various strategies are followed to reduce or eliminate it. Inquiry takes place 'through a one-way mirror' (Guba and Lincoln 1994: 110) in a sort of correspondence between our thoughts/signs and reality. By following rigorous experimental procedures, values, and biases are prevented from influencing outcomes and empirical truth is established through replicable findings. This view of a researcher is discussed later as a 'God's Eye' frame of reference.

Suppe (1977) provides an extensive discussion of the criticisms of logical positivism. Only a brief summary of selected criticisms can be mentioned here. One of the earliest criticisms of logical positivism was by one of its pioneers, Hans Reichenbach (1948) of the Berlin School. He argued that logical positivism could not adequately solve the problem of induction and subsequently the predictive nature of science. The problem of induction is that in using it, it is never possible to arrive at a single theory. The positivistic belief that science, by induction, can ultimately converge on the 'real' truth is thus brought sharply into question.

Quine (1951) asserted the impossibility of having a clear distinction between *analytic* and *synthetic statements* and furthermore, the reduction of complex propositions into clear observational terms. He examined a difficulty first raised by Duhem (1962) that a theory cannot be conclusively falsified, because the possibility cannot be ruled out that some part of the complex test situation, other than the theory under test, is responsible for an erroneous prediction. This difficulty is called the Duhem/Quine thesis (Chalmers 1999: 89).

Popper (1959) showed that logical positivism fails to provide an adequate answer for the demarcation problem. Popper replaced positivism's induction and verification with *abduction* and *falsification*. Following the pragmatist, C. S. Peirce, Popper argued that the process of developing a theory does not begin with an inductive enumeration of observational data, but rather with creative intuition (as will be discussed in Chapter 4). Furthermore, he avoided Hume's radical skepticism by showing that any process of verification (proving) is illusory and should be replaced with a process of falsification (dis-proving). The process of falsification leads to an epistemological Darwinism where the fittest of theories survive empirical refutation. Like Popper, Donald T. Campbell argued for an evolutionary growth of knowledge in which the scientific community selects those models that better fit the problems they are intended to solve (see the section on realism).

Along with Popper, Norman Hanson held that a major defect of logical positivism was that it confines attention only to the finished product of scientific theorizing and gives no attention to the process of reasoning whereby laws, hypothesis, and theories receive their tentative first proposal (Hanson 1958: 71). In 'Patterns of Discovery' Hanson (1958) extended the work of Peirce (see pragmatism) to develop the logic of scientific discovery. He emphasized that theories are not discovered by inductively generalizing from data but rather are *retroductively* inferred hypotheses from conceptually organized data. Hanson viewed observations and facts as theory-laden, and notions of causality as reflecting a certain form of conceptual organization. Causation is not a property of the physical world; it is a way people make sense of the world. He developed a logic of discovery (retroductive reasoning) that reflects the process in which scientific conjectures and laws are developed.

RELATIVISM

We use *relativism* as a general term denoting a set of alternative philosophies of science that emerged in reaction to, or in denial of, positivism. The set includes many variations: historical relativism, social constructivism, post-modernism, critical theory, and hermeneutics. This grouping of philosophies into a single category is based on our judgment, since we cannot cover all their individual viewpoints. However, the perspectives included in our broad category of relativism all break away from the positivist assumption that scientific knowledge is a cumulative, unmediated, and complete representation of reality. They deny a solution to the demarcation problem; emphasize the intertwinement between the genesis and validity of a theory, view reality as socially constructed, and the goal of social science as that of understanding what meanings people give to reality, not only to determine how reality works. Furthermore, they reject the positivistic belief that scientific methods provide a way to develop an objective 'Truth' of the concrete reality in the world. Instead, they believe that scientists construct an image of reality based on their interests, values, and viewpoints in interaction with others. From this standpoint, observations and data give us 'nothing more than facts. The *MBA* truth (small t) is what we make consensually of these facts. And in the social world, truth is therefore collectively constructed.... Truth referents are not in the facts but in the collective interpretation of the facts' (Gioia 2003: 288). We now examine some of the main tenets of the varieties of relativism: historical relativism, social constructivism, postmodernism, critical theory, and hermeneutics.

Some of the first critics of positivism were the historical relativists (Toulmin 1953; Feyerabend 1962, 1975; Kuhn 1962, 1970) and social constructivists (Bloor 1976; Latour and Woolgar 1986). Kuhn (1962, 1970), a historical relativist, called into question the belief that scientific knowledge is cumulative. He argued, instead, that the development of science is dependent on the sociological paradigm agreed upon within the scientific community. He replaced the a priori cognitive structures of Kant with a paradigmatic view that reflected the set of beliefs, values, assumptions, and techniques that guided the scientist. Kuhn viewed scientific knowledge as progressing in a cycle of three phases. The first phase is normal science, where one particular paradigm has control over a scientific community. The second phase is a crisis where abnormal or inexplicable observations arise. Finally, the last phase is revolutionary science where a new paradigm replaces the old paradigm. The replacement of the old paradigm is through a consensus of the scientific community and not through correspondence with reality as had occurred with positivism. Furthermore, the acceptance of a new paradigm presupposes *incommensurability* with other paradigms because of the absence of an agreed-upon, objective criterion for comparing the truth claims of alternative paradigms.

In a similar way, Feyerabend (1962, 1975), Toulmin (1953), and other historical relativists argue for the idea of a socially constructed nature of scientific knowledge. However, they differ in some historical interpretations and conclusions. For example, Toulmin construed scientific theories as neither true nor false but more or less adequate answers for observed irregularities. These irregularities occur when the current theories break down or are unable to provide an adequate answer. Moreover, the development of new scientific theories is based on a *Weltanschauung*, which is an evolving socio-conceptual framework similar to Kuhn's paradigm. However, unlike Kuhn's view that paradigms change all at once, Toulmin construed the change in Weltanschauung as more or less gradual.

Perhaps the strongest negation of positivism is *postmodernism*, which is skeptical of modern science, technology, and social transformations produced by the Enlightenment. The demarcation between modern and postmodern eras is unclear, but it is claimed to have started with Nietzsche in the late nineteenth century (Dallmayr 1987; Sim 2001) and reached its epitome in the second half of the twentieth century during a period of unprecedented socio-economic and technological transformation. Postmodernism is an eclectic school of thought that encompasses post-industrialism, post-capitalism, and post-structural forms of thought. One common theme is skepticism about the major foundations of Western thought, and in particular positivism being a product of the scientific and mathematical developments of the nineteenth and early twentieth century (Alvesson and Deetz 1996; Sim 2001). This skepticism undermines the attainment of truth, the criteria determining truth, and even its very existence. It is based on *anti-essentialist* and *anti-foundationalist* notions about the nature of reality and the ways of knowing reality respectively. Overall, postmodernism denies positivism's logico-linguistic turn to the analysis of science through the use of propositions, blurs the distinction between observable and theoretical terms, and more importantly denies the distinction between the genesis and validity of a theory.

Anti-essentialism refers to a rejection of the essence of phenomena and the causal mechanisms underlying them. The essentialist notion is the cornerstone of scientific inquiry. As Sim (2001) suggests, essentialism regards the attainment of truth, meaning, and origin as its goal. This parallels the Hobbesian and Humean critiques of Aristotelian essences, which consisted of the distinction between 'what' an object is and 'how' it is. Hence, postmodernism rejects the possibility of capturing the essence of the phenomenon and subsequently rejects its existence.

Anti-foundationalism refers to the rejection of foundational or self-evident beliefs required in the pursuit and acquisition of knowledge. Hence, postmodernism rejects the basis of epistemology that asserts the existence of self-justifying or self-evident first principles that guide scientific inquiry.

Postmodernism's anti-essentialist and anti-foundationalist rejections have implications for our conception of the word 'truth,' which lacks a common intrinsic feature that permits us to judge our theories. According to Rorty (1979), the conception of truth has become nothing but a sign of approval or agreement given to promote one theory over others (Engel 2002). An extension of this particular theme lies at the heart of Jean Baudrillard's denial of the possibility of distinguishing between reality and simulation in our postmodern world (Sim 2001). According to Baudrillard, the world is a 'simulacra,' where reality and simulation are intertwined and undistinguishable (as often experienced when playing virtual reality games).

According to Cahoone (1996), postmodernism denies the distinction between the presence of an entity and its representation. One aspect of this criticism stems from the complexity, difficulty, and to a certain extent impossibility of representing the world in an unmediated and holistic fashion. Another aspect stems from the denial of linguistic essentialism whereby language is viewed as a mirror to objectively represent the presence of an object (Hassard 1994; Alvesson and Deetz 1996). An example is Jacques Derrida's deconstruction, which denies the possibility of using language to represent reality. He supports his denial by demonstrating that we think only in signs and that the process of signification is an endless shifting from sign to sign which can never be terminated by reducing the signifying process to some transcendental starting-point or end-point. This leads Derrida to state that there is nothing outside the text that is represented. Furthermore, Rorty claims that different languages constructed within different socio-cultural contexts are incommensurable and thus knowledge is incommensurable. This inevitability of incommensurability means that a consensus as a generalizable epistemic standard is rejected.

Next, Cahoone (1996) argues that postmodernism attempts to show unity as plurality whereby entities are shown to be a product or function of their respective relationship with other entities. Hence, any apparent unities are implicitly repressing their dependency on and relations to others. A proponent of this view is Jean-Francois Lyotard, who rejects the grand theoretical enterprises or 'grand narratives' that serve only to justify our actions. He believes in a multiplicity of alternatives to explanation or mini-narratives, where any claim to a unitary or linear progression is a suppression of other possible alternatives. Scientific knowledge becomes a plurality incapable of legitimizing itself and based on multiple language games (Gasche 1988). As discussed in the next section, this notion of selves is rooted in the William James's construal of pragmatic philosophy.

Postmodern theorist and feminist scholars (such as Martin 1990) have deconstructed and surfaced a number of voices or interests that are typically 'marginalized' in positivistic accounts of social organization or behavior.

In the guise of technocracy, instrumental rationality has pretenses to neutrality and freedom from the value-laden realms of self-interest and politics. It celebrates and 'hides' behind techniques and the false appearance of objectivity and impartiality of institutionalized sets of knowledge, bureaucracy, and formal mandates. Not surprisingly, technocracy is promoted by each of the management 'specialisms' as they claim a monopoly of expertise in their respective domains. Human resource specialists, for example, advance and defend their position by elaborating a battery of 'objective' techniques for managing the selection and promotion of employees (Hollway 1984; Steffy and Grimes 1992). Strategic management institutionalizes a particular way of exercising domination through legitimizing and privileging the 'management' of the organization-environment interface, producing some actors as 'strategists' and reducing others to troops whose role is to subordinate themselves to implement corporate strategies (Alvesson and Willmott 1995; Shrivastava 1986). The concept of technocracy draws attention to some of the darker and more disturbing aspects of so-called 'professional management.' It points to a restricted understanding of human and organizational goals; those that are identified and validated by experts. By associating management with technocracy and its instrumentalization of reason, the domination of a narrow conception of reason is at once exposed and questioned. (Alvesson and Deetz 1996: 203–4)

Hence, what positivists' thought were impartial, objective, and value-free accounts of science, relativists have shown to serve the interest and values of people in power. Moreover, Zald (1995) claimed that 'Most of the "brute facts" that are subject to enumeration in positivistic social science gain their force because of the cultural/social meanings in which the subjects participate. Explanation in the causal sense must give way to, or be embedded in, hermeneutic unveiling and interpretation' (Zald 1995: 456).

Critical theory emerged from the Frankfurt school. Its founders included among others Max Horkheimer (1895–1973), Theodor Adorno (1903–69), and Herbert Marcuse (1898–1979). They adopted a Marxist framework to oppose the destructive effects of capitalism. The aim of critical theory was to diagnose the problems of modern society and identify the nature of the social change needed to produce just and democratic societies. Critical theory shares some commonalities with postmodernism although a key difference is that it maintains hope that knowledge can lead to emancipation and progress. Habermas (1979, 1984, 1987, 1990), a second generation critical theorist, adopts a conventionalist position that deploys a consensus theory of truth, as a regulative standard to assess the extent of systematically distorted communication. He also avoids extreme relativism because he assumes that through ideal speech communication, we might attain a consensual view of truth.

The last major relativistic perspective reviewed here is *hermeneutics*. Originally focused on interpreting the meaning of the Scriptures, hermeneutical philosophers expanded their scope into philology (the science of linguistic understanding and the study of interpretative processes and beings) and many additional areas beyond biblical interpretation, including the social sciences. Although positivists focused almost exclusively on epistemology, hermeneutical philosophers (such as Heidegger 1927/1962; Gadamer 1960/1975; and Bernstein 1983) emphasized that epistemological issues are strongly related to the ontological positions we might take.

As against the positivists who assumed it is possible to gather knowledge about entities that are observed independent of the observer, hermeneutics questioned this shallow approach to epistemology:

It argues that how we view the existence of objects in the extra-mental world is *a function of* how we frame our own existence and relationship with the environment. (By 'extra-mental reality,' I mean the world as it exists independently from how an individual perceives it.) Our perception of the outside world is a function of how we perceive our own position in and relationship with the phenomena—in the past, present, and future. We therefore, need a better understanding of the reference frames we use to make sense of this relationship and the extent to which these frames confuse us or help us clarify and focus our thought processes—especially if we want to develop a proper understanding of the processes taking place in the world. (Hendrickx 2002: 341)

Margaretha Hendrickx applies this hermeneutical perspective by contrasting a positivistic 'God's Eye frame' with a critical realist 'participant frame' that Mr. Jones, a hypothetical management researcher, might take to conduct research. Hendrickx (1999: 344) uses Figure 2.2 to illustrate ways that Mr. Jones might make connections between Popper's (1979) 'Three World View': (1) a material world illustrated by the globe; (2) a world of mental states and processes as illustrated by the human figure, and (3) an emergent

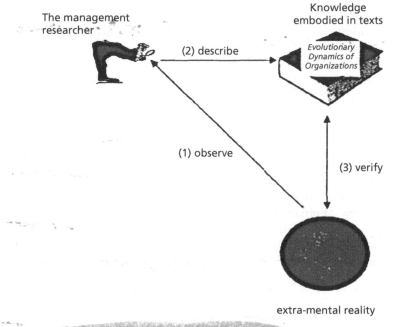

Figure 2.2. God's Eye frame of reference: triangular reasoning

Source: Hendrickx (1999: 344).

world of products of individual and collective human minds, represented by the book.

In the God's Eye frame, 'the world consists of some fixed totality of extra-mental objects. There is exactly one true and complete description of "the way the world is." Truth involves some sort of correspondence relation between words or thought-signs and external things' (Putnam 1981: 49). Here, the researcher views him/herself as a value-neutral observer of real things existing in the world (illustrated by arrow 1). Arrow 2 stands for the relation between the researcher's mental interpretation of the observations and his/her mental model as represented by linguistic signs in a text. Arrow 3 represents the relation between the linguistic signs in the text and the real-world phenomena.

The God's Eye point of view inspires Mr. Jones to think of his relationship with phenomena under investigation as one of the sides of a triangle (Figure 2.1). He functions in this triangle as a (very complicated) mirror. His research activities may be broken down in primarily three tasks, 'observing,' 'describing,' and 'verifying.' First he *inductively* observes what is happening in the world. The reflected photons fall on his eyes' retinas and induce an electron cascade that leads to the creation of photo-graph-like images of the phenomena in his brain. Via a very complex set of biochemical and neurological reactions, these images are translated in patterns of dots on paper or digital signals stored on a computer disk. Mr. Jones describes what he observes in the world. He then generalizes his empirical findings in hypotheses and deductively tests (and observes) whether the postulated relations hold true.

This triangular reasoning squeezes Mr. Jones out of the world, so to speak. He believes that with proper training, he is capable of transcending his own subjectivity, as if he was able to turn his values and preferences off as easily as he turns his computer on to write up his research findings. It is the job, the duty, of Mr. Jones to publish articles with 'true' descriptions of what happens in corporations. He believes that it is possible to obtain the value-neutral state of mind of an outsider. . . . He perceives his relation-ship with these as independent of time, space, and mind, as if he is like God. . . . He believes that what he sees is the way the phenomena in the extra-mental world are. (Hendrickx 1999: 342–3)

A participant frame of reference views the researcher as an active participant in the domain he/she attempts to study and understand. Although this frame has also been called the 'internal' view (Evered and Louis 1981) and 'pragma-tists' worldview' (Putnam 1981; Rorty 1982), Hendrickx (1999: 375) prefers the term 'participant' for being neutral on us-vs.-them and inside-vs.-outside dichotomies that are implicit in the God's Eye frame. Figure 2.3 presents Hendrickx's depiction of the participant frame.

Mr. Jones now thinks of himself as participant in a discourse about ways to help companies succeed in the long run [the research problem being investigated]. He perceives himself as a voice in a universal conversation, in which the various points of view of actual persons reflect their various interests and purposes (Putnam 1981: 49–50). One of these purposes is to find the most clarifying lens with which to discover [and represent the problem and its resolution].

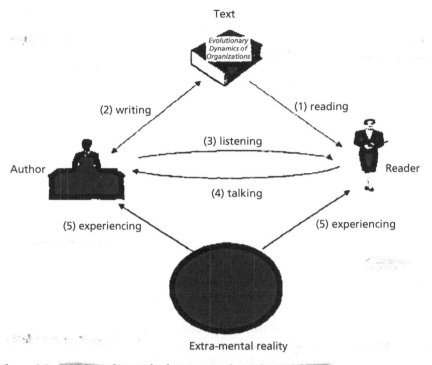

Figure 2.3. Participant frame of reference: quadrangular reasoning

Source: Adapted from Hendrickx (1999: 345).

In the participant worldview, a management researcher explicitly acknowledges that he is the product of a certain history and culture. Thus, Mr. Jones realizes that he knows as much as he learned from the books that he read, the experiences he underwent, and the conversations in which he participated. He has come to terms with the subjective nature of what he knows and understands the futility of attempting to reason in a value-neutral way. Instead, Mr. Jones talks openly about his research values and investigates whether they make sense after all. Mr. Jones attempts to understand whether or not his espoused values are the values he *actually* uses in his research. He also wants to know the extent to which his values in use are consistent with values benefiting the human species as a whole (Campbell 1979: 39; 1982: 333–4). His values motivate him (Campbell 1993: 36). He looks upon his research questions as issues with practical consequences for him, his neighbors, and the top management teams he studies. (Hendrickx 1999: 346)

Hendrickx illustrates Mr. Jones' participant frame of reference in a quadrangle, as depicted in Figure 2.3. As a participant, the researcher performs the roles of an investigator and author with other co-investigators, co-authors, or readers engaged in the discourse. The extra-mental real world and the text or model represents the material and socially-constructed worlds, respectively, that the participating researcher(s) and others construct by experiencing, talking, listening, reading, and writing.

So, compared to the God's Eye view, where the Other is either an onlooker like Mr. Jones, or alternatively, someone down there to be observed, the participant frame of references does not classify readers and writers as a function of whether they know less or more; rather it implies that they know something different. (Hendrickx 1999: 346–7)

Hendrickx (1999: 341) concludes by advocating the participant frame of reference and rejecting the God's Eye frame. She states that a God's Eye frame tends to encourage an authoritative and dogmatic attitude on the part of the author, which promotes close-mindedness and intolerance of alternative perspectives. Such an attitude is not conducive to listening to and learning of the viewpoints of others about the real-world phenomenon or alternative ways to represent it. A participant frame of reference requires an open-minded attitude that encourages engagement and learning with others.

PRAGMATISM

Pragmatism is an American philosophical school of thought that emerged in the late nineteenth century with Charles Sanders Peirce (1839–1914). In an article, 'How to Make our Ideas Clear,' Peirce (1878/1997) introduced the term *pragmatism*, a term derived from Kant and traced back to the Greek word action. Pragmatism sought to reconcile rationalism and empiricism by showing that knowing and doing are indivisibly part of the same process. In philosophy of science, pragmatism was viewed as an alternative to logical positivism and was aligned with instrumentalism, which is the view that scientific theories are not true or false but are better or worse instruments for prediction (Misak 2001). Some philosophers went further to assert that Peirce's thought not only provides an alternative to logical positivism, but actually repudiates, in advance, some of its major developments (Rorty 1961). According to Meyers (1999) pragmatism espouses three theories: (1) a theory of the mind, where beliefs are hypotheses and ideas are plans of action; (2) a theory of meaning, where ideas can be clarified by revealing their relationship with action; and (3) a theory of truth, where beliefs are true when they succeed in guiding action and prediction. Pragmatism is multifaceted and seems to vary according to each pragmatist (Lovejoy 1908). To minimize confusion we focus on the main arguments and criticisms of three pioneering pragmatists—Peirce, James, and Dewey—and two contemporary scholars—Rorty and Rescher.

Peirce introduced the pragmatic maxim of ascertaining the meaning of an idea in terms of the practical consequences that might conceivably result from the truth of that conception. The sum of these consequences constitutes the meaning of the conception (Rescher 2000: 9). Peirce viewed meaning as an inference for repeatable actions, both as habitual behavior in a reoccurring situation over time and as generalizations of actions to larger contexts or different situations (Dewey 1916). In his article 'Fixation of Belief,' Peirce states that the function of beliefs is to commit us to action. This criterion for truth bears not only on the success of the application, but also on the extent to which it sustains a long term commitment from the scientific community. Peirce acknowledged the fallibility of inductive scientific inference. Instead, he proposed a method of scientific discovery through systematic observation and creative inference.

Peirce introduced abduction or retroduction as a creative mode of discovery that follows neither inductive nor deductive modes of inference. 'Induction was widely believed to be the basic process in science. Peirce denied this, arguing that induction serves not to initiate theory but rather to test it' (Mounce 1997: 17). As discussed in Chapter 4, abduction is a hypothetical inference, framed to solve a problem. The new conception is not final. Further inquiry will reveal problems that can be solved only by framing a fresh conception (Mounce 1997: 17).

Peirce's belief in science and the oneness of truth was rooted in an ontologically realist stance. He defends his realist stance by arguing that there is no reason to believe that a mind-independent reality does not exist. He suggests this belief is harmonious with our practice of science. He states:

There are real things, whose characters are entirely independent of our opinions about them; those realities affect our senses according to regular laws, and, though our sensations are as different as our relations to the objects, yet, by taking advantage of the laws of perception, we can ascertain by reasoning how things really are and any man, if he have sufficient experience and reason enough about it, will be led to the one true conclusion. (Peirce 1878/1997: 21)

Peirce intended pragmatism to be a rational and empirical substantiation of knowledge claims (Rescher 2000). He construed the meaning of a term or proposition as constituted by its practical consequences and its truth by its success to satisfy the intended aims. These aims, which included successful prediction and control, were the aims of science.

William James (1842–1910), a contemporary of Peirce, elaborates upon and alters Peirce's philosophical approach in his seminal lectures in 1907 on *Pragmatism* (James 2003). In these lectures, James describes the current dilemma of philosophy as a difference in temperament between rationalism and empiricism. He contends that individuals inevitably exhibit characteristics of both sides of the debate. Thus, in order to continue the abstractness of rationalism and the particularism of empiricism he proposes pragmatism:

You want a system that will combine both things, the scientific loyalty to facts and willingness to take account of them, the spirit of adaptation and accommodation, in short, but also the old confidence in human values and the resultant spontaneity, whether of the religious or of the romantic type. (James 2003: 9)

For James, pragmatism provides a method to settle metaphysical disputes because through it one compares the practical consequences of adopting alternative views. Two alternative or rival views are identical if their practical consequences are identical. Thus, the goal of philosophy is to discover the difference between rival views based on their consequences to different individuals. James described his version of pragmatism as being a compromise between empiricism (which claimed that an objective world commands thought) and idealism (which claimed that subjective thoughts construct the world). He construes pragmatism as a less objectionable but more radical version of empiricism. Pragmatism replaces abstraction, a priori reasons, and fixed principles with concrete facts and action. It is this emphasis on experience that James uses to depict action or practice, which lies at the heart of pragmatism, as a means for solving metaphysical problems and developing a theory of truth. He states:

Theories thus become instruments, not answers to enigmas in which we can rest. It agrees with nominalism for instance, in always appealing to particulars; with utilitarianism in emphasizing practical consequences; with positivism in its disdain for verbal solutions. (James 2003: 24)

James adopted a realist ontology and asserted the existence of a reality independent of our cognition. He states, 'The notion of a reality independent of either of us, taken from ordinary experience, lies at the base of the pragmatist notion of truth' (James 1908: 455). According to James, the truthfulness of a theory is evident through its success as an instrument that is loyal to past experience but also is able to transcend it to generate new facts and to hold so long as it is believed to be 'profitable for our lives' (James 2003: 34). In contrast to Peirce (who was influenced by Kant), James was influenced by the British empiricists such as Locke, Hume, and Mill. James, therefore, viewed pragmatism quite differently from Peirce. While Peirce viewed pragmatism as a methodology for converging on a fixed standard, James invited pluralism. He entertained a diversity of views about a phenomenon that allowed not only for differences among individuals, but even different inclinations and viewpoints within individuals (Rescher 2000: 19).

James interprets pragmatism as: (1) a method to solve metaphysical disputes by which one compares the practical consequences of adopting alternative views; and (2) a theory of truth where truth is verification, which is consistent with our beliefs and experience. Truth is made and can change over time. James refuses the rationalistic relationship between mind and world, which presupposes a passive reality. He contends that this relationship is and should be viewed as pragmatic, future looking, and dynamic, which presupposes an active reality in line with Darwinian evolution.

John Dewey (1859–1952), a student of Peirce, viewed pragmatism as a means to attain societal goals. While Peirce's pragmatism was theoretical and oriented to natural science, and James's was personalistic and psychological, Dewey's pragmatism was communalistic and society-oriented. Dewey's position was intermediate between Peirce and James and emphasized its social aspect by viewing truth as a 'matter of communally authorized assertability' (Rescher 2000: 27). Like Peirce, Dewey refers to his version of pragmatism as 'instrumentalism,' which is grounded in *scientific realism* as a means to remove doubt through social consensus.

The presupposition and tendencies of pragmatism are distinctly realistic; not idealistic... Instrumentalism is thus thoroughly realistic as to the objective or fulfilling conditions of knowledge. (Dewey 1905: 324–5)

According to Rescher (2000), Dewey differs from Peirce in his conception of social consensus. Dewey's view is that social consensus is not based on epistemic factors (empirical evidence) but on socio-political factors. Dewey contends that the success of theories is based on their ability to realize the goals of societal improvement and development.

Two contemporary pragmatists, Richard Rorty (1931–) and Nicholas Rescher (1928–), take clearly different views of pragmatism. Rorty (1980), influenced by James and Dewey, adopts a postmodern view of pragmatism. To Rorty, pragmatism is subjectivistic, anti-foundationalistic, and anti-essentialistic, where truth and validity lose any type of decisive weight and lack any generalizable epistemic standards. Rorty illustrates his anti-essentialism by arguing that truth does not have an essence or any type of isomorphic correspondence with reality. Therefore, any attempt at a progressive accumulation of truth is fruitless. For Rorty, the consequences of knowledge in practice provides a way to state something useful about truth. He believed that all the vocabulary of isomorphic pictures, models, and representations of reality should be replaced with one of practical consequences and implied actions. Rorty states:

The whole vocabulary of isomorphism, picturing, and mapping is out of place here as indeed is the notion of being true of objects. If we ask what objects these sentences claim to be true of, we get only unhelpful repetitions of the subject terms—'the universe,' 'the law,' 'history.' (1980: 723)

In making these remarks Rorty was probably reacting to the formal *syntactical view of theories*. However, other philosophers—such as Suppe (1989), Giere (1999), Morgan and Morrison (1999)—had a less relativistic response by replacing this syntactical view with a *semantic view* of theories. In this view models (rather than correspondence rules) provide the interpretation for the theory. As discussed in Chapter 6, models mediate between theories and data (Morrison and Morgan 1999: 5).

Rescher (2000), following Peirce, adopts a more realistic view of pragmatism and repudiates Rorty's relativistic pragmatism. Rescher proposes three steps to realign pragmatism with its Peircian roots: (1) pragmatism should be construed as a philosophical system that holds 'success' as epistemic for effective prediction, control, and explanation; (2) success is objective and independent of personal preferences; and (3) pragmatism is a method and not a doctrine.

PARSIMONY ?

Rescher emphasizes pragmatic success as inextricably intertwined with the scientific enterprise. Principles of efficacy in prediction and effective intervention in nature are essential to pragmatic success and are the foundations of scientific inquiry. Rescher provides a pragmatic justification for realism, which maintains that there is a real world—a realm of mind-independent, objective physical reality—out there, even though our abilities to understand it are severely limited. He emphasized that the stable aim of science is to provide useful models of reality. To Rescher (2003), realism is only justified by the fact that our knowledge of reality is itself fallible and we can never fully comprehend its complexity. The existence of a mind-independent reality is not the result of scientific inquiry, but a presupposition of inquiry. As discussed in the next section, Rescher argues that it is pragmatically useful for scientific inquiry to presuppose realism.

REALISM

Realism contends that there is a real world existing independently of our attempts to know it; that we humans can have knowledge of that world; and that the validity of our knowledge is, at least in part, determined by the way the world is. Realism is a philosophical theory that is partly metaphysical and partly empirical. It transcends experience but is testable by experience (Leplin 1984). This section discusses some of the historical underpinnings of realism followed by some of its variations including: scientific realism, conjectural realism, realistic pragmatism, and critical realism (evolutionary critical realism).

Historically, realism was concerned with the existence of unobservable entities that lie beyond human perception. Rescher (1987) traces the debate regarding unobservables to three schools of thought: instrumentalism (historically known as nominalism), realism, and approximationism (historically known as conceptualism). As discussed before, instrumentalism rejects the existence of unobservables and regards any reference to such entities in scientific theories as a means or tool to help explain the observable phenomena. In contrast, realism accepts the existence of unobservables and contends that scientific theories reference and capture such entities as they exist in the real world. Finally, approximationism asserts the existence of unobservables; however, it contends that scientific theories roughly capture these unobservables as they exist in the real world. In other words, a weak form of realism adopts a loose isomorphic representation of reality, whereas the strong form of realism contends a direct isomorphic relationship, and instrumentalism repudiates any type of isomorphism.

Chalmers (1999) simplifies the debate to be between anti-realism versus realism. Anti-realism (like instrumentalism) restricts scientific theorizing to the observable and avoids any metaphysical/speculative claims. For anti-realism the criterion of success for a scientific theory is its ability to predict observable phenomena. Here theories simply serve the function of 'scaffolding to help erect the structure of observational and experimental knowledge, and they can be rejected once they have done their job' (Chalmers 1999: 233).

In contrast to positivism and relativism, scientific realism (a strong form of realism) contends that science develops statements that are true at both theoretical and observational levels of phenomena. It claims that science continues to progress by attaining closer approximations of reality. 'We cannot know that our current theories are true, but they are truer than earlier theories, and will retain at least approximate truth when they are replaced by something more accurate in the future' (Chalmers 1999: 238).

Major criticisms of scientific realism were raised by relativists who questioned the belief in absolute truth and approximation to it (Toulmin 1953; Feyerabend 1962, 1975; Kuhn 1962, 1970; Bloor 1976; Latour and Woolgar 1986). The completeness, correctness, and progressively-truer nature of scientific knowledge were at stake. Niiniluoto (1980: 446) states, 'No one has been able to say what it would mean to be "closer to the truth," let alone offer criteria to determine such proximity.'

Several variations of realism developed in response to the criticisms of relativists. Suppe (1977) argued that Kuhn's view of rapid paradigm shifts was historically inaccurate, and rejected his claims of incommensurability among theoretical terms across paradigms. If paradigms are truly incommensurable, how is it possible that scholars compare different paradigms and communicate across the paradigms? Hacking (1983) argued that relativism inappropriately emphasizes the distinction between observable and unobservable entities while neglecting the scientific methods of experimentation that manipulate and control entities to reveal their effects.

Popper (1959) and his followers developed conjectural realism, a moderate realist position. This position emphasizes the fallibilism of scientific knowledge and acknowledges the discontinuous progression of science. Chalmers states:

> So the conjectural realist will not claim that our current theories have been shown to be approximately true, nor that they have conclusively identified some of the kinds of things that are in the world. . . . Nevertheless, it is still maintained that it is the aim of science to discover the truth about what really exists, and theories are appraised on the extent to which they can be said to fulfill that aim. (1999: 240)

Rescher (2003) also responded to the relativists by providing a pragmatic explanation for realism and developing realistic pragmatism. Realistic pragmatism emphasized that the aim of science is to provide a useful model of reality. To Rescher (2003), realism is only justified by the fact that our knowledge of reality is itself fallible, and we can never fully comprehend its complexity. He points out that realism represents a presupposition for inquiry, not a result of it (Rescher 2000: 126).

The commitment to a mind-independent reality is, all too clearly, a precondition for empirical inquiry—a presupposition we have to make to be able to use observational data as sources of objective information. We really have no alternative but to presuppose or postulate it. Objectivity represents a postulation made on functional (rather than evidential) grounds: We endorse it in order to be in a position to learn by experience. What is at issue here is not so much a product of our experience of reality as a factor that makes it possible to view our experience as being 'of reality' at all. As Emmanuel Kant clearly saw, objective experience is possible only if the existence of such a real, objective world is an available given from the outset rather than the product of experience—an ex-post facto discovery about the nature of things. (Rescher 2000: 127)

Rescher (2000) develops six important reasons why a presumption of realism is needed for scientific inquiry:

1. Realism is indispensable for the notion of truth as a correspondence between our ideas and reality. A factual statement cannot be ascertained if there is no final arbiter independent of our cognizing. Rescher (2000: 130) states, 'A factual statement on the order of "There are pi mesons" is true if and only if the world is such that pi mesons exist within it.'
2. Realism is indispensable for the distinction between our subjective thoughts and opinions of reality and reality the way it actually is. Rescher (2000: 131) quotes Aristotle: '...that which exists does not conform to various opinions, but rather the correct opinions conform to that which exists.'
3. Realism is indispensable for communication and inquiry within the scientific community. It is established that the scientific community shares a real world where there are real objects which would '...serve as a basis for inter-subjective communication' (Rescher 2000: 134).
4. Realism is indispensable for communal inquiry within the scientific community. It would be absurd to have a shared focus of epistemic strivings that imperfectly estimate reality when there is no reality. He states, 'We could not proceed on the basis of the notion that inquiry estimates the character of the real if we were not prepared to presume or postulate from the very outset a reality for these estimates to be estimates of' (2000: 132).
5. Realism is indispensable for the very idea of inquiry is hinged upon the conception of an independent reality and the attempts to understand it, albeit not fully. He states, 'Without the conception of reality we could not think of our knowledge in the fallibilistic mode we actually use—as having provisional, tentative, improvable features that constitute a crucial part of the conceptual scheme...' (2000: 132).

6. Finally, realism is indispensable because our conception of causality is dependent on our attempts to empirically understand the real world. 'Reality is viewed as the causal source and basis of the appearances, the originator, and determiner of the phenomena of our cognitively relevant experience' (2000: 133).

Bhaskar (1979, 1998*a,b,c*) developed a form of realism known as critical realism. He and his supporters viewed critical realism as a middle ground between positivism and relativism (Collier 1994; Harvey 2002; Kemp and Holmwood 2003). From relativism, critical realism assumed an anti-foundational stance by acknowledging the fallibilism of our knowledge of reality that is conceptually mediated and theory-laden. It also rejected the existence of axioms or synthetic a priori principles that provided epistemic knowledge of reality (Cruichskank 2002). From positivism, critical realism emphasized empirical experimentation. However, it denied the possibility of generalizing its experimental outcomes because reality is an open system consisting of underlying contingent structures. Moreover, it maintained a mind-independent, stratified reality consisting of underlying structures and mechanisms that determined how things come to behave (*transcendental realism*). It also held that theoretical entities have referential value (i.e., theoretical entities genuinely reflect the way the world is).

To this critical realist perspective, Donald T. Campbell added an evolutionary view of the development and progression of scientific knowledge (Campbell 1989*a,b*, 1990*a*, 1991, 1995; Campbell and Paller 1989; Paller and Campbell 1989). He replaced Kuhn's social constructivist interpretation of scientific development with a selectionist evolutionary epistemology. Scientific progress evolves via a process of blind variation and selective retention. Reality (as opposed to mere opinions) serves as an external arbitrator or common referent in editing beliefs and theories for winnowing out inferior theories. Campbell (1988: 447) states, 'I am an epistemological relativist, but I am not an ontological nihilist.' McKelvey (1999: 384) states, 'His [Campbell] development of evolutionary epistemology reflects his continuing interest in the dynamics of how sciences change in their search for improved verisimilitude in observation and explanation without abandoning objectivist ontological realism.'

According to Azevedo (1997), Campbell shows how the process of blind variation and selective retention of biological evolution applies to science. She states:

Campbell argues convincingly that reality plays a part in editing beliefs, particularly in the sort of environment in which the organism's perceptual mechanisms evolved. Both biological evolution and scientific progress evolve via a process of blind variation and selective retention. Science, seen as a problem solving activity, is continuous with the problem solving activity of all organisms. (Azevedo 1997: 92)

Campbell combined his selectionist stance with a validity-seeking hermeneutics to justify the validity of knowledge based on a consensus among the scientific community. Scientific communities generally do not reach consensus based simply on opinions and beliefs. Scientific communities vary, of course, on the standards used to reach consensus. In the social sciences, the standards or criteria used to reach consensus typically include sound logical arguments and empirical evidence to substantiate the claims that are made. While social scientists debate the nature of the arguments and evidence that they consider legitimate and persuasive, most are willing to accept that: (1) science is a process of error correction; (2) science is based on evidence obtained from outside of the scientists about the world; and (3) while evidence is theory-laden and error-prone, it is nevertheless useful for discriminating between plausible alternative models for understanding a phenomenon in question. This basic method of comparing evidence and arguments between alternative claims is not undertaken to achieve an ultimate Truth; instead, it is to select among competing alternative claims about a question or problem at a given time and context. The theories and models that better fit the problems they are intended to solve are selected, whereas those that are less fit are ignored or winnowed out. Campbell argued that this successive process of comparative selection accumulates into an evolutionary growth of scientific knowledge by the scholarly community.

Discussion and Implications for Engaged Scholarship

In summary, logical positivism was an extension of the Enlightenment and modernism's faith in objectivity, reason, and the progress of scientific knowledge. It emphasized sensory observation and induction as the foundation of scientific knowledge. Underlying this assumption is a value-free and neutral observer and language. It denied all metaphysical statements as having any correspondence with reality and considered them meaningless due to their failure to pass the verifiability theory of meaning or verificationism. This also led to conflating epistemology with ontology. Positivism reduced causal relations or explanations to a Humean constant conjunction of events and emphasized the unity of science or the primacy of the physical sciences as the model for all sciences.

The perspectives that we included in relativism all reacted to positivism's emphasis on certainty, its anti-metaphysical attitude, its reliance on sensory observation, and its modernistic values. Relativism represents a host of philosophical schools of which just a sampling was described including: historical relativism, social constructivism, postmodernism, critical theory, and hermeneutics. These schools converged on their construal of truth as being socially constructed and theory-laden. They adopted an anti-essentialist stance that denied science of its objectivity and empirical/rational basis and denied any privileged way of acquiring knowledge of it.

Pragmatism developed as an alternative to the historical debates between rationalism and empiricism although more recently variants of pragmatism provide an alternative to positivism. It attempted to reconcile the abstractness of rationalism with the particularism of empiricism. Pragmatism is characterized by the relation of theory and praxis and specifically in the predetermined outcomes of an inquiry. Despite Lovejoy's criticism of the varieties of pragmatisms, they shared a common construal of truth as the success in guiding action and prediction. Ideas were clarified by showing their relationship to practice. Unlike, positivism's emphasis on induction, pragmatism embraced abduction as the mode of scientific discovery. Depending on the pragmatist, they adopted an objective or subjective ontology and epistemology or a combination of both.

Similar to pragmatism's attempt to provide an alternative to the historical debates between rationalism and empiricism, realism was also an attempt to provide such an alternative. More recently, critical realism developed an alternative between logical positivism and the more relativistic positions. Also, similar to pragmatism and relativism, realism consisted of numerous perspectives which shared in common an objective ontology that presupposes the existence of a mind-independent reality and the ability of a theory to capture partial aspects of reality. In contrast to positivism and relativism, more contemporary forms of realism viewed truth as being a process of successive approximations of reality, or verisimilitude. Furthermore, it rejected the positivistic adoption of constant conjunction and the relativistic view of socially constructed causal relations and replaced them with a realistic construal of causal mechanisms that exist independently of our knowledge. Contemporary forms of realism also acknowledge the fallibilism of scientific knowledge and attempt to explain the progression of knowledge using an evolutionary metaphor. Finally, most forms of realism adopt some form of subjective epistemology where there are no predefined or predetermined methodologies or criteria that provide privileged views of reality.

It is tempting to view the four philosophies, especially positivism and relativism, as incommensurate and antithetical to each other. If you adopt this view you will probably choose one philosophy that seems closest to your own preferences and condemn the others as 'unscientific,' 'uncaring,' or perhaps just 'unrealistic.' In contrast and like Schultt (2004: 79), we think there are significant benefits from adopting a more inclusive research philosophy that is open to and integrates some of the differences of alternative philosophies of science. Engaged scholarship represents an example of such integration. Ontologically, engaged scholarship adopts Bhaskarian critical realism with its middle-ground position between positivism and relativism and its layered/stratified/multi-dimensional mind-independent reality. However, it also adopts Rescher's realistic pragmatism to provide a pragmatic justification for its realist stance. With critical realist ontology, engaged scholarship adopts a Campbellian relativist evolutionary epistemology to understand the macro-level accumulation of scientific knowledge and its weak anti-foundationalist methodological stance where there are better warranted methods depending on the phenomenon. It also adopts triangulation across convergent, inconsistent, and contradictory data to understand the micro-level development of more robust scientific knowledge. However, the development of engaged scholarship's philosophical underpinnings also benefited from other philosophical and metaphysical perspectives of which the most influential are discussed below.

REFLEXIVITY

Postmodern and hermeneutic scholars have emphasized the interests, values, and biases that are served by researchers. No inquiry can be objective in the sense of being impartial and comprehensive by including a balanced representation of all stakeholders' viewpoints. Critical theorists point out that meanings and interpretations of organizational life get played out in a context of power relationships. 'Meanings are always politically mediated' (Putnam, 1993: 230). Pragmatic and realist philosophers also emphasized the theory-laden nature of human perception, conceptualization, and judgment. The empiricist view was criticized because of the impossibility of pure, unmediated observation of empirical 'facts' (Mingers 2004: 90). That being the case, engaged scholars need to be far more reflexive in their studies than positivists and empiricists have admitted. Reflexivity is characterized by different types of recursive turns each providing different insights and perspectives (Alvesson and Sköldberg 2000).

ABDUCTION

Peirce argued that induction serves not to initiate theory but rather to test it. The basic process in initiating theory was what he called abduction or hypothetical inference. As discussed in Chapter 4, this form of inference begins by engaging with the world and encountering an anomaly or breakdown that is inconsistent with our understanding or theory of the world. Abduction entails creative insight that resolves the anomaly if it were true. A conjecture developed through abductive inference represents a new plausible alternative to the status quo explanation of a given phenomenon in question. Because it might solve the problem, such an insight merits further development and elaboration as a defensible theory through deductive logic, and then testing through inductive inferences.

SCIENCE IS AN ERROR-CORRECTION PROCESS OF KNOWLEDGE DEVELOPMENT

It is easy to 'throw out the baby with the bathwater.' Philosophers of science have extensively criticized and rejected central tenets of logical positivism and empiricism, which had become the received view of science by the 1970s. Despite the demise of the received view, McKelvey (1999) discusses a legacy of useful principles that withstood criticism and are clearly apparent in contemporary social science.

Many key ingredients of positivism nevertheless still remain in good standing among scientific realists, such as theory terms, observation terms, tangible observables and unobservables, intangible and metaphysical terms, auxiliary hypothesis, causal explanation, empirical reality, testability, incremental corroboration and falsification, and generalizable statements. . . . The received view is ontologically strong, in the sense that it posits an external reality and that successive scientific discoveries and theories over time more and more correctly describe and explain this reality; reality acts as a strong external criterion variable against which scientific theories are held accountable. (McKelvey 1999: 386)

The most fundamental of these principles, we believe, is that science is an error-correction process that is based on evidence from the world rather than merely reflecting the scientist's opinions of the world. Indeed, McKelvey (2002a: 254) asserts that 'the singular advantage of the realist method is its empirically-based, self-correcting approach to the discovery of truth.'

However, the relativists, like the pragmatists Dewey and James, cautioned that 'hard-and-fast, capital-T-Truth is simply an illusion' (Westphal 1998: 3). Ideas and beliefs are nothing but human constructions, shaped by social processes and procedures. Truth is that which gets endorsed and accepted in the scientific community. 'Truth resides in agreement: social consensus does not merely evidentiate truth, but is its creator' (Westphal 1998: 3). We pointed out however, that social science communities do not reach consensus based simply on opinions; they rely on standards of sound and persuasive arguments and empirical evidence for a scientific claim. The persuasiveness of an argument is a rhetorical question. Thus, in addition to logos, the other angles of pathos and ethos of the rhetorical triangle are important considerations (too often ignored) in communicating scientific findings.

MODELS AS MEDIATORS

A key criticism of positivism was its syntactic view of theory (consisting of axiomatic first-order logical relations among theoretical terms, and correspondence rules that gave theoretical terms meaning in terms of their observational consequences). Giere (1999), Suppe (1989), and others replaced this syntactic view with a semantic view of theories in which models (rather than correspondence rules) provide the interpretation of social theories (Morrison and Morgan 1999: 5). This criticism provides a key reason for including model development (in research design) as a core activity in the engaged scholarship process. The semantic view claims that models stand in a mediating relationship between theories and data. McKelvey (2002a) emphasizes that model-centeredness is a key element of scientific realism. He quotes Cartwright as saying, 'The root from theory to reality is from theory to model, and then from model to phenomenological wall' (Cartwright 1983: 4). Like Morrison and Morgan, McKelvey views models as autonomous mediators between theory and phenomena.

Models are viewed as being fallibilistic and perspectival. Because data are theory-laden and error-prone, the challenge is to compare plausible alternative models given our current understanding of the subject matter instead of searching for an ultimate truth. As Giere (1999) explains, models represent alternative claims about a phenomenon in question given current understandings of it, rather than a universal objective theory of the world.

[Science] pits one model, or family of models, against rival models, with no presumption that the whole set of models considered exhausts the logical possibilities. This means that what models are taken best to represent the world at any given time depends on what rival models were considered along the way. And this seems, historically, a contingent matter. So the models of the world held at any given time might have been different if historical contingencies had been different. (Giere 1999: 77)

Azevedo (2002) provides a pragmatic extension of using models for scientific problem solving. A scientific theory is operationalized as a model that is mapped onto reality (the problem). The test of a model is practical: how well does it serve as a map to guide action. Because the process of making and using maps is easily understood, the use of a mapping model of knowledge provides a powerful heuristic for determining the validity of scientific theories. Azevedo (2002: 725) points out that maps and models are constructed with interests in mind. They are selective representations of the world, and their content and format are selected according to their relevance to the problems they are intended to solve. Because the usefulness of a map model can only be assessed by how well it helps to solve the problem of the user, its validity is interest-related as well.

RELEVANCE

Users of research knowledge—both scientific and practical—demand that it overcome the dual hurdles of being relevant and rigorous in serving their particular domains and interests (Pettigrew 2001). However, different criteria of relevance and rigor apply to different studies because their purposes, processes, and contexts are different. Pragmatists (particularly James and Dewey) emphasized that the relevance of knowledge should be judged in terms of how well it addresses the problematic situation or issue for which it was intended. Rescher (2000: 105) maintains that the relevance of knowledge about a problematic situation being investigated may entail any (or all) of the following questions:

- Description (answering *what?* and *how?* questions about the problematic situation);
- Explanation (addressing *why?* questions about the problematic situation);
- Prediction (setting and achieving expectations about the problematic situation);
- Control (effective intervention in the problematic situation); and
- Emancipation (identifying the marginalized and repressed).

One criterion of research effectiveness does not fit all. Pragmatists have emphasized that different criteria of relevance and rigor apply to research undertaken to examine these different kinds of questions.

ENGAGEMENT

A fundamental tenet of critical realism is that a real world exists out there, but our abilities to comprehend it are very limited. The ambiguous, 'buzzing, blooming, confusing' nature of reality exceeds the explanatory capabilities of any single theory or model that a researcher might devise. 'In the absence of unambiguous foundational truth in the social sciences, the only sensible way forward can be conscious pluralism' (Pettigrew 2001: S62). As discussed in Chapter 1, pluralism requires engaging others from different disciplines and functions who can contribute different perspectives and models for understanding the problem domain being examined. Engagement not only requires a different conception of the researcher's role, but also an extension of the philosophers' consensus theory of truth.

Hermeneutics and relativism provide useful guidelines for engagement. Perhaps most fundamental is for researchers to jettison their God's Eye view (illustrated in Figure 2.2) and adopt a participant frame of reference (shown in Figure 2.3) to conduct their studies. In a participant role, a researcher listens to and learns from others who have different perspectives that merit consideration for modeling or mapping a problem domain existing in the world. Moreover, relativism stresses the salience of divergent and often conflicting interests, values, and power of stakeholders in any study, and the impossibility of serving them all. One clear implication is the need for researchers to be reflexive in clarifying whose interests and values are served in their research engagements.

Engaging people from diverse backgrounds and perspectives represents a method of triangulating on a complex problem. Triangulation is the use of multiple sources of information, models, and methods in a study. Research knowledge advances by comparing the relative contributions and perspectives provided by different models. Azevedo (1997) discusses how the coordination of multiple models and perspectives may reveal the robust features of reality by identifying those features that appear invariant (or convergent) across different perspectives. Azevedo reflects the established view in philosophy of science of developing reliable scientific knowledge by identifying those perspectives from a pluralist approach that converge on a common or consensual view of the phenomenon.

But the engagement of different stakeholders in a study often produces inconsistent and contradictory perspectives of a problem domain being examined. Pluralistic perspectives should not be dismissed as noise, error, or outliers—as they are typically treated in a triangulation research strategy. Chapter 9 discusses how these inconsistent and contradictory findings require an expansion of a consensus theory of truth that emphasizes convergence and agreement among investigators and reviewers in a scientific community on reliable and replicable findings. But many real-world problems contain inconsistent and contradictory principles. Rendering such problems as incommensurable denies their reality. Inconsistent and contradictory findings from different stakeholders involved in a study often represent truly pluralistic views of a problem domain that might be explained through methods of arbitrage (linking divergent bits of information and views) and paradoxical reasoning (to reconcile opposing and contradictory findings). As Suppe (1977) insightfully asked of Kuhn's claims of incommensurability, if pluralistic perspectives are truly incommensurable, how is it possible that scholars (and practitioners) can compare different paradigms and communicate constructively across the paradigms? One implication of the practice of engaged scholarship is that philosophers of science need to expand their traditional explanations that emphasize convergent central tendencies to include explanations based on inconsistent findings through arbitrage and contradictory findings with methods of paradoxical reasoning.

THE SOCIAL PROCESS OF SOCIAL SCIENCE

Another important implication of the practice of engaged scholarship for philosophy of science is the social process of conducting research. Positivists might be excused for their admission of a separation between a scientific theory to be tested and the social, psychological, and economic processes in which such a theory might have developed. But an excuse for such a separation between the 'logic of discovery' and the 'logic of testing' a theory should not apply to relativism, pragmatism, and realism. Despite the calls for assessing research with intended actions of the users of research by pragmatists, for a pluralistic comparison of alternative models of a problem domain being investigated by realists, and for a social constructions of the meanings of reality from different stakeholders by relativists, it is striking how little attention philosophers from these different schools of thought have given to the social process in which these perspectives might be realized.

Perhaps philosophers of science have deferred this question to sociologists of science. Studies of working scientists by Garfinkel et al. (1981), Knorr-Cetina and Amann (1990), and Latour and Woolgar (1986) indicate that improvisation underlies the process in which scientists actually construct models, enact experimental runs, design and interpret data, report on their methods and findings, and assign credit for discovery. While such studies are useful descriptions of how scientists engage in their practices, they provide little guidance for action, except for the conclusion that scientists engage in what Levi-Strauss (1966) termed a bricolage, improvising with a mixed bag of tools and tacit knowledge to adapt to the task at hand. The process by which scholars might step outside of themselves and engage others to be informed of the problem domain being examined remains a black box. Subsequent chapters explore possible ways to open this black box by suggesting means and ways to engage relevant stakeholders in problem formulation, theory building, research design, and problem solving.

Conclusion

In conclusion, the purpose of the historical review of key concepts and principles of positivism, relativism, pragmatism, and realism has been to identify some of the conceptual tools and frameworks to understand different views of science, to initiate a process of reflexivity in choosing a philosophy of science that suits your scholarly practice, and to gain a deeper understanding of the philosophical basis of engaged scholarship. We discussed how these philosophies of science have influenced our views of engaged scholarship, and also indicated several areas where the practice of engaged scholarship might advance or extend philosophy of science. As stated at the beginning of this chapter and applied in subsequent chapters, we view engaged scholarship as based on the following key elements of a critical realist philosophy of science:

- There is a real world out there (consisting of material, mental, and emergent products), but our individual understanding of it is limited. In general, physical material things are easier to understand than reflexive and emergent social processes.
- All facts, observations and data are theory-laden implicitly or explicitly. Social sciences have no absolute, universal, error-free truths, or laws as any scientific knowledge.
- No form of inquiry can be value-free and impartial; each is value-full. Some methods are better warranted than others depending on the phenomenon.
- Knowing a complex reality demands use of multiple perspectives.
- Robust knowledge is a product of theoretical and methodological triangulation where evidence is not necessarily convergent but might also be inconsistent or even contradictory.
- Models that better fit the problems they are intended to solve are selected allowing an evolutionary growth of knowledge.

3 Formulating the Research Problem

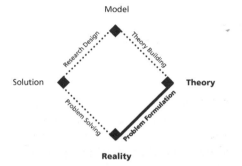

The formulation of a problem is often more essential than its solution, which may be merely a matter of mathematical or experimental skill.
(Albert Einstein quoted in Getzels and Csikszentminhalyi 1975)

It is exceedingly difficult to say something meaningful about the real world without starting in the real world. Observation and description of the real world are the essential points of origin for theories in applied areas.

(Robert Dubin 1976: 18)

Any scientist of any age who wants to make important discoveries must study important problems. Dull or piffling problems yield dull or piffling answers. It is not enough that a problem should be interesting—almost any problem is interesting if it is studied in sufficient depth... the problem must be such that it matters what the answer is—whether to science generally or to mankind.

(P. B. Medawar, Nobel Laureate in Medicine and Physiology, 1979)

Problem formulation is often the first—and most important—task of the engaged scholarship process. Problem formulation plays a crucial role in grounding the subject or problem in reality, and directly affects how theory building, research design, and problem solving tasks are performed. Yet, researchers often overlook or pay little attention to problem formulation. Witness, for example, the glib problem statements in the introduction of most research articles in social science journals. Like other human beings, researchers tend not to be 'problem-minded,' and prefer instead to be 'solution-driven' by focusing on developing and testing models or theories for problems that often remain unclear.

Research is often viewed as a problem solving activity (e.g., Deutsch 1997; Azevedo 2002). Scientific theories are constructed and evaluated with specific interests in mind, and research findings are used to inform decisions about theory and practice. Viewed as a problem solving process, science aims to increase our understanding of complex problems or phenomena that exist under conditions of uncertainty found in the world. This process typically involves steps in recognizing a problem, searching and screening information, evaluating alternatives, and choosing a solution (e.g., Polya 1957; March and Simon 1958; Halpern 1996; Deutsch 1997; McGrath and Tschan 2004). In terms of formulating a research problem, this process translates into four interrelated activities: (1) recognizing and situating a problem; (2) gathering information to ground the problem and its setting; (3) diagnosing the information to ascertain the characteristics or symptoms of the problem; and (4) deciding what actions or questions to pursue to resolve the research problem.

This chapter examines the process of problem formulation in terms of these four activities of situating, grounding, diagnosing, and resolving a research problem. These four activities overlap and are highly interdependent. Except for highly simplified and stylized problems, problem formulation activities seldom unfold in an orderly rational progression over time. Thus, instead of portraying these activities as unfolding in a fixed linear sequence, I view them as a set of parallel activities that researchers undertake simultaneously in varying degrees throughout the problem formulation process. As discussed in this chapter, the relative effort devoted to each of these activities depends on how the problem is perceived, the context in which it exists in the world, and the goals of the study.

Research might be undertaken to examine a wide variety of possible problems. Some research projects might be undertaken to address a particular practical problem, crisis or threat, such as a gap between expectations and outcomes experienced by practitioners in implementing an organizational program, product, or service. If these problems are clearly structured or understood, the problem formulation process may reflect an orderly sequence of activities in situating, grounding, diagnosing, and resolving the problem.

Most research problems are not so well-structured. They often represent anomalies or breakdowns that a scholar encounters in the literature or in practice that are not consistent with the scholar's theory of the world. Scholars often observe something that their theory did not lead them to expect— resulting in a breakdown or anomaly. Anomalies represent diagnostic puzzles that trigger recognition that 'There's something else going on here.'

Finally, the problem motivating a study may deal more generally with exploring an unclear issue or phenomenon in order to find out about reality with no specific end in mind. In other words, the researcher may have only vague impressions of how to situate, ground, diagnose, or resolve a problem. As Abbott (2004: 83) states,

We often don't see ahead of time exactly what the problem is; much less do we have an idea of the solution. We often come at an issue with only a gut feeling that there is something interesting about it. We often don't know even what an answer ought to look like. Indeed, figuring out what the puzzle really is, and what the answer ought to look like often happen in parallel with finding the answer itself.

As these illustrations suggest, a research *problem* is defined as any problematic situation, phenomenon, issue, or topic that is chosen as the subject of an investigation. The problematic situation may originate in either the practical world of affairs, a theoretical discipline, or a personal experience or insight. It may be perceived to represent an unsatisfying circumstance, a promising opportunity, a breakdown or anomaly in expected arrangements, or simply a topic of interest. However one construes the problematic situation, researchers tend to encounter four common difficulties in situating, grounding, diagnosing, and resolving a research problem.

First, a key challenge in situating a problem is deciding what persons or stakeholder groups will be served by the research, and to describe reality from the perspectives of those persons or stakeholders. Implicitly or explicitly, all research is undertaken in service of someone—whether it be the researcher, a funding agency, practitioners, academics, a profession, or any of the above. The point is that problems do not exist objectively 'out there;' they are uniquely perceived and framed by different people. Knowing from whose perspective a problem is being addressed and engaging them in problem formulation is necessary to frame the focus, level, and scope of a research study.

Second, researchers—like other human beings—have limited capabilities in handling complexity. They often use short-cuts or heuristics that produce biased judgments. Needless to say, solving the 'wrong' problem with the 'right' methods, or what J. Tuckey referred to as a Type III error, is costly, demoralizing, and all-too-familiar (Volkema 1995; Buyukdamgaci 2003). Unfortunately, problem formulation is often rushed or taken for granted. As a result, important dimensions of a problem often go unrecognized and opportunities to advance knowledge of the problem are missed (Volkema 1983).

A third difficulty is that the issues that motivate a study are sometimes stated as imaginary pseudo-problems that lack grounding in reality. Too many social science studies suffer from elaborating theories that are often based on an insufficient diagnosis of the problem and its context. As a consequence, theory and research tend to be grounded in myths and superstitions. Those who generalize from concrete experiences or particulars with a problem can answer the questions, *For example? From whose point of view? What is that point of view?* Engaging people who experience and know the problem is necessary to answer these questions. Lacking answers to these questions often leads to unfounded generalizations.

Merton points out that oftentimes in science as in everyday life, 'explanations are provided of matters that are not and never were' (Merton 1987: 21). In legal proceedings, establishing the case is mandatory for pursuing it. Merton (1987) cautioned that an important first element in the practice of science is '*establishing the phenomenon*.' Evidence and arguments should clearly indicate that the phenomenon is enough of a regularity to require and allow explanation. In this way 'pseudo facts that induce pseudo problems are avoided' (Hernes 1989: 125).

A fourth difficulty is that even when problems are grounded in reality, their diagnosis or resolution may not lead to creative theory that advances understanding of the phenomenon or problem. Bruner (1973) points out that a theory or model is a generic representation of the critical characteristics of a phenomenon. For Bruner, grounding theories in reality requires going beyond the information given so that the problem is formulated to have applicability beyond the situation in which it is observed.

This chapter explores ways of dealing with these four common difficulties in situating, grounding, and diagnosing a research problem, and forming a question to study a problem domain. The next four sections discuss each of these key activities in problem formulation. A central theme is the close interplay between theory and reality when formulating a research problem. Abbott reflects this interplay in stating, 'Often one builds out from the problem on the one hand, and from the solution on the other, until the two halves meet in the middle like a bridge built from two banks' (Abbott 2004: 81).

Situating the Problem

All problems, anomalies, or issues motivating a study begin with a perception that something requires attention. Problems are not given by nature, but by how, whom, and why they are perceived. No one can possibly represent all aspects and viewpoints of a problem domain. That being the case, any formulation of a problem is a partial representation reflecting the perspective and interests of the observer. Problems do not exist 'out there' in an objective state of nature. People enact reality and its problems (Weick 1979). Reality is socially constructed (Berger and Luckmann 1966). No one studies the social world as it is, instead, we study reality as it appears to us. A scholar must, therefore, be reflexive and clarify whose point of view and interests are served in a problem or model proposed to represent reality (Van Maanen 1995).

Different people interpret situations in different ways. People who interact and socialize together develop shared beliefs about the nature of things and relationships between them, and shared norms about what they should and should not do. Over time these beliefs may become so institutionalized that they are taken to be 'matters of fact.' Our individual histories are unique, however. Different people interpret situations in different ways because they bring to a situation their own particular mental 'framework' of personal beliefs, attitudes, prejudices, and expectations to make sense of a situation. As a result, Eden et al. (1983: 2–3) point out that people pay attention to certain things, selecting those having a particular significance for themselves, and ignoring the rest.

The 'model' of man we have ... is thus not of an organism responding to some 'stimulus,' nor 'driven' by internal needs of instincts, nor of a person whose thinking and actions are socially 'given.' Rather, it is a human being who acts in the light of the personal interpretations or constructions he (or she) places upon events. (Eden et al. 1983: 3)

One implication of this perspective is that it is impossible to assume, self-evidently and non-problematically, that the way other people interpret a situation, is the same as, or even similar to, the way we interpret that 'same' situation. An event which you or I might see as a major crisis for a particular reason may be seen as a major crisis by someone else for completely different reasons, by another person as a minor difficulty, and yet other people may not even have noticed it at all. No situation is inherently, 'objectively' a problem. A problem belongs to a person; it is an often complicated, and always personal construction that an individual (or like-minded group of people) places on events. (Eden et al. 1983: 8)

When and how a problem is situated largely determines how it is approached and solved. For example, labeling a situation a 'human resources' problem means that it will be approached differently than if it is viewed as an 'organization design' problem or a 'market share' problem. A problem's definition largely determines its solution space. That being the case, when situating the problem we need to be reflexive about whose perspectives will take foreground and background in situating the problem domain. The following dimensions are useful in situating the focal area, level, and scope of the problem domain.

FOCUS AND TIMESPAN

A problem can be viewed as having a foreground and a background, a focal area, and a context (Abbott 2004: 138). For example, studies of businesses often put managers in the foreground and public policy makers or other stakeholders in the background. In this case the focus would be on the problems and situations experienced by managers. The concerns of employees of businesses and other stakeholders would be treated as part of the background or context of the manager's problem domain. So also, local politics, external regulations, and infrastructure in the communities where the business is located would be treated as context in the problem domain. Selecting who is in the foreground and background significantly influences how the research problem is formulated.

Some people may view a given problem in fairly narrow, clear, and static terms experienced by an isolated group of people or institutions at a certain point in time. Others might view the same problem domain as being a general, unclear, and dynamic process diffused among many different groups over long periods of time. These differing perceptions of a problem domain often reflect the differing interests and roles of users. Management practitioners, for example, tend to focus on the immediate and particular problems they are experiencing in running their organizations. Befitting their roles, policy makers tend to be concerned with more general views of problems affecting a larger population of citizens or practitioners.

Ultimately, how a problem domain is specified depends on who is chosen as the users or audience of the research. Most problems are too complex to capture the differing perspectives of all relevant stakeholders. We have no choice but to cut down on the complexity of the problem domain by putting some things and people in the foreground and others in the background.

LEVEL

A problem has a 'level,' in the sense that it may be experienced or noticed at individual, group, organization, industry, or broader levels of analysis. In addition, the factors or events that are thought to contribute to, or be the consequence of, the problem may exist at different levels of analysis. Thus, as Abbott (2004: 138) states, some things are bigger than our focal problem, some are part of the problem (and possibly determine it), and some things that are smaller than it. The choice of level of analysis not only reflects the nature of the problem, but also the disciplinary base that is used to structure or model the problem. For example, psychologists tend to structure their research problems at the individual level, while sociologists tend to view problems from more macro institutional and community perspectives.

Closely related to selecting a level of analysis is the context of the problem domain, which typically includes characteristics broader than or outside of the level at which a problem is examined. For example, the context for studying individual work behavior may include the group, organization, and industry in which the person works. If the level of analysis is expanded to the organization, then many of the group and organization-level characteristics that were before viewed as context are now folded into the problem domain, while more aggregate industry-level factors continue to be treated as part of the environmental context. Of course, choosing the context of a problem domain entails more than just selecting a level of analysis. At a given level, it involves rearranging what things to focus on in the foreground and background and what things to exclude or place outside of your purview.

SCOPE

How deep, how broad, and how long a problem should be studied are never-ending questions of problem scope. Ultimately, the answer is that you study a problem until it satisfies the curiosities and needs of those engaged in the study.

Ideally, the scope of a problem should decrease and become more manageable as you become familiar with it. In practice the opposite often occurs with 'scope creep' where the problem becomes expansive and includes more complex domains as you study a problem. A variety of factors contribute to scope creep. First, it is a constructive sign of learning that the problem of interest may be much larger than initially anticipated, or that it plays into a much larger problem. Research advisors and others engaged in a study may also be learning about the problem, and may suggest a study of related issues and questions.

Another factor that contributes to scope creep is the endless nature of problems in reality. As Rescher (1996: 131–2) states, 'Real things are cognitively opaque—we cannot see to the bottom of them. Our knowledge of such things can thus become more extensive without thereby becoming more complete.' He says that in being real, one can gain new information, which may add to or revise what one has learned earlier. A 'real thing' has features that may exist outside of our cognitive reach. 'As a consequence, our knowledge of fact is always in flux. It is not a thing, but an ever-changing and ever growing manifold of processes' (Rescher 1996: 132).

The focus, level, and scope of a problem domain are often unclear when research begins. Familiarity emerges over time by engaging relevant stakeholders in grounding and diagnosing information about the problem.

Grounding the Problem in Reality

Situating a problem domain and gathering information about it often represent two initial overlapping steps in problem formulation. The more you can ground a research problem in reality from a user's perspective the more you learn to appreciate the multiple dimensions and manifestations of a problem and its solution space. Grounding a problem in reality entails an exploratory study into the nature, context, and what is known about the problem domain. A variety of methods are useful for undertaking this exploration. As discussed later, they include information-gathering activities drawing on personal experiences and direct observations of how a problematic situation unfolds in a particular context, as well as talking with people who experience the problem through casual conversations, interviews, or in group meetings. Reviewing the literature to determine the scope, prevalence, and context of the problem is also needed.

The purpose of these activities is to become sufficiently familiar with a problem domain to be able to answer the journalist's basic questions of *who, what, where, when, why,* and *how* the problem exists. Grounding a problem requires both particular and general answers to these questions. *Particular* answers provide up-close and personal descriptions of the problem based on first-hand observations of a specific case or two. Particular answers provide concrete and vivid details of a specific problem. *General* answers are needed to show that the particular case is not unique; instead it is an instance of a much larger or pervasive problem. Typically the general answers are based on indirect statistical evidence obtained from literature reviews of prior research on the problem.

Daily examples of using both particular and general descriptions of problems are found in the introductory paragraphs of feature stories in many newspapers. Usually, the first paragraph in the stories provides a particular up-close and personal answer to the journalist's questions. A typical format is the following:

> Each week for the past six months *(when)*, Joe Blow, a 45-year-old machinist *(who)* has been seeing his psychiatrist for moods of depression *(what)* that have become worse since he was laid off from his job *(why)* that he held for 20 years at AMC Engineering located in this industrial Midwest town *(where)*.

The second paragraph provides general answers to the journalist's questions about the pervasiveness of the problem. It might read as follows:

> Joe Blow is not alone. A study by University researchers (Wanberg et al. 2005) reported that there were 8349 mass layoffs in 2001 *(when)* in the US *(where)*, which led to 1.7 million individuals losing their jobs *(who)*. Researchers are finding that job loss has a negative influence on most every indicator of mental and physical health. For example, studies demonstrate that job loss is associated with increased anxiety, depression, sleeping problems, alcohol disorders, divorce, and child abuse (e.g., Dooley et al. 1996) *(why)*. Joe Blow and millions like him *(who)* are posing a major question of what to do about the problems associated with job lay offs?

At this point the story might go in several possible directions, depending on the writer's perspective. If the writer takes a human resource development perspective, the story might focus on what training and counseling services are being provided by companies to help individuals, like Joe Blow, make the transition and find a job. Alternatively, the writer may reflect a public policy concern, and question how government might curb corporate human-resource abuses of layoffs and their resulting pain and health care costs on former employees and society. In addition to illustrating the journalist's questions, this example illustrates a point discussed later that many different stories or diagnoses of a problem are often grounded in the same data or observations of reality.

Answering the journalist's questions provides useful criteria for grounding a research problem by obtaining particular and general answers to who, what, where, when, why, and how the problem exists. When beginning a study researchers are seldom sufficiently familiar with a problem domain to be able to answer these questions in particular and in general. And if they think they know the answers to these questions, then it is important to determine who may answer the questions in similar and different ways and why.

Problem formulation is not a solitary exercise; instead it is a collective achievement. Grounding a problem requires the researcher to step outside of him/herself, and to be open to and informed by the interpretations of others about the problem domain. As Bruner (1986: 133) states, 'Reflection and "distancing" are crucial aspects of achieving a sense of the range of possible stances—a metacognitive step of huge import.' Most problems tend to exist in a 'buzzing, blooming, and confusing' reality. The world is too rich and multi-layered to be captured adequately by any single person. Therefore, a pluralist approach to problem formulation is essential. It is only by obtaining and coordinating perspectives of other key stakeholders that robust features of reality can be distinguished from those features that are merely a function of one perspective (Azevedo 1997: 189–90).

Diagnosing the Problem

Grounding a problem domain through careful observation and data collection provides the raw materials for diagnosing a problem. Diagnosis entails a disciplined, yet open-minded, application of models or theories in order to ascertain the specific nature of the problem in context. Becoming familiar with a phenomenon existing in reality supplies multiple opportunities to diagnose expected and unexpected things. Expected things are those that conform to our model of reality; we view them as well-structured problems for which known solutions or interventions are believed to exist. Unexpected things are those that do not conform to our model of reality. They represent anomalies or breakdowns that lead us to recognize that we have an ill-structured under-standing of the problem domain. Further study may indicate that existing solutions to the anomaly are inadequate; a new solution needs to be created or discovered.[1]

Breakdowns are instances when expectations are not met, something does not make sense, or when one's assumption of coherence is violated (Agar 1986: 20). Breakdowns play a central role in bringing problems to our attention. Some anthropologists advise researchers to 'use surprise, the unexpected, or a sense of difference as cues to what to study' (Rosenblatt 1981: 200). Alvesson (2004) suggests that a really interesting breakdown means that an empirical 'finding' cannot easily be accounted for by available theory. The breakdown is, thus, not an outcome of our ignorance, naivety or narrow-mindedness. The surprise should be the reaction likely to be experienced by other members of the research community who are supposed to be able to understand/explain the empirical observation/construction triggering the breakdown.

When some anomaly is perceived in a given context, our repertoire of conceptual models or perspectives limits the range of possible explanations we might develop to appreciate the phenomena in an intelligible way. For example, I enjoy watching birds alight on the bird feeder outside of my kitchen window. However, I am not an ornithologist or experienced bird watcher. As a result I am not likely to recognize or discover if a bird of a new species might land on my bird feeder. As Louis Pasteur said, chance of discovery favors the prepared mind. A prepared mind is not only familiar with particulars of the problem in context, but also has a repertoire of plausible alternative theories or models for representing and explaining the problem. Each theory provides an expected scenario of reality.

A repertoire is important for discovery. Serendipity as described by Merton (1973), and the recurrent theme of 'chance' discovery... implies that the scientist has an available agenda of problems, hypotheses, or expectations much larger than the specific problem on which he works, and that he is in some sense continually scanning or winnowing outcomes, particularly unexpected ones, with this larger set of sieves. (Campbell 1988: 418)

Familiarity with a problem domain increases the likelihood of identifying deviations from normality that merit attention as being important or novel. The likelihood of discovering new explanations for these deviations is largely dependent upon our repertoire of alternative theories. Each theory can serve as an alternative thought trial or conceptual experiment with the phenomena.

---

[1] Breakdowns can occur at any time in the research process—from the initial period of scouting around to determine 'what's-going-on-here' to the writing-up phase when particular theories are applied to particular sorts of evidence. Van Maanen (1995) suggests that breakdowns and surprises are often retrospective matters. This does not make them any less valuable, but it does limit the extent to which we can 'know' our preconceptions at the outset of a study (without experience there is nothing to startle us to recognize them) or our theories (without trying them out on our materials).

Diagnosing problems as being expected or unexpected (breakdowns) lead to different, yet related patterns of problem diagnosis. The former entails solving a problem by selecting from a set of pre-enumerated solutions, while the latter leads to constructing a new solution (Clancey 1985). Research on problems with known solutions tends to represent theory testing or evaluation research projects. In contrast, research on problems with unknown solutions is more challenging because it requires the construction or discovery of new theory. These two related patterns of problem diagnosis are now discussed in greater detail.

Diagnosis is a process of classifying observations of a phenomenon into known categories that are amenable to problem solving. In simple classification, data may directly match solution features or may match features after being abstracted. For example, to identify what kind of bird I see alighting on my bird feeder, I look at the pictures and features of birds in my guidebook to identify the kind it resembles. The essential feature of this simple classification is that I select from a set of pre-enumerated solutions. This does not mean, of course, that I have the 'right answer;' it is just that I have only attempted to match the data against known solutions, rather than construct a new solution. I may have made errors in observing the bird or in matching its features with the most similar one in my guidebook, so my conclusion is a hypothesis (that I will probably not bother to test, given the situation).

As this example illustrates, in simple classification, data elements tend to directly match solution features. For more typical ill-structured problems, the process of diagnosis is more complex. Simon (1973: 181) examined these kinds of ill-structured problems, 'defined as a problem whose structure lacks definition in some respect.' He proposed a strategy for classifying complex systems of ill-structured problems into well-structured problems at micro or modular levels of system architectures. Simon observed that the tricks that have worked in relatively well-structured domains are often extended to ill-structured domains.

He used the example of an architect, who from long term memory and experience knows the basic end states of designing a house subject to client constraints. The design of a house acquires structure by being decomposed into various problems of component design, which converts an ill-structured problem into well-structured sub-problems. Problems are well-structured in small components, but ill-structured overall. Expert specialists (or subcontractors) can be consulted to perform the component tasks in a well-structured manner. This may create problems of neglecting interrelations among various well-structured sub-problems. The danger of such inconsistencies is mitigated by a reliance on the architect's long-term memory or design blueprints; certain ways of dividing the whole task into parts will do less harm to interactions than other ways of dividing the task.

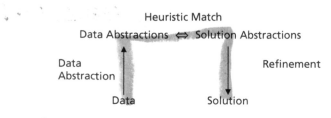

Figure 3.1. Inference structure of problem diagnosis
Source: Clancey (1985: 296).

An initial stage of laying down general (and tentative) specifications is followed by stages in which experts are called up ('evoked') to introduce new design criteria and component designs to satisfy them. At a later stage, there is attention to inconsistencies of the component designs, and a search for modifications that will continue to meet most of the criteria, or decisions to sacrifice certain criteria in favor of others. Each small phase of the activity appears to be quite well-structured, but the overall process meets none of the criteria set down for well-structured problems. (Simon 1973: 194)

Simon notes that when the problem space remains unchanged during problem solving, assimilating new information is not an issue. But when the problem space is subject to change and unanticipated events emerge during the process, then it is necessary to consider how solution models are modified or reconstructed as the problem diagnosis process unfolds.

In practice, diagnosis tends to be solution-driven. Its steps involve classifying data into problematic symptoms or categories, aggregating the classifications to infer the problem, heuristically selecting a solution that is known to be appropriate for the problem, and then refining its application to the case at hand. Clancey (1985) illustrates and describes the general structure of inference in diagnosing problems with Figure 3.1.

Problems tend to start with objects in the real world, so it makes sense that practical problem solving knowledge tends to associate problems with types of objects—people, patients, products, programs, or organizations. For example, in medical diagnosis, basic observations about the patient are classified into symptoms and abstracted to patient categories, which are heuristically linked to disease categories, and then refined to prescribe a treatment for the disease of a particular patient. The steps in this diagnostic process include: (1) data classification and aggregation; (2) heuristic matching of a problem and a solution; and (3) refining the solution to fit the case. Each of these steps are now discussed.

DATA CLASSIFICATION AND AGGREGATION

Classifying observations into conceptual categories is perhaps the most central and important inference that is made in problem formulation (as well as theory building, research design, data analysis, and problem solving activities discussed in later chapters). In the medical example, classifying patient data into symptoms and aggregating the symptoms into a patient disease category involves a reasoning process of defining and generalizing data elements from subclasses to higher abstractions of classes. The very process of classifying terms and aggregating them into more general and abstract concepts changes what we know and how we view a phenomenon. As Hanson discussed, researchers do not merely inspect the world and receive data about problems, we interact with the world and interpret the data in ways that fit our understanding of the world.

The language in which we speak and think and the circumstances in which we find ourselves speaking and thinking in that language contribute to the formation and constitution of what and how we think and hence, what and how we actually perceive. This is not to say that our language *produces* what we think about, or produces what we perceive, anymore than the plaster mold produces the bronze statue, or the recipe produces the cake. It is rather just to suggest that perhaps the form of language exercises some formative control over our thinking and over our perceiving, and over what we are inclined to state as the facts (and indeed how we state those facts). What we call 'facts' are almost always stated in *that clauses*, that some linguistic element we encounter in *seeing* when we consider Seeing That. (Hanson 1969: 184)

In defining terms, seldom do problem solvers follow the Aristotelian notion of concept definition in terms of its necessary constitutive properties as discussed in the next chapter. Instead, general schema are used that include incidental and typical manifestations or prototypes of behaviors. The definitional links are often non-essential, 'soft' descriptions. The meanings of concepts depend on what we ascribe to the links that join them. Thus, in practice we jockey around concepts to get a coherent network. Complicating this is a tendency to use terms that confound causes, effects, and indicators of concepts without understanding the links in a principled way. For example, definitions of problems in organizations are typically based on deviations from normal patterns. But the meaning of 'normal' depends on everything else happening to the organization, so inferring a problem always involves making some assumptions.

HEURISTIC MATCHING OF PROBLEM AND SOLUTION

Unlike data aggregation, a heuristic inference makes a great leap. For example, it is one thing to aggregate indicators of work teams having difficulties in problem solving and decision making, and quite another to leap to the inference that the problem is team leadership. Such an inference is often uncertain, based on assumptions of typicality, and is sometimes just a poorly understood correlation. An essential practical characteristic of heuristics of this type is that they reduce the time and effort spent searching for information and diagnosing a problem by skipping over intermediate means–ends or causal relations. Clancey points out that the disadvantage of this problem diagnosis heuristic is the likelihood of error.

[Heuristic inferences] are usually uncertain because the intermediate relations may not hold in the specific case, or may not be observable, or may simply be poorly understood. While not having to think about intermediate connections is advantageous, this sets up a basic conflict for the problem solver—his inferential leaps may be wrong.... There are unarticulated assumptions on which the interpretation rests.... Yet, we might know enough to relate data classes to therapy classes and save the patient's life! (Clancey 1985: 307, 311)

REFINING SOLUTION TO THE CASE

Once a general solution is selected for the problem category, it must be refined or adapted to fit the particular patient or case. Several solutions shown by evidence and expert consensus to be correct for a given problem are often not implemented in fields of medicine (Denis and Langley 2002), human resources (Anderson et al. 2001; Rynes et al. 2002), and management (Rogers 2003; Tranfield et al. 2003). Chapter 9 discusses in greater detail the error-prone process of deducing particular solutions for individual cases from general solutions or models that are based on statistical evidence of a population or sample. For example, the patient may have been classified into the wrong subclass or archetype of a disease category. The classification system may be too general and not specify the boundary conditions or contingencies of membership. The specific context or position of the individual case in the distribution of the population sample may not be understood. As a consequence, a solution category that is correct for a patient subclass or archetype may not apply or may be incorrect for the individual patient. Action research that diagnoses and implements a solution to solve the problem of a client is plagued with these kinds of particularistic problems of diagnosis and intervention.

RELATIONS AMONG DIAGNOSTIC STEPS

Thus far the flow of inference among the diagnostic steps has proceeded from data to conclusions. However, the actual order of search and inference between models of solutions and data are often reciprocal. This is evident in the following kinds of questions that problem diagnosis often entails:

- Are data about a problem supplied or must they be requested?
- If the data are requested, what alternative solution models and question-asking strategies should be used?

- If new data are received, how should they be used to make inferences?
- If, as is typical, alternative inferences of problems and solutions exist, how does one decide which inference path to believe?

Clancey (1985: 324) notes that a 'triggering' relation between data and solutions is pivotal in almost all descriptions of heuristic classification inference.

We say that 'a datum triggers a solution' if the problem solver immediately thinks about that solution upon finding out about the datum. However, the assertion may be conditional (leading to an immediate request for more data) and is always context dependent (though the context is rarely specified [or clearly understood]). A typical trigger relation is 'Headache and red painful eye suggests glaucoma'—red, painful eye will trigger consideration of headache and thus glaucoma, but headache alone will not trigger this association.... In general, *specificity*—the fact that a datum is frequently associated with just a few solutions—determines if a datum triggers a solution concept ('brings it to mind') in the course of solving a problem.

Heuristic triggers facilitate three kinds of non-exhaustive search techniques between data and solutions:

1. *Data-directed search*, where one works forwards from data to abstractions, matching solutions until a satisfactory or plausible set of alternative inferences have been made.
2. *Solution- or hypothesis-directed search*, where one works backwards from solutions, collecting evidence to support them.
3. *Opportunistic search*, where one combines data and hypothesis-directed reasoning. Here heuristic rules trigger hypotheses, which lead to a focused search, and new data may cause refocusing. Opportunistic search is not exhaustive because the reasoning tends to be limited to a finite set of plausible connections between data and solution classes.

The solutions developed with these heuristic methods may represent nothing more than conjectures that require empirical research and testing. In medical care, those solutions that are substantiated by research are known as 'evidence-based' interventions, while those that are selected for adoption by panels of professional experts are typically referred to as 'best practice' guidelines. Since these best practice guidelines are based on expert opinions rather than scientific evidence, they are often the subject in 'calls for research' through clinical trials or evaluation research in order to empirically test the efficacy of the guidelines.

GOING BEYOND THE DATA GIVEN

As noted in the introduction, even when problems are grounded in reality, a common difficulty is that their diagnosis may not lead to creative theory that advances understanding of the phenomenon or problem. Bruner (1973) argues that creativity requires going beyond the data given. He discusses the cognitive learning problem of encountering an anomaly or breakdown that is inconsistent with what we know. He points out that a theory or model is a generic representation of the critical characteristics of a phenomenon. For Bruner, grounding theories in reality requires going beyond the information given so that the problem is formulated as having applicability beyond the situation in which it is observed. This kind of creative problem formulation involves an 'emptying operation' in which the scholar strips or abstracts away idiosyncratic details of the situation observed in reality. In so doing he/she learns something generic about the problem that generalizes to a broader set of situations existing in reality. Bruner observes that initial descriptions of a problem tend to be much too complex. In the beginning there is often not a strong classification scheme for distinguishing the 'wheat' from the 'chaff.' As a result, one may not see a blight in the forest because of the trees.

Henderson (1967) provides a good example of the 'emptying operation' that Bruner discusses by reviewing how Hippocrates, known as the father of medicine, described the sickness and death of Philiscus.

> Philiscus lived by the wall. He took to his bed with acute fever on the first day and sweating. Night uncomfortable.
>
> *Second day.* General exacerbation; later a small clyster moved the bowels well. A restful night.
>
> *Third day.* Early and until midday he appeared to have lost the fever; but towards evening acute fever with sweating, thirst, dry tongue, black urine. An uncomfortable night, without sleep; completely out of his mind.
>
> *Fourth day.* All symptoms exacerbated; black urine. A more comfortable night, and urine of a better colour.
>
> *Fifth day.* About midday slight epitasis (nosebleed) of unmixed blood. Urine varied, with scattered, round particles suspended in it, resembling semen; they did not settle. On the application of a suppository the patient passed, with flatulence, scanty excreta. A distressing night, snatches of sleep, irrational talk; extremities everywhere cold, and would not get warm again; black urine; snatches of sleep towards dawn; speechless; cold sweat; extremities livid. About midday on the sixth day the patient died. The breathing throughout, as though he were recollecting to do it, was rare and large. Spleen raised in a round swelling. Cold sweats all the time. The exacerbations on even days.

Henderson (1967) notes that Hippocrates made three kinds of observations to describe the process of death. First, there are simple descriptive observations made in the first part of the illness. These observations are condensed to the very limit and uncolored with diagnostic abstractions. Then, there are repetitive patterns observed over time in the case that are used to diagnose uniformities over time in the development of the patient's illness. Finally, (and not described here) are uniformities that Hippocrates observes across cases, which represent recurrences in different cases of single events or event sequences. These uniformities are generalized into more abstract representations of patient categories, such as 'Facies Hippocrates' or the face at death:

'Nose sharp, eyes hollow, temples sunken, ears cold and contracted with their lobes turned outward, the skin about the face hard and tense and parched, the colour of the face as a whole being yellow or black.'

Through cumulative observations of his patients, Hippocrates moves step-by-step toward the widest generalizations within his reach. Henderson (1967) concludes that such methodical descriptions of reality are necessary to develop a science that deals with similarly complex and various phenomena.

Problem Solving: The Research Question

In practice, the solution to a problem solving process is the application of a particular intervention that solves the problem identified. In research, however, the solution to a problem formulation process is often a research question that merits scientific investigation to better understand the problem and its resolution. As stated before, grounding and diagnosing a problem domain typically reveal many interesting and important research issues and questions that might be studied. For example, in terms of the structure of inference in Figure 3.1 a diagnosis of a given problem may trigger any one or more of the following research questions.

1. *Problem classification and aggregation questions:*
    - What kind of problem is this; does it fit known problem categories?
    - What are the defining characteristics or symptoms of a particular problem or disease? How do they cause the problem or disease?
    - Is a better coding system available for identifying and classifying the components or symptoms of a particular problem or disease?
    - In what contexts, situations, or contingencies do different kinds of problems arise?
    - How do the elements or symptoms of problems originate and grow into disease categories?
2. *Heuristic matching of problem and solution questions:*
    - What specific solutions are appropriate for this problem, or variations of this problem?
    - What are the strengths and weaknesses of alternative solution models for this kind of problem?
    - How and why does a solution solve a problem; what are the causal relationships among its components?

- Would a new solution address the problem more effectively than the status quo?

3. *Refining the solution to the case at hand:*
   - What are the relative merits of alternative solutions for the problem exhibited in this particular case?
   - Why are evidence-based solutions to this problem not adopted or implemented?
   - How should solutions be modified or adapted to fit the local situation?
   - What are the particular contexts or contingencies in which a solution is beneficial or harmful?

Obviously, in any given study it is impossible to examine all of these and other questions that may emerge during problem diagnosis. Priorities need to be established by formulating a specific question that will be addressed in a research project. The research question often represents the end to the problem formulation process for researchers, for it identifies the specific question from among a host of other possible questions that will be the focus of an empirical investigation. The research question not only narrows the focus of a study to manageable dimensions, it also establishes a pragmatic criterion for evaluating the relevance and quality of a research project. A research study is successful to the extent that it answers the question it was intended to address.

Selecting the research question is a key decision in focusing a research project. Seldom is the research question selected at one time and in a once-and-for-all fashion. Instead, the problem formulation activities of situating, grounding, and diagnosing the problem provide numerous trials and opportunities to formulate, reframe, and modify research questions. Honing in on the research question entails a clarification of the focus, level, and scope of the problem domain from the perspective of the research users. It should be grounded in the sense that the research question directly addresses a critical aspect of the problem as it was observed in reality. And the question should be important in identifying a critical gap, assumption, or anomaly that requires further theory building and testing.

A number of common-sense suggestions (too often ignored) merit consideration in formulating a research question. In outline form, they include the following:

- A research question should end with a question mark (?), not a period (.). Too often research questions are stated in a form that implies or preordains a solution. Good research questions provoke inquiry by being stated in ways that permit and entertain at least two or more plausible answers to the question.
- The research question should directly address a key part of the problem observed in reality. Too often there is a disconnect between statements of the question and the problem.

- Consider the consequences of the research question. Will it resolve a key part of the problem from the user's perspective? Will it substantially improve the situation for the user? Will it advance knowledge/competence for the user?

The art of formulating good research questions is easily as important as the art of developing clear answers. Indeed, Jerome Bruner adds that the art of cultivating such questions and keeping them alive is crucial to the mindful and lively process of science making, as distinguished from what may appear in a finished scientific report. 'Good questions are ones that pose dilemmas, subvert obvious or canonical "truths," force incongruities upon our attention' (Bruner 1996: 127).

Problem Formulation Techniques

BIASES IN HUMAN JUDGMENTS

A researcher is exposed to many biases in human judgment when engaging others in problem formulation. Considering others' views taxes our limited capacities to handle complexity and maintain attention to particulars. Research shows that human beings lack the capability and inclination to deal with complexity (Kahneman et al. 1982). This is true not only of the researcher, but also the individuals a researcher talks to about a problem domain. People tend to quickly eliminate a problem and be 'solution-minded,' (i.e., focus on solutions prematurely at the expense of not adequately defining the problem). Techniques that extend the duration of problem-mindedness by triangulating on multiple methods and perspectives to represent the problem decrease the likelihood of unintended bias in interpretations.

Research on individual attribution and decision making has found that individuals systematically deviate from a rational ideal in making decisions, causal judgments, social inferences, and predictions (Bazerman 1986; Cialdini 1993). Individuals tend to rely on a limited number of heuristic principles to reduce information complexity. These heuristics allow individuals to solve complex problems by applying more simple judgmental operations. When applying these heuristics, individuals filter information in ways that bias their assessments and inferences, leading them to make systematic, predictable errors in judgment. Bazerman (1986) summarizes these heuristics and their resulting biases (see Table 3.1).

A variety of techniques have been suggested for decreasing bias and increasing problem solving creativity in individual reasoning and decision making by Polya (1957), Bransford and Stein (1993), Halpern (1996), among others. A common theme in this literature is that individuals monitor their cognitive

Table 3.1. Biases in individual and group decision making

Bias	Description
A. Biases emanating from the availability heuristic	
1. Ease of recall	Easily-recalled events, based upon vividness or recency, are judged to be more numerous than events of equal frequency whose instances are less easily recalled.
2. Retrievability	Information that is easy to search for and obtain is more salient than that which is difficult to retrieve.
3. Presumed associations	Overestimating the probability of two events co-occurring based upon the number of similar associations that are easily recalled.
B. Biases emanating from the representativeness heuristic	
1. Insensitivity to base rates	Ignoring base rates in assessing the likelihood of events when other descriptive information is provided—even if it is irrelevant.
2. Insensitivity to sample size	Failing to appreciate the role of sample size in assessing the reliability of sample information.
3. Misconceptions of chance	Expecting that a data sequence generated by a random process will look 'random,' even when the sequence is too short for those expectations to be statistically valid.
4. Regression to the mean	Ignoring the fact that extreme events tend to regress to the mean on subsequent trials.
C. Biases emanating from anchoring and adjustment	
1. Insufficient anchor adjustment	Making insufficient adjustments from an initial anchor value (derived from past events, random assignment, or whatever information is available) when establishing a final value.
2. Conjunctive & disjunctive events	Overestimating the probability of conjunctive events and underestimating the probability of disjunctive events.
3. Overconfidence	Being overconfident of the infallibility of judgments when answering moderately to extremely difficult questions.
D. Two more general biases	
1. The confirmation trap	Seeking confirmatory information for what you think is true and neglecting a search for disconfirmatory evidence.
2. Hindsight	Overestimating the correctness of a predicted outcome after finding out whether or not an event occurred.
E. Biases emanating from group decision making	
1. Groupthink and conformity	Group pressures to conform to others depress group members from considering divergent views.
2. Risky shift	Group decisions are either more conservative or extreme than the average of group members' individual decision.
3. Conflict avoidance	Seeking cohesiveness and avoiding expressing ideas that may be disagreeable or opposing to group members.
4. Falling into a 'rut'	Focusing on evaluating an idea once expressed, rather than introducing more new ideas in group discussion.

Sources: Bazerman, M. (1986). 'Biases', in B. M. Staw (ed.), *Psychological Dimensions of Organizational Behavior*, 2nd edn. Englewood Cliffs, NJ: Prentice Hall, pp. 199–223. Delbecq, A., Van de Ven, A., and Gustafson, D. (1975). *Group Techniques for Problem Solving and Program Planning*. Reading, MA: Addison Wesley.

biases by engaging other informants to provide information and interpretations of the problem domain. This is particularly true for problems where information from people with different perspectives about the problem is important. One-on-one interviews, group meetings, surveys, and other techniques can be used to gather this information. Different techniques provide different kinds of information. For example, the information gathered from brainstorming or focus group meetings often provides an overall gestalt appreciation of a problem that seldom emerges from individual interviews or survey techniques. But use of group meetings to gather information to ground a problem must be done with caution and with careful structuring of the group process.

Group decision biases often skew decision making away from a rational ideal. As the bottom rows of Table 3.1 outline, four of the most common group decision biases are groupthink, risky shift, conflict avoidance, and falling into a 'rut.' In a classic study of group process, Janis identified the phenomenon called 'groupthink' (Janis and Mann 1977). In groupthink situations, group pressures for conformity deter the group from considering all of the views of its members. Risky shift is another group decision bias. Researchers including Kogan and Wallach (1967) found evidence that group decision making is sometimes more conservative than individual decisions. But more often, group decision making tends to be more extreme than the average of group members' individual decisions.

Delbecq et al. (1975) describe several causes of bias in group decision making. Group members in many cultures may be expected to conform, causing them to withhold opinions contrary to the dominant view. Some individuals may be hesitant to express their opinions due to personality characteristics like shyness. Group members may lack the communication skills to adequately present their ideas. Others skilled in impression management techniques may be able to dominate group discussion, even though they lack substantive expertise on the topic at hand. Some group members may be particularly egocentric and unwilling to consider the views of others. Status and hierarchy may affect group discussion, with more junior or low-level members deferring to the opinions of senior or high-level members.

COGNITIVE MAPPING

One technique that is particularly useful for representing a problem as perceived by an individual or group is cognitive mapping. The technique is not necessarily intended to reflect a logical or rational analysis of a situation. Instead, cognitive mapping is a modeling technique designed to represent a person's ideas, beliefs, values, attitudes, and their inter-relationships in a form that is amenable to study and analysis. Bryson et al. (2004) and Eden et al. (1983) describe the technique for constructing a problem as perceived by an individual. The technique could also be used in a group setting. In outline form, the technique consists of the five steps illustrated in Figure 3.2.

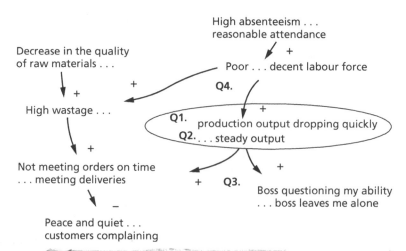

Figure 3.2. Steps in developing a cognitive map of a problem

Source: Eden, C., Jones S., and Sims, D. (1983). *Messing About in Problems: An Informal Structured Approach to their Identification and Management*. Oxford: Pergamon Press, fig. 4.2, p. 42.

1. In the center of a piece of paper or a flip chart, write a label for the problem.
   - An agreed-upon label is usually what is noted as the problem, such as 'production output dropping quickly.'
2. Ask 'What is a satisfactory alternative to this circumstance?'.
   - Find out what the person thinks about his/her own circumstances (rather than the official or politically correct point of view).
   - Ask the individual to describe an opposite alternative that may resolve the situation, such as 'steady output.'
3. Ask 'Why does this matter to you? Why are you worried about it? What are its consequences?' How a concept is used and what it is contrasted to provide the meaning in that context. It also identifies the construct poles (i.e., its connotative links).
   - Identify the psychological (not necessarily 'logical') opposites for each construct (negation).
   - Use arrows with positive or negative signs to identify psychological implications of causality among poles of constructs.
4. Ask 'What reasons come to mind as explanations for the problem label. What are its antecedents?'
   - At this stage the problem is beginning to take shape in an explicit model as the individual sees it. Others may see it quite differently. For example, they may have the same constructs, but they differ in the structure of relationships or arrow.
5. Elaborate.
   - Think backwards and forwards to elaborate the problem to encourage creative expression of the issue.

- What is happening is that the nature of the problem is gradually changing as articulation and modeling take place.
- This is not a scientific model of an 'objective' reality. It is a cognitive mapping of an issue as one person sees it.

Bryson et al. (2004) and Eden et al. (1983) discuss numerous examples and applications of this cognitive mapping technique for problem formulation.

GROUP PROCESS TECHNIQUES

Brainstorming techniques are useful for obtaining ideas about the characteristics of problems from groups of individuals who experience or are knowledgeable informants about a problem domain. Brainstorming techniques structure group decision processes in ways to minimize bias or render them less problematic in group formulations of a research problem. One of the most widely used methods of group brainstorming is the Nominal Group Technique (Delbecq et al. 1975). Figure 3.3 outlines the structured steps of a nominal group meeting that is conducted for the purpose of generating ideas about a topic, problem, or issue. The meeting begins by giving group participants a sheet of paper on which they are asked to write all of their individual ideas

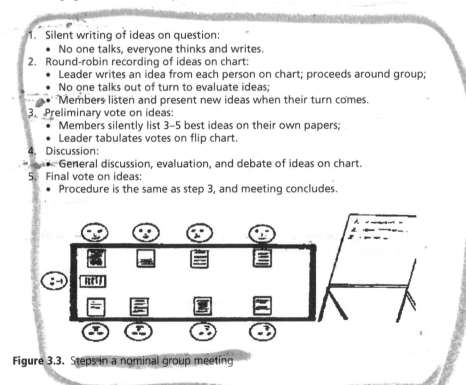

1. Silent writing of ideas on question:
   - No one talks, everyone thinks and writes.
2. Round-robin recording of ideas on chart:
   - Leader writes an idea from each person on chart; proceeds around group;
   - No one talks out of turn to evaluate ideas;
   - Members listen and present new ideas when their turn comes.
3. Preliminary vote on ideas:
   - Members silently list 3–5 best ideas on their own papers;
   - Leader tabulates votes on flip chart.
4. Discussion:
   - General discussion, evaluation, and debate of ideas on chart.
5. Final vote on ideas:
   - Procedure is the same as step 3, and meeting concludes.

Figure 3.3. Steps in a nominal group meeting

A. **Silent writing of ideas on question:**
  - provides focus, time for creativity without interruptions;
  - avoids conformity, competition, & status problems;
  - avoids evaluation and jumping to conclusions.
B. **Round-robin recording of ideas on chart:**
  - forces equal sharing and participation;
  - encourages more ideas through 'hitch-hiking';
  - depersonalizes ideas & tolerates conflicting ideas.
C. **Clarification of each idea on chart:**
  - clarifies each idea before jumping to conclusions;
  - each idea is as important as another before vote.
D. **Preliminary vote on priorities:**
  - allows 'trial run' & avoids premature conclusions;
  - provides focus on important issues;
  - silent voting forces equality & avoids influence of others.
E. **Discussion of preliminary vote:**
  - encourages minority opinions & clarifies misunderstandings;
  - promotes attacking ideas on wall (not people);
  - provides preparation for decision.
F. **Final vote on priorities:**
  - provides written 'minutes' of group ideas & decision;
  - promotes sense of accomplishment & conclusion;
  - motivates involvement in future efforts.

Figure 3.4. Reasons for steps in nominal group meeting silent writing of ideas on question

Note: For further information, see Delbecq, A., Van de Ven, A., and Gustafson, D. (1975). *Group Techniques for Program Planning*, Scott-Foresman Pub.

about a question or problem. Then, in round-robin fashion each individual is given a turn to present his/her idea. Other members are not permitted to evaluate the idea at this time. Each person takes a turn until all ideas are presented. Then, there is time for discussion and members to vote on the ideas they view as being most valuable. This limits the possibility for any one individual to 'take over' and dominate the discussion, allowing for a wider range of possibilities for the group to consider (Delbecq et al. 1975). Additional reasons for each step in the nominal group process are outlined in Figure 3.4.

Another technique for overcoming some of the cognitive biases of group decision making is the Delphi technique where group members do not meet face-to-face; instead they respond to questions that are proposed and tabulated by a group coordinator using electronic discussion boards or email. In this format, individual participants can engage in the process anonymously, negating the potential effects of status and hierarchy and possibly allowing those who are shy or lack verbal communication skills to participate more fully in the process.

Other possible group techniques that inhibit group decision biases include dialectical inquiry and devil's advocacy as described by Schweiger et al. (1989). As applied to problem formulation, brainstorming techniques focus on generating as many problem statements or components as possible, while dialectical methods focus on evaluating and choosing a representation of the problem from a few competing alternatives. In dialect-ical inquiry, a decision making group might be divided into two subgroups. One subgroup develops an argument for a particular problem statement supported with reasons, evidence, assumptions, and qualifications. Another subgroup may do the same for a competing formulation of the problem. The groups then present their arguments and engage in a debate by attempting to bolster their argument and negate those of the other group. A panel of judges or reviewers is often called upon to choose the winning argument or to develop a synthesis that attempts to combine the strengths and minimize the weaknesses of the two arguments. Alternatively, the groups themselves continue debating their assumptions and conclusions until they agree on a problem statement.

In devil's advocacy, the second subgroup criticizes the assumptions and recommendations of the first subgroup, but does not propose new solutions. The first group revises its assumptions and recommendations and presents them again to the second subgroup, and the process continues until the group agrees on a problem statement. These techniques can be used to engage an open debate and to examine a more inclusive set of ideas than a traditional consensus technique that does not incorporate an established norm of debate.

Concluding Discussion

This chapter discussed the process of formulating a research problem in terms of four interdependent activities: situating, grounding, diagnosing, and resolving a problem. These four activities are highly interdependent and typically occur in parallel throughout the problem formulation process. A variety of suggestions and considerations in performing each of the problem formulation activities were also discussed. In summary, they are outlined below.

SITUATING THE RESEARCH PROBLEM

- Identify whose point of view and interests are to be represented in problem formulation.
- Clarify who are the intended users, clients, and audience of the research.
- Who/what is the foreground and background in focusing on the problem?
- What is the level of analysis and context of the problem domain?
- What is the scope of the problem: how deep, how broad, and how long will the problem be studied?

GROUNDING THE RESEARCH PROBLEM

- Address the journalists' questions of who, what, where, when, why, and how does the problem exist.
- Describe the particular problem up close; give an example, anecdote, and an experience with a problem.
- Describe the problem in general; present evidence and studies on the prevalence and context of the problem's existence.
- Talk to people who experience the problem or issue.
- Conduct interviews and nominal groups with people who know about the issue/problem.
- Review the literature to understand and situate the problem.

DIAGNOSING THE RESEARCH PROBLEM

- Classify elements or symptoms of the problem into categories.
- Aggregate categories to infer a problem.
- Heuristically match the problem and potential solutions.
- Does a solution exist for the problem or must one be created?
- Refine the solution to the case at hand.
- What anomalies or breakdowns surfaced in your diagnosis?

SELECTING THE RESEARCH QUESTION

- What part of the problem merits research attention and focus?
- State the question in analytical terms by relating or comparing key concepts.
- Connect the research question to your description of the problem.
- Ensure that you indeed have a question and not a statement.
- Permit and entertain at least two plausible answers to the question. Alternative answers increase independent thought trials.
- Bring your question full circle by considering its consequences:
  - Will the answer solve a key part of the problem from the user's perspective?
  - Will it substantially improve the situation for the user?
  - Will it advance knowledge/competence for the user?

Some years ago, the *Journal of Management Inquiry* featured a debate between Paul Lawrence and Karl Weick about the merits and demerits of undertaking problem-driven or theory-driven research. This debate included the question of who should be the primary user or client of management research. Herbert Simon argued that research in a professional school should both advance knowledge in a scientific discipline and enlighten the practice of management. The arguments advanced by Lawrence and Weick appear to reflect the differing viewpoints of scholars from the reality and theory bases of the Engaged Scholarship Diamond Model. Weick views problem formulation from a theoretical perspective, while Lawrence examines it as a real-world phenomenon. But Weick and Lawrence are not just good role players; they have had many successes in their scholarly careers by successfully completing all the activities of the Diamond Model. Murray Davis (1971, 1986) provides an insightful synthesis to this debate by examining what makes research interesting and classic. He argues that the better we know our audience, the better we can frame or position our research problem and question to the prevailing assumptions of the readers/users of our research.

Paul Lawrence (1992: 140) argues that significant behavioral science originates from problem-oriented research rather than from theory-oriented research. He states that behavioral scientists make a big mistake if they do not ask users and research participants what needs to be studied, and how our theories and knowledge may be inadequate. He suggests seven steps for undertaking behavioral science research:

1. Select an important emerging human problem to study, based on careful listening and observations and being explicit about the value choices involved.
2. Do some initial field scouting of the problem to make an initial assessment of key parameters.
3. Examine relevant theory for promising hypotheses and conceptualizations.
   - Note: this is the third step, not the first.
   - Theory is a good guide for framing, not selecting, the research question.
4. Select research methods after the research question and propositions are chosen.
5. Collect data systematically.
6. Analyze data and generalize the findings.
7. Present results so they are useful for action by responsible problem solvers and academicians.

Lawrence outlines seven advantages of problem-oriented research:

1. One is more likely to develop usable findings and findings that are actually used.
2. Problems link micro and macro levels of analysis.
3. By identifying important problems, the research is practical.

4. It is easier to gain access to study sites and secure funding.
5. The research usually identifies some performance measures as dependent variables.
6. One is more likely to discover new and better organizational forms and social inventions.
7. The chief advantage is that problems are a powerful way to identify gaps in our theory/knowledge.

Weick (1992) argues the case for theory-driven research. All theories are about practice and practicality, and the trick is to discover those settings and conditions under which they hold true. He discusses three criteria for selecting research problems: knowledge (choose problems in areas where you have a thorough understanding), dissatisfaction (choose problems that reflect a healthy, active opposition to existing knowledge and methodology), and generalizability (choose variables and situations that are universal and common rather than unique and rare). A theory-based approach is a continuing effort to find those contexts where a theory holds true (Weick 1992: 172). This formulation emphasizes the process of diagnosis. The particular problem is a pretext to look for a pattern that is more generalizable, more abstract, something that applies to people in general (Meehl 1995); it is an exercise in sense making. In problem-focused work, the particular is a context rather than a pretext and consists of a self-contained story, tied together by its own logic. Different logics will generate different studies, and different stories will suggest different remedies (Weick 1992: 172).

Because of the theory-laden nature of all observations and data, I emphasized that problem-driven and theory-driven research are inextricably connected. Problem formulation and theory building follows an abductive form of reasoning, which is neither inductive nor deductive. Abduction begins by recognizing an anomaly or breakdown in our understanding of the world, and proceeds to create a hypothetical inference that dissolves the anomaly by providing a coherent resolution to the problem. As will be discussed in the next chapter, in the social sciences this logic of discovery is typically followed by a logic of testing in which the consequences of the hypothesis are derived through deduction and the consequences are tested by induction.

I discussed the close connections between theory and practice in situating, grounding, diagnosing, and solving a problem. Lawrence and Weick suggest that the distinction between problem- vs. theory-focused research is neither descriptive nor useful for understanding the process of problem formulation. Theories have problems just as problems have theories (Weick 1992: 176). Problem formulation requires theoretical categories; and theories are used to represent reality. Theories and problems alternate as temporally lagged logics or stories. One person's problem is another person's solution (theory). Therefore, the question of whether research is problem- or theory-driven reflects a one-sided view of the research process. Subsequent chapters will demonstrate that the distinction between problem- and theory-driven research is also not helpful for theory building, testing, and application.

4 Building a Theory

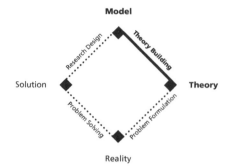

> For our own sakes, we must attend as much to how scientific hypotheses are caught, as to how they are cooked.
>
> (Norwood Russel Hanson 1959: 35)

> It is not so much the world which is logical or illogical as men [and women].
>
> (Stephen Toulmin 2003: 5)

Introduction

This chapter examines the theory building activities illustrated in Figure 4.1 of the engaged scholarship process. The central objective of theory building is to develop plausible and interesting conceptual models that answer a question about the problem as formulated in the last chapter. A central theme of engaged scholarship is the close interplay between theory and reality. In the last chapter this theme emphasized that formulating a research problem requires robust theories and concepts. This chapter applies the theme to theory building. Building a theory requires intimate familiarity with the problem domain. Problem formulation and theory building go hand in hand. Another theme is engagement. Just as problem formulation requires involvement of those who experience and know the problem domain, theory building is greatly enhanced by engaging knowledge experts in relevant disciplines and functions.

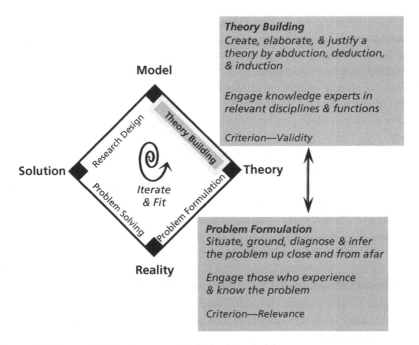

Figure 4.1. Theory building in engaged scholarship model

Theory building involves three activities: (1) conceiving or creating a theory; (2) constructing or elaborating the theory; and (3) justifying or evaluating a theory. These activities entail different types of reasoning: abduction is used for conceiving a theory, logical deduction for constructing a theory, and inductive reasoning for evaluating a theory. Much can be learned about the scientific enterprise by examining these patterns of reasoning. While abduction is a different form of reasoning from deduction and induction, they are closely related. Peirce argued that *abduction*, which initiates theory, requires *induction* in order that the theory may be tested through its consequences. But these consequences are derived through the process of *deduction* (Mounce 1997: 18).

Abductive reasoning usually begins with a surprising observation or experience. This is what shatters our habit and motivates us to create a hypothesis that might resolve the anomaly. Abduction is an inferential procedure in which we create a conjecture that, if it were correct, would make the surprising anomaly part of our normal understanding of the world. For example, I might be astonished to find that 'Mary is strong.' But if I came up with a hypothesis that 'All athletes are strong,' then my anomaly would dissolve by concluding that 'Mary is an athlete.' This form of abduction represents the first of three kinds of reasoning in theory building (Lachs 1999: 78–9).

The second step in constructing a theory uses deductive reasoning to elaborate and identify the consequences of the hypothesis so that it may be open to observation. Deduction involves arriving at a 'result' based on applying a 'rule' or hypothesis to a case. For instance the rule might say, 'All athletes are strong' and when applied to a case 'Mary is an athlete' produces a result 'Mary is strong' (Bartel and Garud 2003). The second section of this chapter discusses basic principles of logical deductive reasoning to elaborate a theory.

Having deduced the conditional consequences of the claim, we can proceed to evaluate and test a theory using inductive reasoning. The third section of this chapter discusses how the logical 'validity' of a theory is typically evaluated in terms of the strength of its argument. In the next chapter we examine how the empirical 'truth' of a theory is evaluated in terms of how well the operational model of a theory fits observations of the world. This requires checking whether the predicted observations are reliable. In the process we repeatedly assess the probable truth of the hypothesis by determining the ratio of successful observations. The result is a judgment of probability. Scientific knowledge largely consists of such judgments, which means that we cannot know anything with certainty and that with time even our hypothesis might turn out to be false.

I discuss these three different theory building activities and modes of reasoning in sequential order. In practice, they represent an iterative cycle. The initial cycle tends to follow a temporal sequence of theory conception, construction, and evaluation activities using abductive, deductive, and inductive reasoning, respectively. Because these activities and modes of reasoning are interdependent, they mutually influence each other over time. The simple temporal sequence transitions into a multiple parallel progression in subsequent iterations of the cycle. Theory building typically requires numerous repetitions of the cycle. I have never experienced or witnessed completing the process of theory creation, construction, and evaluation activities in only one or two trials. Many different trials—often engaging other people—of creating, constructing, and evaluating a theory are needed to build a theory that withstands the criticisms of the status quo and thereby advances scientific and practical knowledge about the problem or question being investigated.

Not all scholars may choose to perform all three activities of creating, constructing, and evaluating theories. Some emphasize creating theories (e.g., Alvesson 2003; Mintzberg 2005), some constructing and modeling theories (e.g., Blalock 1969; Whetten 2002), while others focus on testing theories already constructed (Shadish et al. 2002; Singleton and Straits 2005). Although scholars may express different preferences and styles in creating, constructing, and evaluating theories, all three activities are important skills for theory building. Not all research projects, of course, may require equal attention to all three theory building activities. For example, a study may only require theory evaluation if it is undertaken to test an existing theory already published in the literature.

Conceiving a Theory

The first step in theory building is conceiving the germ of an idea that may become a theory. This idea may be a 'half-baked' conjecture in response to an anomaly that violates our understanding of how things are expected to unfold. For example, most people view interruptions as impeding the work of teams in organizations. However my colleague, Prof. Mary Zellmer-Bruhn, was surprised to find that teams she was observing in her field studies learned more when their work was interrupted by events, such as losing team members, changing tools and technology, and organizational restructurings. What explains this anomaly? She reasoned by abduction that interruptions might be occasions for teams to reflect on what they were doing and 'get out of their ruts' in following mindless routines. If this idea is correct, she concluded that interruptions may provide teams opportunities to learn new ways to do their work better, and thereby resolve the anomaly (Zellmer-Bruhn 2003).

Unexpected things that trigger recognition of anomalies are frequently encountered, often on a daily basis. They prompt us to question our theories or understanding of the world. We cannot, of course, study all the anomalies we encounter. A central purpose of the problem formulation process discussed in the last chapter is to select priorities among the research problems and questions that are most important to study.

By definition, anomalies represent disconfirmations of our theories. Being human and subject to all kinds of biases, including the confirmation trap, we may choose to deny or ignore anomalies. As Carlile and Christiansen (2004) state, 'If you set out to prove your theory, an anomaly is a failure. But if your purpose is to improve a theory, the anomaly is a victory.' This form of openness 'allows us to transcend our particular viewpoint and develop an expanded consciousness that takes the world in more fully' (Nagel 1986: 5). Schon (1987) maintains that in situations of ambiguity or novelty, 'our thought turns back on the surprising phenomenon, and at the same time, back on itself.' This can be described as abductive reflection-in-action.

Such reflection, in fact, is one way that new knowledge is created. The logic of discovery or creativity (as distinguished from a logic of verification or testing) consists of a process of reasoning that Charles Peirce and Norman Hanson called *abduction*, also referred to as *retroduction* (Peirce 1931–58; Hanson 1958). This form of reasoning begins when some surprising anomaly or unexpected phenomenon is encountered. This anomaly would not be surprising if a new hypothesis or conjecture was proposed. The anomaly would be explained as a matter of course from the hypothesis. Therefore, there is good reason for developing the hypothesis for it might explain the phenomenon along with its anomaly.

Abductive reasoning assumes that observations and facts are theory-laden; that is, viewed through a conceptual pattern. Part of this view is a function of the meanings we attach to the terms within a context; part of it is a function of the generalizations, hypothesis, and methodological presuppositions we hold in a context. The theories we might create to explain anomalies are enabled and constrained by our existing repertoire of theories and methods.

Locke et al. (2004) point out that prior scholarship is probably the most obvious inspirational resource for making sense of data. They explain this as follows:

In imaginative work, however, theory is not placed in a dominant and constraining relation to data from which it imposes and affirms a pre-considered order. Used as an inspiration resource to make new sense of data, theory is multidisciplinary, treated pluralistically, and is used to open up new possibilities. When various theoretical frames are placed in tension with data, with each other, and with one's own frame, the interaction of observation and variety in theories can provide new theoretical questions and refine research foci. The interactions can create opportunities for seeing new interpretations that conflict with prevailing views or originate in different perspectives. Further, taking a multidisciplinary approach to theory facilitates the purposeful creation of contradictory ideas by bringing to our work both our learning and the thinking from outside the discipline; as we integrate and recombine insights and work from other fields, we generate new insights and ideas, and can rearrange familiar concepts with new understandings. (2004: 3)

Given the theory-laden nature of observations and data, we do not view the world with a 'blank slate.' We view reality from our theoretical viewpoint or perspective. Theories put phenomena into meaningful systems. A theory is a pattern of conceptual organization that explains phenomena by rendering them intelligible. From the observed properties of phenomena, we reason our way toward a keystone idea from which the properties can be explained. Thus, instead of thinking of theory creation as being analogous to drafting on a clean sheet of paper, it is more helpful to think of it as one of erasing, inserting, revising, and re-connecting ideas scattered on many papers that are scribbled full of experiences, insights, and musings of ours and others. This analogy fits nicely with contemporary definitions of creativity as representing recombinations of old ideas in new ways (Van de Ven et al. 1999: 9).

Peirce and Hanson argued that a theory is not pieced together inductively from observed phenomena, nor is it deduced from axioms or premises; it is rather an abductive process that makes it possible to observe phenomena as being of a certain sort, and as related to other phenomena. Alvesson (2004) criticizes those who view 'grounded theory building' as an inductive process in which researchers are advised to approach field observations without preconceived theories and 'let the data speak for themselves' (Glaser and Strauss 1967; Eisenhardt 1989; Strauss and Corbin 1994). He argues that this form of grounded theorizing from a 'blank slate' misconstrues the process of theory creation and gives an impression of rationality through emphasizing procedures, rules, and a clear route from empirical reality to theory via data, which are viewed as representing objective and impartial facts. Following Peirce and Hanson, I argue that researchers and practitioners create or discover theories through a process of abduction—not by induction or deduction. Nonaka observes that 'people do not just passively receive new knowledge; they actively interpret it to fit their own situation and perspectives. What makes sense in one context can change or even lose its meaning when communicated to people in a different context' (Nonaka 1994: 30).

Whereas the process of abduction begins with recognizing a breakdown or anomaly, it ends with a *coherent resolution*. Agar (1986: 22) states that

a coherent resolution will (1) show why it is better than other resolutions that can be imagined; (2) tie a particular resolution in with a broader knowledge that constitutes a tradition; and (3) clarify and enlighten, eliciting an 'aha' reaction from members of different traditions. . . . A successful resolution will also do more than resolve a single breakdown. The coherence that results must apply in subsequent situations.

Bruner's (1973, 1996) work on learning as going beyond the information given is helpful in considering the creativity and generality of a coherent resolution. Like Peirce and Hanson, Bruner notes that a theory or model is a generic representation of the critical characteristics of a phenomenon. For Bruner, this implies that grounding theories in reality requires going beyond the information given so that the hypothesis is formulated as having applicability beyond the situation in which it is observed. This kind of creative abductive leap leverages learning. It is learning about the critical aspects of a problem so that other things can be solved with no further research or learning required. It is fundamentally an 'emptying operation' in which the scholar strips or abstracts away idiosyncratic details of the situation observed in reality. In doing so he/she learns something generic about the problem that generalizes to a broader set or type of situations existing in reality.

An important qualification in carrying out Bruner's emptying operation is that it threads a fine line between informed generalizability and mere speculation. The ability to perform this 'emptying operation' depends on a scholar's repertoire of experiences and theoretical frameworks. A scholar with several years of experience in formulating research problems and going through the process of engaged scholarship is going to get better at performing an 'emptying operation' that is truly illuminating, as compared to a new researcher with little past experience or exposure to alternative perspectives of others about the problem domain.

Weick (1989) provides a useful way to think about Bruner's (1996) 'emptying operation.' He credits Crovitz (1970) with the idea that models as described in journal papers include two kinds of words: those referring to general concepts that might appear in any paper (y words), and words referring to substantive issues that are specific to particular articles (x words). The ratio of x words to y words suggests how much jargon the article contains. Jargon-laden articles have not been emptied in such a way that they might go beyond the information given. For example, if we delete the x-words (or reconceptualize them into y-words) and keep the y-words, then we have a generic structure for theorizing about subjects across many cases. The key point in Bruner's suggestion of going beyond the information given through a 'cleaning operation' is to remove the idiosyncratic words and ideas that are incidental to our argument, and to focus instead on making connections between the y-words that are central to a generalizable argument. This process of emptying theories of incidental x-words is crucial, for they often prevent us from 'seeing the forest because of the trees.' Parsimonious theories are preferred not just because of simplicity, but more importantly because they tend to go beyond the information given by having been emptied of incidental details.

'If a picture is worth a thousand words, then one well-wrought guess is worth a thousand pictures.' A well-wrought guess, of course, is usually and rather grandly called 'a hypothesis.' What is important about a hypothesis is that it derives from something you already know, something generic that allows you to go beyond what you already know.... Being able to 'go beyond the information' given to 'figure things out' is one of the few untarnishable joys of life. One of the great triumphs of learning... is to get things organized in your head in a way that permits you to know more than you 'ought' to. And this takes reflection, brooding about what it is that you know. The enemy of reflection is the breakneck pace—the thousand pictures. (Bruner 1996: 129)

The time from recognizing an anomaly to proposing a resolution (or new theory) can vary greatly. Although Peirce wrote of abduction as being a flash of inspiration, Campbell (1988: 410) provides a more reasonable evolutionary account of the long process and time it often takes to conceive or create a theory that resolves a breakdown.

A problem is posed for which we must invent a solution. We know the conditions to be met by the sought idea; but we do not know what series of ideas will lead us there. In other words, we know how the series of our thoughts must end, but not how it should begin. In this case it is evident that there is no way to begin except at random. Our mind takes up the first path that it finds open before it, perceives that it is a false route, retraces its steps and takes another direction.... It is after hours and years of meditation that the sought-after idea presents itself to the inventor. He does not succeed without going astray many times; and if he thinks himself to have succeeded without effort, it is only because the joy of having succeeded has made him forget all the fatigues, all the false leads, all of the agonies, with which he has paid for his success.... The important thing to notice is that the good flashes and the bad flashes, the triumphant hypothesis and the absurd conceits, are on an exact equality in respect to their origin. (Campbell, 1988: 417)

Campbell (1988) took a 'blind' view of random variations. That is, saying that the origins of insights are random is to say that observers are often blind to the process and simply do not know how variations emerge. This overlooks the question of whether the statistical pattern in the emergence of new ideas follows a stochastic random process. For the individual scholars engaged in the task, the process of abduction is probably not random. Because observations are theory-dependent on our preferences, experiences, and academic backgrounds, we are predisposed to make particular insights. For instance, in the process of creating a theory sociologists take as a starting point the cultural, normative, or critical theories as opposed to rational choice theories. These theories, which become academic world views, program how problems and possible solutions are framed. So, while we may be blind to how variations evolve, they are guided by our penchant to explain phenomena based on our experience and discipline.

Taking his cue from Campbell, Weick (1989) describes theory building as an evolutionary trial-and-error process of thought experiments in variation, selection, and retention of plausible conjectures to solve a problem or make sense of a phenomenon. As applied to theory building, *variation* is the number of different conjectures we develop to make sense of a problematic situation. *Selection* involves developing and applying diverse criteria for choosing among these conjectures. *Retention* is the elaboration and justification we provide for the chosen conjecture (as discussed in the next section of this chapter). Because the theorist rather than nature intentionally guides this evolutionary process of disciplined imagination, theory creation is more like artificial selection than natural selection. Theorists both choose the form of the problem statement (as discussed in the last chapter) and declare when their thought trials have solved their problem (which is focused on here). Weick elaborates this evolutionary process of theory building as follows.

VARIATIONS IN THOUGHT TRIALS

As we have seen, when faced with an anomaly or problem, we generate conjectures to resolve it. By abductive reasoning we rely on the knowledge and experiences that we have or can access to come up with these conjectures, usually in the form of if-then statements. These thought trials in developing conjectures can vary in number and diversity; that is, the heterogeneity and independence of thought trials. Weick (1989: 522) argues that *a greater number of diverse conjectures is more likely to produce better theory than a process that generates a small number of homogeneous conjectures.*

Weick notes that 'given the tendency of humans to exhibit grooved, habituated, redundant thinking this requirement is difficult to achieve unless disciplined imagination is applied to increase independence in the variations of our thought trials.' One strategy that Weick advocates is to use a strong classification system in which an event or issue clearly falls into a category, or can be examined in terms of several clearly different categories. *Variations in thought trials within one category should be associated with fewer breakthroughs than would variations that originate in more than one category* (Weick 1989: 522).

Those who argue for dialectical oppositions (Astley & Van de Ven, 1983), the cultivation of paradox (Quinn and Cameron 1988), conceptualization at more than one level of analysis (Staw et al. 1981), and micro–macro linkages (Knorr-Cetina and Cicourel 1981) can be viewed as people suggesting that heterogeneous thought trials are more likely than homogeneous thought trials to solve theoretical problems. (Weick 1989: 522)

For example, Scott Poole and I have proposed four different ways for developing theories that resolve apparent paradoxes either between theories or between an anomaly observed in reality and our theories about the phenomenon (Poole and Van de Ven 1989). First, accept the paradox or inconsistency, and learn to live with it constructively with the principle of balance between oppositions or 'moderation in all things.' Second, clarify levels of reference from which different perspectives of the problem arise (e.g., part–whole, micro–macro, or individual–society) and the connections among them. Third, take into account time for exploring when contradictory assumptions or processes each exert a separate influence on the problem. Fourth, introduce new concepts that either correct flaws in logic or provide a more encompassing perspective that dissolves the paradox. These four methods represent a classification system for conducting multiple independent thought trials in developing conjectures about an anomaly.

Developing a strong classification system of independent thought trials is greatly facilitated by obtaining the different perspectives of people from different disciplinary specialties, functional backgrounds, and role orientations. These people can participate in theory building activities in a variety of ways—as members of a heterogeneous or interdisciplinary research team, as research advisors, or simply as participants in a brainstorming meeting. Another way is to review the literature and examine the different approaches or perspectives that have been taken to address the problem. The point is that individual scholars have limited classification systems. Engaging and leveraging independent thought trials typically requires reaching out and either talking to or reading works by others who can offer perspectives and classifications of the problem domain that are different from our own. Weick (1989: 52) notes that any method 'that short circuits memory, foresight, or preference in the generation of thought trials increases the independence of these trials.'

SELECTION AMONG THOUGHT TRIALS

How are we to choose from among the many conjectures or independent thought trials that might be obtained from engaging others' viewpoints? Weick's answer is the same as for thought trials—apply many diverse selection criteria in a consistent way to each conjecture. Specifically, he offers the following proposition.

The greater the number of diverse criteria applied to a conjecture, the higher the probability that those conjectures which are selected will result in good theory. Furthermore, selection criteria must be applied consistently or theorists will be left with an assortment of conjectures that are just as fragmentary as those they started with. Every conjecture can satisfy some criterion. Thus, if criteria are altered each time a conjecture is tested, few conjectures will be rejected and little understanding will cumulate. (Weick 1989: 523, italics added)

If theory creation improves when many diverse criteria are applied consistently to select conjectures, the next question is what criteria might be used? A lay person might answer by suggesting that the most important criterion is to select the conjecture that is valid—i.e., the one that withstands verification and testing. This answer, however, is premature and misdirected. It is premature in the sense that the validity of a conjecture can neither be determined by, nor is it the motivation for, abductive reasoning. While verification and testing conjectures are central evaluation criteria of inductive reasoning, validation is not a criterion of abductive reasoning. Hanson (1958) distinguished between the reasons for accepting a hypothesis from the reasons for suggesting a hypothesis in the first place. The former are reasons for verifying a hypothesis, whereas the latter are reasons that make a hypothesis a plausible type of conjecture—the logic of discovery or creation. Abduction is a creative hypothetical inference framed to solve a problem.

It is not mere extension of ordinary experience. Rather it offers a perspective quite different from the ordinary one. Indeed, it offers a new conception of the matter of which an object is composed, on which, for certain purposes, will replace the ordinary conception. Moreover, the new conception is not final. Further inquiry will reveal problems that can be solved, only by framing a fresh conception. (Mounce 1997: 17)

A criterion of validity may misdirect and censure our selection of conjectures to only those that are believed to be valid. To be valid, the conjectures are likely to be uncreative, already known, and obvious. Hence, they do not advance new understanding of the problem or anomaly. This is not to say that the validity of a conjecture should be ignored all together. After all, the purpose of abductive reasoning is to create conjectures that may resolve the problem or reframe the phenomenon being investigated in a new way. Instead, it is to recognize that valid conjectures are difficult, if not impossible, to determine at the time of their conception. However, as discussed later in the chapter, attempts to verify conjectures selected and determine which should be retained may occur sometime later. Thus, the abduction of conjectures and hypotheses does not depend on their validity.

This process of abductive reasoning amplifies a conclusion drawn by Weick (1989: 525) that '*plausibility is a substitute for validity*' in selecting conjectures. If it is not possible to determine the validity of a conjecture at the time of its conception, then plausibility is the next best option. A conjecture is plausible when it appears to be reasonable, believable, credible, or seemingly worthy of approval or acceptance, even though it may or may not be true (*Random House Unabridged Dictionary*). Plausibility is in the eyes of the beholder. It is a multi-dimensional criterion reflecting our unique assumptions and interests. Weick, for example, discusses his plausibility criteria as the extent to which a conjecture is interesting, obvious, connected, believable, beautiful, or real in the problem context.

In general, the extent to which a conjecture is plausible is largely based on subjective judgments of people who are engaged in the process and have different experiences with and knowledge of the problem domain. Diverse experiences and knowledge provide a base of assumptions for assessing conjectures of trials that mimic experimental tests. Relying on Davis's (1971, 1986) analysis of how one's assumptions trigger judgments of what is 'interesting' and 'classic,' Weick describes the assumption test of a conjecture as follows.

The assumption is a distillation of past experience. When that assumption is applied to a specific conjecture, the assumption tests the conjecture just as if an experiment had been run. When a conjecture is tested against an assumption, the outcome of that test is signified by one of four reactions: *that's interesting* (assumption of moderate strength is disconfirmed), *that's absurd* (strong assumption is disconfirmed), *that's irrelevant* (no assumption is activated), and *that's obvious* (a strong assumption is confirmed). Those four reactions are the equivalent of significance tests, and they serve as substitutes for validity. The judgment *that's interesting* selects a conjecture for retention and further use. That judgment is neither capricious nor arbitrary because it is made relative to a standard that incorporates the results of earlier tests. That standard takes the form of an assumption, and the conjecture is compared with this standard during theorizing. (Weick 1989: 525)

When a conjecture confirms a strongly-held assumption, it may be viewed as either obvious or classic. But what appears obvious to one person may be viewed as classic to another. Thus, Weick (1989) raises the question: For whom might a conjecture not be obvious? An answer to this question can help identify the boundary conditions inside of which a conjecture appears plausible but outside of which it does not.

To appreciate the implications of this plausibility criterion for selecting conjectures, it is helpful to summarize the basic architecture of interesting and classic theories, as described by Davis (1971, 1986). Basically, a classic work speaks to the primary concerns or assumptions of an audience, while an interesting theory speaks to the secondary concerns of an audience. Davis (1986) describes the common attributes of a classic theory as follows:

- It starts with an anomaly that a fundamental problem exists (in society, for example) that needs to be explained.
- Through abduction it identifies a novel factor that caused the anomaly, and traces the ubiquitous effects of the factor on society. This factor collides with and undermines an assumption that the audience holds or values dearly.
- An elaboration of the theory provides hope by suggesting a way to control or live with the factor. The theory is simple enough on the surface for generalists to appreciate, but has a subtle core that is sufficiently ambiguous and complex to challenge and motivate specialists to engage in further research to refine the theory.

In contrast, Davis (1971) discusses how interesting theories negate a secondary assumption held by the audience and affirm an unanticipated alternative. An interesting theory has the following architecture: It begins with a claim that what seems to be X is in reality non-X. However, if non-X is viewed as a small difference from X, then the theory is boring or trivial. If non-X is viewed as very different from X, then the theory is discredited as an absurd 'crackpot' idea of a lunatic. Interesting theories deny weakly-held, not strongly-held, assumptions of the audience.

Davis's descriptions of classic and interesting theories have important implications for selecting conjectures. First, the reputation of a conjecture hinges on knowing the assumptions of the intended audience or users of a study. Second, a necessary (but not sufficient) condition for an interesting or classic study is the formulation of a conjecture that denies a weakly- or strongly-held assumption *of the intended audience*. Therefore, the more we engage and the better we know our audience, the better we can select and frame our conjectures to the prevailing assumptions of the intended audience of our work.

Constructing the Theory

Once the germ of a promising conjecture has emerged through a process of abduction, our mode of reasoning switches to deduction to elaborate the conjecture and construct it into a complete theory. Constructing a theory involves articulating and elaborating a conjecture into theoretical terms, relationships, and conditions when they apply. Basic principles of logical deductive reasoning provide the toolkit for theory construction. Whereas abduction is a mode of reasoning for conceiving a theory, logical deduction provides the tools for constructing the theory.

With the demise of positivism in the philosophy of science came a skepticism of the use of mathematical logic, such as a first order predicate calculus to deduce hypotheses from theoretical premises or axioms. Most philosophers have concluded that axiomatic theorizing may be fine for mathematical puzzles, but is not appropriate for theorizing about real-world phenomena where few, if any, axioms or scientific laws exist from which social theories can be derived (Giere 1999; Toulmin 2003). But *syntactical* techniques of axiomatization should not be confused with more general *semantic* techniques used to formalize a theory (Suppe 1977: 114). Indeed sound logical reasoning remains as important as ever to elaborate the semantic meaning of theories and identify the boundaries of concepts and their relationships.

Logic provides the language and core principles needed to articulate the 'anatomy' of a theory. This section reviews this language of terms used to describe theories, and the principles of logic for relating the terms. They reflect the norms and conventions that have evolved over the years to guide logical reasoning, to distinguish the logician's notions of 'validity' and 'truth,' and to search for plausible alternative models or theories for explaining a research question.[1]

A theory simplifies and explains a complex real-world phenomenon. A good theory not only *describes* the who, what, and where of a phenomenon being investigated, but also *explains* the how, when, and why it occurs (Whetten 1989). *A theory is an explanation of relationships among concepts or events within a set of boundary conditions.* Figure 4.2, adapted from Bacharach (1989) is a diagram of the core components in this definition of a theory. These components include *terms* (concepts, constructs, variables, or events), *relationships* among terms (propositions and hypothesis), *assumptions* (boundary conditions within which these relationships hold in time, space, and value contexts), and *explanations* (arguments that provide reasons for the expected relationships).

Another aspect of a theory is the *level of abstraction* of terms and relationships. Terms vary from those that are abstract and theoretical to those that are concrete and observable. As Figure 4.2 illustrates, a theory may be viewed as a system of concepts, constructs or variables, in which the abstract concepts

---

[1] I confess that some readers of earlier drafts of this section found it somewhat dull and dense reading. Although I made attempts to improve the readability of this section, I also think that this review of the principles of logic that serve as building blocks for theory construction may not become interesting and meaningful until they are put to use, as I will do in later chapters. Useful and more extended discussions of the logic of scientific reasoning are provided by Kaplan (1964); Stinchcombe (1968); Freeley (1976); Giere (1984); Ramage and Bean (1995); Singleton and Straits (1999); and Toulmin (2003).

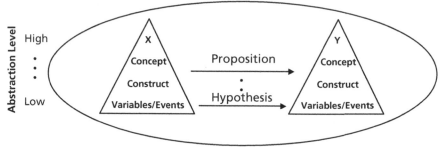

Figure 4.2. Illustration of a theory

Source: Adapted from Bacharach (1989).

and constructs are related to each other by propositions, and the more concrete variables or events are related to each other by hypotheses. This entire system is bounded by a vast number of assumptions, with only the most important or obvious ones stated explicitly, while the vast majority of assumptions remain implicit and tacit. This section discusses each of these components of a theory.

TERMS AND DEFINITIONS

The most basic element of logical analysis is the *term*. A term is whatever is meant by a word or phrase (Singleton and Straits 1999: 41). We can stipulate the meaning of a term, but cannot affirm or deny that it is either true or false.

A useful convention in social science has been to distinguish the meanings of terms by their levels of abstraction, ranging from broad and general to narrow and specific. Anthropologists would say that abstract descriptions of a term tend to be *etic* (from afar), general (broad impersonal scope), and less embedded in context. At the other end of the scale, concrete descriptions of a term tend to be *emic* (up-close), particularistic (often uniquely personal), and situated in a specific context. Following Kaplan (1964), the meanings of the following terms are often distinguished by their levels of abstraction:

- *Theoretical Concepts*: An abstract term that is semantically defined by its association or usage with other terms that are not directly observable.
- *Theoretical Constructs*: A middle-range term that references constitutive components of a concept, but the component parts are not directly observable.

- *Observable Variables or Events:* An operational term that specifies the activities or operations necessary to measure it.

For example, the *social structure of an organization* might be defined[2] at theoretical (concept or construct) and observable (variable or event) levels of abstraction as follows:

- At the most abstract conceptual level an organization's social structure might be defined as the formal (not informal) configuration of roles and authority relationships existing among participants within (not outside of) an organization. A role refers to the expected set of behaviors of a person occupying an organizational position, and authority refers to the formally prescribed power relationships among roles in an organization.
- At a construct level, organizational social structure might be analytically separated into three components of authority relationships among roles: (1) centralization of decision making authority; (2) formalization of rules, policies, and procedures; and (3) complexity, or the number and interdependence of role relationships.
- At a concrete level, the formalization of rules (one construct of the social structure concept) might be observed by measuring the number and specificity of rules in job manuals for various role positions in the organization.

Kaplan's classification of terms into these three levels of abstraction is useful for distinguishing between grand theories (relations among very general and abstract concepts), middle-range theories (relations among theoretical constructs or events that are less general and more specific than concepts), and operational theories (relations among observed variables or incidents). I discuss Kaplan's three levels of abstraction when discussing the merits and demerits of grand, middle-range, and operational theories at the end of this chapter.

A more simple way to classify terms by levels of abstraction is to distinguish between theoretical and observable terms. This classification satisfies most theory building purposes. For example, as Figure 4.2 illustrates, Bacharach (1989) refers to concepts and constructs as theoretical terms, and variables as an observable term. In this usage, *propositions* are considered statements of relationships between concepts and constructs (i.e., among abstract theoretical terms), while *hypotheses* are defined as relationships between variables or events (i.e., among concrete observable terms).

---

[2] The definitions in this example are based on a Weberian view of bureaucracy, as discussed by Hage (1995). These definitions would be very different if one adopted alternative theories of social structure (c.f., Scott 2003: 18–20). This example introduces the paradox of conceptualization, discussed later—good theories are necessary to classify and define concepts; but robust concepts are needed to develop good theories.

As the example of defining organizational social structure illustrates, there are two basic ways to define the meanings of terms at different levels of abstraction: semantic and constitutive definitions. A *semantic definition* describes the meaning of a term by its similarities and differences with other terms. Reference to synonyms and antonyms, as well as metaphors and analogies are useful heuristics for developing semantic definitions. A *positive* semantic definition of concept A, for example, would be to say that it is similar to concepts B, C, and D. A semantic definition by *negation* of the concept A would be to say that A is not like concepts E, F, or G. For example, the definition of the concept of organization social structure included the positive semantic terms of formal role and authority relationships within an organization, and by negation excluded informal external organizational relationships. Both positive and negative semantic definitions are required to clarify the meaning of a concept. Positive definitions identify the properties of a term, while definitions by negation locate the boundaries of a term. 'Terms that are defined by negation are determinate; those defined without negation are indeterminate' (Osigweh 1989).

A *constitutive definition* describes a term with reference to its component parts. For example, concept A consists of a1, a2, and a3 components. Constitutive definitions entail descending the ladder of abstraction. For example, the construct and variable constitutive definitions of the concept of organization social structure above descended the ladder of abstraction by specifying some of the component theoretical and observable terms of the concept.

Semantic and constitutive definitions respectively classify the meaning of a concept by extension and intention, more commonly referred to as breadth and depth.[3] While semantic definitions specify the meaning of a concept by *extension* (i.e., how it is similar to and different from other concepts at the same level of abstraction), constitutive definitions locate the meaning of a concept by *intention* (i.e., what component terms comprise the concept at lower levels of abstraction, and what more aggregate terms the concept is a member of at high levels of abstraction).

---

[3] In Chapter 5 we extend this discussion of semantic and constitutive definitions of terms for developing variance theories that are based on relationships between variables, and process theories that are based on temporal progressions among events. These variables or events may pertain to individuals, groups, organizations, or more aggregate levels of collective behavior. In this chapter I focus on the more general issue of using semantic and constitutive definitions for climbing the ladder of abstraction among terms. However, it is important to distinguish the organizational unit of analysis to which these terms refer from the level of abstraction of those terms. In other words, the terms I use to describe the properties of units at any organizational level may vary in their levels of abstraction.

This discussion of traveling the ladder of abstraction for terms should also not be confused with a philosophical debate about whether the world can be divided into metaphysical idealizations and theoretical laws versus empirical and instrumental objective facts. In Chapter 2 the theory-laden nature of all observations and 'facts' was discussed. At issue here is articulating and reasoning across levels of abstraction of the terms used. By 'theoretical' I mean an abstract formulation of a term, and by 'observable' I mean a concrete formulation of that term.

Osigweh proposes two maxims for descending and climbing the ladder of abstraction with a term. First, descend the abstraction ladder from a universal concept to specific situational constructs by spelling out the attributes that characterize the concept. Second, climb the ladder in a way that retains precision by decreasing the number of attributes and properties that are instantiated or embedded in the intended meaning of a term (Osigweh 1989: 585). Osigweh (1989) advises making concepts travel so they fit precisely a variety of applications—don't stretch their meaning beyond reason.

The purpose of defining terms, of course, is to classify the subject matter into clearly distinct and important categories. Just as classification of phenomena is critical to problem formulation, it is central to theory construction. What makes definitions of terms significant is that they classify the universe into ways that are critical to a theory; or as Plato said, they 'carve at the joints.' 'A significant concept so groups or divides its subject-matter that it can enter into many important propositions about the subject-matter other than those which state the classification itself' (Kaplan 1964: 52).

Inherent in classifying a phenomenon into significant concepts is the paradox of conceptualization. Kant emphasized that concept formation and theory formation in science go hand in hand. As noted in the last chapter, the appropriate conceptualization of a problem already prefigures its solution. 'The proper concepts are needed to formulate a good theory, but we need a good theory to arrive at the proper concepts' (Kaplan 1964: 53). The better the subject matter is classified, the better the theory. The better the theory, the sharper the classification of the subject matter.

Kaplan (1964) cautions, however, against being overly compulsive about clear-cut definitions. All definitions and classifications of concepts remain ambiguous in two respects—semantic openness and operational vagueness.

Semantic openness refers to that fact that the meaning of many terms can only be specified in relation to how they are used together with other terms. As a consequence, 'what begins as the effort to fix the content of a single concept ends as the task of assessing the truth of a whole theory' (Kaplan 1964: 63). The theory as a whole is needed to give meaning to its terms, even those parts of the theory where the terms in question do not explicitly appear. Concepts are implicitly defined by how other concepts and propositions in a theory are treated. The semantic (or systemic) meaning of a concept is always open, for the set of classifications and propositions making up a theory is never complete. Furthermore, the semantic meanings of terms are dynamically open, for they inevitably change with time.

Even at the concrete level some operational vagueness will still remain after we provide clear constitutive definitions of terms. 'Facts are *indefinitely* indefinite: however fine a mesh we use, finer differences slip through the measurement net. And the more discriminations we make, the more opportunities we create for classification errors between borderlines' (Kaplan 1964: 65).

Thus, even though the objective of semantic and constitutive definitions is to clearly specify the meaning and usage of terms, they always remain vague in some respects. Lines are and must be drawn for the pragmatic purpose of being sufficient to address the problem. Kaplan notes that the demand for exactness can have the pernicious effect of inducing premature closure of our ideas and a dogmatic (rather than a critical) attitude. Tolerance of ambiguity is important for scientific inquiry.

RELATIONSHIPS AMONG CONCEPTS

A proposition is a declarative sentence expressing a relationship among some terms. Logicians distinguish the following four kinds of propositions. They provide deeper insights on defining terms and formulating relationships among them.

1. A *categorical proposition* denotes or assigns things to classes (i.e., categories), such as Aristotle did when he claimed, 'all men are mortal.' We make categorical propositions when assigning observations into categories, such as discussed in the last chapter when diagnosing problems by classifying social behaviors into problem or disease categories.
2. A *disjunctive proposition* classifies things into mutually exclusive categories. A disjunctive proposition such as 'this person is either a male or female' seems unproblematic because human beings only consist of two sexes. However, a statement that classifies a student as 'either very bright or studies a lot' is dubious because these categories are not mutually exclusive and the student may fit neither category. Disjunctive propositions are divergent; they differentiate classes of things or theories. A disjunctive proposition is the forerunner of a 'crucial proposition' (discussed later).
3. A *conjunctive proposition* classifies things into multiple categories that the things reflect, such as 'Jane read this and found it interesting.' Conjunctive propositions are integrative; they connect things or bridge terms. A conjunctive proposition is the logic underlying survey questions with multiple response categories, whereas a disjunctive proposition underlies questions with answer scales that force respondents to select only one of multiple options.
4. A *conditional proposition* consists of two simple statements joined by the words 'if' and 'then.' For example, if today is Friday, then tomorrow is Saturday. In a conditional proposition, the 'if' statement is the *antecedent* and the 'then' statement is the *consequent*. A conditional proposition asserts that the antecedent implies the consequent. The consequent is true if the antecedent is true. In scientific discourse, conditional

propositions are often used to specify relations between the antecedent and the consequent either by definition or by cause.

A constitutive definition of a term is a conditional proposition where the consequent follows from the antecedent by the very definition of the antecedent. For example, if the figure is a triangle, then it has three sides. Scholars typically descend the ladder of abstraction by using *deductive conditional propositions* to define the constitutive components of concepts into constructs and then into observable variables or events. A highly condensed example might look like this:

IF   :   The concept of organization social structure consists of the degrees of formalization, centralization, and complexity;

AND :   The construct of formalization is observed by the number of rules and degree to which people follow rules (variables);

AND :   The construct of centralization is indicated by the variables, discretion people have deciding what and how work is done;

AND :   The construct of complexity is indicated by the degree and number of interdependencies among organizational participants in doing their work;

THEN: Organization social structure is operationally defined as the number of rules, degree of rules followed, task discretion, and indicators of task interdependence among organizational participants.

Construct validity is a term frequently used in social science that has specialized meaning to logicians. The *construct validity* of deductive conditional propositions is established by showing that each consequent follows its antecedent by the very definition of the antecedent. The consequent is true if the antecedent is true.

In a *causal conditional proposition*, the antecedent causes the consequent. A physical science example is that if metal is immersed in nitric acid, then it will dissolve. A social science example is that if an organization grows in numbers of employees, then the structure of the organization will differentiate into more departments and hierarchical levels at decreasing rates (Blau and Schoenherr 1971). In these examples of 'if–then' conditional causal propositions, the antecedent (immersing metal in nitric acid or increasing the number of employees) causes the consequent (the metal dissolves or the organization structure differentiates). The logical structure of many hypotheses in the social sciences are of this form of causal conditional propositions. As discussed later, the 'validity' of a causal conditional proposition is established by argument, whereas its 'truth' is established empirically.

The principles discussed above for traveling the ladder of abstraction for concepts also apply to relationships. I noted that propositions and hypotheses differ by levels of abstraction: propositions are relationships among theoretical concepts or constructs, while hypotheses are relationships among concrete observable variables or events. Notwithstanding the varying usage of the terms 'proposition' and 'hypothesis' in many journals, it is important to distinguish abstract theoretical propositions from concrete observable hypotheses of a theory. Kaplan noted this by distinguishing between concatenated and hierarchical forms of theories.

A *concatenated theory* tends to consist of many concepts that are related into a configuration or pattern of hypotheses. As the bottom of Figure 4.3 illustrates, this pattern often converges on some central concept or dependent variable, with each of the independent variables representing a factor that plays a part in explaining the dependent variable. As a result, a concatenated theory is also called a 'factor theory' (Kaplan 1964: 298). Less complementary adjectives include 'bullet' or 'laundry list' theories (Bromiley 2004). As these adjectives suggest, concatenated theories often consist of numerous hypotheses that are seldom generalized to more abstract theoretical propositions. Explanations of concatenated theories tend to focus on individual hypotheses among the independent, dependent, moderating, or mediating variables in the structural causal model as illustrated in the bottom of Figure 4.3. Concatenated theories tend to focus on only one level of abstraction—usually the concrete level of variables and hypotheses. Seldom are attempts made to

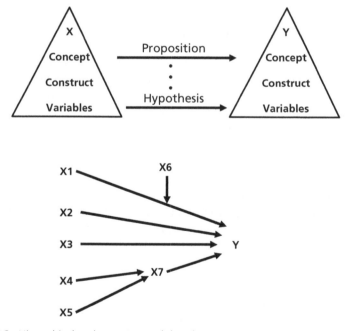

Figure 4.3. Hierarchical and concatenated theories

generalize and travel with the hypotheses that relate observable variables to more abstract propositions that relate to theoretical constructs. As a result, concatenated theories tend to provide a broad and extensive, rather than deep and intensive, understanding of a phenomenon.

In contrast, a *hierarchical theory* is one whose hypotheses are presented as deductions from (or inductions to) one or a few basic propositions following the principles for developing causal conditional propositions. As the top of Figure 4.3 illustrates, the hierarchy represents logical relationships among concepts or constructs as the ladder of abstraction is ascended by inductive reasoning or descended by deductive reasoning. Following Osigweh's (1989: 585) maxims, we climb the abstraction ladder by extending the breadth of hypotheses into more general propositions, while reducing their connotation (thereby increasing simplicity).

Concatenated and hierarchical theories reflect different rungs on the ladder of abstraction. Concatenated theories often reflect operational hypotheses among observable variables, while hierarchical theories are propositions among theoretical constructs. Concatenated theories can be transformed into hierarchical theories by climbing the ladder of abstraction. As we climb we rise to fewer and more general propositions as we move from conclusions (hypotheses) to the premises that entail them (propositions and assumptions) (Kaplan 1964: 298).

LOGICAL DEDUCTIVE REASONING

In logic an *argument* is a set of two or more propositions of which a conclusion is claimed to follow either necessarily or probably from the premises. An argument provides a way to explain our reasoning for a theoretical proposition or an observable hypothesis. The hypothesis is the *conclusion* or the *claim* of the argument. All the other statements that we use to justify the hypothesis are the *premises* of the argument. Once the reasoning for a hypothesis is formulated, then it can be transformed into the logical structure of an argument. A hypothesis is justified by showing that it is the logical conclusion of a valid argument (Giere, 1984: 33).

The most common kind of argument studied by logicians is the *syllogism*. It is an argument composed of three propositions: two premises and the conclusion that the premises logically imply. The basic structure of a syllogism is as follows.

> major premise: All men are mortal
> minor premise: Socrates is a man
> conclusion : Therefore, Socrates is mortal

To analyze the logical structure of reasoning for a theory, we first identify the premises (i.e., reasons, evidence, and assumptions) given for a hypothesis (the conclusion), and arrange them into this syllogistic structure in order to determine the validity or invalidity of the argument. Whereas terms are judged as to their meanings, and propositions primarily as to their truth, syllogisms are judged in terms of their validity (Wheelwright 1962: 14). The validity of a syllogism depends solely on the relationship between its premises and its conclusions. We do not need to know whether the premises or conclusions are empirically true. We only need to know whether the conclusion would be true if the premises were true. The validity or invalidity of a syllogism is independent of the truth of its premises. Hence, as Singleton and Straits (1999: 43) discuss, we can have a valid syllogism consisting of false propositions:

All students are MBAs. (false)
Some robots are students. (false)
Therefore, some robots are MBAs. (valid, but false)

And it is possible to have an invalid syllogism consisting of true propositions:

All butterflies can fly. (true)
All crows are birds. (true)
Thus, all crows can fly. (not valid, but true)

Validity refers to the relation between premises and conclusion, which can be determined by examining the logical structure of the argument. Logicians typically substitute the letters 'p' for the antecedent and 'q' for the consequent of conditional 'if–then' propositions, and 'r' for additional premises in the case of a chain argument. These symbols are applied below to recognize the form of reasoning in a few of the most common types of conditional arguments used in scientific reasoning. The notes below each argument explain why the first three conditional arguments have a valid form, while the last two are not valid.

Forms of Syllogisms: Causal Conditional Arguments

1. *Affirming the antecedent*

   If p, then q   If a firm practices TQM,[4] then it will be successful.
   p   ACO practices TQM.
   Therefore, q   Therefore, ACO will be successful.

---

[4] TQM is an abbreviation for Total Quality Management, which includes a variety of quality management practices such as those advanced by Deming, Juran, and Six Sigma, which have been adopted by many companies worldwide.

Notice that the first premise says that q (success) will be true if p (practicing TQM) is true. The second premise asserts that p is true (ACO practices TQM). If this conditional statement is true and if the antecedent is true, then the consequent must be true also—which is just what the conclusion states. In short, it is impossible that q be false if both premises are true. This satisfies the definition of a deductively valid argument.

2. *Denying the consequent*

   If p, then q   If a firm practices TQM, then it will be successful.
   Not q   ACO is not successful.
   Therefore, not p   Therefore, ACO does not practice TQM.

   The first premise is the same as in the first argument. But the second premise says that q (success) is not true. So, p (practicing TQM) cannot possibly be true either. If it were, q (success) would be. But q is not. As noted below, this deductive form of denying the consequent turns out to be quite similar to inductive arguments used in scientific reasoning to reject a hypothesis.

3. *Chain argument (hypothetical syllogism)*

   If p, then q   If organization trust increases, then transaction costs de-
                  crease.
   If q, then r   If transaction costs decrease, organizational profitability
                  increases.
   If p, then r   If organizational trust increases, then organization profit-
                  ability increases.

   Conditional chain arguments like this can be constructed with any number of premises. There are two requirements for a valid chain argument: (1) the consequent of each premise must be the antecedent of the next premise; and (2) the conclusion must have the antecedent of the first premise as its antecedent and the consequent of the last premise as its consequent. The chain argument is one of the simplest and most common ways to logically derive hypotheses from propositions.

4. *Fallacy of affirming the consequent*

   If p, then q   If a firm practices TQM, then it will be successful.
   q   ACO is successful.
   Therefore, p   ACO practices TQM.

   This argument proceeds with the second premise, affirming the consequent of the conditional first premise. Arguments of this form often sound quite convincing, but are not valid.

5. *Fallacy of denying the antecedent*

   If p, then q   If a firm practices TQM, then it will be successful.
   Not p   ACO does not practice TQM.
   Therefore, not q   ACO is not successful.

This form of conditional argument proceeds with the second premise denying or negating the antecedent of the first premise. Although invalid, such arguments can also sound very persuasive. Arguments of this form are invalid by the meaning of conditional statements. 'The conditional statement says that the truth of the antecedent is sufficient for the truth of the consequent. It does not say that the falsity of the antecedent is sufficient for the falsity of the consequent' (Giere 1984: 62).

There are many other forms of deductive arguments besides conditional arguments. Readers are encouraged to review them in Giere (1984), Ramage and Bean (1995) and Freeley (1996). In general, Singleton and Straits (1999: 48) provide the following three useful rules for assessing true and false premises, valid and invalid arguments, and true and false conclusions.

- If all the premises are true and the argument is valid, the conclusion *must* be true.
- If all the premises are true and the conclusion is false, the argument *must* be invalid.
- If the argument is valid and the conclusion is false, at least one premise *must* be false.

These statements are useful to remember for evaluating deductive reasoning. Applying them can help you become an excellent reviewer of proposals and arguments that may deal with subjects you know little about. Freeley (1996: chaps. 8–10) provides a useful review of tests, cogency, and obstacles to clear syllogisms or arguments.

This section has briefly reviewed how logicians can analyze relations among propositions irrespective of their truth. Scientists have the broader goal of establishing knowledge about the empirical world. They evaluate both the validity of their reasoning and the empirical truth of their statements. It is easy to see the relevance of deductive logic to scientific inquiry. 'The reasoning from theories to hypotheses should be deductively valid, for *if the argument by which a testable conclusion is deduced is invalid, then it is pointless to investigate the truth of the conclusion or the hypothesis*' (Singleton and Straits 1999: 50, italics added).

Justifying the Theory

The foregoing review of basic components and logical principles for theory construction has introduced most of the key ideas for justifying a theory. Theories can be justified in two ways: by testing their empirical fit with the world using inductive reasoning, and by presenting rhetorical arguments of the logical validity, credibility, and persuasiveness of a theory. Both of these approaches are necessary to justify the empirical and conceptual bases of a theory. Hence, they compliment, and do not substitute for, each other. The next two sections discuss these two approaches for justifying a theory.

INDUCTIVE REASONING IN SCIENCE

The prior section noted that in order to be valid, the conclusion of a deductive argument cannot go beyond the content of the premises. Deduction therefore 'only tells us things we know already,' even though we may not have realized that before the deductive reasoning process unfolded (Kemeny 1959: 113). Induction, on the other hand, involves the drawing of conclusions that exceed the information contained in the premises. As Bruner (1973) discussed, because science seeks to establish general knowledge that goes beyond the data given, it must use inductive reasoning. Inductive reasoning presents a claim that the conclusion is probably true if the premises are true. In its simplest form, an inductive argument has the following logical structure.

All observed members of p are q   X% of observed members of p are q
Therefore, all p are q   Therefore, X% of p are q

As discussed below, inductive generalizations are stronger the more the observed instances and members of p vary.

This general form of inductive arguments is one reason why scientific reasoning cannot yield certainty. Even if we could be certain of our premises, the best inductive scientific argument would not guarantee the truth of our conclusion. Thus, the very nature of scientific reasoning introduces an unavoidable possibility of error. Giere (1984: 45), like Bruner (1973), points out that another characteristic of inductive arguments is that they are knowledge expanding; that is, their conclusions contain more information than all their premises combined. It is because of this feature of inductive arguments that science can be a source of new knowledge. These error and expansion features of inductive arguments are related. It is only by giving up the certainty of truth that inductive arguments can be knowledge expanding.

A hypothesis can be rejected because (as we have seen) it is valid to inductively deny the consequent:

If p, then q   If the hypothesis is true, then the predicted fact is true
Not q   The predicted fact is not true.
Therefore, not p   Therefore, the hypothesis is false. (Valid)

But a hypothesis cannot be proven because that would amount to the fallacy of affirming the consequent:

If p, then q   If the hypothesis is true, then the predicted fact is true.
q   The predicted fact is true.
Therefore p   Therefore the hypothesis is true. (Not valid)

There may be more than one explanation for an observed result; other hypotheses may explain the result as well.

If a theory can only be disproved and never proven, how might we gain confidence in the plausibility of a theory? In a nutshell, the answer is (1) develop many diverse tests of the hypothesis; and (2) rule out plausible alternative hypotheses. These two strategies strengthen the inductive conclusion that the hypothesis is more probable in comparison with alternatives, although by deduction it can never be proven to be true.

The greater the number and variety of tests that do not reject a hypothesis, the more credible it is. The idea of strengthening conclusions by increasing the number of diverse applications of a proposition represents the theory justification analogue of the theory creation idea discussed before of expanding variations in thought trials. A greater number of diverse conjectures (hypotheses) is not only more likely to produce a better, but also more convincing theory than a process that generates a small number of homogeneous conjectures or hypotheses. For example, a proposition on work participation and productivity that applies to a wide range of situations and levels (such as for individual employees, work teams, organizational democracy, and larger community networks) is clearly preferable to one that only applies to a single object. A theory with a greater ratio of diverse hypotheses to propositions is more plausible than one with a low ratio (Bacharach 1989: 509). That is, a theory with a proposition that sustains five diverse hypotheses is more credible than when it can justify only one or two homogeneous hypotheses.

The credibility of a theory is a function of its probability of rejection. A *hypothesis must be improbable of being true relative to everything else known at the time excluding the theory being tested* (Giere 1984: 103). Although we can never prove the truth of a theory, our confidence in its plausibility or credibility increases when it is subjected to tests that are more likely to be rejected. Vague or commonplace hypotheses are difficult to reject and, as a result, are less credible than hypotheses that are highly unlikely (but not impossible) to be true given our existing state of knowledge. As Singleton and Straits (1999: 53) note, 'Larger numbers of observations produce stronger inductive arguments *if* the generalization is limited in scope and precision. And generalizations consistent with established knowledge are more probable than those that are not consistent.'

Fortunately, at the time of theory building, the degree of strength or credibility of inductive generalizations can be designed into the theory. Singleton and Straits (1999: 52–3) discuss five useful design principles that should be taken into account simultaneously when building theories.

1. *Similarity of observations.* The more the observable hypotheses that are derived from a theoretical proposition are alike, the weaker the theory.

2. *Dissimilarity of observations.* The more ways that observed instances of hypotheses differ from one another, the stronger the argument.
3. *Scope and precision of generalization.* The more sweeping the generalizations from a theory, the less likely it is to obtain supporting evidence. Inductive generalizations can be altered in two ways: by specifying the entities or things to which the hypotheses apply, and by changing the precision of inductive conclusions. Stating that all or X% of people are satisfied is more precise but less probable than the conclusion that 'most people are satisfied.'
4. *Number of observations.* The greater the number of observed instances, the stronger the argument. However, if the additional observed instances are all alike (as in 1 above), then the probability of the conclusion will not change.
5. *Known relevance.* The greater the relevance of the generalization to prior knowledge, the stronger the argument. When inductive conclusions are not compatible with well-established knowledge, then they are viewed as being less probable (Singleton and Straits 1999: 52–3).

Another way to increase the credibility of a theory is to rule out plausible alternative hypotheses. The comparative method is perhaps one of the most basic principles for advancing scientific knowledge. The credibility or truth of a theory is not determined in an absolute sense by evaluating whether a hypothesized relationship exists or not. As discussed in Chapter 6, statistically significant tests of null hypotheses are seldom significant in practice because prior research may have already found evidence for the relationship. The important question is whether the proposed relationship represents a substantial advance over the current state of knowledge. The credibility of a theory is judged by comparing it with rival plausible alternative theories at the time of the investigation. At a minimum, to be credible a new theory should provide a better explanation for a phenomenon than the status quo explanation. Suppe (1977) and Giere (1999) cite Bacon for his initial proposal to compare rival plausible alternative theories. The better a theory survives both logical and empirical comparisons with rival theories, the more plausible and credible the theory.

Fortunately, the number of alternative theories that actually provide rival explanations for a given phenomenon in the literature at any given time tends to be very small. In my particular field of organization and management studies, I typically find only two or three theories seriously contending as rival alternative explanations for a given research question. In his historical review of the sociology of knowledge, Collins (1998) found no more than five or six theories competing to explain a phenomenon at a time. The more that one of these rival alternative theories can be disconfirmed through logical arguments or empirical tests, the more credible the surviving theory is. The greater the number of comparative tests with rival theories to which a theory is subjected, the more credible it is.

Stinchcombe (1968*b*) discusses how this basic inductive process of science should lead scholars to design *crucial experiments* where evidence in support of one theory implies the rejection or negation of a rival alternative theory. In other words, we should carefully examine the consequences of our claims whose negation may be implied by the alternative theory or argument. This results in a disjunctive conditional proposition that rules out a plausible alternative theory.

BUILDING THEORETICAL ARGUMENTS

Kaplan (1964: 302) pointed out that, 'A hypothesis may be as much confirmed by fitting it into a theory as by fitting it to the facts. For it then enjoys the support provided by the evidence for all the other hypothesis of that theory' in comparison with other theories. The method of argument provides a rhetorical strategy for justifying the conceptual basis of a theory.

Arguments are produced for many purposes. In this section I focus on scientific and professional discourse where an argument is presented in formal defense of a claim (a theory, proposition, or hypothesis). As used here, argument does not refer to its commonplace meaning of people having unpleasant and pointless disputes or verbal fistfights. Instead, an *argument* refers to an explanation with reasons and evidence for a theory. Argument in this sense is an essential mode of inquiry because it is a way of explaining why our proposed theory is better than others. Not all theories are equal. Some theories can be supported with better reasons and evidence, and with fewer qualifications and possible rebuttals than others. Without the discipline of critical reasoning that arguments entail, it is often difficult to convince yourself and others of the pros and cons of your theories in comparison with others.

An argument is also a central means of communicating a proposed theory and attempting to convince others that it is correct. The relative contribution or advance to knowledge of a new theory is rarely self-evident, and not accomplished by asserting strongly-held beliefs or ideologies. If it is to be considered credible, sound arguments are needed for a proposed theory in comparison with others so that listeners can assess those arguments and judge which is the stronger or more plausible theory. Thus, once we have conceived of and constructed a theory, a further step of developing an argument is needed to explain and defend it.

A good argument doesn't merely repeat conclusions. Instead it offers reasons and evidence so that other people can make up their own minds for themselves. . . . That is how you will convince others: by offering the reasons and evidence that convinced you. It is not a mistake to have strong views [i.e., beliefs]. The mistake is to have nothing else. (Weston 2000: xii)

While crafting an argument provides many opportunities for learning, revising, and improving our theory, the argument itself does not reflect this journey of learning and conceptual development. Giere (1984: 10) notes that the process of convincing others of what one has created or discovered is very different from the process of discovery itself. Scientific reasoning, as found in professional scientific journals, does not include the many activities and independent thought trials that may go into creating or discovering a theory (as discussed in the first section of this chapter). Instead, it typically includes only the argument of reasons, evidence, qualifications, and reservations for the proposed theory or claim. The British logician, Stephen Toulmin (2003) points out that an argument is a retrospective justification of a theory.

An argument makes good on our claim that the conclusions arrived at are acceptable conclusions. . . . Logic is concerned with the soundness of the claims we make—with the solidity of the grounds we produce to support them, the firmness of the backing we provide for them—or, to change the metaphor, with the sort of case we present in defense of our claim. (Toulmin 2003: 6–7)

As noted before, it has been customary since Aristotle to analyze the logical structure of arguments by setting them out as a syllogism, consisting of three propositions: minor premise, major premise, and conclusion. Although analytically simple and elegant, Toulmin (2003: 87) argues that a syllogism is not sufficiently elaborate or candid for presenting a practical substantial argument that has the objective of persuading an audience rather than analyzing formal logic. Toulmin adopted an audience-based courtroom metaphor of argument where jurisprudence governs how claims-at-law are put forward, disputed, and determined.

Toulmin's courtroom model differs from formal logic in that it assumes (1) that all assertions and assumptions are contestable by 'opposing counsel,' and (2) that all final 'verdicts' about the persuasiveness of the opposing arguments will be rendered by a neutral third party, a judge or jury. Keeping in mind the 'opposing counsel' forces us to anticipate counter-arguments and to question our assumptions; keeping in mind the judge and jury reminds us to answer opposing arguments fully, without rancor, and to present positive reasons for supporting our case as well as negative reasons for disbelieving the opposing case. Above all else, Toulmin's model reminds us not to construct an argument that appeals only to those who already agree with us. (Ramage and Bean 1995: 102)

This courtroom model of argumentation applies equally well to scientific discourse, where the judge and jury are the members of a professional or scientific community, and the 'opposing counsel' tends to be those individuals who subscribe to the theories or models being negated or replaced in the argument. More specifically, in the case of the journal review process, the jury consists of two or three anonymous reviewers of each paper while the judge is the journal editor. In the case of competitive research grants, the jury consists of the review panel and the judge is the program funding officer. While reviewers also perform the opposing counsel role, it is ever-present in the many other papers and proposals competing for the same limited journal space and research funding. Although politics and chance influence this process, most scientists believe that arguments trump politics and chance in governing this highly competitive market for ideas.

Logic and jurisprudence help to keep in the center of the picture the critical function of reason. The rules of logic are not laws, but standards of achievement which a person in arguing can come up to or fall short of, and by which achievement can be judged. A sound argument, a well-grounded or firmly-backed claim, is one which will stand up to criticism. (Toulmin 2003: 8)

The Toulmin structure of argument consists of the following elements: background, claim, grounds, warrants, backing, qualifications, and possible rebuttals. Toulmin's method of argument has become perhaps the most widely diffused and adopted form of argumentation in western society. It is the leading form of argumentation taught in English-speaking schools (Ramage and Bean 1995) and used by debate clubs throughout secondary and higher education (Freeley 1996). Instruction in Toulmin's structure of argument is available in many excellent textbooks (Ramage and Bean 1995; Freeley 1996; Weston 2000; as well as three editions of *The Uses of Argument* from 1958–2003 by Toulmin himself). Several educators have created publicly accessible websites for introducing and practicing Toulmin's method of argument.[5] Some of these textbooks and web sites use slightly different terminology for various elements of an argument, as outlined below. However, these are differences of style rather than substance.

background	problem, question, context of the claim
claim	conclusion, answer, or hypothesis
reasons	major premise, warrants, or logic underlying the claim
evidence	minor premise, grounds, or data backing the reasons
qualifiers	boundary conditions and assumptions when claim holds
reservations	limitations or grounds for rebuttal of a claim

We now discuss how these elements of the Toulmin system might be used to craft an argument in support of a theory that we have created. Figure 4.4 illustrates how these elements are related. Readers are referred to other textbooks and web sites just mentioned for more extensive treatments and applications of the Toulmin method of argumentation.

[5] See, for example: http://writing.colostate.edu/Google.com identifies many additional web sites with the keyword 'Toulmin structure of argument.'

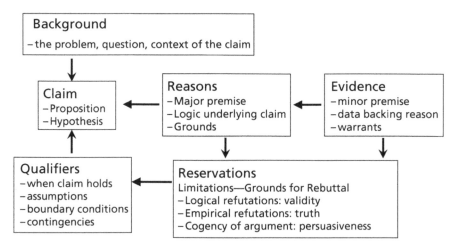

Figure 4.4. Toulmin structure of argument

Source: Toulmin, S. (2003). *The Uses of Argument*, updated edn. Cambridge: Cambridge University Press.

BACKGROUND

An argument assumes a specific context or background. To start with we need to present the problem or question being investigated in a particular context. This background statement is needed for several reasons.

First, as discussed in Chapter 3, understanding the nature and context of the research problem and question is needed to motivate an argument. Explanations of the problem or question—why it is important in the context in which it resides, how it has been addressed in the past, and what is incomplete or unsatisfactory with past treatments—open the mind of a listener and set the stage for claiming a new theory to answer the question.

Second, this background statement is also needed to determine whether the case merits argumentation. Establishing the case is mandatory for pursuing it in legal proceedings. At issue is whether our theorizing has progressed to the point of having a theory or proposal that is ready for justification. Too often we rush prematurely to make an argument for a case that has not yet been adequately conceived or constructed. The quotation in the chapter introduction by Hanson (1959: 35) merits restatement: 'For our own sakes, we must attend as much to how scientific hypotheses are caught, as to how they are cooked.' Several iterations of the activities discussed in sections I and II of this chapter are typically needed to 'catch' (conceive and create) a theory. As most fishermen and women have experienced, you lose the fish if you try to bring it in before setting the hook. Premature theory justification often destroys or evaporates theory creation.

An argument begins by specifying the problem and question to be addressed and the possible solutions that merit consideration. To determine if we have a justifiable case that warrants consideration, Toulmin suggests that it is common to (1) set out the alternative solutions requiring consideration to a question or problem; (2) identify a particular solution that is unequivocally indicated by reasons and evidence; and (3) rule out some initial possibilities in light of the evidence (Toulmin 2003: 21).

Third, it is important to consider the assumption base of the intended audience in addressing these issues. Like a plaintiff in a courtroom, the more we know the assumptions of the judge, jury, and defendants, the better we can tailor and direct the argument.[6] Some members of the audience may not be aware of the problem or why it is important. For those who are aware of the issue, they may not share similar assumptions about the problem and ways to address it. An effective starting-point in any communication is to appeal to shared assumptions, values, or standards that the audience grants. If the audience accepts our assumptions, then we have a starting place from which to build an effective argument. If our audience doesn't accept our starting assumptions, then other formulations of the problem, case, or beliefs are needed until we find common ground with our audience (Ramage and Bean 1995: 100).

THE CLAIM

The claim is the theory, proposition, or hypothesis that we propose as an answer to the question or problem being investigated. A claim is the central conclusion that we are trying to establish by our argument. To be effective, claims should be specific, discriminating, and simple assertions. For example, a claim that 'group brainstorming techniques increase group decision-making effectiveness' is too general, while 'the nominal group brainstorming technique increases the number of ideas generated by a group on a problem-solving task' is more specific. However, neither of these propositions are discriminating for they leave the alternatives and key conditions unspecified. A more discriminating proposition would be that 'nominal and delphi group brainstorming techniques generate more ideas than conventional discussion groups composed of seven members when working on a problem solving task for one hour.' Crucial to a discriminating proposition is inclusion of the alternatives that are being negated in comparison with the ones being affirmed.

---

[6] There is no better way to learn the mindset of a reviewer than to be one. Reviewers of scientific journal articles and research grants are pro bono volunteers. Most journal editors and program organizers have an ongoing search for volunteers. If their reviews are penetrating and constructive, these volunteers are often invited onto the editorial board or research panel.

These examples represent relatively simple propositions because each is stated in a single sentence that is relatively easy to understand (for those who know about brainstorming groups). Indications of propositions that are too complex are those that entail a highly complex sentence with many adjectives, qualifications, and prepositions. A claim may also be too complex if it needs to be re-read several times to be understood. As Weston (2000: 60) advises, first state your claim or proposition simply, and elaborate it later when discussing other elements of the argument.

Arguments should be restricted to focusing on a single claim. This is an important implication of hierarchical and concatenated theories discussed in the last section. Hierarchical theories facilitate clarity of exposition and energy in crafting a single argument that focuses on the central theoretical proposition from which one can descend the ladder of abstraction to logically derive and explain many diverse concrete hypotheses. In contrast, concatenated theories seldom take advantage of the parsimony provided by the ladder of abstraction, either by descending the ladder to logically derive hypotheses from propositions, or by climbing the ladder to infer how various hypotheses conceptually aggregate to reflect a theoretical proposition.

Concatenated theories, consisting of many logically different hypotheses are difficult to justify. Not only do they require crafting multiple arguments, one for each hypothesis, but also reconciling inconsistencies between arguments. This creates an unmanageable complex problem for the proponent and the audience. Given the same space and time limitations, a proponent is more likely to craft a single strong elaborate argument for a proposition than many equally strong 'mini'-arguments for each hypothesis. An audience is more likely to follow the line of reasoning and be convinced by a single coherent argument than by a series of shorter, different, and often inconsistent arguments.

REASONS AND EVIDENCE

Reasons are statements explaining the logic underlying the claim for why the claim is correct or true, and evidence is the grounds—data, facts, statistics, testimony, or examples—backing the reasons. In terms of a syllogism, reasons are the major premises for a claim, and evidence includes the minor premises grounding the reasons for the claim. In most arguments, several reasons are presented for the claim and a variety of evidence to support each reason. For example, we might state that 'there are three reasons for my claim, and a variety of studies in the literature support each reason.' Then presumably we would go on to discuss each reason and the literature supporting each reason for the claim.

Given that there are typically many reasons and extensive evidence for a claim, the question is which reasons and what evidence should be presented in an argument? Space and time limitations force us to present only the most important reasons and evidence. As discussed in the prior section, the reasons and evidence presented for a claim should be logically valid. In other words, we select the reasons that represent the major premises and the evidence reflecting the minor premises that provide the strongest and most direct chain of reasoning to logically derive the claim. If an argument cannot be presented in a logically valid way, then it may be pointless to pursue it further.[7]

For example, to substantiate the logical validity of the claim that 'the nominal group technique generates more motivated and satisfied participants to a task than does the Delphi technique,' one could reason that 'face-to-face group meetings facilitate greater social-psychological interactions, norms, and sentiments among members than do electronic discussion groups where members do not meet face-to-face (the major premise).' As evidence one might present two minor premises: (1) nominal groups meet face-to-face in a structured meeting format while Delphi group members do not meet face-to-face and only submit their ideas to a question via electronic media; (2) studies (for example, by Van de Ven and Delbecq 1974) have found that the structured format of nominal groups (silent writing of ideas on paper, round-robin recording of ideas, discussion, and independent voting) inhibits the negative effects of conventional discussion groups (e.g., falling into a rut, evaluating rather than generating ideas, and voting in conformance with members of higher status), but facilitates positive effects of belonging to the group and satisfaction with group decisions. The chain of reasoning from these major and minor premises leads to the logical inference of the claim.

QUALIFICATIONS AND ASSUMPTIONS

Once we have considered the reasons and evidence for the claim, then we are in a position to qualify the claim by specifying the boundary conditions within which the claim applies, and outside of which the claim is not assumed to hold or be true. Boundaries and assumptions are critical because they set the limitations for applying a proposed theory or claim. Dubin (1976) emphasized that all theories are contingency theories because each is based on a host of bounding assumptions. They include the values and interests of researchers and users of a study, as well as analytical limits on the time, space, and magnitude of relationships specified in the claim.

Values are the implicit assumptions by which a theory or claim is bounded. Bacharach (1989: 498) cites Max Weber for pointing out that 'the value-laden nature of assumptions can never be eliminated. Yet, if a theory is to be properly used or tested, the theorist's implicit assumptions which form the

---

[7] Chapter 8 expands on this discussion by pointing out that an intended audience may wish not only a logical explanation for a claim, but also strategic and deep explanations that respond to their own pragmatic interests in understanding the meanings and uses of an argument.

boundaries of the theory must be understood.' Fortunately, there is growing acceptance of Weber's conclusion. Reflecting on a decade of theorizing, Weick (1999) observes a growing reflexivity in recent management literature.

More straightforward boundary conditions of a theory are analytical assumptions of time, space, and magnitude of relationships. Spatial boundaries are conditions restricting the use of a theory to specific units of analysis (e.g., specific types of organizations, locations, or contexts). Temporal contingencies specify the dates and durations of time over which the proposition or theory applies (Bacharach 1989).

Finally, Toulmin (2003) points out that we may need to qualify the degree of certainty or confidence in the evidence and reasons used in support of the claim. Qualifiers (e.g., 'very likely,' 'probably,' or 'better than an alternative') state the extent to which our reasons and evidence fit the case under consideration, and whether special facts may make the case an exception to the rule or whether our claim is subject to certain qualifications.

RESERVATIONS AND LIMITATIONS

No argument for a claim or theory is perfect. Every argument has some limitations or objections that can represent the grounds for rebutting or refuting the claim. As Figure 4.4 indicates, validity, truth, and persuasiveness represent three common grounds for refuting an argument. These evaluation criteria can help us detect and replace or repair flaws in our arguments. 'As advocates, we should prepare our refutation with the same care that we prepare other elements of our argument. Effective refutation is rarely the result of improvisation, but comes from careful analysis and preparation' (Freeley 1996: 283).

As discussed in section II of this chapter, the logical *validity* of an argument is the degree to which the claim is a logical conclusion in the chain of reasoning from the major premises (the reasons) and minor premises (the evidence). Paraphrasing Freeley (1996: 170–1), a number of questions are useful for assessing logical reasoning:

- Are the reasons solid? Have good reasons been given to establish the foundation of the claim? Have better reasons been used in the literature?
- Are the reasons and evidence sufficient to justify the claim? Are additional evidence and reasons needed to back the claim?
- Have sufficient reasons and evidence been provided to anticipate rebuttals or reservations of the argument?

A second common ground for refuting an argument is the extent to which the evidence that is used to support the reasons are considered *truthful* (i.e., survive empirical testing). Freeley (1996: 127–48) discusses a variety of tests of credible evidence that emerge from a long history of argumentation. Stated as questions, they provide a useful checklist for evaluating the evidence used in any argument:

- Is the evidence relevant, critical, and sufficient?
- Is the evidence clear, consistent within itself and with other known evidence?
- Is the evidence verifiable?
- Is the source of the evidence competent, unprejudiced, and reliable?
- Is the evidence statistically sound, cumulative, and current?

Finally, the logical elements of an argument discussed in this section will be expanded in Chapter 8 to include the *persuasiveness* of an argument. Justifying a theory represents an art in building a convincing argument. What makes an argument convincing and, therefore, utilized is a rhetorical question (Van de Ven and Schomaker 2003). Rhetoric is the use of persuasion to influence the thought and conduct of one's listeners. To Aristotle, the art of persuasion comprises three elements: (1) *logos*—the message, especially its internal consistency as discussed in this section (i.e., the clarity of the argument, the logic of its reasons, and the effectiveness of its supporting evidence); (2) *pathos*—the power to stir the emotions, beliefs, values, knowledge, and imagination of the audience so as to elicit not only sympathy, but empathy as well; and (3) *ethos*—the credibility, legitimacy, and authority that a speaker both brings into and develops over the course of the argument or message (Barnes 1995). As discussed in Chapter 8, logos, pathos, and ethos together shape the persuasiveness of any communication. The persuasiveness of a theory is in the 'eyes' of the listener (not just the speaker), and requires appreciating the context and assumptions of the audience or listeners.

We are reminded again of the importance of framing a study with a reflexive attitude about whose perspectives and interests are to be served by the claim. Knowing the values and interests of stakeholders in the intended audience of a study is crucial for formulating the research problem, the question, selecting an interesting conjecture, and presenting a convincing argument for the theory. A convincing theory is not only a function of presenting a valid argument, but also of the degree to which the speaker is viewed as a credible witness and is able to stir the human emotions of listeners.

CAN A THEORY BE GENERAL, ACCURATE, AND SIMPLE?

Three criteria are commonly used to evaluate a theory: it should be general, accurate, and simple. Thorngate (1976) postulated that it is impossible for a theory of social behavior to be simultaneously general, accurate, and simple. Like Weick (1999), I question if this postulate is correct, and discuss some possible ways for developing general, accurate, and simple theories using some of the logical principles of theory building discussed in this chapter.

Weick (1999: 800) selects the following quotation from Thorngate to summarize his postulate:

The impostulate of theoretical simplicity dictates that we shall never see a general, simple, accurate theory of social behavior. In order to increase both generality and accuracy, the complexity of our theories must necessarily be increased. Complex theories of social behavior will be viable only to the extent that the complexities of social behavior are organized. However, there is reason to believe that much social behavior is not organized beyond a 'local,' or situation-specific level. Even if it is organized beyond this level, there is faint reason to believe that the organization is simple. Complex theories of social behavior may be easily constructed in an attempt to describe the organization, but the ethics and pragmatics of research set severe limits on the complexity of theories that can be subjected to empirical test. Herein lies the ultimate irony of our discipline [social psychology]: Precise and complex theories may hold the promise for being general and accurate, but in the end they are untestable as those which are simple and vague. (Thorngate 1976: 134–5)

Many organizational scholars have expressed agreement with Thorngate's postulate that any social theory entails inevitable tradeoffs between being general, simple, and accurate (Langley 1999; Pentland 1999; Weick 1999; Van de Ven and Poole 2005; among others). For example, Weick (1979: 36) illustrates Thorngate's postulate using the metaphor of a clockface with general at 12:00, accurate at 4:00, and simple at 8:00, as illustrated in Figure 4.5. Weick (1999: 801) states that the point of this representation is to see the tradeoffs among the three criteria. 'An explanation that satisfies any two characteristics is least able to satisfy the third characteristic.'

Is Thorngate's postulate correct, or does Weick's clockface metaphor lock us into thinking of tradeoffs rather than complements among general, simple, and accurate theories? 'A way of seeing is a way of not seeing' (Poggi 1965). For example, another spin on Weick's clock metaphor is that a theory will appear general, simple, and accurate twice a day—it's just a matter of when you look. Continuing this playfulness, the clockface might represent different times around the world. Then we might conclude that a given theory can simultaneously be general in Europe and New Zealand, accurate in India and California, and simple in Asia and Brazil—it's a matter of where you look. Pressing this far-fetched metaphor a bit further leads to a reasonable conclusion that the generality, simplicity, and accuracy of a theory may be a function of time, proximate viewpoint, and cultural context. Slight variations of meta-phors can lead us to think very differently about things.

By relaxing his clockface metaphor and applying a few of the basic principles of logical reasoning as discussed in this chapter, Weick (1999) changed his position. He observed the following contradiction in Thorngate's postulate.

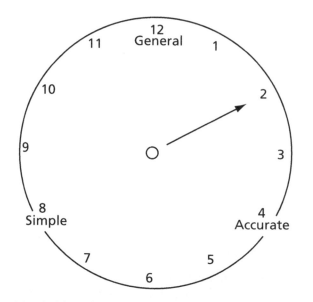

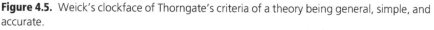

Figure 4.5. Weick's clockface of Thorngate's criteria of a theory being general, simple, and accurate.

Source: Weick, K. E. (1979). *Social Psychology of Organizing*, 2nd edn., fig. 2.1, p. 36.

If, as Thorngate asserts, it is true that it is impossible for an explanation of social behavior to be simultaneously general, accurate and simple, then that assertion is false. It is false because the assertion itself IS general (it applies to all explanations), IS simple (it is summarized in one accessible sentence), and IS accurate (it is a valid prediction). Thus, Thorngate's general, accurate, simple explanation for the impossibility of a theory itself shows that such a theory is possible. Humans who are able to wind themselves into and out of tangles such as this need all the help they can get when they develop theory. (Weick 1999: 802)

To explore how and why we might work ourselves out of this tangle, let us examine three propositions in Thorngate's statement of his postulate (quoted above).

The first proposition in Thorngate's postulate is that, 'In order to increase both generality and accuracy, the complexity of our theories must necessarily be increased.' Although this may often happen, it need not if we travel the ladder of abstraction correctly. Thorngate's proposition may be a result of incorrectly climbing the ladder of abstraction by widening the extension and increasing the connotation of concepts, resulting in concepts that are stretched to become vague pseudogeneralizations that are not necessarily more complex; instead they become meaningless. If logical steps in climbing the ladder of abstraction are applied correctly, then increasing the generality of a theory should maintain its accuracy by decreasing its complexity. As Osigweh (1989: 584) points out, climbing the ladder of abstraction involves extending the breadth of a concept (generality) while reducing its properties or connotation (thereby increasing its simplicity).

The second proposition in Thorngate's quotation is that 'complex theories of social behavior will be viable only to the extent to which the complexities of social behavior are organized. However, there is reason to believe that much social behavior is not organized beyond a 'local' or situation-specific level.' In this statement Thorngate appears to reflect the *principle of local determination*. Kaplan (1964: 300) observes that

It is often felt that only the discovery of a micro-theory affords real scientific understanding of any type of phenomenon because only it gives us insight into the inner mechanism of the phenomenon. Underlying this position is what might be called the principle of local determination: the radius of the explanatory shell can be made indefinitely small. Local determination is determinism conjoined to a denial of action-at-a-distance in space or time: whatever happens anywhere is capable of being explained by reference to what is to be found there. (Kaplan 1964: 300)

Simple theories are economical. 'But contracting the explanatory shell is by no means always a move in the direction of economy' (Kaplan 1964: 300). For example, it is not obvious that a cognitive psychological explanation of human behavior is more simple, general, or accurate than an institutional sociological explanation. Local determination appears to reflect the disciplinary disposition of the researcher. While a researcher's inclinations cannot be ignored in theory development, neither should the nature of the research question or problem being addressed. Selecting the radius of a theory's explanatory shell (i.e., its generality, accuracy, and simplicity) is a choice that should match the perspective and scope of the problem domain as perceived by key stakeholders of the study.

A third proposition in Thorgate's postulate quoted above is that 'Complex theories of social behavior may be easily constructed in an attempt to describe the organization, but the ethics and pragmatics of research set severe limits on the complexity of theories that can be subjected to empirical test.' Clearly, the greater the complexity of a theory, the more difficult it is to test. But Thorngate's statement addresses the complexity problem only from the researcher's viewpoint. He does not mention the consequences of complexity for the audience or consumers of theories. For them, the limiting factor of complex theories is not their testability; it is the amount of complex information people can simultaneously process at a time.

From an engaged scholarship perspective, the complexity (as well as the generality and accuracy) of theories is more in the eyes of the audience than it is in the testing capacities of the researcher. Theories that exceed Miller's (1956) 'magical number' (of seven plus or minus two) exceed the information processing capabilities of most readers. Beyond this number of $7+$ or -2 factors, hypotheses, or findings in a study, members of an audience become numb and lose their capabilities to discern what is general, simple, or accurate in a theory of social behavior. Theories that exceed Miller's magical number may be a product of not clearly formulating the research problem as well as not traveling the ladder of abstraction in crafting an understandable hierarchical theory out of a concatenated 'laundry list' of possible explanatory factors.

This interpretation of Thorngate's postulate links the generality, accuracy, and simplicity of a theory with climbing the ladder of abstraction and considerations of the intended audience. Like any claim, there are boundaries to these links. An important qualification is Merton's (1968) proposal to develop theories of the middle range. Merton describes a middle-range theory as being less abstract than grand social theories (such as proposed by Parsons or Engles) that are often too remote from social phenomena to accurately account for what is observed in specific empirical contexts. On the other hand, middle-range theories are a level more abstract than observed particulars for identifying the classes or archetypes of problems of which particular cases are a part. Middle-range theories are close enough to observable activities within contexts to permit empirical testing and generalization to propositions (Merton 1968: 39).

Theories tend to be constructed and justified to fit the existing body of knowledge. Hence we should expect, as Merton (1968) describes, that while middle-range theories are not logically derived from general abstract theories, once developed and tested, they may provide important empirical evidence for one or more general theories. This is because grand abstract theories tend to be sufficiently loose-knit, internally diversified, and mutually overlapping to subsume a number of middle-range theories. More accurate and specific empirical evidence and more contextual theorizing of middle-range theories contribute to improving and grounding general theories. In return, this increases the generality or radius of the explanatory shell of the middle-range theory subsumed by a general theory. In this way, middle-range theories can contribute to bridging and adding to scientific knowledge.

Conclusion

Writers often express different views about theory building. They range from those emphasizing theory creation and arguing that trivial theories are produced by hemmed in methodological strictures that favor validation rather than imagination (Weick 1989; Mintzberg 2005), to those emphasizing the need for clear definitions, internal logical consistency, and verifiability (Bacharach 1989; Peli and Masuch 1997; Wacker 2004). In part these writers are right in describing one theory building activity and wrong in ignoring other activities involved in theory building. Many of these differences dissolve when it is recognized that theory building is not a single activity. Instead it involves at least three activities—creating, constructing, and justifying a theory.

This chapter examined these three theory building activities and discussed how they entail different patterns of reasoning: abduction is used for conceiving a theory, logical deduction for constructing a theory, and inductive reasoning and argumentation for evaluating and justifying a theory. I conclude that much can be learned about theory building by understanding and developing skills in these patterns of reasoning.

CONCEIVING A THEORY BY ABDUCTION

The first step in theory building involves an abductive reasoning process of conceiving the germ of an idea that may become a theory. This idea may be a 'half-baked' conjecture that was created in response to an anomaly that violates our understanding of the world. Abduction is a creative form of reasoning that is triggered by encountering anomalies and ends by selecting a plausible or coherent solution that might resolve the anomaly.

A useful model for understanding the dynamics of abductive reasoning in theory creation is an evolutionary model of variation, selection, and retention of thought experiments, as proposed by Campbell (1988) and Weick (1989). Variation is the number of different conjectures that are developed to make sense of an anomaly observed in a problematic situation. Selection involves the application of different criteria for choosing among these conjectures. Retention is the elaboration and justification of theories for the chosen conjecture.

Representing abductive reasoning as an evolutionary process, Weick (1989) introduced several useful propositions for increasing the number of independent thought trials in generating and selecting conjectures for addressing anomalies. In particular, this chapter discussed three of these propositions. First, the number and diversity of thought trials in generating conjectures increases the likelihood of producing better theory. Second, the diversity of criteria applied to a conjecture increases the likelihood that those conjectures that are selected will result in good theory. Third, since it is not possible to determine or test the validity of a conjecture at the time of its conception, then plausibility is a substitute criterion for validity in selecting conjectures.

Engaged scholarship represents a strategy for implementing these propositions. Engaging and obtaining the diverse perspectives of other people increases the independence of thought trials for developing conjectures, and for applying diverse criteria in choosing among the conjectures. Moreover, the more we engage and the better we know the perspectives and assumptions of key stakeholders, the better we can select and frame conjectures that are plausible to the intended audience of a study.

CONSTRUCTING A THEORY WITH LOGICAL DEDUCTIVE REASONING

Once a plausible conjecture has emerged through a process of abduction, then the mode of reasoning switches to deduction to elaborate the conjecture and construct it into a complete theory. A theory was defined as an explanation of relationships among constructs within a set of boundary conditions. I reviewed some of the basic principles of logical deductive reasoning, for they provide the toolkit for theory construction. Constructing a theory involves articulating and elaborating a conjecture into theoretical and observable terms, developing propositions and hypotheses that relate these terms, and specifying the conditions when they apply. I emphasized that sound logical reasoning remains as important as ever to elaborate the semantic meaning of theories and identify the boundaries of concepts and their relationships. I reviewed the distinction logicians make between the logical 'validity' and empirical 'truth' of an argument. This distinction is important because if a theory is not logically valid, then it is pointless to investigate its empirical truth by designing and implementing either variance or process research models, as discussed in the next three chapters.

JUSTIFYING A THEORY WITH INDUCTIVE REASONING AND RHETORICAL ARGUMENTS

I discussed how theories can be justified in two ways: by testing their empirical fit with the world using inductive reasoning, and by presenting rhetorical arguments of the logical validity, credibility, and persuasiveness of a theory. Both of these approaches are necessary to justify the empirical and conceptual bases of a theory. Hence, they compliment, and do not substitute for, each other.

By inductive reasoning, a theory can only be disproven and never proven. If that is the case, I discussed how we might gain confidence in the plausibility of a theory? The proposed answer is to (1) develop many diverse tests of the hypothesis; and (2) rule out plausible alternative hypotheses.

- The greater the number and variety of tests that do not reject a hypothesis, the more credible it is. The credibility of a theory is a function of its probability of rejection.
- Another way to increase the credibility of a theory is to rule out plausible alternative hypotheses. At a minimum, to be credible a new theory should provide a better explanation for a phenomenon than the status quo explanation.

These two strategies strengthen the inductive conclusion that the hypothesis is more probable in comparison with alternatives, although by deduction it can never be proven to be true.

Stinchcombe (1968*b*) suggested that this basic inductive process of science should lead scholars to design *crucial experiments* where evidence in support of one theory implies the rejection or negation of a rival alternative theory.

An argument provides a rhetorical strategy for explaining and justifying a theory. Not all theories are equal; some can be supported with better reasons and evidence, and with fewer qualifications and possible rebuttals than others. Without the discipline of critical reasoning that arguments entail, it is often difficult to convince yourself and others of the pros and cons of a theory in comparison with others.

I proposed and discussed the Toulmin (2003) structure of argumentation for explaining and justifying a theory. The Toulmin method arranges the elements of an argument into statements of: (1) the background context, problem, and question being examined; (2) the claim, or the central proposition, hypothesis, or theory being advanced; (3) the major reasons or explanations supporting the claim; (4) evidence backing the reasons; (5) qualifications of the boundary conditions and assumptions for the claim; and (6) reservations, including limitations or grounds for rebuttal of the claim. Critical in developing these elements of an argument are the assumptions and perspectives of the audience being addressed. It reminds us again of the importance of being engaged and in framing a study with a reflexive appreciation of whose perspectives and interests are being served in an argument.

The chapter concluded with a discussion of three criteria commonly used to evaluate a theory: generality, accuracy, and simplicity. Thorngate (1976) postulated that it is impossible for a theory of social behavior to be simultaneously general, accurate, and simple. Like Weick (1999) I questioned if this postulate is correct, and explored possible ways for developing general, accurate, and simple theories by climbing the ladder of abstraction and incorporating the perspectives of the intended audience. An important qualification to this discussion is Merton's (1968) proposal to develop theories of the middle range; theories that lie in between and can bridge concrete hypotheses among observable variables or events and grand universal propositions among abstract concepts.

5 Variance and Process Models

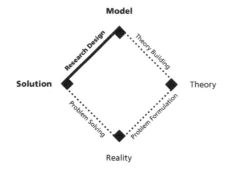

This chapter introduces the research design activities illustrated in Figure 5.1 of the engaged scholarship process. It assumes that an empirical research study is being designed for the purpose of developing or testing a theory as discussed in Chapter 4 to examine a research problem and question as formulated in Chapter 3. Since a theory is not directly observable, it needs to be transformed into an operational research model. This chapter introduces two basic models—variance and process models—that are commonly used for designing social research to study different kinds of questions and propositions. The two models adopt different epistemological assumptions, hypotheses, and instruments for representing the theory and phenomenon being investigated. Following this overview, the next two chapters discuss operational steps and decisions in designing a variance model (Chapter 6) and process model (Chapter 7).

To begin, it is important to distinguish a *theory* from a *model*. Social scientists do not directly observe or test theories; instead, they examine models (McKelvey 2002*a*). Models are partial representations or maps of theories. In addition, models consist of a host of instruments, procedures, assumptions, and manipulations that are used to apply scientific methods of observation and analysis. This includes all the assumptions of variance and process models discussed in this chapter. Morgan and Morrison (1999) argue that these models do not simply represent operational versions of a theory. Instead, because the models include a host of instrumental assumptions and

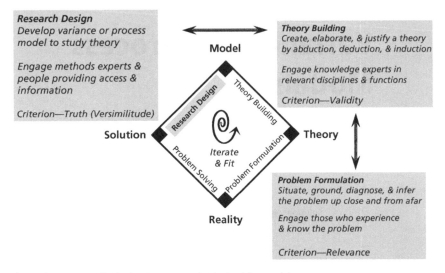

Figure 5.1. Research design in engaged scholarship model

practices that are not reflected in the theory itself, models occupy an autonomous role in scientific work and serve as *mediators* between theories and data.

It is common to think that models can be derived entirely from theory or from data. However, if we look closely at the way models are constructed we can begin to see the sources of their independence. It is because they are neither one thing nor the other, neither just theory nor data, but typically involve some of both (and often additional 'outside' elements), that they can mediate between theory and the world. (Morrison and Morgan 1999: 10–11)

A research model is an instrument for linking theory with data in terms of function, representation, and learning. First, a model functions like a tool or instrument that is independent of the thing on which it operates and connects, just as a hammer is separate from the function of connecting the nail to the wall. Research models function as tools or instruments and are independent of, but mediate between theories and the world; and like tools, can often be used for many different tasks. Models also serve as instruments that can be used to learn about the world and about theories. As a tool of investigation, a research model provides ways to represent some aspects of the world and some aspects of our theories about the world.

Hence, the model's representative power allows it to function not just instrumentally, but to teach us something about the thing it represents . . . [But] just as one needs to use or observe the use of a hammer in order to really understand its function; similarly, models have to be used before they will give up their secrets. In this sense, they have the quality of a technology—the power of the model only becomes apparent in the context of its use. Models function not just as a means of intervention, but also as a means of representation. It is when we manipulate the model that these combined features enable us to learn how and why our interventions work. (Morrison and Morgan 1999: 11–12)

Variance and process models are used to empirically examine two different types of research questions that are often asked about an issue being studied:

- *What* are the antecedents or consequences of the issue?
- *How* does the issue emerge, develop, grow, or terminate over time?

These 'what' and 'how' research questions represent a 'fork in the road' for designing and conducting social research. The two research questions require different methodologies that are based on fundamentally different assumptions and epistemologies.

'What' questions entail a variance model (Mohr 1982) or 'outcome-driven' (Aldrich 2001) explanation of the input factors (independent variables) that statistically explain variations in some outcome criteria (dependent variables). 'How' questions require a process model or 'event-driven' explanation of the temporal order and sequence in which a discrete set of events occur based on a story or historical narrative (Bruner 1991*a*). In terms of causality, 'what' questions require evidence of co-variation, temporal precedence, and absence of spurious associations between the independent and dependent variables (Blalock 1972). 'How' questions require narratives explaining an observed sequence of events in terms of a plot or an underlying generative mechanism that has the power to cause events to happen in the real world and the particular circumstances or contingencies that occur when these mechanisms operate (Bruner 1991*a*; Tsoukas 1989).

While the vast majority of social science research to date has focused on 'what' questions, there has been a growing interest in studying 'how' questions. Process studies are fundamental for gaining an appreciation of dynamic social life, and developing and testing theories of 'how' social entities adapt, change, and evolve over time. However, because most researchers have been taught a version of variance modeling and because methods for process modeling are perhaps less well developed, researchers tend to conceptualize process problems in variance terms. 'One can see the "law of the hammer" in operation here: Give a child a hammer and everything seems made to be hit; give a social scientist variables and the general linear model, and everything seems made to be factored, regressed and fit' (Poole et al. 2000: 29). As a consequence, researchers often make the mistake of using the wrong methods to study their research question.

For example, a researcher studying innovation who is trained in variance methods is inclined to decompose a sequence of innovation events into a series of input–output analyses by viewing each event as a change in a variable (e.g., the number of product innovations), and then examining if changes in this variable are explained by some other independent variable (e.g., R&D

investment). From a variance theory perspective, events represent changes in variables, and these changes are the building blocks of process in an input-process-output model. But since a process question is not whether, but *how*, a change occurred, we first need a story that narrates the sequence of events that unfolded as the innovation emerged from concept to implementation. Once the sequence or pattern of events in a developmental process is found, then one can turn to the 'what' questions about the causes or consequences of the event sequence.

Given these differences between 'what' and 'how' questions and their close correspondence with variance and process models, respectively, I make three basic suggestions for designing and conducting a social science study:

1. Understand your research question, and select the methodology appropriate for examining the research question (not vice versa).
2. Understand the assumptions as well as the strengths and limitations of the variance and process models that you select to examine your research question.
3. Assess variance and process models on their own terms; not in terms of the other.

This chapter elaborates these three suggestions. It begins with an overview of variance and process models as two fundamentally different epistemologies for social research. The two models capture basic distinctions between research studies undertaken to investigate either: (1) variance or causal questions of 'what causes what;' and (2) process questions of 'how things develop and change over time.' The basic assumptions underlying these different models are then discussed. These differing assumptions explain how and why variance and process models are incommensurable in some respects. Therefore, contrary to the commonplace practice of using a universal set of criteria for evaluating social science research, I argue in Chapters 6 and 7 that process and variance studies should be designed and evaluated based on their own unique criteria.

Having distinguished the two models, I conclude that it is important to appreciate their complementary relationship. Answers to a 'what' question typically assume or hypothesize an answer to a 'how' question. Whether implicit or explicit, the logic underlying an answer to a variance model is a process story about how a sequence of events unfolds to cause an independent (input) variable to exert its influence on a dependent (outcome) variable. Thus, one way to significantly improve the robustness of answers to 'what' (variance theory) questions is to explicitly examine the process that is assumed to explain why an independent variable causes a dependent variable.

Similarly, answers to 'how' questions tend to be meaningless without an answer to the corresponding variance theory questions of 'what caused it?' or 'what are its consequences?' As Pettigrew (1990) argues, theoretically sound and practically useful research on change should explore the contexts, content, and process of change through time. Just as change is only perceptible relative to a state of constancy, an appreciation of a temporal sequence of events requires understanding the starting (input) conditions and ending (outcome) results.

Two Basic Epistemologies

Two basic epistemologies underlie the different approaches that are necessary to study research questions dealing with 'what' and 'how.' Bruner (1986) distinguished them as representing two basic types of human intelligence: the paradigmatic, logico-scientific (variance) mode of thought and the narrative (process) mode of thought. He describes them as follows:

There are two modes of cognitive functioning, two modes of thought, each providing distinctive ways of ordering experience, of constructing reality. The two (though complementary) are irreducible to one another... Each of the ways of knowing, moreover, has operating principles of its own and its own criteria of well-formedness. They differ radically in their procedures for verification. (Bruner 1986: 11)

Bruner notes that we have relatively little knowledge about how narrative understanding works compared to the vast literature on paradigmatic thinking and its methods. Although recent research in many fields is filling this void, much remains to be done.

Aldrich (2001) distinguishes the 'what' and 'how' questions in terms of outcome-driven and event-driven research, as follows.

Outcome-driven explanations are built backward, from an awareness of observed outcomes to prior causally significant events. Two related problems are introduced with this strategy. First, it often leads to investigators' selecting on the dependent variable, a well-known research bias. Second, even though we might include all organizations—those that have experienced the event and those that have not—we still observe them at only one point in time. Figure 5.2 gives a graphic example of an outcome observed at Time 1 that is then linked backward to events occurring earlier. (Aldrich 2001: 118)

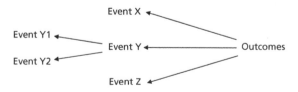

Figure 5.2. Outcome-driven explanations

Source: From Aldrich (2001), adapted from Elder et al. (1988).

In contrast to outcome-driven explanations, event-driven explanations are built forward, from observed or recorded events to outcomes. Researchers pick certain kinds of events a priori and then record their occurrences over time. No simple rules exist for such designs, and some events can figure in more than one narrative. Moreover, most events we observe probably have no obvious consequences, thus requiring that researchers have strong a priori theoretically grounded notions of the expected causal process. Figure 5.3 gives a graphic example of events observed over time, which are then linked forward to outcomes occurring later. Note that later outcomes are themselves events, with subsequent consequences. (Aldrich 2001: 119)

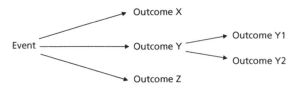

Figure 5.3. Event-driven explanations

Source: From Aldrich (2001), adapted from Elder et al. (1988).

Aldrich (2001) notes that researchers often get into trouble because they do not make explicit distinctions between event-driven and outcome-driven studies of organizational and other social processes.

One contributing factor may be that two different definitions of 'process' are often used in the literature: (1) a category of concepts or variables that pertain to actions and activities; and (2) a narrative describing how things develop and change (Van de Ven 1992). When the first definition is used, process is typically associated with a variance model (Mohr 1982), where an outcome-driven explanation examines the degree to which a set of independent variables statistically explain variations in some outcome criteria (dependent variables). The second meaning of process takes an event-driven approach that is often associated with a process study of the temporal sequence of events (Abbott 1988; Pentland 1999; Poole et al. 2000; Tsoukas 2005).

Mohr (1982; Poole et al. 2000) first distinguished variance and process approaches to social scientific research, and the distinction has been quite influential in organizational studies. In general terms, a variance model explains change in terms of relationships among independent variables and dependent variables, while a process model explains how a sequence of events leads to some outcome. The two approaches yield quite different conceptualizations of change and imply different standards for judging research on change and development in social entities. Figure 5.4 illustrates the two models.

While influential, Mohr advanced a rather restrictive view of variance and process models. Others have advanced broader interpretations of variance and process representations of social action (Abell 1987). Abbott (1984, 1990, 2001) compared stochastic and narrative explanations in sociology. Bruner (1991*a*) and Polkinghorne (1988) present general introductions to theories of narrative in the human sciences in which they highlight the differences between narrative explanation and traditional causal analysis in social science. Barnett and Carroll (1995) distinguish between the 'content' and 'process' of change. Content refers to what actually changes in an organizational entity, while process examines how the change occurs. Content studies tend to focus on the antecedents and consequences of organizational change, while process studies examine the sequence of events over time as change unfolds in an organizational entity. Poole et al. (2000) elaborate and discuss narrative process and causal variance modeling. They point out the different assumptions, implicit or explicit, that scholars make when they adopt variance and process models.

The common thread running through these works is the difference between scientific explanations cast in terms of independent variables causing changes in a dependent variable, and explanations that tell a narrative or story about how a sequence of events unfolds to produce a given outcome.

Variance methods seek explanations of continuous change driven by deterministic causation, with independent variables acting upon and causing changes in dependent variables. An example of the variance method of research on organizational change is a study by Schoonhoven et al. (1990). They applied event-history analysis to examine differences in the speed with which new ventures in the US semiconductor industry ship their first products for revenues. Schoonhoven et al. (1990) found that the speed of shipping the first products (the dependent variable) was significantly predicted by firms with: (1) lower levels of technological innovation; (2) lower monthly expenditures; (3) a founding organization structure that included both manufacturing and marketing positions; (4) more competitors in the

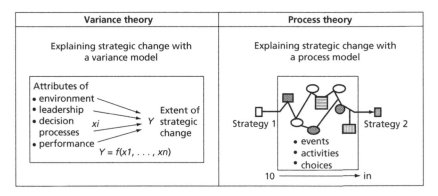

Figure 5.4. Two approaches to explaining strategic change

Source: After Mohr (1982) in Langley (1999).

marketplace; and (5) their foundation in the Silicon Valley region (the independent variables).

In contrast, Gersick (1994) provides an example of a process model of organization change undertaken to understand the development of a new company start-up. She examined how a start-up company regulates its development strategy over time. Gersick analyzed key decisions, events, and strategies in this start-up over time based on monthly interviews with start-up leaders and venture capitalists and board meeting observations. Gersick found two forms of temporal pacing that regulate momentum and change in an organization's strategy. One form of pacing is time-based, with reorientations initiated at temporal milestones, the other is event-based, with actions initiated when the right event occurred. These two pacing types fostered systematically different patterns of momentum and change in the new start-up.

As the study by Schoonhoven et al. (1990) illustrates, variance models explain change in terms of relationships among independent variables and dependent variables, while the study by Gersick (1994) exemplifies a process model that explains how a sequence of events unfolds over time. The two methods yield quite different conceptualizations of change and imply different standards for judging research on change and innovation. Table 5.1 provides a summary comparison of the two methods based on the discussion in Poole et al. (2000).

THE VARIANCE MODEL

As noted before, the variance approach focuses on variables to represent the important aspects or attributes of the subject under study. Explanations take the form of causal statements or models that incorporate these variables

Table 5.1. Comparison of variance and process approaches

Variance approach	Process approach
Fixed entities with varying attributes	Entities participate in events and may change over time
Explanations based on efficient causality	Explanations based on final, formal, and efficient causality
Generality depends on uniformity across contexts	Generality depends on versatility across cases
Time ordering among independent variables is immaterial	Time ordering of independent events is critical
Emphasis on immediate causation	Explanations are layered and incorporate both immediate and distal causation
Attributes have a single meaning over time	Entities, attributes, events may change in meaning over time

Source: Adapted from Poole et al. (2000: 36).

(e.g., X causes Y which causes Z). An implicit goal of variance research is to establish the conditions necessary to bring about an outcome. Variance models employ experimental and survey research designs, grounded in the general linear model that underlies most common statistical methods, including ANOVA, regression, factor analysis, and structural equation modeling.

Poole et al. (2000) discuss six key assumptions underlying variance models. These six assumptions combine to enable the study of causal relationships among variables in an analytically sophisticated way. However, as the six assumptions show, this instrumentation creates a highly restrictive representation of the phenomena being studied.

1. *The world is made up of fixed entities with varying attributes.* In a variance model the basic units of analysis are entities that maintain a unitary identity through time. These entities possess a fixed set of variable attributes that are assumed to reflect any significant changes in the entity (Abbott 1990). For example, in a study of employee job satisfaction, the employee is taken as the basic entity. The focus of the research is on characteristic attributes of the employee, such as gender, age, tenure, work, incentives, etc. Changes and levels in these variables for a sample of employees represent the essential measurement tasks, and the goal of the research is to represent relationships among these and other variables.

   The variance approach assumes that any significant changes in the entities being studied (e.g., employees) are captured by the variables. The entities are, in effect, settings within which the variables act. To form a proper explanation, it is necessary to identify the variable attributes that are essential to the process under study. Variables constitute the primitive terms used in theories. Hence, both causes and outcomes of change and development must be framed as variables. Employing this mode of explanation requires one to 'variabilize' the world, that is, to view the order underlying observed phenomena as comprised of variables standing in relationship to each other.

2. *Efficient causality is the basis of explanation.* Aristotle distinguished four causes—literally, *aitia,* 'answers to the question' of why change occurs (Aristotle 1941; Randall 1960)—material, formal, efficient, and final. Respectively, they indicate that from which something was made (material cause), the pattern by which it is made (formal cause), that from which comes the immediate origin of movement or rest (efficient cause), and the end for which it is made (final cause) (Ross 1949). Variance models are explicitly concerned with efficient cause, tending to downplay other sources of change. Mohr explains, 'An efficient cause is a force that is conceived as *acting on* a unit of analysis (person, organization, or entity) to make it what it is in terms of the outcome variable (morale, effectiveness, and so on) or change it from what it was. It may be thought of as a *push-type* causality'

(1982: 40). For example, organizational rewards encouraging innovative behavior, top management team support, and an entrepreneurial climate act on an individual to increase the likelihood that the person will initiate a new venture. Each cause in a variance theory is assumed to function as an efficient cause. Other types of causality, such as final causality that posits that phenomena are influenced by the ends to which they are tending, are not regarded as valid generative mechanisms.

3. *The generality of explanations depends on their ability to apply uniformly across a broad range of contexts. One criterion for evaluating variance explanations is their generality.* In the variance view, the generality of a causal mechanism refers to the domain of cases and contexts in which it is able to operate *uniformly and consistently* at all levels of both independent and dependent variables. The broader this domain, the more general the explanation provided. Causes are assumed to operate 'at equal speed' and in the same way across all cases (Abbott 1990). The generative mechanism is also assumed to be continuously efficacious across time; independent variables are always operating on dependent variables in a continuous fashion as the process unfolds. When causal relationships between independent variables and a dependent variable are not uniform over cases or time, researchers search for additional variables in the context that may account for the unexplained variance. For example, when relationships between entrepreneur personality variables and new venture performance proved unstable, entrepreneurship researchers began to search for other variables to explain new venture performance.

4. *The temporal sequence in which independent variables influence the dependent variable is immaterial to the outcome.* When several independent variables are included in a model, the time order in which the variables come into operation makes no difference in the level of the outcome, so long as the theory employs a time frame in which they can all operate or trigger. The level of outcome variable Y is the same whether variable X occurs before variable Z or vice versa, so long as their influence is fully brought to bear on Y. This is consistent with the general linear model, which employs linear combinations of independent variables to predict dependent variables. This combinatorial process yields equivalent results no matter which independent variable operates first.

Variables that act in grossly different time frames are commonly separated into two different explanatory theories, distinguished as being at 'macro' and 'micro' levels. For instance, variables affecting new business initiation might be partitioned into three sets on the basis of temporal duration—variables that influence individual creativity and innovation in business, variables that influence business planning, and variables that influence initiation and diffusion of business in society.

Initially the focus would be on developing a theory or model for each level. Once this has been accomplished, the interrelationship of the levels is addressed.

A minimal time unit is also assumed. Since many variance models assume causation to operate continuously over time, the existence of variables that require time to be partitioned into bits of definite length presents a thorny conceptual problem (McGrath 1988; Abbott 1990). For independent variables to be in continuous operation on a dependent variable, all variables—independent and dependent, categorical or continuous—must be susceptible to measurement at the same point in time and the temporal unit of measurement must be equal for all variables. Otherwise, variables of different statuses are included in the same model. As temporal units grow finer and finer, the model breaks down because eventually the unit is so fine that at least one variable cannot be realized in the time frame, and measurement becomes impossible.

5. *Explanations should emphasize immediate causation.* Causal relationships in variance models assume that at each point in time the variables in the model contain all the information needed to estimate their values at the next point in time (Abbott 1990). The variance approach reduces development and change to a sequential list of the results of a deterministic or stochastic model: 'A set of initial values faces the model and produces new values that in turn face the model and so on; the immediate past is perpetually producing the future...' (Abbott 1990: 146). Because of this, extended narratives or accounts involving long sequences of actions are not required for a valid explanation. It is not necessary to know the particular twists and turns of an entity's history to explain it, because any effects of the past that matter in the present are represented in the immediate past state of the entity. For example, founding team characteristics that matter to new venture performance at time 3 are assumed predictable from the state of the venture at time 2. The possibility that unique effects of founding team characteristics could interact with the state of the venture at later points in time in ways unpredictable from previous states is not considered by the variance approach.

6. *Attributes have one and only one causal meaning over the course of time.* Because variance models operate continuously and uniformly over time, they treat each variable as though it has the same status or meaning throughout the process. A variable such as entrepreneurial orientation is required to have the same meaning and place in the model at time 100 as it had at time 1 if the data are to 'fit' the model. This assumption is a logical result of variance model assumption 1, in that entities can only remain fixed if their attributes retain a unitary identity and meaning over the course of time.

Given its prevalence, it is easy to presume that the variance approach represents the basic, objective approach of social science. However, as we have seen, variance research is based on a certain way of constructing reality, a certain way of cutting up the world into researchable pieces. The variance approach works perfectly well for examining research questions about comparisons among entities or causal relationships among variables. However, its assumptions prove very restrictive for studying how social entities develop and change. An alternative scientific methodology has been articulated in recent years for addressing process research questions.

THE PROCESS MODEL

Like the variance approach, a process model provides general explanations, though its criteria for generality differ. Unlike some other perspectives critical of variance research, the process approach does not reject quantitative methods. It utilizes any methods that can help make sense of change and development processes. However, the form of narrative explanation places certain restrictions on the type of data that should be used and the nature of models that can be employed. The process approach also assumes that explanation occurs by specifying generative mechanisms. The generative mechanism in narratives, a particular form of process modeling, hinges on plots that differ in form from those employed by variance approaches.

Variance models also rely on stories to undergird explanations. However, these stories are 'mininarratives' which give an in-depth understanding of a causal process and justify links among variables, but do not form an integral part of the explanation itself. The explanatory work in variance models is done by a continuously operating causal model. In contrast, a process model explains development in terms of the order in which things occur and the stage in the process at which they occur. In narrative methods the plot in the story itself is the generative mechanism.

Thus, the process approach offers a model of scientific explanation that differs in several ways from the variance model. The contrasting assumptions of the two models are displayed in Table 5.1. Process approaches to the study of how change and development occur can be characterized by six contrasting assumptions to those of variance models.

1. *The world is made up of entities that participate in events. These entities may change over time as a result.* The unit of analysis in the narrative approach is an evolving central subject that makes events happen and to which events occur (Abbott 1988). While attributes of an entity may change, the entity itself may also change through a number of processes—through transformation into a different type of entity, merger with another entity, division

into two different entities, and death or dissolution. For example, the temporal development of a new business may entail qualitative changes, including being merged with another company, split up, spun off, or terminated during the course of study. These processes cannot be represented adequately in a set of variables, because they have to do with qualitative change in the entity. 'Entity processes' (Abbott 1992) are enacted through sequences of events and can themselves be coded as macro-level events, that is, as discontinuous occurrences that represent qualitative shifts.

While discriminating choice of variables is important in forming variance models, process explanations hinge on discerning the central subjects and the types of events that mark qualitative changes in these subjects. *Central subjects* are individual entities (people, groups, organizations, machines, and other material artifacts) around which the narrative is woven. It is important to note that the term 'subject' does not refer to human subjectivity, but rather to the actor(s) participating in the narrative.

Events are the natural units of the social process; events are what key actors do or what happens to them. The process perspective explicitly focuses on events rather than variables because of the inherent complexity of developmental processes (Abbott 1990). The variance approach would regard events as a combination of particular values of many variables. Abbott (1990) states that, 'The narrative analyst views events as the natural way to simplify the social process. Rather than disassembling complex particulars into combinations of supposedly independent variable properties . . . such an analyst views direct conceptualizing of the observed events as the best way to simplify the complex flow of occurrences' (p. 142). Poole et al. (2000: 41) add that the process approach also views events as the most valid representation of what occurs in development and change processes.

2. *Final and formal causality, supplemented by efficient causality, is the basis for explanation.* Process theories focus on critical events and conjunctions of events to explain development and change, and hence they hinge on necessary causality. Each causal event imparts a particular direction and moves the developing subject toward a certain outcome. This influence is necessary for development and change to proceed down a particular path. However, subsequent events, conjunctions, and confluences also influence the subject, and may alter the direction imparted by earlier events. Because causal influences come to bear 'event-wise'—through one or more events—rather than continuously, no cause can be sufficient in narrative explanation.

Narrative explanations employ efficient causality to explain the influence imparted by particular events and, often, to explain the mechanics of transitions between events and between more macro-level units, such as phases. However, narrative explanation also admits other forms of causality, especially final causality and formal causality. Micro-moves are from event to event (and even some larger transitions are explicable in terms of efficient causes). However, explaining why larger patterns evolve requires a broader causal scheme. In Mohr's (1982) terminology, narrative explanation requires a *'pull-type causality*: X [the precursor] does not imply Y [the outcome], but rather Y implies X' (p. 59). In Sarasvathy's (2001) terminology, a pull-type causality relies upon 'effectuation' processes that are more general and ubiquitous than causation processes.

For example, final and formal causality, or effectuation, of new venture performance may occur where the entrepreneur adopts systems and structures expected by venture capitalists such as detailed performance goals. A desire to be seen as a legitimate new business may pull the entrepreneur toward developing goals valued by venture capitalists, which then may pull the entrepreneur toward the set of systems and structures needed to reach these goals.

3. *The generality of explanations depends on their versatility.* Like variance theories, process theories are evaluated on their potential generality. The generality of a narrative explanation, however, stems not from its uniformity and consistency, but from its *versatility*, the degree to which it can encompass a broad domain of developmental patterns without modifying its essential character. The broader its domain—the greater the variety of cases, contexts, events, and patterns to which the theory can be applied— the more general the explanation. A key difference between process and variance explanations is the use of terms such as 'encompass' and 'adapt' as opposed to variance explanations, which use terms such as 'uniform and consistent operation.' These process terms capture a basic quality of narrative process explanation, which attempts to discern a common process in a range of complex and seemingly disparate events and sequences.

A defining feature of process narratives is their inherent complexity. The events that comprise them are complicated. Process narratives with the same 'plot' often differ considerably in specific sequences due to the particular conjunctions of causes and contextual factors operating in specific cases. Narrative causality is 'loose' in that it specifies only the pattern or form that arranges events in space and time; therefore, it does not exert the deterministic influence over events that efficient causes exert in variance theories. Moreover, in process theories, efficient causation is event-centered and hence may be intermittent and uneven over time. As a result, narratives explainable in terms of the same theory may vary considerably in the nature and patterns of events that transpire. For instance, a life-cycle theory of new venture development may posit a general set of stages through which all new ventures pass, but the exact sequence of stages experienced by a particular new venture or the observed length of time a new venture spends in each stage may vary considerably.

4. *The temporal sequence of events is critical.* The preceding assumption implies that the order in which causal forces come to bear is crucial in narrative accounts. The order in which events occur determines when efficient causes come into play; while the duration of events and the continuity across events determines how long these causes operate. Differences in temporal order can make large differences in outcomes.

In group decision making, for example, if groups start with solutions, the solution orientation acts to narrow their frame of reference, and later attempts to define the problem will generally be constrained by the frames implied in the solutions first entertained. On the other hand, groups that start with a broad search for understanding the problem are not so constrained and therefore may consider a much wider range of solutions during subsequent solution phases. The order in which the events 'solution development' and 'problem diagnosis' occur brings different causal forces to bear. In the case of the solution-oriented group, there is a strong framing effect. The problem-oriented group is driven by forces enabling and constraining search behavior, and only later experiences solution-framing effects. The different temporal orderings result in quite different outcomes (Maier 1970).

5. *Explanations should incorporate layers of explanation ranging from immediate to distal.* Explanations of development at any point rely on all prior events and associated causal influences. In process theories, history cannot be encapsulated in the immediate past state of the entity (as it is in variance models), because the ordering and context of previous events is critical to narrative explanation. Within the same narrative framework, the particular histories of individual cases may lead them to take different paths to different outcomes. To subsume these differences under a common theory, it is necessary to show how the sequence of events for each case resulted in a unique causal history that caused the narrative to unfold in different ways.

This creates an interesting situation: whereas a particular cause may operate for only a limited time in a process model, in a sense it never ceases to influence the entity, because it forms part of the entity's history. A new venture start-up founded to commercialize a technological innovation that is subject to a strict regulatory regime, such as federal approval of a new drug or safety device, bears the influence of this regime long after regulatory requirements have been satisfied. The particular characteristics of the product and its ultimate success or failure are shaped by its history and the measures taken in response to regulation.

The different durations of events are related to a second reason that process models must allow for versatile causal analysis. Efficient causal factors are associated with events, and to the extent that one event runs longer than another, its causal influence is more enduring. In a childcare program, for example, the influence of the state licensing and regulatory process may stretch over months or years. However, the influence of a county board to turn down financing comes to bear in a short period of time. While duration per se has no relation to the importance of a cause, the possibility of causes with different time horizons forces process models to look back much further than the previous state of the entity.

6.   *An entity, attribute, or event may change in meaning over time.* As noted before, the process approach presumes that the unit of analysis may undergo metamorphosis over time. So the entity, for example a new business, may be fundamentally transformed into a different type of unit, merge with another unit, or go out of existence over the course of its life span. In the same vein, an attribute of the entity may change its essential meaning as the entity develops; what strategic planning is will be fundamentally different for a small start-up than for the larger firm it grows into. Finally, events may also change in meaning. For example, an event 'denied funding' is likely to mean very different things to a nascent product development team than to the project team that has shepherded an innovation through several years. To a young new venture team, denial of funding is likely to constitute a catastrophe that threatens the very life of the project; to the experienced team it represents an unfortunate but survivable event and sets in motion plans for obtaining interim funding from 'soft' sources. This does not represent different interpretations of the same event, but rather fundamentally different meanings for the two events.

Concluding Discussion

I have argued that different research questions require different research models. Social science researchers tend to focus on two kinds of research questions:

- What are the antecedents or consequences of something?
- How does something develop and change over time?

A variance model is appropriate for the first kind of question, and a process model is needed to address the second kind of question.

This chapter reviewed the philosophical assumptions underlying variance and process research models, and discussed how they represent two distinct modes of inquiry. Research assumptions, hypotheses, and procedures take different shapes in variance and process studies. Although it is possible to maintain these distinctions, researchers often confuse and mix various principles of these two distinct research models. When it comes to research design, 'the devil is typically found in the details.' As a consequence, 'there is a tendency to miss either one target or the other, often by virtue of trying, and inevitably failing, to mix the two together' (Mohr, 1982: 36). Following Mohr's advice, I treat these models separately by focusing on steps in designing variance research models in Chapter 6 and process models in Chapter 7.

Sometimes researchers mistakenly adopt a variance model to study process questions. This is understandable because most social scientists have been taught a version of variance modeling and received little training in process models. As discussed in this chapter, an unfortunate implication is that if the researcher's repertoire is limited to variance modeling, he/she is severely limited to casting process dynamics into general linear relationships among variables. Process models tend to be more complex than variance methods due to the complexity of events, the need to account for temporal connections among events, different time scales in the same process, and the dynamic nature of processes.

As discussed in Chapter 7, process models employ eclectic designs that identify or reconstruct the process through direct observation, archival analysis, or multiple case studies. Analysis of process data requires methods that (1) can identify and test temporal linkages between events and also overall temporal patterns (Poole et al. 2000); and (2) can cope with the multiple time scales that often occur in processes (where some events extend for years, other events embedded in them run for shorter periods, and others embedded within these run for even shorter periods) (Langley 1999).

Both variance and process models strive for generality, but with a process model, generalization depends on *versatility*, 'the degree to which it can encompass a broad domain of developmental patterns without modification of its essential character' (Poole et al. 2000: 43). A versatile process explanation can 'stretch' or 'shrink' to fit specific cases that may differ in their tempo and time span. For instance, the punctuated equilibrium model of organizational change (Tushman and Romanelli 1985; Gersick 1991) is highly versatile because it can be applied to processes that take a week, to processes that take years, and to a wide range of different processes, including organizational change, group development, and the evolution of technology.

Having distinguished between the two general types of questions addressed by variance and process models, it is important to see their complementarity. The two types of questions are highly related and both are important for understanding organizational change. To answer the 'what' question, one typically assumes or hypothesizes an answer to the 'how' question. Whether implicit or explicit, the logic underlying an answer to a variance theory is a process story about how a sequence of events unfolds to cause an independent (input) variable to exert its influence on a dependent (outcome) variable. For example, to say that R&D investment and entrepreneurial orientation causes new corporate venture businesses is to make important assumptions about the order and sequence in which R&D investment, opportunity recognition, and new venture start-up events unfold in an organization. Thus, one way to significantly improve the robustness of answers to the first (variance model) question is to explicitly examine the process that is assumed to explain why an independent variable causes a dependent variable. To do so requires opening the proverbial 'black box' between inputs and outcomes, and to take process seriously by examining temporal sequences of events.

Similarly, answers to process questions tend to be meaningless to their users without an answer to their corresponding variance questions. For example, to propose that new businesses proceed through a general set of life-cycle stages but may do so in different sequences may prompt a question of what factors cause the different sequences observed. One way to improve the answers to process theory questions about how businesses pass through life-cycle stages is to search for start-up characteristics that influence differences in progression through such stages. As Pettigrew (1990) argues, theoretically sound and practically useful research on change should explore the contexts, content, and process of change through time. Just as change is only perceptible relative to a state of constancy, an appreciation of a temporal sequence of events requires understanding the starting (input) conditions and ending (outcome) results. In short, answers to both questions are needed to appreciate the inputs, processes, and outcomes of social life.

6 Designing Variance Studies

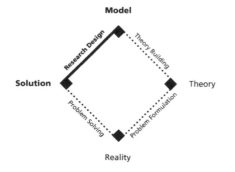

This chapter reviews basic steps and decisions in designing a variance research model. At its core, a variance research model consists of a causal conditional proposition. The basic structure of a causal conditional proposition consists of an 'if–then' statement of the relationship between one or more causes and effects. As introduced in Chapter 4, these 'if–then' statements are called *propositions* when the causes and effects are stated in abstract theoretical terms, and they are called *hypotheses* when these 'if–then' causes and effects are stated in concrete observable terms. Empirical study of a theoretical proposition requires that it be translated into hypotheses among observable terms. A central task of research design is transforming a theory into an operational research model.

A variance research model represents the theory from a particular *perspective* as a causal *relationship* among *variables* of *units* that are *sampled, measured,* and *analyzed* in accordance with *experimental design procedures.* This chapter unpacks the terms in this statement, for they constitute the essential tasks of developing a variance research model. Table 6.1 outlines eight key issues, decisions, and suggestions for clarifying the components of a variance research design. By necessity these issues are discussed in sequential order. In practice they are highly interdependent and need to be treated in an iterative manner.

Variance modeling is the dominant type of social science research. Many good texts and resources are available for addressing the eight issues in

Table 6.1. Key issues, decisions, and suggestions for variance research design

Issues	Decisions	Suggestions
1. The research question and perspective	What is the causal conditional proposition or question? For whom & for what is the study being conducted?	Variance research is geared to 'if–then' causal questions. Involve key stakeholders in research design.
2. Unit of analysis	What individual or collective properties are being studied?	Clarify the unit of analysis and unit of observation. Distinguish analytical, relational, & global properties of collectives.
3. Causal model	What is the variance research model?	State causal conditional relationships in the variance research model. Select proximate and controllable causes.
	How to probe (not prove) causation?	Causation between variables indicated by covariation, temporal precedence, & no spurious factors.
4. Experimental design	Is this a randomized, quasi, or non-experimental design?	Adopt experimental logic to control for extraneous effects. Evidence of causation is strongest with randomized experimental design.
5. Sample selection and size	What criteria are used to select units, constructs, observations, & settings?	Focus on construct validity in theoretical sampling. In population sampling, be clear about target population before drawing a sample.
	How many cases should be included in the sample?	Select the number of cases that equate statistical and practical significance.
6. Measurement	Sample indicators of variables	Achieve construct validity with constitutive definitions.
	What is the frame of reference of measures? How to measure variables: manipulate, use primary or secondary sources?	Guard against systematic & unsystematic measurement biases. Each method has strengths and weaknesses.
7. Data analysis	What procedures to follow in data collection & tabulation? What techniques should be used to analyze and interpret the data?	Standardize procedures to remain flexible & open to novel insights. Use the techniques that fit the research question and model. Conduct workshops with key stakeholders to gain feedback on study findings.
8. Validity	What are the threats to validity of study findings?	Minimize threats to the internal, statistical, external, & construct validities of the study.

designing variance research models. My objective in this chapter is not to introduce new methods for dealing with these eight research design issues. Instead, it is to identify and suggest how principles of engaged scholarship can greatly facilitate and guide decision making on these eight issues. These suggestions are outlined in the right column of Table 6.1.

An important limitation of this chapter is that it only provides a general picture of the issues involved in developing a variance model. Shadish et al. (2002) and Singleton and Straits (2005) offer more extensive and sophisticated treatments than provided here of the technical considerations in addressing the issues listed in Table 6.1. I refer to these texts throughout the chapter.

There are many instances where the technical decisions in designing a variance study can be informed by, and reflexive of, the interests and perspectives of key stakeholders. Principles of engaged scholarship—identifying, involving, and negotiating the perspectives of key stakeholders—are not only necessary for understanding the purposes and interests served by a study, but also for incorporating their values, interests, and tacit knowledge into the design of a study. I argue that researchers who engage others in the design and conduct of their studies are more likely to develop research findings that penetrate more deeply and have greater impact for theory and practice about the research question being examined than those researchers who 'go it alone.'

To begin, variance studies are typically modeled to examine questions or hypotheses from a particular *perspective* about *relationships* between *variables* of the *units* or entities being examined. The first three issues in Table 6.1 focus on these three key terms. Subsequent issues in Table 6.1 deal with basic issues in designing a study.

The Research Question and Perspective

I noted before that no social science research can be unbiased, impartial, and value-free; instead, it is inevitably instantiated with the interests and values of particular stakeholders. Most studies entail at least three key stakeholders: the researcher(s), the intended users or audience, and the sponsors of the research. The interests and perspectives of these three stakeholders are not always the same. That being the case it is crucial for engaged scholars to identify, negotiate, and choose whose interests and perspectives are featured in the study. As noted in Chapter 2, a researcher is not being reflexive if he/she takes a 'God's eye view' of these questions; rather, a 'participant view' is more likely to produce decisions that reflect the interests of key stakeholders in a study. At a minimum, engaged scholars should talk with stakeholder representatives to review and verify their decisions in designing a study.

Taking a reflexive viewpoint can be very helpful in deciding who to involve as advisors or collaborators in formulating the research question and making the operational decisions necessary for developing the research model. These decisions include selecting the units of analysis; the key variables and relationships, as well as designing the study; accessing, collecting, and analyzing the data; and applying the results in ways that advance science and practice. Making these decisions typically requires deep tacit knowledge of the particular context and potential uses of a study. Reviewing the prior research literature on a research question is necessary, but it does not substitute for engaging in discussions with these stakeholders about alternative ways to address the issues and decisions listed in Table 6.1.

The Unit of Analysis

The entities (individuals, collectives, or objects) being studied are referred to as the *units* of analysis. Ordinarily, the unit of analysis is easily identified as who or what is to be described or analyzed in a study. For example, individuals are typically the unit of analysis in studies of job satisfaction, work motivation, or leadership, while organizations are the unit of analysis in studies of organization design, structure, change, or performance. In these examples, the research question dictates who or what is to be described, analyzed, and compared.

Identifying the unit of analysis, however, may not be so simple when examining various properties of collectives that exist in a nested hierarchy of individuals in groups of organizations and more encompassing social collectives. Some properties of organizations, such as culture, are not directly observable; instead a researcher may have to rely on various social artifacts (e.g., certain policies, privileges, events, or practices) that serve as proxies or indicators of organizational culture. Alternatively, a researcher may have to rely on the responses of individual informants and aggregate them to describe the larger social phenomenon of organizational culture. Conversely, a researcher may only have access to organizational-level records or informants (e.g., upper-level managers) to obtain information about individuals within the organization.

In these examples, the unit of observation is different from the unit of analysis. Drawing conclusions about a unit of analysis on the basis of information gained from a different unit of observation can lead to individualistic and ecological fallacies. The *individualistic fallacy* (also referred to as an *atomistic fallacy*) occurs when incorrect inferences are made about a larger collective unit from micro-level data. For example, an obvious individualistic fallacy is to conclude that an organization is 30 years old because its individual members are on average 30 years old. *Ecological* fallacies are more common. They occur when incorrect inferences about individuals are made based on organizational properties. For example, an organization indicted for many fraudulent behaviors does not imply that all individuals within the organizations behave fraudulently.

Lazarsfeld and Menzel (1969) provide a useful framework for making clear distinctions between global, relational, and analytical properties of collectives nested in social aggregates (individuals, groups, organizations, and more encompassing collectives). For example, if the unit of analysis is the group, its *global* properties are macro-characteristics of the group itself, which are not based on any information about individual members, such as group size, goals, and age. *Relational* properties of a group deal with characteristics describing linkages of group members to each other, such as power, interdependence, and conflict among members of the group. *Analytical* properties of groups refer to characteristics of its members that are independent of relational and collective properties of the group, such as each member's age, education, and tasks.

Global data are not aggregated because they are obtained on the collective itself. Additional information about the collective can be obtained by aggregating member and relational data in various ways to the collective unit of analysis. Analytical properties of collectives can be obtained by performing mathematical operations (such as computing means and standard deviations) on member data, whereas structural properties can be computed from relational data. For example, from member data on the amount of education and training of each unit member, one can compute the heterogeneity of skills of personnel in the group (e.g., as the standard deviation of education and training among members). From relational data on the frequency of communications between each member and others in a group, one could compute structural properties of the total (sum) communications among members or construct a sociogram of the centrality of communications in the group.

A basic source of error in aggregating data from individuals to groups is not being clear about whether group properties are intended to have parallel meaning with individual properties. In the preceding examples, the average amount of participation by unit members and the total communications among members are analytical and structural properties of groups, respectively, which have a similarity of meaning to the member and relational properties on which they are based. However, heterogeneity of skills and centrality of communications apply only to the unit collective and have no parallel meaning to the unit of individual members. In general, Lazarsfeld and Menzel (1969: 507) state that, 'Whereas correlations, standard deviations, and similar measures always have a meaning peculiar to the group level, averages, proportions . . . [and sums] may or may not have a parallel meaning on the individual level.' They describe this 'lack of parallel meaning' with an illustration of a 'hung jury' that cannot reach a decision because individual jurors have firm but inconsistent convictions.

Lazarsfeld and Menzel (1969) do not provide a prescription for avoiding troublesome aggregation issues in moving from individual to collective levels.

These issues are perhaps better addressed on an individual study basis where the intended and observed meanings of properties at the individual and group levels can be assessed.

Useful and insightful treatments of these multi-level issues in theory development, data collection, and analysis have been provided by Rousseau (1985) and Klein and her associates (Klein et al. 1994; Klein et al. 1999; Klein and Kozlowski 2000). They emphasize that underlying any aggregation procedure are assumptions of how the micro and macro properties of collectives are functionally related; that is, in what specific ways properties of members and collectives have similar and dissimilar meanings. The more these functional relations are made conceptually explicit, the easier it is to detect and correct aggregation errors, and thereby learn the concrete meanings of concepts from different units of analysis.

The Causal Model

As is evident in the foregoing discussion, relationships among characteristics of units are of primary interest in variance research models. The characteristics of units that vary by taking on different values, categories, or attributes are called *variables* (Singleton and Straits 2005: 48). Hypotheses specify the expected relationships among these variables of a unit or entity. In variance research models, these hypotheses typically consist of causal conditional statements. Typically, these causal conditional hypotheses are stated verbally in an if–then form (e.g., 'if X then Y,' or 'if more X then more Y'). They are often stated mathematically in the form of a functional equation ($Y = f(X)$, which reads 'if X is this value, then Y is that value') (Singleton and Straits 2005: 66). Whether expressed verbally or mathematically, formulating an analytical statement of this causal relationship is critical for guiding the design and conduct of a variance research project.

Philosophers have debated the meanings of cause, effect, and causation for centuries (see a review in Shadish et al. 2002: 3–7). Briefly, the debate contrasts essentialist versus probabilist meanings of causation. *Essentialists* focus on the *causes of effects* by arguing that causation requires showing that the independent variables are necessary and sufficient conditions for the effect to occur in the dependent variable (i.e., X is a full cause of Y). In contrast, *probabilists* focus on the *effect of causes* by taking a manipulative account of causation where X causes Y when the experimenter manipulates X, and observes outcomes in Y. (Here there is no presumption that X is the full cause of Y.)

In organization studies an essentialist account of causation is illustrated in Mohr's (1982) discussion of necessary and sufficient conditions in causal relationships. He stated that 'in a variance theory *the precursor (X) is a necessary and sufficient condition for the outcome (Y)*' (Mohr, 1982: 38; italics in the original). He argued that if X only serves as a sufficient condition then the causal theory is unsatisfactory, for a change in Y might occur without a change in X (since X is not necessary). What makes Y occur when X does not? We might theorize that X is a cause of Y and may have found important cases where X sometimes causes Y, but this falls somewhat short of providing a necessary and sufficient explanation for Y.

Most social scientists adopt a probabilistic or manipulative view of causation, and reject an essentialist view of causation (Cook and Campbell 1979: 15). This is so for several reasons. First, most social phenomena cannot be isolated in closed systems as is necessary to evaluate essentialist views of causality (Bhaskar 1975). Second, given the reflexive nature of human behavior, outside variables typically impinge on a dependent variable, and effects are inevitably influenced by factors or events other than those hypothesized. Hence, observed causal relationships between independent and dependent variables will be probabilistic. Probabilistic relationships are viewed as weak to essentialists who seek explicit functional laws that express inevitable relationships among a set of observables, and in this sense provide a complete causal understanding of a particular event (Cook and Campbell 1979: 15). However, such an essentialist view of causation is an unrealistic and misleading aspiration. All social science can do is *probe but not prove a causal hypothesis* (Campbell and Stanley 1963).

Charles Sanders Peirce and David Hume (among others) argued that causality is not a property of the world; instead it serves as a way for humans to make sense of the world. It is something inferred from an observed association between events. Variance researchers typically regard causal relationships as the heart of scientific explanation.

Even if such relationships cannot be 'proven' empirically (just as no generalization can be proven by scientific evidence), [variance] researchers have found it useful to think causally (Blalock 1969: 6) and have found working with causal hypotheses to be a very productive way of doing science. (Singleton and Straits 2005: 58)

How do we know if cause and effect are related? The classic answer, attributed to the nineteenth-century philosopher John Stuart Mill, focuses on three criteria for inferring a causal relationship between variables:

- covariation or correlation between presumed cause and effect;
- temporal precedence of the cause occurring before the effect; and
- absence of spurious factors that may confound the cause–effect relation.

These three criteria are now discussed from the viewpoint of formulating the research question or hypothesis.

COVARIATION

If one variable is to be a cause of another, the variables must be statistically associated. If there is a change or manipulation of the independent variable and no change in the dependent variable, then the independent variable does not produce or cause the dependent variable.

Of course, covariations among variables are rarely perfect; but statistically significant correlations are plentiful.

In the social sciences, causal relationships often are implied from comparatively 'weak' associations. One reason for this is that many measurements in the social sciences are relatively imprecise. The primary reason, though, is that in explaining human action, multiple causes may independently or jointly produce the same or similar effects. A weak association may mean that only one of several causes has been identified, or it may mean that a causal relationship exists, but not under the conditions or for the segment of the population in which the weak association was observed. (Singleton and Straits 2005: 58)

When formulating the research question, application of the covariation criterion involves a dual judgment about (1) whether an association among variables implies a meaningful causal relationship; and (2) if other potentially more important and relevant factors should be considered. The causal relationships of greatest practical significance tend to be those involving manipulable and putative causes; the ones we can do something about and are within our reach. Research models that address a research question by examining proximate and controllable causes for an effect are preferred to distal and uncontrollable causes.

For example, if one is studying the question of increasing organizational innovativeness (the dependent variable) from the perspective of its managers, the selection of causal factors within the organization (such as the amounts of investment, attention, communications, and rewards devoted to innovative behavior) are more proximate and controllable than other possible causal factors external to the organization in the industry, region, or country, that may be too distant for the managers to influence in the short run. In general, proximate and controllable causes are more likely to covary with intended effects than are distal and uncontrollable factors.

DIRECTION OF INFLUENCE

A second criterion of a probable causal relationship is that a cause must precede its effects, or at least the direction of influence should be from cause to effect (and not vice versa). At a minimum this criterion requires a clear statement and explanation of the direction of influence among variables in the hypothesis. The causal direction in some relationships in organizational research can only be conceived to operate in one direction. For example, the founding characteristics imprinted at the birth of an organization influence its subsequent behavior and likelihood of survival (Stinchcombe 1965). It is difficult to imagine how the causal relationship may go in the reverse direction.

But the direction of influence is often not so easy to determine in social research. Consider, for example, the proposition that decentralization increases organizational performance because when more people participate in making decisions that affect their work they make more accurate decisions and are more motivated to implement them than centralized decisions. In the reverse direction you could argue that organizational performance causes decentralization because high performance increases organizational slack and lessens the perceived need for centralized control.

As this example suggests, hypothesized causal relationships should be specified and explained with a reasonable argument. Whenever possible, variance studies should also be designed to empirically examine the direction of relationships. In experiments this is done by manipulation, while in survey designs it is done with repeated observations of the variables in question. Statistical procedures are often used to examine temporal precedence by comparing lead and lag effects among the independent and dependent variables. Lead effects of the independent variable on the dependent variable should be clearly stronger than lag effects to provide evidence for the direction of the hypothesized causal relationship.

NONSPURIOUSNESS (ELIMINATION OF RIVAL HYPOTHESES)

A well-known maxim is that 'correlation does not prove causation.' This is so because a correlation does not show the direction of a relationship (as just discussed). It is also because correlations do not rule out alternative explanations for a relationship between two variables. A presumed causal relationship may be due to an extraneous factor that renders it to be a spurious relationship. Therefore, to infer a causal relationship from an observed correlation, there should be good reason to believe that there are no confounding factors that could have created an accidental or spurious relationship between the variables.

Singleton and Straits (2005: 60) provide the example of a positive correlation between the number of firefighters at a fire and the amount of damage done. This does not imply that more firefighters cause more damage. The reason for the correlation is that the size of the fire determines both the number of firefighters summoned and the amount of damage. In other words the relationship is an incidental consequence of a common cause—size of the fire—which is an antecedent extraneous variable in this example.

Developing a research question or hypothesis that is not spurious requires careful consideration of the extraneous factors that may confound a causal relationship. Of course it is not possible to consider all factors. One can only attempt to consider and evaluate the effects of the most plausible factors based on knowledge gained from prior research and the particular context and setting in which the research is conducted. The plausible extraneous factors that may confound a hypothesized causal relationship can be handled in a number of ways.

First, through randomization, three characteristics of experiments make it possible to control for most extraneous factors: (1) random assignment of units to treatment and control groups; (2) manipulation of the presumed cause (the treatment) and measurement of the outcome in both the treatment and control groups; and (3) comparative observations to see whether variation in the cause is related to variation in the effect. Randomization reduces the probability that observed differences between treatment and control groups are due to extraneous factors.

In non-experimental survey designs, extraneous factors are typically dealt with by holding them constant in a statistical analysis of cause-and-effect relationships. Of course, one can statistically control only for those variables that have been measured as part of the research. The effects of any unknown or unmeasured variables cannot be assessed.

At the time of formulating a causal research question or hypothesis, the researcher should not only consider control variables, but also possible moderating and mediating variables that may influence the cause-and-effect relationship being studied. The magnitude of a causal relationship may change drastically in different situations or contingencies. In other words, various levels or categories of these contingencies may moderate the causal relationship. For example, Burns and Stalker's (1961) organizational contingency theory proposes that a mechanistic structure leads to high performance in stable and predictable environmental conditions, while an organic structure produces high performance in unstable and uncertain organizational environments. According to this theory, the relationship between organization structure and performance would be spurious if one did not include the antecedent moderating effects of environmental contingencies.

Extraneous variables may also intervene in the relationship between the independent and dependent variables. The identification of an intervening variable or mechanism linking the independent and dependent variables may strengthen the causal relationship:

Indeed, this is sometimes advocated as a fourth criterion—in addition to association, direction of influence, and nonspuriousness—for establishing that one variable causes another.... For example, one may argue that the belief that smoking causes lung cancer will be enhanced considerably if and when it is established that certain chemical agents from cigarettes produce cancerous cells. Knowing the causal process through which smoking produces cancer would provide one last shred of evidence against a spurious correlation. (Singleton and Straits 2005: 63)

Identifying mediating variables provides a deeper and more proximate understanding of the intervening mechanisms that may explain a causal relationship.

A CAUSAL MODELING PROCESS

Whetten (2002) provides a useful graphical strategy for developing and displaying a causal model in addressing a research question. Using Post-It Notes (PIN) and a flip chart (or poster) he proposes the following four steps for constructing a causal model. These steps are illustrated in Figure 6.1.

1. List the variables in your causal model. Write one variable on each PIN. Begin with the core construct you are trying to understand, and tape it in the center of your poster. Then add related constructs that might represent causes, effects, and correlates of your core construct. Place the dependent variables (effects) to the right side, and antecedent (independent or causal) variables on the left. Place mediating variables between the variables they mediate, and place moderating variables above or below the relationships they are believed to moderate.
2. Draw arrows indicating various relationships among the variables in the model. Display the direct causal sequence in your model by drawing the central causes as arrows from antecedents (on the left) to your core construct, and effects as arrows pointing to consequences (to the right) of your core construct. Insert arrows to and from mediating variables as indirect relationships between expected causal relationships, and arrows from moderating variables to the relationships being moderated.
3. List the assumptions or boundary conditions of the causal model by drawing a box around the model and writing the conceptual and contextual assumptions outside of the box. These statements should indicate how far generalizations from the causal model might be extended to theory and population.
4. List inside the box plausible alternative factors that may be extraneous or rival explanations for the core construct of interest. These factors may need to be measured and either statistically controlled or compared as plausible rival explanations to those proposed in the causal model.

Whetten's graphical approach provides a concrete methodology for engaging others (research team members and stakeholders) in model building. When all participants are provided a PIN pad, each member can brainstorm and write key variables on PINs, paste them on a board, and explain/negotiate reasons for

1. List the variables in your model (one on each PIN)
   - Focal construct, possible causes, effects, correlates
   - Assess the scope, abstraction level, & categories of variables
   - Unit of analysis: individual, group, organization, industry, country
2. Draw relationships indicating roles of constructs in model:
   independent, dependent, moderating, mediating, categoric, sequential effects
3. List assumptions & boundary conditions outside of box.
4. List rival alternative factors and control variables inside of box

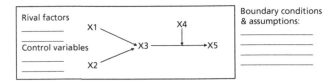

Figure 6.1. Whetten's causal modeling steps

Source: Whetten, D. (2002). 'Modeling-as-Theorizing: A Systematic Methodology for Theory Development,' in D. Partington (ed.), *Essential Skills for Management Research*. Thousand Oaks, CA: Sage, p. 58.

placement of the variable in the emerging causal model. Further group discussion and editing of variables in the model can result in a collective development and understanding of the causal model being examined in a research project.

Experimental Designs

Due largely to the influence of Campbell and Stanley (1963), Cook and Campbell (1979), and Shadish et al. (2002), causal models in the social sciences are typically classified into randomized, quasi-, and non-experimental designs. While authors vary in how they classify studies into these three basic designs, I treat them as follows:

1. *Randomized experiment*: a study in which units are assigned at random to receive treatment and alternative conditions that are deliberately manipulated either by the researcher or by nature to observe their effects.
2. *Quasi-experiment*: a study in which units may not be randomly assigned to conditions, and the treatment and alternative conditions are not deliberately manipulated. Instead, they are produced by naturally occurring events and compared to observe their effects. As defined here, quasi-experiments are often referred to as survey research studies. Some survey designs are simply correlational studies of the size of relationships among variables.
3. *Non-experiment*: a descriptive case study that may lack a control group. The researcher observes and compares a unit or case in terms of some naturally occurring conditions or events.

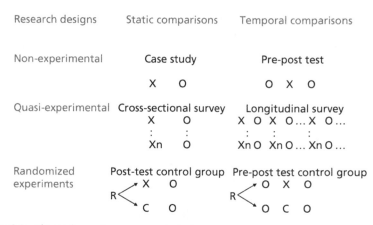

Figure 6.2. Alternative variance research designs

These three designs can be undertaken to examine static causal models at one point in time or change over several points in time. Figure 6.2 illustrates these alternative variance research designs. Key features of these three designs are now summarized.

RANDOMIZED EXPERIMENTS

The key features of experiments are that various treatments (the independent causal variable) are manipulated by the researcher, units (people or groups) are assigned by chance (e.g., by coin toss or use of a table of random numbers) to the treatments, and then compared by measuring the effects (dependent variables). These key features of a randomized experiment are illustrated in Figure 6.3.

Key Ingredients:
1. Manipulated independent variable (treatment X)
2. Measured dependent variable (Y)
3. Treatment & control groups treated exactly alike except for one receiving experimental treatment.
4. Random assignment of units to experimental groups
5. Observed difference, Δ, attributed to treatment effect.

Figure 6.3. Illustration of a randomized experiment

If implemented correctly, random assignment creates two or more groups of units that are probabilistically similar to each other on the average. Hence, any outcome differences that are observed between those groups at the end of a study are likely to be due to the treatments, not to differences between the groups that already existed at the start of the study. Further, when certain assumptions are met, the randomized experiment yields an estimate of the size of a treatment effect that has desirable statistical properties, along with estimates of the probability that the true effect falls within a defined confidence interval. (Shadish et al. 2002: 13)

Shadish et al. (2002: chap. 8) discuss many variations of randomized experimental designs. Two of the most basic designs are shown at the bottom of Figure 6.2. As the post-test control group design illustrates, the basic randomized experiment requires at least two conditions (a treatment and control group), random assignment of units to conditions and a post-test assessment of the units. This post-test control group design is ideally suited for examining atemporal (or static) research questions of whether the treatment and control conditions produce an observable effect or difference on selected outcome measures (dependent variables). In contrast, the pre-test-post-test control group design is used for examining temporal questions dealing with the relative change over time of treatment and control conditions in terms of effects or dependent criteria. Comparisons between pre-test and post-test provide ways to measure the relative growth, decline, decay, or stability of effects over time for units that are randomly assigned to treatment and control groups.

Randomized experiments can be conducted in a laboratory or in a controlled field setting. Random clinical trials are required by the US Food and Drug Administration to determine the safety and efficacy of all kinds of

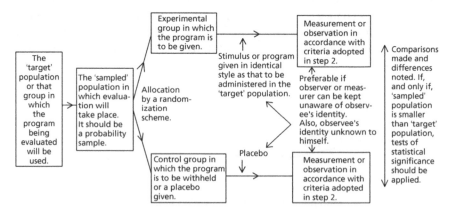

Figure 6.4. Design of an experiment for evaluation research

Note: This flow chart illustrates optimum principles and sequence to be followed in conducting a valid experimental design to evaluate a health program. (Reproduced from Greenberg, Bernard G. and Mattison, Berwyn F., 'The Whys and Wherefores of Program Evaluation,' *Canadian Journal of Public Health*, vol. 46, July, 1955, p. 298.)

Source: Suchman, E. A. (1967). *Evaluation Research*. New York: Russell Sage, p. 92.

medical devices, interventions, and drugs before they are approved for public release and application. They have also become the preferred protocol for evaluation research. Figure 6.4 illustrates the principles and procedures of a randomized experimental design for evaluating a social program, as developed by Suchman (1967).

Whether performed in the 'field' or the laboratory, a randomized experiment is ideally designed to mirror the criteria for establishing a probable cause-and-effect relationship.

- It demonstrates covariation between independent and dependent variables.
- It makes clear the temporal precedence of variations in independent and dependent variables.
- Through randomization it rules out most spurious effects or third-variable explanations.

See Shadish et al. (2002: chap. 8) for a more elaborate discussion and application of randomized experimental designs.

QUASI-EXPERIMENTAL SURVEY DESIGN

The key features of quasi-experiments are to examine the effects of naturally occurring treatments in the world by observing and classifying them into groups and comparing their effects in terms of a set of measured outcome criteria. The middle of Figure 6.2 illustrates these key features of quasi-experiments in terms of cross-sectional and longitudinal surveys. In either design, the researcher first identifies the naturally occurring conditions found in the world and classifies them into different levels or treatments in the population. Units are then randomly selected (if possible) at different levels or treatment categories of the population. All units (or cases) are treated alike and measured on all variables, typically using survey methods. Statistical procedures are used to analyze presumed causal relations between independent and dependent variables after controlling for plausible spurious variables.

Quasi-experimental studies share a similar purpose with randomized experiments—to obtain empirical evidence of a causal relationship between independent and dependent variables. However, quasi-experimental studies may be more problematic because there is more risk of causal inference than with randomized experiments. This is because quasi-experimental studies lack random assignment and manipulated control over treatment and alternative conditions. Units may self-select their own treatment conditions or be assigned to them by teachers, managers, regulators, or others according to some non-random administrative selection criteria. In addition, a naturally occurring treatment condition may not be administered in consistent ways.

As a result, quasi-experimental studies are subject to a number of threats (discussed below) that limit the extent to which observed results can be attributed to the treatment(s) being investigated.

For example, in a managerial study of the effects of Six Sigma quality improvement practices, a researcher might identify and compare groups of companies in a population that have and have not implemented a Six Sigma program. However, pre-test measurements reveal considerable variations among companies within and between groups in ways and degrees to which they have implemented or not implemented Six Sigma. This might lead the researcher to transform the independent variable from Six Sigma treatment and control conditions to an interval scale of the degree to which Six Sigma is implemented. Each interval in this scale is presumed to reflect different naturally occurring levels or conditions in which the companies in the sample have implemented Six Sigma. Presuming that a reliable scale can be developed, the researcher then measures it and other selected outcome criteria in a survey administered to all companies in the sample. Based on an analysis of the survey data, the researcher is confronted with the question of what kind of causal inferences can be drawn from observed relationships between levels of Six Sigma implementation and outcome criteria?

In quasi-experiments [like this], the researcher has to enumerate alternative explanations one by one, decide which are plausible, and then use logic, design, and measurement to assess whether each one is operating in a way that might explain any observed effect. The difficulties are that these alternative explanations are never completely enumerable in advance, that some of them are particular to the context being studied, and that the methods needed to eliminate them from contention will vary from alternative to alternative and from study to study. However, quasi-experimental researchers may still have considerable control over selecting and scheduling measures, over how nonrandom assignment is executed, over the kinds of comparison groups with which treatment conditions are compared, and over some aspects of how treatment is scheduled. (Shadish et al. 2002: 14)

Because quasi-experiments do not use random assignment and controlled manipulation of treatment conditions, researchers must rely on principles of control by design and statistics to show that alternative explanations are implausible. In terms of control by design, researchers can add design elements (e.g., observation of more pre-test time points, additional control groups, and other plausible explanatory variables) in order to address the confounding of treatment effects or the plausibility of other threats (discussed below) to the validity of causal inferences. In addition to design control, quasi-experimental researchers can use a variety of statistical controls that attempt to hold constant or remove confounds from estimates of causal relationships. Shadish et al. (2002) provide a detailed and useful review of techniques for control by design and control by statistics that social researchers might use to draw plausible causal inferences from quasi-experiments.

NON-EXPERIMENTAL CASE DESIGNS

Because case studies often lack random assignment, a control group, and a sufficient number of cases to statistically examine cause-and-effect relationships, many commentators doubt the potential of such designs to support causal relationships (Shadish et al. 2002: 18). Yin (2003), however, discusses a number of productive ends in describing a unit or case in terms of some naturally occurring conditions or events in order to reveal a previously unstudied phenomenon, to develop a grounded theory or to generalize the findings to a theory. Yin (2003) provides a useful discussion of concepts and methods for conducting case studies with these ends in mind.

He points out that comparative analysis of a given case (e.g., an organization) can often be achieved by comparing several subunits or perspectives of participants embedded in the overall case, as well as by observing two or more cases that provide contrasts or comparisons on the research question being investigated. These comparisons often rely on qualitative data that provide greater richness and nuance in understanding the nature or development of a phenomenon than variations among quantitatively measured variables and their statistical relationships. As a consequence, non-experimental comparative case studies are often useful for grounded theory building and theoretical inference (construct validity), while experimental designs are useful for theory testing and sample inference (external validity).

Critical for achieving these non-experimental objectives is the method of comparative analysis, which is perhaps the most basic element of scientific investigation. The *method of comparative analysis* emphasizes that knowledge of any phenomenon is never absolute; it is always relative to another case or standard. Sometimes this standard is clearly evident in a theoretical expectation or hypothesis that can be used to assess an observed phenomenon. With such a clearly formulated theory, a case study can be used in a replication logic to disconfirm a theory. For example, if a theory hypothesizes that all swans are white, and a case study observes the existence of a black swan, then the theory is not replicated; it must be wrong.

Most social scientific cases are not sufficiently specific for using replication logic to disconfirm a theory. Instead, detailed qualitative and ethnographic case studies are used to ground the development of a theory. As discussed in Chapter 3, grounded theory building often begins with the recognition of an anomaly or breakdown in a case that is either not consistent with or explained by our theories of how the world works. In such instances, intimate familiarity with the phenomenon from qualitatively rich case studies can provide the information needed to engage in abductive reasoning. Abduction is a creative leap in formulating a conjecture that, if correct, resolves or dissolves the anomaly. This conjecture represents the first step in creating a theory that advances a new, but yet untested, explanation of how the world works.

One kind of anomaly that researchers occasionally encounter is the appearance or recognition of a totally new social form or pattern. This novel phenomenon may be viewed as being so new to the world, or so misunderstood by a community of researchers or practitioners that it deserves careful systematic description. Such revelatory cases provide new empirical data that must be taken into consideration in related studies by subsequent researchers and in related practices by professionals in the field. Descriptive revelatory case studies thereby have the potential for making important contributions that advance scientific knowledge and professional practice.

Sample Selection and Generalization

Social researchers conduct their studies in localized and particularistic settings, and yet wish to generalize their findings to the broadest possible domains of theory and population. Because of resource constraints and other practical necessities, researchers can only examine a restricted range of *units* (e.g., the sample includes only the people in a population who are accessible and consent to participate in a study), of *constructs* or *treatments* (e.g., the operational research model examines only a few of many possible treatments or variables from the theory on which it is based), of *observations* (e.g., only a few observable indicators are used to measure theoretical constructs), and of *settings* (studies are inevitably conducted at a particular place and point in time).

There is a tension between the localized nature of research findings provided by a particular study and the more generalized inferences researchers wish to draw from their studies. Researchers usually aim to generalize their results to broader domains of units, constructs or treatments, observations, and settings than examined in a given study (Cronbach 1982). They often want to connect study findings to theories with broad conceptual applicability, which requires generalization to abstract theoretical constructs from the operational models and treatments that are used to represent these constructs in a given study. They also want to draw causal generalizations to a broader population of people (units), observations, and settings than were included in a particular study. Cook and Campbell (1979) and Shadish et al. (2002) refer to these two basic kinds of causal generalizations as construct validity and external validity. *Construct validity* refers to inferences that are made about the constructs and theories that are represented in an operational research model. *External validity* refers to generalizations of study findings to variations in persons, settings, treatments, and measurement variables.

Sampling provides a basic strategy for addressing these tensions. Sampling is a process of selecting subsets of units, constructs or treatments, observations, and settings in order to draw conclusions about entire sets. Although research methodology texts typically focus only on selecting units and settings from a population, the sampling idea applies equally well to selecting variables and treatments for constructs in a theory, and for selecting observations to measure these constructs. The measurement section below deals with sampling indicators of variables and constructs. Summarized here are considerations in sampling variables from theoretical constructs and sampling units and settings from a target population.

Since it is often not practical to observe all constructs in a theory and all cases in a target population, the major considerations in sampling constructs, units, and settings is to ensure that the range of variations in the target theory and population are adequately represented in a study. As noted above (and in Table 6.1), the sampling of constructs and cases depends on the research question and the unit of analysis (individuals, groups, programs) being observed and compared in the study. The discussion below focuses on the variety of constructs in a theory and units in the population, how many should be chosen for a study, and by what method?

THEORETICAL SAMPLING

Chapter 4 discussed the use of deductive conditional propositions for developing constitutive definitions of terms and the levels of abstraction between theoretical constructs and observable variables in a theory. These ideas are placed into action when sampling operational variables or treatments in a research model from abstract constructs in a theory.

Chapter 4 noted that a constitutive definition of a term is a conditional proposition where the consequent follows from the antecedent by the very definition of the antecedent. Transforming a theoretical construct into an operational variable requires descending the ladder of abstraction by using *deductive conditional propositions* to define the constitutive components of concepts into constructs and then into observable variables. For example, adopting a Weberian theory of bureaucracy (Hage 1965; Hall 1972), the following deductive conditional propositions might be used to develop operational variables of the concept of organization structure.

IF : The concept of organization structure is the degrees of formalization, centralization . . . and other constructs;

AND: The construct of formalization is observed by the number of rules and degree to which people follow rules (variables);

AND: The construct of centralization is indicated by the variables, and the discretion people have deciding what and how work is done;

(and) . . . other constructs of the concept structure are indicated by other variables;

THEN: Organization structure is operationally defined as the number of
rules, degree of rules followed, task discretion...(and variables
of other constructs of the concept of organization structure).

The *construct validity* of this set of deductive conditional propositions is established by showing that each consequent follows its antecedent by the very
definition of the antecedent. The consequent is true if the antecedent is true.

As this example illustrates, many other constructs and variables could
be used to operationally define Weber's concept of structure. Moreover,
constitutive definitions of other theories of organization structure would
result in many other operational variables. The point is that the variables
included in any research model represent a sampling of many possible observable variables of a construct both from a given theory and from different
theories. That being the case, it is crucial to select only those operational
variables of the theory that are most important or relevant for addressing
the research question being investigated.

This principle also applies to sampling hypotheses from propositions
because the principles of traveling the ladder of abstraction for concepts also
apply to propositions. Chapter 4 noted that a theory consists of propositions
and hypotheses that differ by levels of abstraction: propositions are relationships among theoretical constructs, while hypotheses are relationships among
observable variables. Hypotheses are sampled deductions from one or a few
basic propositions using causal conditional propositions. Following Osigweh's
(1989: 585) maxims, we climb the abstraction ladder by extending the conceptual breadth of hypotheses into more general propositions, while reducing their
connotation (thereby increasing simplicity). As we climb, we rise to fewer and
more general propositions as we move from conclusions (hypotheses) to the
premises that entail them (propositions and assumptions) (Kaplan 1964: 298).

Conceivably, an infinite number of hypotheses can be derived from a theoretical proposition (Dubin 1976). However, any research model includes only a
small sample of observable hypotheses that can be deduced from, or induced to,
a theoretical proposition. That being the case, Stinchcombe (1968b) and Giere
(1999), among others recommend a sampling strategy of selecting only those
hypotheses that represent diverse tests of a proposition. The greater the number
of divergent hypotheses that do not reject a proposition, the more credible the
proposition. A second way to increase the plausibility of a theoretical proposition is to rule out hypotheses derived from rival alternative propositions. At a
minimum, to be viewed as credible, hypotheses derived from a new proposition
should provide better explanations of a phenomenon than hypotheses reflecting
the status quo explanation. Stinchcombe (1968b) discusses how this basic
inductive process of science should lead researchers to design *crucial experiments*
where evidence in support of one theoretical proposition implies the rejection or
negation of a rival alternative proposition.

Over the course of a study, researchers often change their initial under-standings of the conceptual domain being studied. Theoretical sampling is seldom static; it is an ongoing sensemaking process (Weick 2005). Shadish et al. (2002: 21) note the following:

There is a subtle interplay over time among the original categories the researcher intended to represent, the study as it was actually conducted, the study results, and subsequent interpretations. This interplay can change the researcher's thinking about what the study particulars actually achieved at a more conceptual level, as can feedback from readers. But whatever reconceptualizations occur, the first problem of causal generalization is always the same: How can we generalize from a sample of instances and data patterns associated with them to the particular constructs they represent? (Shadish et al. 2002: 21)

POPULATION SAMPLING

In addition to drawing inferences to theory, researchers also want to gener-alize study findings to various people (units), settings, and outcomes in a population. If the population of interest is known, then it is possible to identify the variations in units, settings, and outcomes that exist in that population. The basic sampling strategy is to ensure that the range of vari-ation in the target population is adequately represented in the study's sample of observations. Singleton and Straits (2005: chap. 5) provide a useful review of the major steps in sampling design, which is a plan of how cases are to be selected for observation. This plan involves three major steps: (1) define the population; (2) construct the sampling frame; and (3) implement a probabil-ity or nonprobability sampling strategy.

The first step is to identify the target population, which is the particular collection of units and settings to which a researcher would like to generalize study findings. Singleton and Straits (2005: 113) credit the sociologist, Ken-neth Bailey (1982), for noting an important distinction between experienced and novice researchers in how they approach sampling:

The experienced researcher always gets a clear picture of the population before selecting the sample, thus starting from the top (population) and working down (to the sample). In contrast, novice researchers often work from the bottom up. Rather than making explicit the population they wish to study, they select a predetermined number of conveniently available cases and assume that the sample corresponds to the population of interest. Consider a sample consisting of 'randomly' chosen passersbys at a shopping center on a Saturday afternoon. What could this sample possibly represent? There is simply no way of knowing until an intended or target population is defined. (Singleton and Straits 2005: 113)

Defining a target population depends upon the unit of analysis and the research question, and involves specifying the cases that are to be included and excluded in the population. If the unit of analysis is individuals, some combination of exposure to the independent variables or treatments being investigated and the selected demographic characteristics such as age, gender, race, and education is typically used. For example, in a study of how health-care physicians and managers solve problems, Schultz (2001) stratified his target population into individuals who obtained a medical degree (MD) or managerial degree (MBA or MHA) and who varied in age, gender, and years of experience working in supervisory positions of managed healthcare systems. In this experiment Schultz randomly assigned individuals from the two strata of educational degrees in the target population to two problem solving tasks, and then compared their results by statistically controlling for their age, gender, and years of working experience.

As this example suggests, defining the target population is closely related to constructing the sampling frame, which identifies the set of all cases from which the sample is actually selected (Singleton and Straits 2005: 116). This is the second step and can be done by either listing all the cases in the population or by developing a rule that defines membership in the population. Oftentimes it is not possible to identify all members of a target population. A census listing of all members of a target population may not exist. Instead, researchers often rely on a rule stipulating criteria for inclusion and exclusion in the target population. For example, Schultz developed and used a rule that all members of his target population must be working in a supervisory role in a managed healthcare system; anyone not satisfying these conditions was excluded from his target domain. However, his sampling frame was ambiguous with respect to the geographical location of the target population. As a result, the rule that Schultz used to specify his sampling frame did not provide a geographical basis for sampling individuals from different regions in the US and other countries that are generally known to have different healthcare cultures and practices.

The third major step in sampling is to select cases from the target population as defined by the sampling frame developed in step two. Singleton and Straits (2005) discuss two general procedures—probability and nonprobability sampling—that are typically used to select a sample that is representative of a target population in a study. Probability sampling includes simple random sampling, stratified random sampling, and cluster sampling.

- *Simple random sampling* consists of a random selection from the entire population that makes it equally possible to draw any combination of cases from the target population. Using a table of random numbers to select cases from a population, for example, random sampling has the scientific advantage of applying the principles of probability sampling theory to calculate sampling error and estimate sample precision.

- In *stratified random sampling*, the population is divided into strata and independent random samples are drawn from each stratum. This strategy is particularly appropriate for selecting and comparing naturally occurring events or treatments in a target population that are difficult to manipulate experimentally. For example, comparisons between married and divorced couples on child rearing behaviors may only be possible by stratifying the target population into married and divorced couples and then randomly selecting couples from each stratum to examine their parental behaviors.
- *Cluster sampling* is often used when it is impossible or impractical to list all members of a target population. In cluster sampling, the population is broken down into groups of cases, called clusters, which consist of natural groups, such as geographical states, regions and cities, or types of organizations, such as colleges, churches, and businesses.

Nonprobability sampling refers to the non-random selection of cases for a study. Singleton and Straits (2005) discuss a variety of nonprobability sampling procedures, including convenience, purposive, and quota sampling. Since nonprobability samples are not randomly selected, they have two weaknesses: no control for investigator biases in selecting units and not being able to predict variations among sampled units based on probability sampling theory.

SAMPLE SIZE

A final sampling decision is determining the appropriate number of cases to sample in a study. Sample size considerations include: (1) the heterogeneity of the populations; (2) the desired precision in determining magnitudes of effects; (3) the type of sampling design; (4) the availability of resources; and (5) the number of breakdowns planned in data analysis (Singleton and Straits 2005: 140). A discussion of the mathematical statistical analysis for determining the power of tests to achieve statistical significance is beyond the scope of this chapter. Statistical textbooks and web sites are widely accessible for calculating the size of sample required in a study to estimate the power of significance tests for various statistical models.[1]

One consideration that is often overlooked in determining sample size is equating statistical significance with practical significance of a test. Walster and

---

[1] See, for example the following web sites—*Supercourse—Survey sample size* from the University of Pittsburgh (at: http://www.lib.umn.edu/libdata/link.phtml?page_id=1187&element_id=34881); *Statistical considerations for clinical trials* from Harvard University (at: http://www.lib.umn.edu/libdata/link.phtml?page_id=1187&element_id=34882); *Statistics Calculator* and *Power Calculator* from UCLA (at: http://www.lib.umn.edu/libdata/link.phtml?page_id=1187&element_id=34884); *The Survey System* from Creative Research Systems (at: http://www.lib.umn.edu/libdata/link.phtml?page_id=1187&element_id=34885).

Cleary (1970) pointed out that classical hypothesis testing methods do not necessarily lead researchers to make rational decisions. They argue that the problem is not with classical methodology, but with the way it is used. Conventional procedures for determining the power and statistical significance of a test are often not consistent with the practical significance of a test. It is well known that a researcher can control the power of a statistical significance test by manipulating sample size. But this form of statistical significance should not be confused with practical significance. The latter reflects a judgment by users of study findings on what magnitudes of effect and levels of probability they consider trivial versus those large enough to convince them of altering their behavior with respect to the test in question. For research findings to be relevant to users, Walster and Cleary (1970) advise researchers to select a sample size that equates this qualitative notion of practical significance with statistical significance.

Measurement and Frames of Reference

Once a set of variables has been selected to represent the constructs of interest in a research model, then attention can turn to measuring these variables. Measurement is the process of assigning numbers or labels to variables of units in order to represent their conceptual properties (Singleton and Straits 2005: 76). Fundamentally, measurement represents a problem of conceptualization. Typically, it begins by descending the ladder of abstraction to recast theoretical constructs into observable variables, and select procedures and indicators to measure these variables in ways that are reliable (i.e., replicable) and valid (i.e., capture their intended meanings).

In the physical sciences variables are typically measured with standardized instruments, for example, to find the temperature, mass, density, and force of material objects. In contrast, social scientists examine individual and collective properties that often cannot be observed directly, are too complex for any one person to observe, and for which no uniform or standardized measures exist. As noted in the second section of this chapter on units of analysis, many individual attitudes and behaviors (such as job satisfaction and learning) are based on psychological constructs that cannot be observed directly; they require individuals to express their subjective perceptions and attitudes through the use of questionnaires and interviews. In addition, many properties of collective units of analysis are too complex for one to observe. Organizations, for example, typically consist of many people, groups, and levels with diverse goals, structures, and activities. Measuring these collective properties must often rely on informants, such as top or middle-level managers. However, research demonstrates that perceptions of a few managers are often not generalizable to the entire organization (Dearborn and Simon 1958; Porter 1958).

The frames of reference that individuals take in answering questions dramatically influence their judgments (Guilford 1954; Smith et al. 1969). When two persons with different frames of reference are exposed to the same situation or stimulus, they select different aspects as pertinent to their judgments and provide different summary evaluations of that situation. Frames of reference are the internal standards or cognitive filters a person uses in describing or evaluating a situation (Helson 1964). As applied to measurement, it is useful to examine at least two interlocking issues that influence a respondent's frame of reference: (1) the immediate characteristics of the stimulus or situation to which a person is exposed; and (2) the systematic and unsystematic ways in which individuals respond to the stimulus or situation as a result of prior experiences, dispositions, and roles.

The first issue requires an examination of how a respondent's frame of reference is influenced by the composition of the measurement instrument itself and the setting in which respondents complete it. Specifically, as the top of Table 6.2 outlines, the nature, complexity, referent, and time perspective of

Table 6.2. Development and evaluation of a measurement instrument

Frames of reference in developing a measurement instrument
- Perceptual selectivity in determining human judgments is dramatic. A frame of reference is the cognitive filter a person uses to respond to questions:
    1. Time perspective of questions.
    2. Behavioral, cognitive, or emotional phenomena.
    3. Descriptive or evaluative measures.
    4. Number of intervals or points on answer scale.
    5. Anchors or cues on answer scales.
    6. Unit of analysis.
    7. Respondent or informant role.

Evaluating a measurement instrument
Intrinsic validity—do the measures capture the intended constructs?
- Reliability estimates
    Repeated, parallel, split half, & multiple measurements
    Coefficient alpha and the number of items in index
    Breadth of construct being measured
- Convergent & discriminant validity
    Factor analyses of all items from several indices
    Multi-trait, multi-method matrix
    Median correlations with other items
    Parallel measures

Extrinsic validity—what are the measures in the instrument good for?
- Conform to theory
- Discriminate different types of units
- Predict or explain criterion/outcome
    Concurrent validity
    Predictive validity

Source: Van de Ven and Ferry (1980).

questions and the anchor points on an answer scale have been found to significantly influence a respondent's frame of reference at the point of measurement (Smith et al. 1969; Van de Ven and Ferry 1980). To the extent that a measurement instrument takes these factors into account explicitly, a researcher can control one of the major sources of variation in respondents' frames of reference and thereby have a better understanding of the judgments made by people about the individual and the organizational phenomena of interest. Van de Ven and Ferry (1980: 57–74) provide a useful discussion of the key factors to consider in structuring the frame of reference of questions in a questionnaire or interview instrument.

In addition to the effects due to composition and administration of the measurement instrument itself, there are systematic and unsystematic effects on frame of reference due to the position, past experiences, and predilections of the respondent. The systematic effects include those individual differences in respondents that are known, as a result of previous theorizing or research, to influence respondents' judgments in predictable ways. For example, judgments about individual and group behavior in organizations have been found to differ systematically when respondents occupy different positions and levels in an organization (Porter 1958; Ghiselli 1973; Bouchard 1976). These systematic differences are addressed by developing and implementing a data collection plan that samples respondents or informants from diverse organizational positions and roles. Depending on the variables that are measured, the responses of multiple and diverse informants are then compared and averaged to obtain aggregate scores of organizational groups. Unless there are good reasons to believe that the judgments of one particular informant group are more important or accurate than another, the responses of different informant groups are typically weighted equally in the aggregate collective score (Van de Ven and Ferry 1980).

In studies of job satisfaction and other attitudinal characteristics of organizations (e.g., climate and morale), perceptions have been found to differ systematically among respondents of different age, gender, education, social background, and job tenure in the organization (Smith et al. 1969; Dunnette 1976). These individual difference factors are commonly used as stratification variables when reporting norms for instruments measuring various attitudinal dimensions of jobs and organizations. One reason for this strategy is to statistically control for differing frames of reference of respondents when evaluating a measurement instrument. When these individual difference factors are not explicitly included in a research model, they are often measured and treated as extraneous variables (as discussed before).

The unsystematic effects on frame of reference include a host of unknown predilections, personality orientations, and contextual factors within respondents that influence their individual judgment of a given stimulus in different ways. For example, a sickness in the family, a recent extremely happy or sad incident, and the psychological mood of a respondent at the time of data collection undoubtedly influences his/her answers to questions (Guilford 1954). However, these kinds of influences on frames of reference are unsystematic in the sense that they are expected to be randomly and normally distributed among the sample of respondents or informants and will therefore cancel out statistically when judgments are averaged together. These kinds of unsystematic disturbances on frames of reference are the basis of the argument for obtaining the perceptions of many judges or informants to measure various organizational phenomenon. Classical test theory demonstrates that reliability of a measure increases by increasing the number of judges (Lord and Novick 1968).

Many additional tasks, beyond the scope of this chapter, are involved in developing and evaluating measurement instruments and procedures. Some of the tasks involved in evaluating a measurement instrument are outlined at the bottom of Table 6.3. Readers are referred to Singleton and Straits (2005) and Van de Ven and Ferry (1980) for useful discussions and examples of the process of measurement in social research, and procedures for evaluating various indicators of the reliability and validity of a measurement instrument.

Data Analysis

Scientific inquiry involves a repetitive interplay between theoretical ideas and empirical evidence. Data analysis takes place whenever a research model and data are compared. This comparison occurs whenever the researcher struggles to bring order to, or to make sense of, his/her observations. I suggest below that an engaged scholar should not struggle alone; much help is available if he/she involves other research colleagues, users, and practitioners.

Different methods of data analysis are appropriate for different variance research models. There is no need to enumerate them here since several excellent sources are available for guidance. Yin (2003) and Miles and Huberman (1994) provide useful ways to tabulate, display, and analyze case study data obtained from documents, archival records, interviews, direct observations, participant observations, and physical artifacts. Singleton and Straits (2005) emphasize survey research methods, and discuss methods to edit, code, enter, clean, and document survey data in computer files before steps are undertaken to analyze the data. Pedhazur and Schmelkin (1991) and Neter et al. (2005) provide detailed discussions with examples and software of descriptive and inferential statistics for analyzing multivariate causal models with survey data. Finally, Shadish et al. (2002) focus on analyzing data in order to draw generalized causal inferences from experimental and quasi-experimental designs.

Whatever the data analysis methods and research models that are compared, one thing is clear. A single pass in making sense of data and models is seldom sufficient. Numerous iterations are typically required, and this process is greatly facilitated by engaging others in each iteration. I have found it useful to begin by conducting a preliminary analysis of the research question, model, and data analysis, and then conducting two workshops—one with research colleagues and one with key users or practitioners from the organizations in which the research is being conducted. The workshop with research colleagues tends to provide very useful feedback for refining the analytical aspects of the research model, data analysis procedures, and situating the findings in the research literature. Review sessions with users and practitioners often generate a different kind of feedback dealing with the potential applications and implications of study findings, as well as exploring ways to modify the model and data to examine the research question in more penetrating or relevant ways. Sometimes this includes further data collection that host organizations are often happy to provide (since they raised the further research question). I typically conclude these workshops by indicating that the research team will investigate the most plausible suggestions made and schedule another review session to share the findings. I also ask for volunteers who are willing to help or advise the research team to undertake the next iteration of analyzing study data.

And so the next iteration of the process unfolds, culminating with a second round of workshops in which the revised study findings are presented in a report and discussed. Feedback from the second workshops are typically useful for refining the study report, and for concluding the study. In several instances my research team was invited to continue or expand the research into a longitudinal study with the support and collaboration of research colleagues, users, and practitioners.

I have learned several lessons from conducting these research workshops. First, inviting feedback on research findings can easily lead to 'scope creep' of the research agenda into unexpected and distracting directions. Being clear about your research question and agenda are critical for being open to suggestions and negotiating them in ways that add value and direction to the research objectives. Second, some of my greatest insights and learning experiences about research questions have come from these research workshops with colleagues, users, and practitioners. These learning insights would not have been gained had my research team not involved others in analyzing and reporting the findings. Among the insights were learning different ways to interpret and construct study findings, and understanding the threats to the validity of a study (discussed next) and how these threats might be ameliorated. Although these engaged scholarship principles of involving others in data analysis and interpretation entail much more work than 'going it alone,' the insights and learning gained from engaging a community of research colleagues, users, and practitioners are 'priceless.'

Validity

Shadish et al. (2002: 34) define validity as the approximate truth of an inference or knowledge claim of a causal relationship based on evidence that supports that inference as being true or correct. They ground their concept of validity in a correspondence theory that says that a claim is true if it corresponds to the observed world. Philosophers have argued that correspondence theory is compromised because the data to which a claim is compared are themselves theory-laden and so cannot provide a theory-free test of that claim (Kuhn 1962). While recognizing that correspondence theory is vulnerable to this criticism, they point out that among variance researchers this correspondence theory is 'the nearly universal scientific concern of gathering data to assess how well knowledge claims match the world. Scientists also judge how well a given knowledge claim coheres with other knowledge claims built into accepted current theories and past findings' (Shadish et al. 2002: 35).

Over the years Campbell and his colleagues (Campbell 1957; Campbell and Stanley 1963; Cook and Campbell 1979; Shadish et al. 2002) have developed a validity typology that has been widely adopted by social scientists. The typology consists of four related criteria for assessing four kinds of inferences typically drawn about causal inference from an experimental study: statistical conclusion validity, internal validity, construct validity, and external validity. Shadish et al. (2002: 38) define these criteria as follows.

1. *Statistical conclusion validity* refers to the appropriate use of statistics to infer whether the presumed independent and dependent variables covary.
2. *Internal validity* refers to whether their covariation resulted from a causal relationship.
3. *Construct validity* refers to whether inferences can be generalized to higher order constructs that represent sampling particulars in a study.
4. *External validity* refers to whether inferences of causal relationships hold over variations in persons, settings, treatment, and measurement variables.

Thus, while internal and statistical conclusion validity focus on whether a cause-and-effect relationship is evident in a particular study, construct and external validity refer to generalizations of the study to theory and populations of interest, respectively. These four criteria for evaluating the

Table 6.3. Threats to validity of experimental results

Internal validity: Is the relationship causal or would the relationship exist in the absence of any treatment or variation in the independent variable? Checklist of threats:
1. History.
2. Maturation.
3. Instrumentation.
4. Testing.
5. Statistical regression.
6. Selection.
7. Mortality (attrition).
8. Ambiguity about direction of causation.
9. Contaminations equalizing groups.

Statistical conclusion validity: Are the results due to chance? Possible threats:
1. Statistical power: sampling the wrong number of observations where statistical significance does not equal practical significance.
2. Fishing expedition: maximizing on chance with numerous statistical tests.
3. Reliability of measures.
4. Reliability of treatments—lack of standardization of procedures.
5. Random irrelevancies in experimental settings.
6. Random heterogeneity of respondents.

Construct validity: Do the model findings generalize to the theory? Possible threats:
1. Invalid constitutive definitions of theoretical and empirical terms.
2. Mono-method bias—use of only one procedure to measure variables.
3. Hypothesis guessing—participants guess the hypothesis.
4. Evaluation apprehension—participants present positive impression.
5. Experimenter expectancies that bias the data.
6. Confounding levels of constructs.
7. Interaction of different treatments.
8. Interaction of testing and treatment (especially with pre-testing).
9. Restricted generalizability across constructs.

External validity: Do the findings generalize to the intended population? Possible threats:
1. Not knowing what treatment caused the effect when multiple treatments are used.
2. Did pre-test affect treatment that limits inferences beyond experiment participants?
3. Inferring results beyond the pool of selectively recruited participants?
4. Inferring results to other settings or organizations than those examined?
5. Inferring treatment results to different historical settings.
6. Unrecognized side effects of treatment.

Sources: Campbell and Stanley (1963); Cook and Campbell (1979); and Shadish et al. (2002).

quality of experimental findings are discussed in detail by Shadish et al. (2002; chaps. 2 and 3). Table 6.3 provides a summary reference of the criteria often used to assess threats to these four kinds of validity in experimental studies.

Conclusion

This chapter reviewed some of the basic issues, decisions, and suggestions in designing a variance research model. A variance research model represents the theory as a causal conditional relationship among variables of units that are sampled, measured, and analyzed in accordance with experimental design procedures. I discussed eight key issues that are normally addressed in designing a variance research study. They are the following:

1. Any study reflects the perspectives of certain stakeholders and assumes much tacit knowledge of the particular research context or setting. Researchers are often not aware of the values and assumptions underlying their scientific practices. They become apparent by involving key stakeholders in developing the research question, identifying the key variables and relationships in a research model, and in designing the research. Involving key stakeholders in these issues increases the likelihood that study findings capture the perspectives and tacit knowledge embedded in a research question and model being examined.

2. A research study should clearly identify the unit of analysis, which refers to the entities or objects being studied. Typically, the research question stipulates the entities or objects being examined. However, the units of analysis may not be so simple when examining social collectives existing in a nested hierarchy of individuals in groups or organizations and more encompassing collectives. In these cases the unit of analysis may not be the unit of observation, and special precautions should be taken to avoid individualistic and ecological fallacies.

3. A variance research model consists of one or more causal conditional 'if–then' propositions that are assumed to hold in specified conditions. Most social scientists adopt a probabilistic or manipulative view of causation, and rely on covariation, temporal precedence, and the absence of spurious factors to indicate causation between independent and dependent variables. To deal with plausible spurious or extraneous factors, researchers often add a number of control, moderating, and mediating variables to their causal model. This makes the model more complicated and difficult to examine empirically. In general, parsimonious models are preferred to complex ones due to an ease in understanding and empirical examination. When multiple causal relationships are at play, researchers might include only those factors that are proximate and controllable from the perspective of the key study units or users.

4. Causal models can be examined with a wide variety of randomized, quasi-, and non-experimental designs. Although evidence of causation is strongest with randomized experimental designs, random assignment, and manipulation of treatments are often not possible in a given study. Pragmatic constraints often require researchers to adopt less-than-ideal designs for addressing research questions. That being the case, it is important to assess how any study is vulnerable to threats of validity (see point 8 below), and explore ways for dealing with them.

5. In most social science studies there is tension between the local and particular nature of a research study and the general inferences researchers would

like to draw from their studies. These tensions are addressed by sampling the units, constructs, observations, and settings that are examined in the research. These sampling decisions should be guided by the construct validity of generalizations to an intended theory and the external validity of generalizations to a target population. Furthermore, the sample size or number of cases observed should be chosen to equate the statistical significance of a test with its practical significance to key stakeholders or users of a study. It makes little sense for a study to produce statistically significant findings that are considered trivial by key stakeholders.

6. Measurement is fundamentally a conceptual problem. Typically, the first step in measurement requires defining theoretical constructs into observable variables, and then selecting procedures and indicators to measure these variables in reliable and valid ways. Frames of reference dramatically influence how individuals answer questions and provide data to a researcher. As noted in Chapter 1, social science researchers only obtain the information that organizational participants or respondents are willing to provide. The more a researcher is aware of respondents' frames of reference, the better the measures and their interpretations. As Table 6.2 outlined, the composition of questions in a measurement instrument largely determines how responses are to be interpreted. In addition, a variety of individual difference factors (age, gender, role, experience, personality) influence frames of reference in systematic ways. These systematic factors are typically measured and controlled statistically to examine causal relationships. Finally, the unsystematic effects on frames of reference are assumed to cancel out statistically if the size and distribution of responses in a sample reflects a normal distribution.

7. Data analysis occurs whenever a research model and data are compared. Many research methodology texts provide extensive methods and statistical programs for analyzing data to examine different variance research models. A key suggestion in this chapter is that researchers use the techniques that fit the research question and model. To guide this process, I suggested that researchers conduct workshops with research colleagues and key users or practitioners to obtain feedback on preliminary study findings.

8. No study is perfect. To varying degrees, each is subject to some combination of threats to internal, construct, external, and statistical validities. Assessing the design of a study in terms of these criteria (as listed in Table 6.2) provides a useful checklist of the strengths and weaknesses of a study.

Research design is typically viewed to be a technical project undertaken by researchers trained in experimental research design and statistics. Understanding the technical considerations in experimental design, sampling, measurement, statistical analysis, and inference are crucial to scientific inquiry. Hopefully this chapter has shown numerous instances in which these technical decisions need to be informed by the interests and perspectives of the key stakeholders of a study. Principles of engaged scholarship—identifying, involving, and negotiating the perspectives of key stakeholders—are not only necessary for understanding the purposes and interests served by a study, but also for incorporating their values, interests, and tacit knowledge into the design of a study. Researchers who engage others in the design and conduct of their studies are more likely to develop research findings that penetrate more deeply and have greater impact for theory and practice about the research question being examined than those researchers who 'go it alone.'

7 Designing Process Studies

There is a growing interest in understanding processes of change and development in individuals, groups, organizations, and other social entities. Process studies are undertaken to examine research questions dealing with how things change and develop over time. Chapter 5 reviewed the philosophical assumptions underlying process research and how they differ from variance models. This chapter discusses some of the operational issues and decisions involved in designing process models to either develop or test a process theory. These issues, outlined in Table 7.1, include: clarifying the meanings and theories of process, designing field studies to address process questions, observing and collecting data about process events over time, and analyzing these data into coherent and useful process theories.[1] By necessity these issues are discussed in sequential order. In practice they are highly interdependent and need to be treated in an iterative manner. Poole et al. (2000) provide a more detailed book-length treatment of these issues.

Following a discussion of the process research design issues listed in Table 7.1, this chapter presents an example of designing a study to evaluate an influential process model of organizational growth developed by Greiner (1972). The example also illustrates how valuable insights and learning can be gained by engaging in conversations with others when designing research—in this case between the process theorist (Prof. Larry E. Greiner) and modeler (me).

The chapter concludes on a motivational note addressing concerns often expressed by junior faculty and doctoral students about the amounts of time, resources, and contacts needed to conduct longitudinal process studies.

---

[1] This discussion does not exhaust the issues that confront process researchers, but in my experience it covers most of the critical choices in designing field process studies of organizational innovation and change. Other good sources for designing longitudinal organizational studies include Galtung (1967), Huber and Van de Ven (1995), Kimberly and Miles (1980), and Miller and Friesen (1982).

Table 7.1. Key issues, decisions, and suggestions for process research in field studies

Issues	Decisions	Suggestions
Formulating the process research plan		
1. Meaning of process	A category of concepts or a developmental sequence?	Process research is geared to studying 'how' questions.
2. Theories of process	Examine one or more models?	Apply and compare plausible alternative models.
3. Reflexivity	Whose viewpoint is featured?	Observe change process from a specific participant's viewpoint.
4. Mode of inquiry	Deductive, inductive or retroductive?	Iterate between deduction and retroduction.
5. Observational method	Real-time or historical observations?	Observe before outcomes are known.
6. Source of change	Age, cohort or transient sources?	Develop parallel, synchronic, and diachronic research design.
7. Sample diversity	Homogeneous or heterogeneous?	Compare the broadest range possible.
8. Sample size	Number of events and cases?	Focus on number of temporal intervals and granularity of events.
9. Process research designs	What data analysis methods to use?	Match data analysis methods to number of cases and events.
Measuring & analyzing process data		
1. Process concepts	What concepts or issues will you look at?	Begin with sensitizing concepts and revise with field observations.
2. Incidents & events	What activities or incidents are indicators of what events?	Incidents are observations; events are unobserved constructs.
3. Specifying an incident	What is the qualitative datum?	Develop decision rules to bracket or code observations.
4. Measuring an incident	What is a valid incident?	Ask informants to interpret and verify incidents.
5. Identifying events	What strategies are available to tabulate and organize field data?	Apply a mix of qualitative and quantitative data analysis methods.
6. Developing process theory	How to move from surface observations to a process theory?	Identify five characteristics of narrative theory.

Process questions of how things change and develop over time require longitudinal data that can be obtained either from historical archival files or from a real-time field study of a change process. Whether the data are obtained from archival sources or from field studies, I advise researchers not to go it alone; instead, they should engage and collaborate with other scholars (typically senior colleagues) who are conducting process studies or have access to longitudinal process data.

Formulating the Research Plan

CLARIFY MEANINGS OF PROCESS

Process studies are centrally concerned with how change unfolds in the entities or things being studied. This chapter focuses on organizational change to exemplify methods for designing process studies. *Organizational change is defined as a difference in form, quality, or state over time in an organizational entity* (Van de Ven and Poole 1995). The entity may be an individual's job, a work group, an organizational subunit, strategy, or product, the overall organization, or a community or population of organizations. Change can be empirically determined by longitudinal observations of the entity over two or more points in time on a set of dimensions, and then noticing a difference over time in these dimensions. If there is a noticeable difference we can say that the entity has changed. Much of the voluminous literature on organizational change focuses on the nature of this difference, and the processes that explain how it unfolds.

Two different definitions of 'process' are often used to explain change: (1) a category of concepts or variables that pertain to actions and activities; and (2) a narrative describing how things develop and change (Van de Ven 1992). As discussed in Chapter 5, when the first definition is used, process is typically associated with a 'variance theory' methodology (Mohr 1982), where an outcome-driven explanation examines the degrees to which a set of independent variables statistically explain variations in some outcome criteria (dependent variables). The second meaning of process takes an event-driven approach that is often associated with a 'process theory' explanation of the temporal order and sequence of change events based on a story or narrative (Abbott 1988; Pentland 1999; Poole et al. 2000; Tsoukas 2005). These two definitions represent very different views of process, and the definition that researchers adopt influences the questions they ask, the research methods they employ, and the contributions they make. Hence, at the outset of a study, it is important to clarify the meanings of process.

Process as a Category of Concepts

Studies of process in the social sciences typically treat process as a category of concepts of individual and organizational actions, such as communication frequency, work flows, decision-making techniques, as well as strategy formulation, implementation, and corporate venturing. In this usage, process refers to a category of concepts that can be distinguished from other categories of concepts, such as organizational environment, structure, and performance. Like these other categories, process concepts are operationalized as variables and measured as fixed entities (variables), the attributes of which can vary along numerical scales from low to high. Studies that adopt this definition of process typically examine research questions dealing with the antecedents or consequences of change. As discussed in Chapters 5 and 6, these kinds of questions call for a variance research design of the causal factors (independent variables) that statistically explain variations in some outcome criteria (dependent variables).

Some researchers who are wedded to defining process as a category of concepts may argue that one can decompose an observed sequence of events into a series of input-process-output analyses by viewing each event as a change in a variable (e.g., as the difference between nonexistence at the beginning state and existence at the ending state of the entity) and then determining whether state transitions are explained by some other independent variables. From this perspective, events represent changes in process and output variables in an input-process-output model, and the essential influence can be captured by measuring these variables and estimating the likelihood of occurrence using stochastic methods like event history analysis (Tuma and Hannan 1984). However, if the research question is *how*, not *if*, a change occurred, then an answer requires a narrative describing the sequence of events that unfolded while the change occurred. Once the sequence or pattern of events in a developmental process is found to exist, one can turn to questions about the causes or consequences of events within the process pattern.

Thus, to understand how processes of change unfold, researchers may need to alter their typical ways of modeling and methods of analysis. Rather than first generalize in terms of variables, researchers should first generalize in terms of a narrative history or a story. Only in this way will the key properties of order and sequence of events be preserved in making theoretical generalizations about processes of social change and development.

Process as a Developmental Event Sequence

A second meaning of process is a sequence of events or activities that describe how things change over time. Whereas the first definition of process examines changes in variables over time, this definition of process takes a historical developmental perspective, and focuses on the sequences of incidents, activities, or stages that unfold over the duration of an entity being studied. Table 7.2 exemplifies this meaning of process by outlining a sample of well-known process models of decision making, strategic planning, and organization development.

While the process models in Table 7.2 are concerned with the development of very different things, they are strikingly similar in two respects. First, with the exception of Cohen et al.'s (1972) garbage can model, research on all the other process models are based on cross-sectional observations or retrospective case histories in a variety of organizations. The stages or phases of activities in each model were inferred either from organizational historical self-reports or by categorizing cohorts of groups or organizations into the stages or phases. My understanding is that in no instance was any one organizational unit actually observed over time to go through all the stages or phases of any model shown in Table 7.2. Thus, there is a great need and opportunity for systematic longitudinal research to substantiate and elaborate these process models of development.

Second, in contrast with the first meaning of process as a category of variables, variables are not the centerpiece of the process models in Table 7.2.

Table 7.2. Sample of developmental process models in strategic management literature

Authors and Summaries	Beginning	Activity phases or stages		End
Strategic decision models				
Mintzberg et al. (1976) —Field study of 25 strategic, unstructured decision processes	1. Identification phase —Decision recognition routine —Diagnosis routine	2. Developmental phase —Search routine —Design routine		3. Selection phase —Screen routine —Evaluation–choice routine —Authorization routine
Cohen, March, and Olsen (1972) —Garbage can model of decision making	Decisions are probabilistic intersections of relatively independent streams within organizations of: —choices —problems —solutions —energy of participants			
Quinn (1980) —Case studies of nine major corporations	Fourteen process stages beginning with need sensing and leading to commitment and control systems. Flow is generally in sequence but may not be orderly or discrete. Some of the process stages are the following: 1. Sense need 2. Develop awareness & understanding 3. Develop partial solutions 4. Increase support 5. Build consensus 6. Formal commitment			
Strategic planning models				
Gluck, Kaufman, and Walleck (1980) —Study of formal planning systems in 120 companies	1. Basic financial planning —meet budget	2. Forecast-based planning —predict the future	3. Externally oriented planning —think strategically	4. Strategic management —create the future
Lorange (1980) —Normative model of corporate strategic planning	1. Objectives setting —identify relevent strategic alternatives	2. Strategic programming —develop programs for achieving chosen objectives	3. Budgeting —establish detailed action program for near-term	4. Monitoring —measure progress toward achieving strategies 5. Rewards —establish incentives to motivate goal achievement
Organization development models				
Scott (1971) —Stages of corporate development	1. Single product, channel, & entrepreneurial structure	2. Single product, channel, & functional structure		3. Multiple products, channels, & division-alized structure
Greiner (1972) —Stages of organizational growth through evolution and revolution	1. Growth through creativity —Leadership crisis	2. Growth through direction —Autonomy crisis	3. Growth through delegation —Control crisis 4. Growth through coordination —Red tape crisis	5. Growth through collaboration —Crisis of ?

Source: Ven de Ven (1992). 'Suggestions for Studying Strategy Process: A Research Note', *Strategic Management Journal*, 13: 171.

Instead, the central focus of developmental process models is on progressions (i.e., the nature, sequence, and order) of activities or events that an organizational entity undergoes as it changes over time. As the table exemplifies, a linear sequence of stages or phases of development is a common form of progression in these process models. For example, a rational process of decision making is typically viewed as a sequence of separable stages (e.g., need recognition, search, screen, and choice activities) ordered in time and with transition routines to make adjustments between stages (March and Simon 1958). Many social processes reflect far more complex progressions than simple linear sequences of stages or phases.

There are many other forms of progression that are useful for thinking about and observing developmental processes. The child development psychologists, van den Daele (1969; 1974), Riegel (1969), and Flavell (1972), for example, propose a vocabulary of developmental progressions that goes beyond simple unitary stages. As Table 7.3 illustrates, the vocabulary includes *multiple*, *cumulative*, *conjunctive*, and *recurrent progressions* of *convergent*, *parallel*, and *divergent* streams of activities as a developmental process unfolds over time. This vocabulary is useful for appreciating alternative forms of developmental progressions, which in turn, is central to understanding the

Table 7.3. A vocabulary for examining developmental progressions

Alternative Progressions of Events

- simple unitary progression
  - A sequence of the form   U ⟶ V ⟶ W

- multiple progressions
  - Development can follow several paths
  - Forms: parallel, divergent, and convergent

PARALLEL	DIVERGENT	CONVERGENT
U ⟶ V ⟶ W		
U ⟶ V ⟶ W		
U ⟶ V ⟶ W		

- cumulative progressions
  - More than one stage may belong to a unit at a time.
  - Forms: by addition, substitution, or modification
    - U ⊃ a   ⟶ V ⊃ a b   ⟶ W ⊃ a b c
    - U ⊃ a   ⟶ V ⊃ b   ⟶ W ⊃ b c
    - U ⊃ a   ⟶ V ⊃ a b   ⟶ W ⊃ c

- conjunctive progressions
  - Events in one path are related or influence events in another path of a multiple progression
  - Relations may be probabilistic, inclusive, or mediated

- recurrent progressions
  - Repeating strings of events over time

Source: Adapted from van den Daele (1969). 'Qualitative Models in Developmental Analysis', *Developmental Psychology.*

second meaning of process. It provides the analytical terms needed to make clear distinctions between the various process models in Table 7.2.

1. A *Unitary Progression* is a simple linear sequence of the form U → V → W, where U, V, and W represent qualitatively different patterns, stages, or phases of activities or behaviors. This model assumes that each stage may consist of any number of subsets of activities, but that these subsets must occur in an ordered progression. If a developmental progression has no more than one subset of events over time, it is called a simple unitary progression, as illustrated in Table 7.2 by the two strategic planning models and Scott's (1971) stage model of corporate development.

2. *Multiple Progressions* assume that developmental processes follow more than a single path. Three common forms of multiple progressions among event sequences are the parallel, divergent, and convergent progressions illustrated in Table 7.3.

    In multiple progressions a temporal sequence of events may reflect more than one pathway at a given time in the ordered progression. For example, in the strategic decision process study of Mintzberg, Raisinghani, and Theoret (1976) in Table 7.2, more than one feasible path (or routine) of decision diagnosis, search, or evaluation might be pursued in each respective stage of identification, development, and selection. These paths diverge from each other at the beginning of each stage, proceed in parallel progressions during each stage, and converge at the end to complete each stage. As this example suggests, any developmental progression that has more than one subset of parallel paths at a time is called a multiple progression. A description of how multiple progressions of events diverge, proceed in parallel, or converge over time provides a useful vocabulary for making process statements about specific stages or the overall developmental pattern of a developing entity over time.

3. A *Cumulative Progression* (in unitary or multiple models) assumes that elements found in earlier events or stages are added and built upon in subsequent events or stages (as they are assumed to be in Lorange's (1980) and Scott's (1971) models in Table 7.2). Complete cumulation means that every event from each stage is carried from its onset until the end of the developmental progression. Of course this seldom happens, since losses of memory, mistakes and detours, and terminated pathways all imply partially cumulative or substitution progressions (as illustrated in the bottom two tracks in Table 7.3). Such partial cumulation is reflected in Quinn's (1980) 'logical incremental' model of a long sequence of 14 stages, which distinguishes it from a cumulative progression implied by a rational model of decision making.

    A cumulative progression may take the form of addition, substitution, or modification (Flavell, 1972). In *addition*, a later-occurring event supplements an earlier-occurring event. The outcomes of two events E1 and

E2 may coexist and are both equally available for E3. For example, in Scott's (1971) model of corporate development, a multiple products divisionalized structure is largely produced by the addition (with slight modification) of a stage 1 single product entrepreneurial structure with a stage 2 single product functional structure. With *substitution* the outcomes of a later event largely replace those of an earlier one. More precisely, E2 deletes or subtracts the effects of E1, and replaces them by adding those of E2. For example, in Greiner's (1972) model of organizational growth, crisis at the end of each stage leads the organization to shift (or substitute) its focus and transition into the next qualitatively new stage. In *modification* a later event represents 'a differentiation, generalization, or more stable version of the earlier one' (Flavell 1972: 345). In this case the outcome of E1 is revised or modified in E2. For example, in the strategic planning model of Gluck et al. (1980) in Table 7.2, the planning process and focus of each prior stage is modified and made more elaborate in the next stage.

4. *Conjunctive Progressions* (in unitary, multiple, or cumulative models) posit that the elements of subsets may be related. Conjunctive events are causally related events, meaning that events in one pathway may influence events in other pathways of a multiple progression. Of course what is related at one time may be viewed as unrelated at another. Therefore, strict causality among events is difficult to establish.

   Conjunctive progressions may be probabilistic, inclusive, or mediated. *Probabilistic* relationships between events occur when the trajectories of multiple paths of activities happen to intersect. Such is the form of conjunction among streams of choices, problems, solutions, and participants' energy in the garbage can model of Cohen et al. (1972). *Inclusion* occurs when the outcomes of earlier events become incorporated into the later one, as often observed with PERT charts. For example, Lorange's strategic programming phase represents the logical inclusion of alternatives from stage 1 into a strategic program in stage 2. In a *mediation* relationship an earlier event or element 'represents some sort of developmental bridge or stepping stone (mediator) to the later one' (Flavell, 1972: 345). So E2 is required in order to move from E1 to E3, which may also pre-empt alternative paths. For example, in Greiner's model crisis events mediate and bridge transitions between evolutionary stages of organizational growth.

5. *Recurrent Progressions* (in unitary, multiple, cumulative, or conjunctive models) are repeating strings of events or activities over time. Although the previous progression models have been treated as nonrecurrent sequences, parts or all of them may repeat over time. For example, what distinguishes Mintzberg's model of strategic unstructured decision processes from the others in Table 7.2 is its attention to repeating

routines, or iterative progressions, within each phase of decision making. Abbott (1990) discusses a variety of techniques for the colligation and measurement of recurrent and nonrecurrent event sequence data.

These alternative models of progression in Table 7.3 do not occur independently. Whether implicit or explicit, every development process model makes a commitment to some form of temporal progression of unitary or multiple sequences of events that may be cumulative, conjunctive, and reoccur over time. This vocabulary of temporal relationships among events can help scholars articulate the meanings of their process models in more operational and discriminating ways than in the past. However, this analysis of process as a sequence of events cannot go far without considering the alternative theories of process that may explain specific developmental progressions.

CLARIFY THEORIES OF PROCESS

Whereas a definition of process indicates one's meaning of process in relation to other uses, a theory of process consists of an explanation of how and why a process unfolds over time. Such a theory is useful not only to ground the conceptual basis of a process study, but also to guide the design and conduct of an empirical study. Thus, the second basic decision for designing a process study is to clarify the theory of process underlying the substantive investigation.

I do not wish to imply that you have a clear process theory in mind before undertaking empirical research so that it can be tested. In my experience, I have never been sure what process theory might be useful to explain field observations. It is precisely because of this ambiguity in not knowing what to expect that a repertoire of alternative models is immensely helpful in making sense of reality. As Pasteur advised, 'Chance favors the prepared mind.'

Viewing process as a developmental progression, Scott Poole and I proposed four basic theories that serve as ideal types for explaining processes of development and change in organizations (Van de Ven and Poole 1995). Figure 7.1 shows that each theory views the process of development as unfolding in a fundamentally different progression of change events, and to be governed by a different generative mechanism or motor.

- A *life cycle* (or regulated) model depicts the process of change in an entity as progressing through a necessary sequence of stages or phases. In terms of the vocabulary introduced before, the typical progression of a life cycle process of change is a unitary, cumulative, and conjunctive sequence of stages, because the content and historical sequence of these stages is

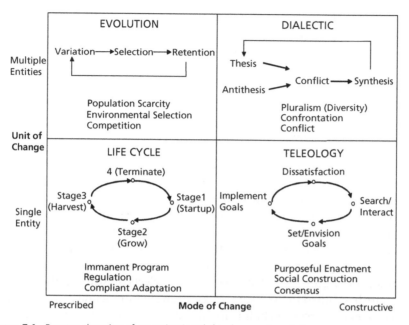

Figure 7.1. Process theories of organizational development and change

Source: Van de Ven, A. H. and Poole, M. S. (1995). 'Explaining Development and Change in Organizations,' *Academy of Management Review*, 20(3): 520.

Note: Arrows on lines represent likely sequences among events, not causation between events.

prescribed and regulated by an institutional, natural, or logical program prefigured at the beginning of the cycle.

- A *teleological* (or planned change) model views development as a cycle of goal formulation, implementation, evaluation, and modification of actions or goals based on what was learned or intended by the entity. This sequence emerges through the purposeful enactment or social construction of an envisioned end state among individuals within the entity. Teleological models of development incorporate the systems theory assumption of equifinality; there are several equally effective ways to achieve a given goal. There is no assumption about historical necessity. Rather, these models rely on agency as the explanatory principle: they posit a set of functions or goals desired by an organizational unit, which it has to acquire in order to 'realize' its aspirations. Development is movement toward attaining a purpose, goal, function, or desired end state.
- In *dialectical* models of development conflicts emerge between entities espousing an opposing thesis and antithesis that collide to produce a synthesis, which in time becomes the thesis for the next cycle of a dialectical progression. Confrontation and conflict between opposing agents generate this dialectical cycle. Stability and change in a dialectical process theory are

explained by the relative balance of power between opposing forces. Stability is produced through partisan struggles and accommodations, which maintain the status quo between oppositions. Change occurs when these opposing values, forces, or events go out of balance. The relative strength, power, or legitimacy of an antithesis may emerge or mobilize to a sufficient degree of force to overthrow the current thesis or state of affairs and produce a synthesis, which then becomes the new thesis as the dialectical process recycles and continues.

- An *evolutionary* model explains change as a recurrent, cumulative, and probabilistic progression of variation, selection, and retention among entities in a designated population. This evolutionary cycle is generated by competition for scarce environmental resources between entities inhabiting a population. As in biological evolution, change proceeds in a continuous process of variation, selection, and retention. Variations, the creation of novel forms, are often viewed to emerge by blind or random chance; they just happen. Selection occurs principally through the competition among forms, and the environment selects those forms that optimize or are best suited to the resource base of an environmental niche. Retention involves the forces (including inertia and persistence) that perpetuate and maintain certain organizational forms. Retention serves to counteract the self-reinforcing loop between variations and selection.

Two dimensions are useful for distinguishing the four process models illustrated in Figure 7.1: (1) whether the unit of change involves one or more entities; and (2) whether the mode of change is prescribed or constructed. Life cycle and teleological theories operate on a *single entity*. In the case of a life cycle model, the development of any entity is governed by a code immanent within the entity or a set of institutional rules to which the entity adapts while changing. While the environment and other entities may shape how an entity adapts, they are strictly secondary to the immanent forces for development within the single entity. Teleological theories also focus on only a single entity's goals, social construction, or envisioned end state to explain development. A teleological theory can operate among many members of an organization or a set of organizations when there is sufficient consensus among the members to permit them to act as a single organizational entity. On the other hand, evolutionary and dialectical theories operate on *multiple entities*. Evolutionary forces are defined in terms of their impact on populations and have no meaning at the level of the individual entity. Dialectical theories require at least two entities to fill the roles of thesis and antithesis.

The generative mechanisms of the four process theories also differ in terms of a second dimension regarding whether the sequence of change events is prescribed *a priori* or whether the progression is constructed and emerges as the change process unfolds. A *prescribed* mode of change channels the development of entities in a pre-specified direction, typically of maintaining and incrementally adapting their forms in a definite, calculable way. A *constructive* mode of change generates unprecedented, novel forms that, in retrospect, are often discontinuous and unpredictable departures from the past. A prescribed motor evokes a sequence of change events in accord with a pre-established program or action routine. A constructive motor, on the other hand, produces new action routines that may (or may not) create an original (re)formulation of the entity. Life cycle and evolutionary theories operate in a prescribed modality, while teleological and dialectical theories operate in the constructive modality.

Most researchers conduct their studies with one model or theory in mind. Working with a single model or perspective of change has the advantage of sharpening and focusing data collection and analysis. A single perspective or model is also easier to operationalize and fit the data. However in Chapter 4, I argued, in contrast, that having two or more models enables the researcher to make stronger inferences by positing a series of critical tests of assumptions that differentiate the models. Another advantage of comparing plausible alternative models is that null results on one model are less likely to leave the researcher in a cul-de-sac of knowing only what is not the case.

Most organizational change processes can be exceedingly complex, and far beyond the explanatory capabilities of any single process theory found in the literature. Typically several different models are needed to capture different aspects of the same process; they complement each other to better understand the process (Pettigrew 1990). Moreover, when researchers and practitioners have only a single perspective or theory, they tend to twist and rationalize facts to fit their model (Mitroff and Emshoff 1979). Consequently, I suggest it is generally better to develop and juxtapose alternative theories and then determine which theory better explains the data or how they can be combined.

The comparative method also facilitates keeping the research focused and manageable. It reduces complexity because it is very difficult to analyze a large array of field data without conceptual guidance. This approach emphasizes that testing a process theory should be based on the relative explanatory power of alternative theories that are available or that can be developed to explain the phenomena. It is also consistent with the principle that knowledge advances by successive approximations and comparisons of competing alternative theories (Lakatos 1978).

FRAME OF REFERENCE TO VIEW THE RESEARCH QUESTION

Once the meanings and theories of process are clear, then a researcher has the basic conceptual foundations for designing a process study undertaken to examine a specific research question about how change unfolds over time.

A crucial step in launching any study is being reflexive about the researcher's role and perspective. As discussed in Chapter 2, a researcher can only observe and recount a partial view of the events that may unfold in a change process (Schein 1987). The view that scientific observations can be impartial or detached has been severely discredited (Popper 1972). Most social scientists now concede that no research is value-free; a researcher should therefore disclose his/her values and perspective (Van Maanen 1995; Alvesson and Skoldberg 2000).

Every act of observing something represents countless choices not to observe other things and perspectives. Any topic or issue can be examined from the viewpoints of many different individuals or stakeholders. Some of these viewpoints are accessible to the researcher, others are not. It is difficult, if not impossible, for a researcher to assume an impartial and detached perspective or to obtain a balanced representation of all stakeholders involved in any complex organizational change process. It is better to be explicit about which stakeholder's interests and viewpoints are favored (and accessible) than to be silent or naïve about whose interests are served and ignored in any study.

Following this recommendation, engaged scholars often aim to see organizational life from the perspective of a specific participant or stakeholder in the process. This often requires more than a detached view of the subject; indeed, researchers may actively participate in the lives of the people and situations that they are studying (Singleton et al. 1993).

This requires a degree of access and engagement with key stakeholders that few researchers have been able to develop. Gaining access is problematic for many researchers because they seldom place themselves into the frame of reference of the stakeholders who sponsor the study or wish to use its results. Typically, managers are key stakeholders in field studies of change in their organizations. Without observing a change process from the manager's perspective, it becomes difficult for a researcher to understand the dynamics confronting managers who are directing the change effort, and thereby generate new knowledge that advances the theory and practice of managing change. If organizational participants do not understand the relevance of a study, there is also little to motivate them to provide access and information to an investigator. The issue here is *not* that researchers become consultants. As discussed further in Chapter 9, the issue is one of engaging key participants in a study in formulating important research questions that capture the attention and motivation of scholars and practitioners alike.

For example, in launching the Minnesota Innovation Research Program (MIRP) (Van de Ven et al. 2000), we found that a useful way to begin formulating a longitudinal field study was to conduct periodic meetings with small groups of managers from various organizations engaged in comparable change efforts or new ventures. In these meetings we discussed the meanings and implications of the research question (e.g., How and why do innovations develop over time?) and explored ways of studying the question so that it might advance theory and practice from a manager's viewpoint. These meetings produced many useful ideas that guided our research, and many participants also agreed to provide access to conduct the research. Moreover, these meetings often identified individuals whom we negotiated with to become study advisors, facilitators, or co-investigators.

MODE OF INQUIRY

Reflecting on their styles of inquiry and clarity of the subject matter, researchers can adopt a continuum of strategies that are grounded in theory or data. While *deduction,* a theory-driven approach, is familiar to most readers, *abduction,* and its relationship to the more popular term, *induction,* may not be. As discussed in Chapter 4, induction refers to the inference we draw from direct observation of a phenomenon that results in assigning a probability of the likelihood of an occurrence in the future. Abduction refers to a conjecture or hypothesis that we invent to explain anomalies or surprising patterns that we observe (Peirce 1955). Such a conjecture or hypothesis should go beyond the information given in a specific case (Bruner 1973). Since abduction more accurately describes the mode of reasoning entailed in grounded theorizing than induction, I use the term abduction instead of induction.

With a deductive approach, the basic steps in designing research might consist of adopting one or more process theories of change (e.g., Figure 7.1), developing an operational template for the theory, and then using it to determine how closely an observed process matches the theory. With abduction, the steps might include observing processes of stability and change over time in a few organizational entities, sorting data into meaningful categories, developing propositions explaining the observations, and corroborating them with a different sample or on the same sample at a different time.

There is a tight iterative cycle between deduction, abduction, and verification in grounded theory building studies. Strauss (1987) emphasized that all scientific theories require that they be conceived, then elaborated, then checked. 'Few working scientists would make the mistake of believing these stood in a simple sequential relationship.... Many people mistakenly refer to grounded theory as "inductive theory"... All three aspects of inquiry (induction, deduction, and verification) are absolutely essential' (Strauss 1987: 11–12). In the course of a longitudinal study, most researchers move back and forth between these modes of inquiry many times.

OBSERVING PROCESSES IN REAL TIME OR RELYING ON RETROSPECTIVE ACCOUNTS

Because change is defined as an observed difference in an organizational entity over time, a process study necessarily entails collecting longitudinal data. These data can be obtained either by observing the sequence of change events as they occur in real time, or by relying on archival data to obtain a retrospective account of the change process. Most studies of organizational change are retrospective, conducted after outcomes are already known before data collection begins. Retrospective studies provide the advantage of knowing the 'big picture'—how things developed and the outcomes that ensued. This *post hoc* knowledge is helpful for interpreting events that unfolded, and for constructing a narrative of the process. When researchers conduct real-time observations of a change process as it unfolds, they do not have this advantage of afterthought and may miss occurrences or events that later can be viewed as critical. Until we have the compass of the entire process, we often have no way of knowing what information is important and what is not.

However, prior knowledge of the outcome of an organizational change may also bias a study. This is especially true if the final assessment valorizes the outcome as a success or failure, effective or ineffective. There is a tendency to filter out events that do not fit or that render the story less coherent, such as censoring minority views.

A promising approach is to initiate historical study before the ultimate outcomes of a change process become apparent. It is even better to observe the change process in real time as it unfolds in the field setting. This approach maximizes the probability of discovering short-lived factors and changes that exert an important influence. As Pettigrew (1985) notes, 'the more we look at present-day events, the easier it is to identify change; the longer we stay with an emergent process and the further back we go to disentangle its origins, the more likely we are to identify continuities.' At one point or another, most field studies of organizational change involve many forms of longitudinal data collection: archival, retrospective, and real-time observations.

SOURCES OF CHANGE

In the study of human development, Schaie (1965) discussed three common sources of temporal change:

1. *Age.* The age or temporal duration of the individual at the time of measurement. This variable represents that part of development and change that is produced by unfolding biological or institutional processes.

2. *Cohort*: The set of characteristics of all individuals who were born at the same time and go through similar developmental processes, such as classes in school. This variable represents the common historical conditions that shape the development of a given cohort.

3. *Transient*: All the temporary or immediate and non-cumulative factors that influence outcomes or the dependent variables at the time of measurement.

Schaie suggests that it is important to design organizational change studies so they can disentangle these three sources of change—those that are due to age, to external factors in the history of the developing organism (cohort), or to immediate external factors (time of measurement). What appears to be a developmental change due to some immanent mechanism could well be due to a cohort effect or to a unique effect at the time of measurement. For example, a sudden shift in morale compared to previous levels may result from a general improvement in social mood at the time of measurement. Interpreting this as a function of solidification of a developing culture would be incorrect, though it would be easy to see why a researcher whose attention focused only on the organization under study might draw this conclusion. In the same vein, what appears to be a general developmental pattern might be due to cohort effects, unique events occurring only to the group of organizations that were founded in a given time and place. By this reasoning, for example, it would be risky to try to generalize principles of effective development of organizational start-ups in the relatively benign 1950s to organizations in the competitive 1990s because they belong to different cohorts. They operated and started under different resource constraints, had employees with different attitudes, and had a different external environment.

This is not to imply that it is impossible to develop generalizable findings concerning development and change. Rather, it is important to consider what source observed changes may originate from and to rule out alternative explanations for the ones we advance. It is also important to consider the limits of our conclusions. Taking into account age, cohort, and time of measurement as well as organization type and context will result in more effective research designs.

Barley's (1990) research design, shown in Figure 7.2, provides a good example of a systematic study of these different sources of change. In his field study of the adoption of a technology (CT scanners), Barley drew comparisons between two parallel hospitals with synchronic (one point in time) observations of different radiology technologies, and with diachronic (repeated over time) observations of CT scanning behavior by radiology department staff. Reflecting on his design, Barley discusses how conclusions can become problematic when the research questions and comparative analysis are not matched correctly.

For example, synchronic data may seem to suggest that similar outcomes are rooted in similar processes. However, similar outcomes may arise from different processes and different outcomes may arise from similar dynamics (Barley, 1990: 186). Only diachronic data can disentangle such possibilities. By itself, a parallel study of a class of events, objects, or activities may also lead to wrongful conclusions. Suppose, for instance, that one were to investigate the effects of new technologies by studying CT scanning in a number of hospitals. Even if one found that all CT scanners occasion similar phenomena, one could not be sure whether the findings would apply to all computationally based imaging devices or only to CT scanners. A synchronic analysis of several technologies conducted in tandem could resolve this issue. In other words, the synchronic, the diachronic, and the parallel represent three distinct axes of comparison that, when used in combination, allow researchers to examine explicitly the spatial and temporal boundaries of their claims. (Barley 1990: 227)

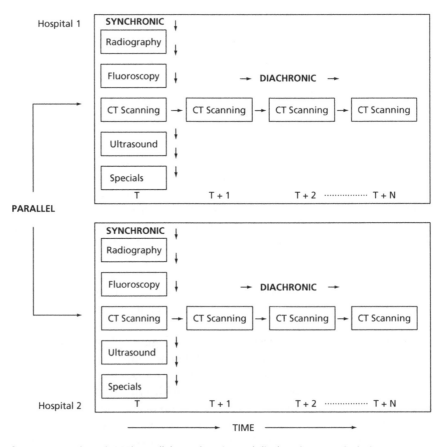

Figure 7.2. Barley's (1990) parallel, synchronic, and diachronic research design

Source: Barley, S. R. (1990). 'Images of Imaging: Notes on Doing Longitudinal Research,' *Organization Science*, 1(3): 226.

SAMPLE DIVERSITY: HOMOGENEOUS OR HETEROGENEOUS CASES

There is no one best sampling scheme for process research. A homogeneous sample has the advantage of keeping to a minimum the multitude of alternative explanations for developmental processes. This is especially advantageous in the case of lengthy sequences of events, because they are particularly vulnerable to accidental or adventitious occurrences that shift the course of development. Comparing cases that are similar in as many respects as possible facilitates identifying whether change processes are due to such transient events or to more basic developmental models, but does not control for cohort effects. A homogeneous sample also facilitates the development and investigation of very precise, focused questions or hypotheses. Hence homogeneous sampling is useful when a well-specified theory of change or development is available. A broad, heterogeneous sample, however, may provide a better opportunity to detect whether sources of change are due to temporal development, cohort, or transient factors.

The comparative method is perhaps the most general and basic strategy for generating and evaluating valid scientific knowledge. This strategy involves the selection of comparison groups that differ in the scope of the population and conceptual categories of central interest to the research. Kaplan (1964: 52) pointed out that scientific knowledge is greatly enhanced when we divide the subject matter into concepts and cases that 'carve at the joints' over the widest possible ranges, types, conditions, and consequences. In this way researchers can develop and evaluate the limits of their propositions.

A broad sampling scheme also permits a researcher to make empirical links between different specialties or schools of thought that have emerged for different organizational settings in which the change process occurs. For example, because organizational structures for business creation are different in small company start-ups, internal corporate innovation projects, and inter-organizational joint ventures, it is widely believed that the process of entrepreneurship in these organizational settings must also be different. Our MIRP studies questioned this conventional belief, and proposed the plausible alternative that creating a new business entails fundamentally the same process regardless of organizational setting. We obtained some empirical evidence supporting this proposition (Van de Ven et al. 1999). The findings suggest that significant benefits and efficiencies can be gained by applying principles of business creation from new company start-ups to internal corporate venturing and inter-organizational joint ventures, and vice versa.

Given the tradeoffs between homogeneous and heterogeneous samples, Pettigrew (1990: 275–7) suggests four useful guidelines for selecting cases to study:

1. 'Go for extreme situations, critical incidents and social dramas.' By choosing unusual cases, cases that are critically important or highly visible cases, researchers select cases in which the process is 'transparently observable.' However, such cases may have nongeneralizable features precisely because they are unusual.

2. 'Go for polar types.' Choose cases that seem very different in terms of the processes under study. For example, compare successful and unsuccessful program start-ups. Or, choose cases that differ from patterns in earlier cases. By successive sampling of polar types, it will eventually be possible to cover the range of possible cases.

3. 'Go for high experience levels of the phenomena under study.' Choose cases that have a long track record of experience with a process. This strategy may not be feasible for some cases: new program start-ups, for example, may best be illuminated by inexperienced entrepreneurs, since they will make the mistakes and experience the learning that highlights key requirements for successful start-ups.

4. 'Go for a more informed choice of sites and increase the probabilities of negotiating access.' Cases must often be selected on the basis of who will cooperate, rather than on grounds of optimal sampling. This, of course, introduces a sampling bias that must be considered in drawing conclusions from the study.

SAMPLE SIZE: NUMBER OF EVENTS AND/OR CASES

The major sample size consideration in variance research studies is the number of cases selected for data collection, as discussed in Chapter 6. The larger the number of cases that are sampled from a population of interest, the more generalizable are the results (provided that the cases are drawn in a representative fashion). Furthermore, in experimental designs, researchers are advised to select the number of cases needed to obtain enough power for statistical tests to equate statistical significance with practical significance in hypotheses testing (Walster and Cleary 1970). Pragmatically, the number of cases selected also depends on the availability of sites and the costs involved in collecting data on each case.

In longitudinal process studies, the central sample size consideration is the *number of temporal intervals or events* obtained on a change process in each case. The number of temporal intervals or events observed depends on what constitutes the 'natural' flow of experience in the organizational change cases being studied. Organizational change processes vary in *temporal duration* and *granularity*. In terms of temporal duration, some organizational change processes, such as group decision making, may occur in committee meetings lasting no more than a few hours. Other change processes, such as the development of technological and administrative innovations, may span several years.

Granularity refers to the preciseness or discreteness of events that are recorded throughout the temporal duration of a case being studied. The granularity of events varies greatly, ranging from events of such large scope that only 5 to 20 might be observed over the period of study to events of such small scope that several thousand occur. Event granularity typically increases with the micro-analytic detail of the change process being investigated.

Events that require a great amount of time and effort to observe and code are likely to be observed in shorter sequences than those less costly to observe. Because there are inherent tradeoffs between the temporal duration and granularity of events that can be sampled, most studies of fine-grained events tend to focus on change processes of relatively short temporal duration, while studies of lengthy change processes tend to adopt coarse-grained events.

PROCESS RESEARCH DESIGNS

There are important implications of the number of cases and events observed in a study for process research design and data analysis. Poole et al. (2000) discuss these implications with reference to their typology of alternative process research designs shown in Table 7.4.

Studies consisting of *few cases, few events* reflect the typical sampling design of comparative case studies. Sometimes there may be few events, not due to paucity of data, but because only a few occur. For example, in a comparative study of strategic decision making where the sequence of search, screen, and choice behaviors are being investigated, there may be relatively few instances of each type of behavior in the case. Alternatively there may be only a couple of instances of the key events (e.g., conflicts) in otherwise lengthy cases. Provided there are enough cases for systematic comparison and induction across the instances, Yin's (2003) comparative case study designs can be utilized.

Table 7.4. Typology of process research designs from Poole et al. (2000)

	FEW EVENTS	MANY EVENTS
Few cases	Summary case studies	Summary case studies Phasic case studies Time series analysis Markov analysis
Many cases	Multivariate analysis Phasic analysis with optimal matching Event history analysis	Multivariate analysis of summary data Phasic analysis with optimal matching Markov analysis Time series analysis

Studies with *many cases, few events* provide many comparative options for the researcher. *Summary measures* for each case can be derived by collapsing the data along the time dimension (e.g., counting the number of conflicts that occur during innovation regardless of when they occurred), or through the use of surrogate measures of temporal order (e.g., did the conflict occur during the first or second halves of the innovation process?). Such measures can then be treated as variables in traditional statistical methods. However, with such pooling of the data, one can lose the temporal order of events that figure prominently in most process research studies.

One method to preserve information about temporal order that clusters cases with similar sequences is *optimal matching*. Poole et al. (2000) discuss that once clusters have been derived, they can serve as the basis for variables that can then be entered into traditional statistical analyses. Alternatively, Tuma and Hannan (1984) discuss how *event history* or *survival analysis* can be used to determine when critical events occur, provided the length of time until they occur is recorded. Supplementary analysis can in some cases divulge causal factors underlying event occurrences (Willett and Singer 1991).

A different set of options are open for studies with *few cases, many events.* Comparative analysis of *qualitative case studies* using Yin's designs are one option. Events can be parsed into *phases* representing coherent periods of activities subsuming two or more events in sequence. These phases can then be used as bounded units to provide temporal divisions in case studies, as Holmes (1997) did in his studies of hostage-taking situations and Van de Ven and Polley (1992) did in their study of a biomedical innovation. Various types of *time series* analyses can also be used when many events are available for each case. These generally involve transforming the event series into some continuous form. In addition, Poole et al. (2000) discuss the application of *Markov analysis*, which preserves the categorical qualities of the event series and enables us to track temporal dependencies among events.

For studies with *many cases, many events* a number of powerful statistical techniques are available. As with the many cases, few events situation, simple *descriptive summaries* of the frequency with which coded events occur provide useful displays for examining stages or phases in the developmental progression. However, with such pooling of the data, one can lose the temporal order of events that figure prominently in most process research studies. *Optimal matching* can be used to derive measures of similarity among the event sequences for the cases and these measures can then be analyzed in at least two ways. First, they can be used as input to cluster analysis and multidimensional scaling techniques that can identify clusters of similar sequences; the resulting clusters can then be used to define variables for causal or correlational analysis, as in Poole and Holmes (1995). Second, these distances can be used to test for causal factors that create the differences between pairs of sequences. Poole et al. (2000) also discuss how *trend analysis* or *multiple time series methods* can be used to identify patterns of change across many cases, provided the events can be used to define continuous variables. *Markov analysis* of multiple cases can provide maps of temporal dependencies among events. Causal factors leading to such dependencies can then be analyzed using *Markovian regression* techniques or other simpler designs.

Measuring and Analyzing Process Data

At the heart of any longitudinal study is measuring and analyzing process data. This section reviews techniques for gathering, tabulating, and analyzing process data. In a typical longitudinal field study, the gathering of data might entail the following procedures:

- survey questionnaires completed by all participants every six months;
- interviews with key managers and participants every six months;
- direct observations of regularly scheduled meetings;
- a diary recording informal discussions with participants; and
- documents and reports from news media and organizational archives.

Whatever data collection methods are used to observe change processes in the field or from archival records, over time data mount astronomically and overload the information processing capacity of even the most insightful mind. Drawing careful inferences requires methods that go beyond subjective 'eyeballing' of raw data to identify patterns. But it is difficult to reconstruct field methods, because they are rarely reported in detail in published field studies. One cannot ordinarily follow how the researchers arrived at their conclusions from hundreds of pages of field observations, even though the reports may be sprinkled with vivid—yet idiosyncratic—quotes from organizational participants. As in variance research, methods for measuring and analyzing process data require explicit and careful attention. Chapter 6 discussed well-established psychometric procedures for survey instrument construction and evaluation. The remainder of this chapter deals with analogous, but less well-established procedures for measuring and evaluating process data. These procedures and decisions are outlined at the bottom of Table 7.1.

PROCESS CONCEPTS

Whether a researcher sets out to develop or test a process theory, the collection of longitudinal data requires a set of categories or concepts. These concepts provide selective focus for observing a change process;

one cannot study everything, and different categories can produce very different findings. When a particular process model(s) is proposed or known beforehand, category development proceeds deductively by operationalizing theoretical constructs into empirical indicators of those constructs. When a grounded theory building approach is taken, these initial categories are best viewed as 'sensitizing constructs' for conducting exploratory research. The categories become clear as they are grounded in field observations. Eventually, these grounded concepts can be codified in a final category system.

A grounded theory-building strategy provides a useful first step in developing some basic concepts and ideas from raw data. To its originators, Glaser and Strauss (1967) and Strauss and Corbin (1990), grounded theory building consists of the following structured steps. Begin with small units of data (incidents) and gradually construct a system of categories or concepts that describe the phenomena being observed. The categories may have several subcategories and dimensions that are gradually elaborated and refined as specific incidents are examined, coded, and compared. As the categories are developed, additional data are examined to verify the properties of the emerging category system. The analysis concludes with the identification of a small number of core categories that serve to integrate the theoretical concepts that are firmly rooted or 'grounded' in the data.

In our Minnesota Innovation Research Program (MIRP), for example, we began with five 'sensitizing categories' to study innovation development: ideas, people, transactions, context, and outcomes (Van de Ven et al. 2000). As is typical in longitudinal studies, our assumptions and definitions of these

Table 7.5. Evolution of innovation concepts during MIRP

	Starting definitions from literature	But we see this in field studies
Ideas	One invention to be operationalized	Reinvention, proliferation, reimplementation, discarding, and termination of many ideas
People	An entrepreneur with a fixed set of full time people over time	Many entrepreneurs, distracted, fluidly engaging, and disengaging in a variety of roles over time
Transactions	Fixed network of people/firms working out the details of an innovative idea	Expanding and contracting network of partisan stakeholders converging and diverging on innovation ideas
Context	Environment provides opportunities and constraints on innovation process	Innovation process constrained and created by multiple enacted environments
Outcomes	Final result orientation: a stable order comes into being	Final results may be indeterminate; multiple in-process assessments and spinoffs; Integration of new order with the old
Process	Simple cumulative sequence of stages and phases of development	From simple to multiple progressions of divergent, parallel, and convergent paths; some are related and cumulative, others not

Source: Van de Ven et al. (1999).

concepts over time changed substantially and became progressively clear with field observations. Table 7.5 compares our starting assumptions of these concepts drawn from the literature at the time, with how we came to view them as a result of two years of field studies. The latter disclosed a different reality from the rather orderly and naïve conceptions of the former. As this example illustrates, the development of research constructs involves an iterative process of conceptualization, observation, and reformulation.

INCIDENTS AND EVENTS

It is useful to distinguish between *incidents* and *events* in a process theory (Abbott, 1984), which are analogous to the distinction between *variables* and *constructs*, respectively, in a variance theory (discussed in Chapter 6). Incidents are operational empirical observations, while events are abstract concepts of bracketed or coded sets of incidents. The stream of incidents, a directly observable first-order set of activities, is translated into a sequence of events, a more abstract second-order construction. This implies that some incidents may be embedded in different conceptual domains and utilized as constituents of different events.

Events may differ in temporal and spatial scope, and as a result, incidents may indicate more than one, overlapping event. For example, a meeting with 'firm Q' can indicate the event 'meeting with a partner,' but it may also indicate a longer event, 'negotiation with firm Q regarding partnership.' Events may be embedded within different types of events of a larger scope. Both levels may be important for understanding the change process, because interwoven narratives clarify it better than either narrative could on its own. Abbott (1992) gives an example from his studies of the rise of professions in society, 'I once set out to explain why there are no psychiatrists in American mental hospitals. The exodus, which dates from 1900–30, reflects not only the rational individual mobility decisions that are specifiable annually, but also outpatient community developments that are specifiable only decadely, and changes in knowledge and social control taking place over even longer periods.'

Another complication is the possibility that the incident–event relationship may change over time (Abbott 1984). The significance of events may change as the process unfolds. The same change is possible in incident–event relations. For example, the first time a potential partner is encountered may signal an expansion of an organizational program, whereas the sixth encounter with a potential partner may signal desperation for ideas or resources. Thus, while events are constructs indicated by incidents, the indication relationship is more complicated for qualitative data than it is for quantitative scores. The assumption of uniformity across respondents and responses in psychometrics and scale theory may not hold for data used to define events. What quantitative analysis would classify as an error may be quite important nuances for qualitative data.

DEFINING AN INCIDENT: A QUALITATIVE DATUM

In survey research, a *quantitative datum* is commonly regarded to be: (1) a numerical response to a question scaled along a distribution; (2) about an object (the unit of analysis); (3) at the time of measurement; which is (4) entered as a variable (along with other variables on the object) into a record (or case) of a quantitative data file; and (5) is subsequently recoded and classified as an indicator of a theoretical construct.

In comparison, we define a *qualitative datum* as: (1) a bracketed string of words capturing the basic elements of information; (2) about a discrete incident or occurrence (the unit of analysis); (3) that happened on a specific date; which is, (4) entered as a unique record (or case) in a qualitative data file; and (5) is subsequently coded and classified as an indicator of a theoretical event.

The basic element of information in a qualitative datum is a bracketed string of words about a discrete incident. Raw words, sentences, or stories about incidents that are collected from the field or from archives cannot be entered into a qualitative data file until they are bracketed into a datum(s). Obviously, explicit decision rules that reflect the substantive purposes of the research are needed to bracket raw words.

In our MIRP studies, the decision rule used to bracket words into a qualitative datum was the definition of an incident that occurred in the development of an innovation (Van de Ven et al. 2000). An incident occurred whenever changes were observed to occur in any one of our five core concepts: innovation ideas, people, transactions, context, and outcomes. When an incident was identified, the bracketed string of words required to describe it included: date of occurrence, the actor(s) or object(s) involved, the action or behavior that occurred, the consequence (if any) of the action, and the source of the information. As with any set of decision rules, discussions among researchers were necessary to define innovation incidents in an operationally consistent manner.

Decision rules may vary in the level of specificity and the temporal duration of incidents they construct. Some rules specify fine-grained definitions of incidents that interpret each action as a separate incident; others adopt coarse-grained definitions that require longer episodes for incidents. The proper granularity of incidents depends on the rates of development of various kinds of processes, and the differing research questions associated with these rates.

For example, Knudson and Ruttan (2000) found that hybrid wheat development was governed by biological laws that require several decades to move from basic research through technology development to market introduction. They observed that hybrid wheat's innovation process had been following this 'biological time clock' for forty years since the late 1950s. In studies of biomedical innovations, Garud and Van de Ven (2000) observed that the rate of development was governed by an 'institutional regulation time clock,' in which the design, testing, and commercial release of devices entailed extensive review and approval steps by the US Food and Drug Administration, sometimes lasting five years. However, rates of development of other processes, such as group decision making (Poole and Roth 1989) or the development of novel administrative programs (Roberts and King 1996; Bryson and Roering 2000) are more rapid and appear to be limited only by entrepreneurial time and attention. As these variations suggest, the temporal scope of organizational change should correspond with the granularity of incidents being observed in the field study. Zaheer et al. (1999) provide a stimulating discussion of these and other considerations in developing temporal metrics.

RELIABILITY AND VALIDITY OF INCIDENT CONSTRUCTION

It is important to establish the reliability of classifying raw data into incidents. An equally important, though often neglected, issue is the validity of this bracketing procedure (Folger et al. 1984; Poole et al. 1987). Researchers often assume that the meaning of incidents is clear, and that establishing reliability is equivalent to showing the meaning of codings is clear. However, attaining reliability among coders simply indicates that the meaning of incidents is clear to the particular group of researchers who designed the coding system, not necessarily to participants or key stakeholders. It is necessary to test empirically whether researchers' classifications coincide with practitioners' perceptions of events. If the evidence indicates inconsistency, then no claims about the meaning of events to the participants are valid. Researchers can still sustain claims about the meaning of the incident from their theoretical position, but no claims about the 'social reality' of the event are appropriate.

Two basic procedures can enhance the reliability and validity of incident coding. First, coding of incidents from raw data sources can be performed by two or more researchers. Consensus among coders increases the consistency of interpretations of the decision rules used to identify incidents. Second, incident codings can be reviewed by key organizational informants. It is useful to ask informants if any incidents are missing or incorrectly described. Based on this feedback, revisions in the incident listings can be made if they conform to the decision rules for defining each incident. Typically, these two steps result in a more complete listing of incidents about the change process being studied.

QUALITATIVE STRATEGIES FOR IDENTIFYING EVENTS FROM INCIDENTS

The next step is to identify theoretically meaningful events from the incident data. Since the temporal sequence of events is a central organizing device for process data, this next step typically consists of identifying the order and sequence of events from observed incident data. Several approaches are available for tacking back and forth between incident data and event sequence categories.

Abductive approaches go first to the data—the incidents—and sift through the various instances, deriving categories from the ground up, using the constant comparative method for identifying concepts from data (Dougherty 2002). Langley (1999) discusses two additional strategies for making sense of process data:

Visual mapping. As the saying goes, 'a picture is worth a thousand words.' A diagram of how incidents unfolded by event categories or actors over time is a useful method for organizing incident data. Visual graphical representations permit the compact presentation of large quantities of information, and are particularly useful for analyzing process data because they allow the simultaneous display of a large number of dimensions, and they show precedence, parallel processes, and the passage of time. Miles and Huberman (1994) provide many different formats with examples of how these graphical displays might be constructed. Meyer (1991) provides a creative application of visually mapping major changes unfolding at different levels of a health care system.

Temporal bracketing. Various categories of events identified through visual mapping can be arrayed over time by phases, stages, or distinct periods of activities. In their study of technology adoption in small manufacturing firms, for example, Langley and Truax (1994) decomposed decision, activity, and context events into three periods: rivalry between projects and management turnover (1987), financial and technical difficulties and union strike (1988), and major project investment stimulated by customers (1989). They observed continuity in the activities within each period and discontinuities between the periods. Importantly, these periods are not 'phases' in the sense of a predictable sequential process but simply a way of structuring the description of events (Langley 1999).

Deductive approaches make use of theory to specify the expected order and sequence of event categories.

Template matching. In this strategy, operational templates of one or more process theories, such as those illustrated in Figure 7.1 and Table 7.2, are used to determine how closely an observed event sequence matches each theory. Allison (1971) used this strategy to examine how well decisions made during the Cuban Missile Crisis reflected three theoretical templates: a rational actor model, an organizational process model, and a political model. He concluded that the second and third models more accurately explained the observed decision process than the first model.

Pentland (1999: 719) poses an important challenge to template matching by asking (with reference to Figure 7.1): 'How can we tell which motor (or theory) is running?' Many specific theories of organizational change are combinations of two or more of basic 'motors' (e.g., life cycle plus teleology). The problem is that these deep structures [process theories] are never directly observed. All we have in empirical research is the 'surface structure' captured in our observations. This is the problem of construct validation; given some data, what is the underlying construct? A number of steps can be taken to enhance the reliability and validity of coding incidents into indicators of event constructs or events into higher-order constructs. Operational definitions and coding conventions can be drafted for the coded constructs, and periodic meetings can be conducted with researchers and other colleagues to evaluate the construct validity of these definitions.

I found that a useful way to conduct such meetings is to begin with an overall presentation of the conceptual model being studied, then give specific definitions of each construct in the model and the measurement indicators to be used (Van de Ven and Ferry 1980). Participants can then be asked to 'suggest better indicators for measuring this construct as defined previously.' Often using a Nominal Group Technique format (see Delbecq et al. 1975), reviewers are provided a brief period to think and respond to the questions in writing. Then a general discussion ensues to obtain group opinions. The qualitative written comments from these review sessions are especially helpful to clarify the different interpretations of constructs and event indicators by participants in the review sessions.

Synthetic strategy. Another deductive approach to analyzing process data is to transform sequence data into summary statistics such as: the total number of events in various categories in the entire sequence or in segments of it; or the total number of phases in the process. This 'synthetic strategy,' as Langley terms it, can then be used to test developmental models with variance analysis. While this transformation is commonly used (e.g., Eisenhardt 1989), care must be taken to preserve the temporal sequence in observed change processes. Too often the categories that researchers use collapse the data over time, and thereby remove the temporal information that is central to any process story.

Poole et al. (2000) point out that in practice, these strategies are frequently combined in a *retroductive* approach. He used this approach to derive his group decision coding system (Poole and Roth 1989). A literature search is undertaken to derive a scheme for categorizing and coding events, and categories are adjusted in view of what is workable and informative after trying them out on the data. This permits the theoretically driven scheme to emerge and adapt in response to the exigencies of the data. Bales and Strodtbeck (1951) used this approach in developing their Interaction Process Analysis.

QUANTITATIVE STRATEGIES FOR CODING EVENT SEQUENCE DATA

The foregoing qualitative approaches to ordering and making sense of event process data are useful for identifying and displaying general patterns in event sequence data. However, they only take us so far. Longitudinal field data on organizational change incidents typically far exceed our limited capacity to analyze qualitative data. Further information reduction strategies are often needed to analyze process patterns in the data.

A limitation of many quantitative coding systems is that they reduce rich qualitative data to a single dimension of meaning. One way to organize multi-dimensional data to analyze change processes is to array them on multiple tracks corresponding to conceptually meaningful categories. The procedure of coding incidents along several event tracks was used in Poole's (1983) studies of decision development in small groups, which coded acts with a three-track coding system that took into account the impact of each incident (a group member's statement) on group work process and group relationships, and also indexed incidents on several topics it referred to. By coding each incident on several conceptually relevant dimensions simultaneously, Poole was able to derive a richer description of group processes than previous studies had achieved.

Abbott (1990) describes methods for analyzing sequence, order, and causal relationships in coded event data. They involve different forms of transforming a chronological listing of coded incidents into dichotomous indicators of event constructs. Such transformations of qualitative codes into quantitative dichotomous variables permits applying various statistical methods to examine time-dependent patterns of relations among the event constructs. *Sequence analysis*, a family of methods concerned with the problem of determining the temporal order among events, is particularly useful for such analyses (Abbott 1984). Analogous to analysis of variance that determines differences or correlations between spatial orders (variables), sequence analysis examines similarities and differences between temporal orders (discrete events).

Poole et al. (2000) review a variety of statistical methods that can be used to identify substantively interpretable time-dependent patterns (or lack thereof) and relationships in event sequence data. These techniques include:

1. Stochastic modeling techniques (e.g., Markov and logit analysis) to examine probabilistic relationships between the occurrence of events.
2. Granger causality and vector autoregression to identify possible causal relationships between dichotomously coded events.
3. Phasic analysis of temporal patterns in event sequence data.
4. Linear time-series regression analysis on incidents aggregated into fixed temporal intervals to examine causal relationships among coded event time series.
5. A variety of diagnostic procedures for examining non-linear dynamic patterns in event time series.

Other statistical methods can also be used to examine the temporal duration and sequence among coded events. For example, 'renewal theory' can be used to examine whether the duration between two consecutive events in a change process are distributed according to some known probabilistic distribution, such as the exponential or more general Weibull distribution. In addition, Tuma and Hannan (1984) show how 'hazard rates' can be computed to determine the likelihood of occurrence of certain coded events based on a set of predictor variables.

FROM EVENT SEQUENCE TO STORY NARRATIVE

A basic scientific goal in conducting longitudinal studies of organizational change is to develop a *process theory of change*. A process theory needs to go beyond a surface description to penetrate the logic behind observed temporal progressions. This explanation should identify the generative mechanisms that cause observed events to happen in the real world, and the particular circumstances or contingencies when these causal mechanisms operate (Harre and Madden 1975; Tsoukas 1989).

Thus, as we move from surface observations toward a process theory, we move from description to explanation. Explanation requires a *story*, and stories can be understood as process theories (Pentland 1999). In narrative theory the story is an abstract conceptual model; it identifies the generative mechanisms at work. At a minimum this story must describe a progression or sequence of events. In narrative theory, however, the 'story' includes a great deal more than just event sequence. In particular, a process theory should include the following features in the story (Pentland 1999: 712–13).

1. *Sequence in time.* Narrative should include a clear beginning, middle, and end . . . Chronology is a central organizing device. The events or actions referred to in a narrative are understood to happen in a sequence.

2. *Focal actor or actors.* Narratives are always about someone or some-thing...There is a protagonist and, frequently, an antagonist as well. The characters may not be developed or even identified by name, but, along with sequence, they provide a thread that ties the events in a narrative together.

3. *Identifiable narrative voice.* A narrative is something that someone tells, so there should always be an identifiable voice doing the narrating. That voice reflects a specific point of view of the key participant or stakeholder chosen in decision 3 (above).

4. *'Canonical' or evaluative frame of reference.* Narratives carry meaning and cultural value because they encode, implicitly or explicitly, standards against which actions of the characters can be judged....But even without any explicit moral, narratives embody a sense of what is right and wrong, appropriate or inappropriate, and so on.

5. *Other indicators of content or context.* Narrative texts typically contain more than just the bare events. In particular, they contain a variety of textual devices that are used to indicate time, place, attributes of the characters, attributes of the context, and so on. These indicators do not advance the plot, but they provide information that may be essential to the interpretation of the events (e.g., knowing that the scene is a wedding changes the significance of the utterance 'I do').

These five steps in theory building are easier said than done. Developing a process theory that embodies these features requires considerable ingenuity and creativity in applying the repertoire of methods described in this chapter. Bruner (1986, 1991b) and Polkinghorne (1988) provide extensive and useful perspectives for developing a narrative understanding of social behavior. But as the development of any skill requires, developing narrative theory requires repeated use and practice of these methods.

Example of Process Research Design with Comments from Larry E. Greiner

This section provides an example of some of the steps and decisions in designing process research. It also illustrates a pattern of interaction among scholars engaged in designing a study to evaluate a particular process model. The example was initially reported in Van de Ven (1992) and is largely reproduced here. It focuses on Greiner's (1972) well-known model of organizational growth outlined at the bottom of Table 7.2.

I sent a draft of this assessment to Prof. Larry E. Greiner at the University of Southern California. He responded with a very useful set of comments that not only clarify, amplify, and correct my initial interpretations of his model, but also exemplify how the meanings, vocabulary, and methods for process research covered in Chapter 7 can facilitate more penetrating and constructive dialogue among scholars whose primary motivations are to learn and better understand how organizations change. In order to show this constructive dialogue, I did not change my initial assessment of the model in the text from that which Prof. Greiner reviewed. With his permission, I include his comments in footnotes to pertinent statements made in the text.

Greiner's model clearly uses the second meaning of process as a developmental sequence of events, and proposes that organizational growth progresses through five stages of evolution and revolution: (1) creativity and leadership; (2) direction and autonomy; (3) delegation and control; (4) coordination and red tape; and (5) collaboration and revitalization.[2]

To evaluate the status of Greiner's applied theory, it is useful to recognize that he implicitly borrows conceptual elements from three of the ideal types of process theories. In so doing, Greiner's model contains a number of conceptual anomalies, which in turn suggest a number of promising areas for further theory building. In the main, the model is rooted in a life cycle theory of change, in which 'historical forces [organization age, size, growth rate, and stages of evolution and revolution] shape the future growth of organizations' (Greiner, 1972: 166). The quest for growth represents an underdeveloped teleological element in the model. Greiner states his position that 'the future of an organization may be less determined by outside forces than it is by the organization's history.... [B]ehavior is determined primarily by previous events and experiences, not by what lies ahead' (p. 166). Beyond this introductory statement, the 'pull' of an envisioned end state of growth is largely ignored by Greiner, as are considerations of alternative paths to achieve the desired end of growth; instead only one particular sequence of developmental stages is discussed. The term 'evolution' is used loosely to describe prolonged periods of growth where no major upheaval (or 'revolution') occurs in organizational practices. Thus, Greiner does not borrow conceptual elements from the ideal type evolutionary theory (as we have described it). He does, however, entertain dialectical theory by observing that 'as a company progresses through developmental phases, each evolutionary period creates its own revolution' (p. 166). However, with the exception of asserting the life cycle

---

[2] Greiner: You might give my article a little context in terms of time and place—since it was written in 1972, one of the first such models, and it was published in HBR [*Harvard Business Review*], which did not want a theoretical discussion. So I was unable at the time to explain the piece theoretically in 'academic' style or to describe the empirical aspects in somewhat more 'messier' form than the HBR artists and editors would allow.... (I might add too that I think the model was the precursor if not the first 'punctuated equilibrium' model—at least Tushman has said this to me.)

view that crises are immanent to each evolutionary stage, Greiner does not explain how these divergent forces emerge out of unitary progressions within each stage, and how these antagonistic forces converge and collide to mediate a synthesis in the next stage, as a dialectical theory would require.[3] As this overly brief critique suggests, a fruitful way to evaluate and extend applied models of process is to anchor the analysis in more basic and general theories of process.

To empirically examine Greiner's model (as formulated in 1972) from a developmental process perspective, one would ask the following kind of question, 'Does organizational growth commonly progress through the sequence of stages that Greiner proposes?' A key conceptual move for addressing this research question is to view Greiner's stages as categories of events, and not to assume that these categories of events occur in any particular sequence of progression over time. Thus, instead of viewing organizational growth as a unitary progression of a linear sequence of stages based on a life cycle theory of change, one is open to more empirical possibilities if the process of organizational growth is viewed in terms of a variety of other models of event progressions and theories of change process.

One way to do this is to adopt a research design as illustrated in Figure 7.3. In comparison with Greiner's initial formulation of the model, this research design redefines the five stages of organizational evolution and the four

---

[3] Greiner: This [sentence] hurts a bit because I tried very consciously to use dialectical explanation (without calling it that to HBR readers) throughout the evolving stages and crises. I think you will see this logic if you go through each stage's description, such as at the end of the Phase 2 description where I write, 'although the new directive techniques channel energy more efficiently into growth (thesis), they eventually become inappropriate for controlling a larger, more diverse and complex organization. Lower level employees find themselves restricted by a cumbersome and centralized hierarchy. . . . thus a crisis develops from demands for greater autonomy by lower level managers (antithesis).' The synthesis link I then make (but perhaps not as explicitly as I should) when I introduce 'Delegation' in stage 3 as lower levels receive more autonomy—though this autonomy is different from the kind they were asking for—and this in turn—becomes the new thesis. You or others might not agree with how I use dialectics or that I don't explain them clearly enough, but I can say that I was very conscious of it at the time, and I do think it is more evident in my more concrete explanations than you note. In fact, I have had past correspondence with some dialectical sociologists about the model's use of dialectics, which was quite uncommon at the time in management literature. I also think it is the dialectics that added the power struggle reality and made the article so successful in managerial reaction.

[But in agreement with you] I would say my model is a reasonably explicit (for an applied business magazine) attempt to combine unitary life cycle with dialectical theories—but not teleological. For me, life cycle explains the 'form' of the unitary stages, while the dialectics explain the underlying dynamics of movement. For example, I put the 'crises' in the model because I could not find data showing the stages as naturally and automatically evolving one after the other. Thus, it is not a model where a future life or end state is assured—(there are even divergent paths which are not really discussed in the article, such as failing to solve a crisis or dying if the crisis continues). My reason for saying it is not teleological is that there is no envisioned end state that pulls the process—for me it is the current dynamics within the organization that are driving it forward—convergence around the thesis of each stage and then running into resistance (antithesis) and requiring reorientation for the conflict to be resolved. The model in fact has no ending and concludes with a question mark.

Substantive Event Categories
Creativity (business idea)   ------------------------

Leadership (founder-manager   ------------------------
transitions)

Professional management   ------------------------
direction

Autonomy demands by   ------------------------
employees

Delegation of responsibilities   ------------------------

Control attempts by top man-   ------------------------
agement

Coordination of decentralized   ------------------------
units

Red tape (resistances to   ------------------------
bureaucracy)

Collaboration (team-building   ------------------------
practices

*Occurrence of Events
over Time*

Figure 7.3. Research design for studying Greiner's model of organizational growth

Source: Van de Ven, A. H. (1992). 'Suggestions for Studying Strategy Process: A research Note,' *Strategic Management Journal*, 13: 185.

revolutionary crises identified within the stages into nine conceptual tracks or categories of events,[4] and shifts time from a vertical to horizontal axis. In so doing, one can not only gain a richer appreciation of how events pertaining to organizational evolution and revolution unfold over time, but also how the multiple tracks of event categories are related and thereby facilitate and constrain the overall process of organizational growth.

Guided by this research design, one could undertake longitudinal study of a number of organizations from birth to maturity. One would gather data on the chronological sequence of activities or events that occurred in the development of each organization. The observed activities could then be coded along the nine event tracks or categories outlined in Figure 7.3. For example, the creativity track would not only include the occurrence of the initial business idea on which the organization was founded, it would also record all events that occurred to further invent, develop, and adapt the business idea (or strategy) of the organization. So also, the delegation track would include all events related to the decentralization of responsibilities, the establishment of

[4] Van de Ven: A careful examination of the conceptual overlap between the nine substantive event categories in Greiner's model would prune the set to a smaller and more manageable number of tracks. However, we will not undertake this needed theory building task in this example.

profit centers and bonuses, top management restraints to managing by exception, and similar indicators of delegation activities described by Greiner (1972: 170–1). Clearly, events pertaining to each substantive event track listed in Figure 7.3 can occur repeatedly during the life of an organization, and often in no necessary temporal order. Recording events along these different substantive categories or tracks (rather than a single track as has been done in the past) greatly liberates one from the erroneous and confining assumption that the life cycle of an organization proceeds in a simple unitary sequence of stages.

Event sequence analysis could begin after the field observations have concluded and events were coded along the conceptual tracks. This analysis would consist of identifying the order and sequence of events for each organization, and then comparing the observed sequence with the proposed sequence of events in Greiner's model. A strong test of Greiner's model would require that all[5] events pertaining to creativity and leadership occur first, direction and autonomy second, delegation and control third, coordination and red tape fourth, and collaboration and revitalization last.

I doubt if empirical evidence from such a study will substantiate Greiner's model of organizational growth because no empirical support has been found for a unitary sequence of stages in other studies of innovation development (see Van de Ven et al. 2000). However, this conclusion is premature because (as stated before) very few longitudinal studies have examined the development of strategic change processes in general, and to my knowledge, no studies have specifically examined organizational growth as a developmental sequence of events along the lines suggested here.[6]

Finally, it is noteworthy that a high level of mutual respect and trust is necessary for engaged scholars to have constructive critical dialogue as this example indicates. Greiner aptly concluded our dialogue with the following comments.

---

[5] Greiner: My only concern here is with your use of the word 'all'—at least I would not argue for 'all,' though I would argue that the 'bulk' of events or the 'median' should occur during these time periods. While the HBR article draws a graphic line at the beginning and end of each stage in its pictorial portrayal to the reader, I have always said that there is bound to be 'slop over' between stages—for example, 'autonomy' concerns don't suddenly die away with initial attempts at 'delegation.'

[6] Greiner: My sample was small, mostly secondary data, and limited largely to industrial/consumer goods companies. So there is a need for a larger more systematic study—and it's interesting that none has been conducted over all these years on my model or any others for that matter. Such a study might go beyond determining if in fact there is the linear order of stages and crises to find out: Are there different growth stages for different industries? Do companies that fail to grow pursue a different order of stages, or do they fail to resolve certain crises?

Future studies don't necessarily have to measure every aspect of every hypothesized stage to begin to check out the model. For example, each stage contains a clear statement about formal organization structure, which is usually public information. So just a pass at this issue would tell us a lot. Other data for other aspects may be harder to come by because they are 'internal' to the companies.

Probably some of this you were unaware of because I could not explicitly discuss it in the article. I don't think my suggestions change your basic points and hopefully they add a little more clarification. . . . Messing with another person's piece of art is always a little tricky. But I hope you know my intentions are good, as I know yours are too.

I suppose you now may be wondering why I never did all of this—and I don't know, though I did get back to it with the professional service firm research this past year. . . . I think if I had read your piece, I might have had some guidance. It's interesting how undeveloped this area of research is. (Greiner, personal communication)

Concluding Comments

Research design invariably requires the exercise of what Aristotle termed 'practical wisdom.' There is no definitive best design for a given project, and any design requires giving up some data in order to focus on others. I outlined a number of methods for moving from data on observed incidents to a process model that does not betray the richness, dynamism, or complexity of a process theory or story. I also presented an example of designing a process model to empirically examine Greiner's (1972) model of the stages of organizational growth. This example and my interchange with Larry Greiner (representing views of the process theorist and modeler) shows that many strategies are possible in designing a process study. Each strategy reduces some aspect of complexity by focusing on some anchor point for guiding the analysis.

Langley discusses the strengths and weaknesses of alternative methods based on Thorngate's (1976) and Weick's (1979) tradeoffs between the *accuracy, generality,* and *simplicity* of any theory.

Some strategies tend to stick closely to the original data, whereas others permit greater abstraction. Close data fitting reflects what Weick (1979) calls 'accuracy.' However, accuracy may act against generality—another desirable quality related to the potential range of situations to which the theory may be applicable. Finally, simplicity concerns the number of elements and/or relationships in a theory. It affects the theory's aesthetic qualities. Simple theories with good explanatory power may actually be preferred to complex ones that explain a little more; as Daft (1983) suggests, good research is more like a poem than a novel. (Langley 1999: 694–5)

Fortunately, the methods discussed in this chapter are not mutually exclusive. They complement each other. Each method can provide useful information for deciding how and what other methods to use in the next step in the analysis. In this sense, the methods serve as building blocks for developing process theories. My experience has been to use all the strategies for analyzing various aspects and questions in the course of designing and analyzing field data on processes of organizational change. In practice my objective is to combine the information that quantitative and qualitative approaches provide for understanding organizational change processes. By themselves quantitative data provide a skeletal configuration of structural regularities, often devoid of life, flesh, and soul. Qualitative data, by themselves, are like an amoeba, rich with life but absent apparent structure. Only by combining quantitative and qualitative data in a balanced way do we come to understand the richness of life in its varied regularities.

Finally, process questions of how things change and develop over time necessarily require longitudinal data. Junior faculty and doctoral students often express concerns about the amounts of time, resources, and contacts needed to conduct longitudinal process studies. These concerns are genuine, but often reflect the mindset of a researcher attempting to go it alone in conducting a study. In keeping with the central theme of engaged scholarship, I advise researchers to seek out and collaborate with other scholars (typically senior colleagues) who have been engaged in studying a process question for some time, who have established trusting relationships with other scholars and practitioners, and who often welcome co-investigators to join and share in the collective achievement of conducting a longitudinal process study.

As discussed in this chapter (issue 5 on observation method in Table 7.1), longitudinal data can be obtained either by conducting a real-time field study of a change process as it unfolds or by obtaining historical archival data that are publicly available or that might be accessible by joining other researchers who collected such data. Collecting primary data involves more work and time than obtaining secondary data because the former requires building relationships with people in field sites, negotiating access, and collecting and tabulating longitudinal data as a change process unfolds. It often takes several years of repeated meetings with practitioners and stakeholders to develop trustworthy ties and to formulate research questions that both academics and practitioners judge worthy of longitudinal research. In addition, collecting longitudinal real-time data is a labor-intensive commitment for an extended period of time. Instead of trying to go it alone, I recommend that researchers (particularly those launching their careers) collaborate with and learn from experienced researchers engaged in an on-going longitudinal process study.

These data collection tasks are already completed when examining secondary data. However, gaining access to archival data and figuring out how the data were collected, how they might be interpreted, and how they might be coded to examine process questions of interest represent challenging tasks. These tasks require careful study and communications with the experts who created and maintain the secondary data files. Fortunately, as Greiner notes, researchers don't necessarily need to measure every aspect of a process model or question being investigated. A preliminary pass at analyzing archival information (often publicly available) may tell us a lot about the process being studied.

In short, whether the longitudinal process data are obtained from primary or secondary sources, I advise researchers not to go it alone; instead, engage and collaborate with other scholars (typically senior colleagues) who are conducting process studies or have access to longitudinal process data.

8 Communicating and Using Research Knowledge

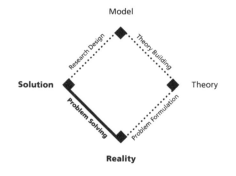

Knowledge for whom? Action for what?

(Suchman 1971)

Many suppliers and users of social research are dissatisfied, the former because they are not listened to, the latter because they do not hear much they want to listen to.

(Lindblom and Cohen 1979: 1)

The problem formulation, theory building, and research design activities discussed in previous chapters set the stage for problem solving in the engaged scholarship model, as shown in Figure 8.1. Problem solving entails a variety of activities undertaken to communicate and apply research findings with an audience. Presumably these findings provide empirical answers to the research questions about the problems that motivated the research. Let us also assume that these study findings meet the dual hurdles of relevance and rigor and have the potential to advance knowledge for science and practice. The question addressed in this chapter is how might these research findings be communicated to and used by intended scientific and professional communities in order to achieve this potential?

Researchers typically respond to this question by writing a report of the research findings including a brief discussion of their implications for theory and practice. Many researchers consider their communication task completed when they publish their report in a scientific journal and make verbal

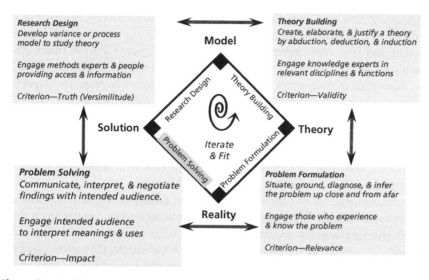

Figure 8.1. Problem solving in engaged scholarship model

presentations of it at professional conferences as well as to host organizations and practitioners who sponsored the research.

This response assumes that communicating research findings entails a one-way transfer of knowledge and information from the researcher to an audience.

According to this perspective, a researcher who communicates 'effectively' is transferring ideas to listeners with minimal spillage (Eisenberg and Phillips 1991). Words contain information, language transfers thoughts and feelings, and listeners extract ideas from transmission (Axley 1984). [This view] evokes an image of communication as easy, effortless, and linear. Miscommunication occurs when no information is received or when the information received is not what the sender intended. According to this view, receivers are typically passive and reactive. (Putnam et al. 1996: 379–80)

The underlying assumption of this view is that if an idea is good enough, it will be used. But there is considerable evidence that research knowledge based on sound empirical evidence is often not used or adopted as intended by either scientists or practitioners. In this chapter I argue that a deeper understanding of communicating knowledge across boundaries and a more engaged relationship between the researcher and his/her audience are needed if research findings are to have an impact in advancing science and practice.

IMPACT OF SOCIAL RESEARCH ON SCIENCE AND PRACTICE

One indicator of the impact and use of published research by the scientific community is the number of times this research is cited by authors in their subsequent articles. Given the need to frame and build current research in the context of past scholarly effort, citations indicate the relationship between current and past scholarship. Using the Social Sciences Citation Index (ISI), Starbuck (2005) conducted a citation count of articles published in American and European management journals. He found that on average the papers in these management journals were cited only .82 times per article per year. Articles in American journals tend to get more citations than foreign journals, especially those not in the English language. My overall conclusion from these data is that papers published in these journals are not cited or used sufficiently to advance subsequent science. A published article is of little significance to science unless other scientists cite it and build on it.

Counting citations overlooks the important question of how prior scholarship is used. Golden-Biddle et al. (2002) examined knowledge use from three award-winning articles occurring over a six-year period in 489 subsequent citations. By analyzing the citation record per focal article, they questioned the prevailing view that knowledge claims remain the same in their movement from the original article to subsequent users. They found the nature and use of knowledge changes dramatically as it is adopted and appropriated. Users selectively interpret and use knowledge as it serves their own purposes, fits their unique situations, and reflects their relations with their practicing community. They conclude that

Selectivity is an overriding feature of how we use knowledge, with the consequence that it is, perhaps necessarily, broken apart in use. Selective use of knowledge claims is an inevitable, frequent, and faithful way of using prior knowledge. But, rather than construing these results as problematic departures from a norm of citing, we suggest they foreground the craft of our knowledge-making.... This study calls on us scholars to become more reflexive and knowledgeable about our use of prior work and the disciplinary craft of knowledge-making. The task is not to become more comprehensive or homogeneous in using knowledge claims from prior work, but rather to pay attention to how we produce work, including selecting and materializing prior knowledge claims. (Golden-Biddle et al. 2002: 30–1)

What about the use of scientific research by practitioners? Studies show that practitioners often fail to adopt the findings of research in fields such as medicine (Denis and Langley 2002; Dopson 2005), human resources (Anderson et al. 2001; Rynes et al. 2002), social work (Small and Uttal 2005), and management (Tranfield et al. 2003; Rousseau 2006). One reason for this is that managers typically do not know the evidence. Rynes et al. (2002) report that less than 1 percent of human resource managers read the academic literature regularly, and Rousseau (2006: 261) observes that consultants who advise them are unlikely to do so either. A common explanation is that scientific knowledge is not put in a form that can be readily applied in contexts of practice. Dopson (2005) points out that while both researchers and practitioners concede that evidence-based practice is a good idea, there is a knowledge boundary between researchers and practitioners. For example, researchers ask the relatively detached question: 'What do the data mean?' In contrast, practitioners ask the relatively involved question: 'What do the data mean for me?' They each view the questions in terms of their occupational interests and their self-image as people doing a good and worthwhile job.

Action scientists such as Argyris and Schon (1996) focus on the behaviors of researchers to explain this lack of implementation of research knowledge. They argue that scientific knowledge will be implemented only if researchers, consultants, and practitioners jointly engage in interpreting and implementing study findings (Whyte 1984; Schein 1987). Academic researchers are criticized for having paid little attention to transferring the knowledge they produce (Beyer and Trice 1982; Lawler et al. 1985). Beer (2001), for example, recommends that researchers take responsibility for specifying how the knowledge that they produce should be implemented. He also discusses how customary knowledge transfer practices often inhibit implementation of proposed solutions, such as the use of authoritarian or coercive styles of imparting knowledge, defensiveness routines by teachers and researchers, and self-interested recommendations by consultants that maintain or increase clients' dependence on consulting services.

Mohrman et al. (2001) empirically examined the perceived usefulness of research by practitioners in a context where researchers were not playing an action-oriented interventionist role. They found that practitioners in ten companies undergoing change viewed research results as useful when they were jointly interpreted with researchers and when practitioners had opportunities to self-design actions based on the research findings. Mohrman et al. (2001: 369) conclude that 'perceived usefulness requires far more than simply doing research in relevant areas.' Moreover, 'it would seem that researchers must do more than work collaboratively with organizational members to understand research findings. Perhaps they must become part of an organization's self-design activities if they wish to promote usefulness' (p. 370).

As these observations and studies suggest, it is one thing to write a research paper, and quite another to transfer, interpret, and implement study findings at the communication boundaries of both scientific and practitioner communities. Estabrooks (1999: 15) points out that 'Many factors get in the way of using research, and empirically, we know very little about what makes research use happen or not happen.' Recently, scholars have begun to reconceptualize knowledge transfer as a learning process in which new knowledge is shaped by the learner's pre-existing knowledge and experience. Individuals are not simply sponges, soaking up new information without filtering or processing. 'Knowledge use is a complex change process in which "getting the research out there" is only the first step' (Nutley et al. 2003: 132). Neither scientists nor practitioners simply apply scientific research; they collaborate in discussions and engage in practices that actively interpret its value to accomplish their tasks.

There is no such thing as 'the' body of evidence: evidence is a contested domain and is in a constant state of 'becoming.' Thus, research is rarely self-evident but varies according to the context in which it is received and deployed. Successful implementation then involves a focus on local ideas, practices and attitudes, and this suggests that the key is to engage the interests and involvement of [potential users— both scientists and practitioners of social research]. (Nutley et al. 2003: 133–4)

Before introducing a framework and method for engaging scientists and practitioners in interpreting and learning from research findings, it is important to clarify that social research is undertaken for many purposes. Different criteria of relevance and use are therefore necessary for communicating and applying research findings.

RELEVANCE

Users of both scientific and practical knowledge demand that it meet the dual hurdles of being relevant and rigorous in serving their particular domains and interests (Pettigrew 2001). However, different criteria of relevance and rigor apply to knowledge for science and practice because their purposes, processes, and contexts are different. As discussed in Chapter 9, these different research purposes may be to describe, explain, design, or intervene in a problematic situation. The pragmatic relevance of each form of knowledge should be judged in terms of how well it addresses the problematic situation or issue for which it was intended (Dewey 1938).

Management scholars debate these and other criteria of relevance. As Brief and Dukerich (1991) discuss, the debate often turns on whether the usefulness of knowledge to managers and organizational practitioners should focus on control and intervention (contain actionable knowledge that prescribes what to do to resolve a problem), or if it should include more broadly other criteria (knowledge that describes or explains a phenomenon, and thereby provides a model for viewing and understanding 'what *may* be, and not to predict firmly what *will* be') (Brief and Dukerich 1991: 328). Argyris and Schon (1996), Beer (2001), Starkey and Madan (2001), and Cummings and Jones (2004) argue that if knowledge is to be useful to managers, it must be actionable. March (2000), Grey (2001), Kilduff and Kelemen (2001), Weick (2001), among others caution against restricting useful knowledge to this control criterion because it is far too narrow, instrumental, and may lead to focusing on shallow and short-sighted questions of performance improvement instead of addressing larger questions and fundamental issues.

The above criteria of relevant knowledge are not mutually exclusive. Indeed, Baldridge et al. (2004) empirically found a positive relationship between the academic quality (number of citations) and practical relevance (judged by a panel of executives, consultants, and human resource professionals) of a sample of 120 articles published in top academic management journals. However, they caution that the relatively low correlation (r = .20) leaves significant room for cases where judgments diverge or there is no relationship at all (Baldridge et al. 2004: 1071).

The relationship between academic quality and practical relevance often evolves over time. Thompson (1956: 110) warned against the pressure for immediately applicable research results because '[it] leads to the formulation of common-sense hypotheses framed at low levels of abstraction, without regard for general theory... and thereby reduces the ultimate contributions of the research to administrative science. Moreover, [it] often leads to the application of ideas whose unintended and unrecognized costs may be greater than their positive contributions.'

Managing Knowledge Boundaries

Recent literature on knowledge management provides important advances for thinking about how researchers might communicate their study findings at the knowledge boundaries with different audiences or communities. These communities may consist of people in different specialized domains, such as occupational and disciplinary specialties. I focus on the boundary between academic researchers and practicing managers as applied to our problem of communicating research findings to intended audiences. But the framework discussed below applies equally well to communicating across other knowledge boundaries, such as between authors and editors, teachers and students, consultants and clients, and people from different disciplines or functions.

Communication among people requires common knowledge of the syntax (structure), semantics (meaning), and pragmatics (use) of language in order to understand each other's domain-specific knowledge. In linguistics, syntax, semantics, and pragmatics represent a hierarchy of communication difficulties. At the most basic and general level is syntax, which is the grammatical structure of sequence, order and arrangement of words and phrases into sentences of a language. At the next interpretive level is semantics, or the meanings that are expressed with the pattern of words and sentences. Finally, at the most specific and personal level is pragmatics where actors apply their meanings of communication to practical uses in particular circumstances and contexts. Semantic interpretation implies syntactical understanding, and pragmatic uses imply syntactical and semantic understandings among communicating parties.

Carlile (2004) proposes that increases in the difference, dependence, and novelty of domain-specific knowledge between people creates progressively complex boundaries of conveying syntactic, semantic, and pragmatic understandings of communications between the actors. These more complex boundaries, in turn, require three progressively more complex processes of knowledge transfer, translation, and transformation. This section explains Carlile's propostion, and subsequent sections of this chapter apply it to the problem of researchers communicating and applying their study findings for science and practice.

According to Carlile (2004), the difference, dependence, and novelty of domain-specific knowledge among people at a boundary determine the complexity of communicating across that boundary.

- *Difference* refers to unique amounts of knowledge (e.g., as between novices and experts) and types of specialized domain-specific knowledge of people at a knowledge boundary. If there is no difference in domain-specific knowledge among people, there is no communication boundary. But as difference in the domain-specific knowledge increases among people, the effort required to share and assess each other's knowledge increases.
- *Dependence* is the degree to which people across boundaries perceive they must take each other's views into account if they are to meet their goals, such as that of co-authors of a paper, teachers and students, consultants and clients, and speakers and listeners. Without dependence, difference is of no consequence. The coordination of dependence among people at a boundary requires a capacity to develop an adequate common knowledge as resources and tasks change. The greater the interdependence, the greater the coordination required through more intensive and rich communications.
- *Novelty* refers to either a lack of common knowledge due to different cultures and contexts of people at a boundary, or to new domain-specific knowledge as might be represented in conveying novel research findings. When novelty arises there is often a lack of common knowledge to adequately share and assess domain-specific knowledge. As novelty increases the vector spreads, increasing the complexity and amount of effort required to share and access knowledge.

Carlile (2004) uses an inverted triangle as illustrated in Figure 8.2 to portray how increases in the difference, dependence, and novelty of knowledge among people at a boundary create syntactic, semantic, and pragmatic communication difficulties, and hence contribute to progressively more complex forms of communication across boundaries.

When a common syntax and lexicon sufficiently specifies the differences and dependences among people at a boundary, the boundary proves 'unproblematic,' and knowledge can be transferred using a conventional information processing view.

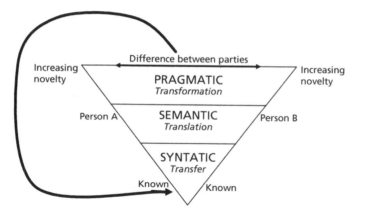

Figure 8.2. Carlile's framework for managing knowledge across boundaries

Source: Adapted from Carlile (2004). 'Integrative Framework for Managing Knowledge Across Boundaries,' *Organization Science*, 15(5): 555–68.

Simply transferring knowledge, however, proves problematic when novelty arises because the current lexicon is no longer sufficient to represent the differences and dependencies now present. The limitation of an information-processing approach occurs because the processing of a common lexicon is assumed to be always a sufficient common knowledge. So while a common lexicon is always necessary, it is not always a sufficient type of common knowledge to share and assess domain-specific knowledge. (Carlile 2004: 558)

The transition from a syntactic to a semantic boundary occurs when novelty makes some differences and dependencies unclear or some meaning ambiguous. When interpretive differences exist in the meanings of research findings or implications, communication requires an interpretive approach (translation) that emphasizes the importance of common meaning to share knowledge between actors. 'Researchers who adopt an interpretive approach recognize how different domains (i.e., thought worlds) naturally generate interpretive differences and so emphasize processes that help create "shared meanings" (Dougherty 1992) or mechanisms "to reconcile discrepancies in meaning" (Nonaka and Takeuchi 1995: 67)' (Carlile 2004: 558).

The transition from a semantic to a pragmatic boundary arises when interactions surface different interests among actors. When people have different interests, they are no longer indifferent to their dependencies on one another. In these situations both domain-specific and common knowledge may need to be transformed to share and assess knowledge at the boundary. The pragmatic boundary emphasizes that knowledge is power, and is 'at stake' for those actors who have developed it (Carlile 2002).

When interests are in conflict, the knowledge developed in one domain generates negative consequences in another. Here the costs for any actor are not just the costs of learning about what is new, but also the costs of transforming 'current' knowledge being used (i.e., common and domain-specific knowledge). These costs negatively impact the willingness of an actor to make such changes. (Carlile 2004: 559)

Carlile importantly points out that managing knowledge at a pragmatic boundary typically requires multiple iterations (as represented by the arrow in Figure 8.2). Through numerous engagements in communicating at the boundary, people get better at developing an adequate common knowledge for sharing and assessing each other's knowledge. As discussed in previous chapters, the engaged scholarship (ES) model calls upon researchers to communicate at the boundary with key stakeholders in problem formulation, theory building, research design, and problem solving. As researchers communicate with stakeholders at each stage of the ES research process, 'they get better at identifying what differences and dependencies are of consequence at the boundary; they improve at collectively developing more adequate common lexicon, meaning, and interests. Through this iterative capacity the invested and path-dependent nature of knowledge can be transformed' (Carlile 2004: 563).

Table 8.1 provides a summary of Carlile's (2004) framework for communicating knowledge across boundaries. He notes that the transition between boundaries is not often easily identified by the people involved. In addition, he views the relationship among the boundaries in Figure 8.2 as a progressively

Table 8.1. Comparison of approaches to communicating knowledge across boundaries

	Knowledge transfer across syntactic boundary	Knowledge translation across semantic boundary	Knowledge transformation across pragmatic, political boundary
Circumstances	Differences and dependencies between actors are known.	Novelty generates different meanings and interpretations.	Novelty generates conflicting interests between actors that impede their ability to communicate knowledge.
Communication	Information processing transferring knowledge from speaker to listeners.	Interpersonal conversations & discourse to interpret and translate new meanings of the text.	Negotiation & heedful accommodation to transform interests or to arbitrage pluralistic interests.
Reasons	Common lexicon and syntax are necessary but not always sufficient to share and assess knowledge across a boundary.	Common understandings of information often require creating new meanings.	Knowledge is power that is 'at stake' when communicated across boundaries. Actors protect/defend their interests when their 'rights' to domain-specific knowledge are threatened.

Source: Adapted from Carlile (2004). 'Integrative Framework for Managing Knowledge Across Boundaries,' *Organization Science*, 15(5): 555–68.

more complex hierarchy. That is, communicating at more complex boundaries still requires the capacities below them. For example, knowledge translation assumes knowledge transfer, and knowledge transformation also requires knowledge transfer and translation processes. I now discuss these boundaries of knowledge transfer, translation, and transformation in greater detail as they apply to the communication of research findings.

KNOWLEDGE TRANSFER

Crossing the theory-practice boundary is typically formulated as a knowledge transfer process where communication is viewed from an information processing perspective, such as when researchers transfer (i.e., send, exchange, relay, and convey) research findings to an audience, typically through written reports or spoken presentations. Carlile (2004) notes that knowledge transfer is an adequate form of communication when the sender and receiver have a common syntax for sharing differences and dependencies in domain-specific knowledge. The major challenge of knowledge transfer is using a communication medium that is capable of transmitting the richness of the information to be conveyed (Daft and Lengel 1984). Some forms and channels of communication do not adequately convey the richness of the message, and hence, receivers obtain simplified, reduced, or filtered portions of the message. As a consequence, receivers may not perceive the message as worthy of consideration or adoption.

Research on the adoption and diffusion of innovations provides useful guidelines for knowledge transfer. An innovation is typically defined as the development and implementation of new ideas, and research findings are innovations when they are perceived by potential adopters to represent new ideas for theory and practice. Rogers (2003) distills the findings of over 4000 studies demonstrating that the adoption of innovations (i.e., new ideas) depends not only on the actors involved but also on the characteristics of the specific innovation in question and on the social context within which the innovation is communicated. The following three propositions summarize much of this research as it applies to the communication of research findings.

First, *research findings are more likely to be adopted and diffused when they are perceived as having a relative advantage over the status quo, are compatible with current understandings of things, are simple to understand, and are explicit, observable, and can be tried out.* As this proposition suggests, researchers can directly influence the potential adoption of research findings by how they craft their reports. Stated in the negative, research findings are NOT likely to be adopted when the report provides no evidence or discussion of: (1) the relative advantage of the findings in comparison with existing or plausible alternative theories or practices; (2) how the findings fit and are compatible with existing knowledge and theories relevant to the findings; (3) what the findings mean in simple and commonly understood language; and (4) explicit ways and examples of how the findings can be applied and implemented in specific contexts and situations.

Second, *research reports are more likely to be adopted when they engage and reflect the views of leading members of the adopting community.* Involving stakeholders (here viewed as potential adopters) in each stage of the engaged scholarship process not only increases the likelihood of incorporating their perspectives but also their voices in research findings. When it is time to communicate research findings, these stakeholders often become 'opinion leaders' (Rogers 2003) who can provide credible information and advice about the research findings to others in their communities. As 'boundary spanners' (people with ties across boundaries that divide their colleagues) they often play an ambassadorial role to other groups, representing the research findings to possible users. Of course, opinion leaders may not be able to overturn a negative reception to study findings, particularly when the report does not accomplish the first proposition. But they can add or subtract momentum to, and can sometimes modify the adoption and diffusion trajectory of research findings.

Adler and Kwon (2005) discuss how social similarity facilitates trust, and thus communication, since socially similar actors are more likely to speak the same language and share the same knowledge and assumptions. People generally will be more receptive to new ideas generated and used by members of their own community than they are to ideas from other communities. Institutional theory highlights this factor in its discussion of mimetic isomorphism (Dimaggio and Powell 1983). Imitation is more likely among actors who already see themselves as similar. Burt (1987) argues that similarity may also be a function of a structurally similar network location rather than direct interaction. These factors all contribute to the bandwagon effects observed in the diffusion of innovations (Abrahmson and Rosenkopf 1993).

The two propositions just presented suggest that adoption and diffusion of research is driven by the intrinsic merits of the research findings (proposition 1) and the characteristics of potential adopters (proposition 2). While important, they underemphasize the role of rhetoric in the diffusion process. Actors are seen as adopting new innovative ideas when they *believe* that they are effective (Strang and Macy 2000). A rhetorical view asserts that these beliefs do not emerge within a social vacuum; they are rhetorically shaped and promoted by speakers and listeners (Green 2004). The next proposition reflects this rhetorical view.

Third, *research reports are more likely to be adopted by a specific audience when they are presented in an argument that is rhetorically persuasive.* What makes information convincing and, therefore, utilized is a rhetorical question (Van de Ven and Schomaker 2002). Rhetoric is the use of persuasion to influence the thought and conduct of one's listeners. To Aristotle, the art of persuasion comprises three elements: (1) *logos*—the message, especially its internal consistency (i.e., the clarity of the argument, the logic of its reasons, and the effectiveness of its supporting evidence); (2) *pathos*—the power to stir the emotions, beliefs, values, knowledge, and imagination of the audience so as to elicit not only sympathy, but empathy as well; and (3) *ethos*—the credibility, legitimacy, and authority that a speaker both brings into and develops over the course of the argument or message (Barnes 1995). As Figure 8.3 illustrates, logos, pathos, and ethos are the elements of the rhetorical triangle. Combined, they shape the persuasiveness of any communication.

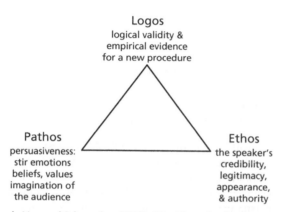

Source: Van de Ven and Schomaker (2002). 'The Rhetoric of Evidence-Based Medicine,' *Healthcare Management Review*.

Argument reflecting logos, pathos, ethos:

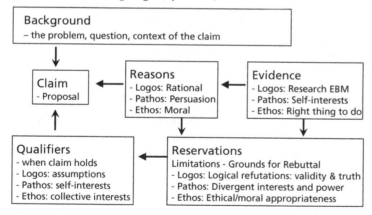

Sources: Toulmin, S. (2003). *The Uses of Argument*, updated edn. Cambridge: Cambridge University Press. Green, A. (2004). 'Rhetorical Theory of Diffusion', *Academy of Management Review*.

Figure 8.3. The rhetorical triangle

Persuasiveness is in the 'eyes' of the listener (not just the speaker) and requires appreciating the context and assumptions of the audience or listeners. For example, Davis (1971, 1986) argues that what influences readers to view a theory as interesting or classical is the degree to which the writer challenges the assumptions of the reader. In a nutshell, a classic work speaks to the primary concerns or assumptions of an audience while an interesting theory speaks to the secondary concerns of an audience. Interesting theories negate an accepted assumption held by the audience and affirm an unanticipated alternative. Therefore, knowledge transfer is not only a function of the logic and data supporting a message, but also the degree to which the speaker is viewed as a credible witness and is able to stir the human emotions of listeners.

Hence, from a rhetorical perspective a researcher can increase the likelihood of influencing his/her intended audience with pathos, logos, and ethos justifications of research findings when crafting a research report. The elements of a rhetorical argument reflecting logos, pathos, and ethos are illustrated at the bottom of Figure 8.3.

Green (2004) explains how pathos, logos, and ethos justifications shape the rationality underlying both the adoption and rejection of research findings.

Pathos appeals connect with the emotions of individuals (e.g., fear, greed, etc.) They are highly passionate appeals to an audience's self-interest that build and construct pragmatic legitimacy.... Emotional appeals have the ability to grab an actor's limited attention, excite the imagination, and direct behavior away from the status quo. Although initially persuasive, emotional appeals are unable to sustain the limited attention of actors. Thus, practices associated with emotional appeals have transient persuasive power that may exhibit fadlike tendencies. (Green 2004: 659)

Logos pleas justify action by appealing to the desire for efficient/effective action and, like pathos, help build pragmatic legitimacy. Whereas pathos appeals are capable of eliciting strong initial reactions, logos justifications are slower at getting actors' attention, because they often require methodical calculation of means and ends. Initially, the call for efficiency/effectiveness is less powerful than a pathos appeal (like fear). However, whereas passionate pleas tend to dissipate quickly, appeals to logic are able to sustain their persuasiveness. (Green 2004: 660)

Ethos appeals justify action by appealing to socially accepted norms and mores. They produce moral legitimacy that rests not on judgments about whether a given activity benefits the evaluator, but rather on judgments about whether the activity is the 'right thing to do.' Ethos appeals are probably the most powerful, with the most enduring impact on taken-for-grantedness. Whereas pathos and logos justifications emphasize individual concerns and interests, ethos appeals focus on social and collective interests. Ethos appeals may have a slower persuasive effect because they typically require more complex cognitive processing than direct appeals to individual interests and because they require the sacrifice of individual interests for social interests. (Green 2004: 660)

Green discusses how appeals to pathos, logos, and ethos may be combined to shape the adoption and diffusion of a message. He proposes that '*a rhetorical sequence that starts with pathos, moves to logos, and ends with ethos will have a rapid rate of initial adoption, a broad diffusion, and a slow abandonment*' (Green 2004: 661). In other words, over the life cycle of a diffusing practice, Green suggests a temporal sequence of messages that emphasize different elements of the rhetorical triangle. 'Whereas pathos may initiate change, logos implement it, and ethos sustain it, each type of appeal may fit with specific periods in the life cycle of a highly diffused practice' (Green 2004: 651). When writing a given report, this temporal sequence could be compressed into the beginning, middle, and end of a report. The introduction would begin with pathos to grab a reader's attention, the body of the paper would elaborate the logos of the message, and a conclusion section would highlight the ethos of the message.

KNOWLEDGE INTERPRETATION AND TRANSLATION

A knowledge transfer metaphor, even when communicated in the richness of a rhetorical triangle typically remains a one-way transmission of information from a sender to a receiver. Although application of Green's rhetorical theory emphasizes the importance of anticipating the needs and assumptions of the audience, the process remains centered on how a speaker conveys his/her message to a listener. The listener's role in knowledge transfer remains relatively silent. But it is never inactive. What happens when the listener does not understand or interpret the study findings as presented by the researcher? How is a listener to apply statistical research findings to a specific individual situation? What if the listener is interested in a different question than the one addressed in a research report? Typically, authors of research reports will not know of these reactions unless they engage in conversations with readers or listeners of a report. As these questions suggest, a research report often represents a first—not a last—step for scholars to engage in conversations with potential users, and thereby gain a broader and deeper appreciation of the meanings of research findings.

In Carlile's (2004) framework, the transition from a syntactic transfer to a semantic translation boundary occurs when novel information from either a speaker or listener makes some differences and dependencies among the speaker and listener unclear or some meanings ambiguous. When interpretive differences of the meanings of research findings or implications exist, communication requires an interpretive approach (translation). This necessitates conversations or discourse to share knowledge between actors. Here, discourse is defined as talking, dialogue, or conversation among researchers and practitioners about study findings. Discourse is needed to create shared meanings as a way to address the interpretive differences among actors (Carlile 2004).

The key features that distinguish knowledge transfer from translation are conversations, sensemaking, and collaboration between the producers and users of research knowledge. Putnam et al. (1996) and Huff (2002) use a conversation metaphor to describe knowledge translation. In the conversation metaphor, *social discourse and interpretation* become the focal processes of communication. Communication consists of interconnected exchanges, for example, message-feedback-response, action-reaction-adjustment, symbolic action-interpretation-reflection, and action-sensemaking (Putnam et al. 1996: 384). Weick's (1979) model of communication as a double interact serves as a useful basic building block of communication and organizing. A double interact between two actors consists of an action-reaction-adjustment, which forms interlocked cycles of interaction for interpreting many plausible meanings of a message.

A variation of Weick's model (which focuses on individuals' cognitive experiences) is a co-production process among speakers and an audience in which communication arises collectively. Through collaboration the participants produce common meanings and coordinate local agreements (Putnam et al. 1996: 385). Meaning surfaces through retrospective sensemaking, co-constructing interpretations, and collaborative storytelling.

Speakers and listeners serve as co-authors who simultaneously construct and make sense of their interactions. Conversations are both the essence and the product of research. In many ways, conversations lay the groundwork for engaging scientific and practitioner communities. Putnam et al. (1996: 393) point out that participants who engage in dialogue suspend defensive exchange, share and learn from experiences, foster deeper inquiry, and resist synthesis or compromise. A research report is not treated as a social fact or as having a 'fixed' meaning. Rather texts are open to multiple and unlimited meanings, interpretations, and action among participants (speakers and listeners) engaged in a text.

Engaging in a conversation or discourse with an audience often requires researchers to take a hermeneutic 'participant view' rather than a 'God's Eye view' of research findings. As discussed in Chapter 2, a 'God's Eye view' portrays a researcher as being the expert authority in presenting research findings that are unambiguously true. In western cultures this often has a mind-closing effect that reinforces dogmatic argumentation and promotes conflict and intolerance (Hendrickx 1999: 341). In contrast, when a scholar reasons in a participant frame of reference, he/she is a participant engaged in a discourse with others about ways to interpret, understand and use the research findings. 'The participant frame of reference does not classify readers and writers as a function of whether they know less or more; rather it implies that they know something different' (Hendrickx 1999: 347).

It is important to recognize, however, that these hermeneutic views may be bound by culture. The extent to which a researcher adopts a participant or God's Eye view depends, in part, on the cultures of people at the communication boundary. Two of Hofstede's (1980) dimensions of national culture—*individualistic vs. collectivistic* and *power distance*—explain significant differences in communication protocols (Lincoln et al. 1986). In a highly individualistic society, there are weak connections among individuals, the self-concept is defined in terms of individual traits, and personal identity is derived from individual achievement. In contrast, in collectivistic societies, there tend to be strong connections among people, self-concept is defined with reference to a societal and cultural context, and personal identity is derived through the in-group and its successes (Gibson and Zellmer-Bruhn 2001). Power distance is the degree to which members of a culture accept and expect that power in society is unequally distributed (Hofstede 1980). These two dimensions have been shown to have a positive correlation, and to reflect the dominant cultural profiles around the world (Bhagat et al. 2002). Individualistic societies tend to have low (small) power distance and collective societies tend to have high (large) power distance.

Yu (2006) discusses how cultural values influence expected patterns of communication. People socialized in individualistic and small power distance cultures emphasize freedom and challenge, favor less centralized and autocratic leadership, and expect to express their voices regardless of their hierarchical positions. In such a culture people prefer a scholar to take a participant's viewpoint in discussing research findings. Conversely, a God's Eye view may be more appropriate for communicating with people embedded in cultures of larger power differences and higher collectivism where there is a greater acceptance of inequalities and authoritarianism. In such vertically-differentiated cultures, making a negative comment, directly raising issues or problems, and arguing with someone in a higher position are often considered offensive behaviors (Yu 2006: 13). Therefore, to minimize the loss of information, formal communications tend to be more effective than informal discussions.

Communicating across cultural boundaries highlights the need for sensitivity and credibility of the speaker in the eyes of the listeners. I learned this the hard way thirty years ago while conducting what was to be a two-day workshop on applying the nominal group brainstorming technique (Van de Ven and Delbecq 1974) for identifying citizen needs in community planning with the tribal council of the Indian Community Action Program in Missoula, Montana. During the break after the opening session the tribal council leader spoke to me, saying 'White man, you got nothin' to tell us. Get your "bleeping" "bleep" out of town.' And I did immediately! I learned then of the importance of indigenous leadership. Outsiders sometimes cannot 'go it alone' to communicate across cultural boundaries; I should have established a relationship with a Native American insider of the tribe to plan and co-present findings in ways that tribal council members would have considered acceptable and credible.

Similar to cultural boundaries, there are many other sources of interpretive differences between researchers and practitioners. Research is rarely self-evident to the practitioner. It varies according to the context in which it is received and deployed. Successful implementation, then, involves a focus on local ideas, practices, and attitudes. This suggests that the key is to engage the interest and involvement of practitioners in interpreting the meanings of a message (Nutley et al. 2003: 133–4).

One common source of interpretive difference between researchers and practitioners is on general statistical scientific findings and the specific individual context in which they may apply. Research findings typically represent a trade-off in utility between the extremes of generic knowledge and local knowledge specific to a context. Statistical conclusions about a sample of cases can seldom be applied to a particular case until one knows the position of a particular case in the general distribution. For example, if research finds that greater education increases job performance, than the individuals who score lower than the average of the sample have much to gain from obtaining more education, but those individuals scoring above average have little to gain from more education. Moreover, population-level findings are often not useful for dealing with specific individual cases. For example, guidelines from evidence-based medicine are often not useful to physicians treating individual patients in their examination rooms (Dopson 2005). This is because evidence-based medical guidelines based on population statistics are often shallow and detached from the rich and detailed historical context of particular patients. While the general evidence-based guideline may be correct, it ignores the context-specific considerations in which it must be applied to each individual patient. Only through conversations between researchers and practitioners do participants come to interpret and understand these complexities and disconnects between general scientific findings and individual context-specific applications.

Another common source of interpretive difference between researchers and practitioners is the different kinds of explanations of research findings that are useful. Chapter 4 pointed out that an audience often wants an explanation that supplements logical deduction with a pragmatic model of other kinds of explanation. An explanation is defined in terms of *verstehen* or understanding that emerges in a dialogue between the answers provided by a speaker and the questions asked by a listener. The purpose of an argument is for the speaker in a dialogue to present reasons to the listener to accept a claim that he/she may doubt. In this dialogue, the speaker anticipates the *why* questions about a claim from the listener, and offers a chain of inferences showing how the claim was derived from major and minor premises. Walton (2004) refers to this sequence of reasoning as a *trace explanation*, which reveals the sequence of inferences that led to the conclusion of the reasoning. However, he notes that trace explanations may not be of interest to the listener who may not be an expert and does not have intricate knowledge of the means–ends causal chain of the claim being discussed.

Instead, a listener may seek an explanation for the purpose of understanding a claim that he/she is willing to accept as factual. In other words, the purpose of the explanation is not to remove doubt that a claim is true, but to understand more in depth what it means. Walton (2004) suggests that a *strategic explanation* may be helpful in some of these cases. Strategic explanations describe the action that can follow the problem-solving strategy stated in the claim.

For example, a strategic explanation for research on nominal group brainstorming techniques might go as follows. 'If your purpose is to generate group satisfaction and commitment to implement a solution to a problem solving process, then use the nominal group technique because people are more willing to implement their own solutions rather than those of someone else, particularly when their solutions are produced by a process that encourages equal, fair, and open participation by all members.' Strategic explanations tend to be action oriented by applying and explaining the implications of a claim in terms of a task being undertaken by the listener. In this sense, a strategic explanation might be viewed as pragmatic advice in using the claim, whereas a trace explanation provides a means–ends analysis of the generative mechanisms that cause the claim.

Finally, Walton (2004) discusses a third type of *deep explanation*, where the speaker uses the knowledge base of the listener, and not just that of the causes and consequences of the claim. A deep explanation requires that the speaker figure out what the listener knows and doesn't know to explain the claim. This is more difficult because the speaker needs to go outside of his/her own knowledge base and connect with that of the listener. A central objective of engaged scholarship is to develop deep explanations of research findings. A deep explanation comes closest to achieving the purpose of an explanation, commonly viewed as transferring understanding between the speaker and listener. Such a deeper form of explanation begins with verbal face-to-face dialogues between the speaker and the listeners, and might end with a written explanation of the proceedings in a report. This deeper form of explanation can be achieved when scholars arrange review meetings or conferences with members of their intended audience in order to verbally present their findings and engage in discussions for the purpose of developing empathy for each others' viewpoints and understandings of the findings.

Requests for deep explanations arise unexpectedly. For example, as a doctoral student I followed my adviser, Prof. Andre Delbecq, to conduct a series of neighborhood block meetings to identify the needs of low income people in Dane County, Wisconsin. It provided the field setting to develop and try out various steps in what became known as the Nominal Group Technique (Delbecq and Van de Ven 1971). I recall a mother with a baby in her arms saying, 'Dr. Delbecq, can you look at my sick baby?' Prof. Delbecq stopped the meeting and said he was not a medical doctor, and asked if there was a doctor in the house. A nurse was present who took the mother with her baby into another room to examine the baby. This mother asked a deep question that profoundly altered people in the room and my understanding of communication and learning. Moved by the incident, an elderly gentleman attending the meeting made a passionate plea for addressing the health care needs of low income people, which surfaced as the top priority in the neighborhood block meeting. After the nominal group meeting I talked with this elderly gentleman. He told me, 'This is the first time in my life that I felt I could speak my mind.' Prof. Delbecq's behavior at the meeting taught me to start where people are at (not where I am at) to entertain deep questions. Moreover, learning does not occur until there is a need for it. Allow listeners to speak their minds if you hope to learn from them.

In summary, research findings are always open to multiple meanings and explanations. A trace explanation typically provides causal reasons and evidence for deriving the findings, as is typically expected of research reports in scientific journals. This traditional form of scientific explanation often needs to be extended and supplemented with strategic and deep explanations for practitioner audiences. Given the fact that scientific and practitioner audiences often have different pragmatic interests in understanding the meanings and uses of research, different research reports are often needed to communicate with them. But given the different meanings, interpretations, and uses of research findings, an engaged researcher should participate in face-to-face meetings and discussions with potential users of a study in order to frame and summarize learning experiences with each audience before writing these reports.

PRAGMATIC AND POLITICAL TRANSFORMATION OF KNOWLEDGE

It is often not just a matter of interpreting and translating the meanings and uses of research findings, but of negotiating interests and making trade-offs between the stakeholders of research findings. Under conditions of conflicting interests, creating common meanings may not be possible; what is required is a process in which participants negotiate and are willing to transform their own knowledge and interests to fit a collective domain. 'When different interests arise, developing an adequate common knowledge is a political process of negotiating and defining common interests' (Carlile 2004: 559).

Evans (1999) provides a good example of the differing interests of researchers and practitioners who are commonly engaged in studies of organizational change.

In organizational settings, managers and employees have a pragmatic interest in understanding 'what works' in terms of human resources, organizational design, or even reengineering interventions. On the one hand, managerial scholars have an overlapping, though not identical, interest in testing their theories about organizational design and human behavior. These interests are overlapping rather than identical because of the different values underlying the positions. In a real sense, they match two underlying philosophies about the nature of causation: the activity theory and the essentialist theory (Cook & Shadish, 1994). In the former, one is interested merely in whether a change has taken place and, to a lesser extent, whether it can be generalized to other situations; in the latter, one is interested in *why* the change occurred. This leads to a rather different emphasis being placed on the types of threats to validity that may occur. Managers are interested in events bringing about change that can be replicated in other situations; researchers are more interested in the internal validity of the study: did the particular stimulus bring about change, or were there alternative causes for the change? Similarly, the manager is more interested in putting together a package of stimuli that can bring about the change, whereas the researcher wants to explore with some precision how the components of that package might work. Both, however, wish to distinguish real change from 'accidental regularities.' (Evans 1999: 325)

As this example suggests, the transition from a semantic to a pragmatic boundary in Carlile's Figure 8.3 arises when communication uncovers different interests among actors that have to be resolved. When actors have different interests, the dependencies between them are not indifferent (James 1907). Knowledge is invested in practice, so it is 'at stake' for those actors who have developed it (Carlile 2002). When interests are in conflict, the knowledge developed in one domain may generate negative consequences in another. Here the costs for any actor are not just the costs of learning about what is new, but also the costs of transforming 'current' knowledge being used (i.e., common and domain-specific knowledge). These costs may negatively impact the willingness of an actor to make such changes.

I learned this the hard way many years ago when conducting an evaluation study by interviewing the professional staff of a planning agency. I presented the findings in a meeting with the board of directors of the planning agency and Charlie, its executive director. The findings were presented by summarizing what I heard and did not hear in terms of my theory of planning. During my presentation Charlie became incensed, and did not speak to me for three years. I knew right away that I had done something profoundly wrong, but did not know what. Reflecting on this painful incident, I came to realize that either as a researcher or consultant, I have no unilateral right to impose and use my theory to evaluate Charlie's or anyone's organization without their informed consent. Any model or theory reflects multiple meanings and interests, some of which conflict with those of the users or the subjects. Hence, use of any theory or model should require negotiated consent of those assessed.

Schultz and Hatch (2005) provide an instructive example of the difficulties of communication when editing a book among scholars across disciplinary boundaries.

We invited scholars with different disciplinary backgrounds and interests to write about organizational identity, image, culture, reputation and corporate branding. While we experienced high agreement among the members of this group that all these constructs were important and interrelated, it turned out to be an immense struggle to define even basic terms such as identity and image, because the different disciplines on which we drew clung to their own definitions. Although these disciplines overlapped, they were far from compatible. In our struggle to make sense of interrelated conceptual differences we ended up using the Tower of Babel myth to describe the belief the group held that they were looking for a lost—or not yet found—common language. More specifically, we used a spatial metaphor to argue that the meaning of each term depends on where in the conceptual landscape an observer stands, each discipline preferring a different position. This experience gave us firsthand knowledge of the cross-functional difficulties managers face when implementing corporate initiatives. (Schultz and Hatch 2005: 340)

I have experienced similar difficulties in coordinating the Minnesota Innovation Research Program (MIRP) that involved over thirty faculty and doctoral students from eight different academic disciplines who tracked fourteen innovation projects in longitudinal field studies from concept to implementation or termination (Van de Ven et al. 1999; Van de Ven et al. 2000). It took one and a half years of monthly meetings among MIRP investigators to reach agreement on five core concepts for studying the innovation process; namely, the innovation process consists of new *ideas* that are developed by *people* who engage in *transactions* or relationships with others and who guide their actions based on judgments of *outcomes* and changing external *contexts*. Like the case described by Schultz and Hatch, all MIRP investigators reached agreement on these five key concepts for studying the innovation journey, but no consensus was reached on operational definitions and measures. Instead of imposing or mandating the use of common operational definitions in all studies, we concluded that they were not needed; instead the differences provided learning opportunities by arbitraging or leveraging the different meanings and measurements of these concepts in different innovations studied by program investigators.

In retrospect, this turned out to be a wise decision, for it enabled the following: several creative variations among MIRP members in studying innovations, group meetings where members shared their different but related research findings, and motivation among investigators in the collective learning experience. When different interests arise, developing an adequate common knowledge is a political process of negotiating and defining common interests. Sometimes agreements are only necessary on overarching working principles, including agreements among participants to disagree on operational details. In pluralistic situations heedful accommodations among participants can provide constructive opportunities for learning by leveraging differences through arbitrage.

Like Schultz and Hatch, I have also worked with companies over many years to apply evidence-based practices of using research results to inform corporate change initiatives across functional boundaries, such as marketing, engineering, R&D, and HRM. People from these different functions often have competing competencies, methods, and mindsets. Their interests are different. As a consequence, research findings are often interpreted as representing competing, conflicting or paradoxical implications for action. Yet, like the MIRP investigators, corporate practitioners share some overarching common interests that facilitate crossing their different functional boundaries. For example, a common interest in economic survival motivates collaboration among people in order to produce changes that respond to customer needs and competitive market conditions. In a few instances, research evidence facilitated collaboration across boundaries. This occurred when corporate practitioners viewed the research findings as neutral grounds on which to recognize and negotiate their differences and enable action.

Negotiating conflicting interest in research knowledge entails risks for all parties at the boundary (i.e., both researchers and practitioners). No findings or applications of research are known with complete certainty. All interpretations and uses of knowledge are inferences. For example, research findings of a study I conducted in a large human services organization in Cleveland were discussed with managers, the conclusion of which was a need for a change in policy that required approval of the board of directors. As we walked to the board meeting to propose the policy change, I will never forget the executive director telling me, 'Van de Ven, I'll have your ass if this doesn't work out.' Thank goodness it worked!

What often makes organizations and real-world problems complex is their paradoxical nature. Research findings about these organizations and problems should, therefore, reflect these paradoxes. Scott Poole and I urged scholars to embrace paradoxical findings, for they provide important opportunities for learning and theory creation (Poole and Van de Ven 1989). In particular, we proposed four different ways to approach apparent paradoxes observed in practice and our theories about the phenomenon. First, accept the paradox or inconsistency, and learn to live with it constructively in a pluralistic world with principles of respect for and balance between oppositions or 'moderation in all things.' Second, clarify levels of reference from which different perspectives or interests of a problem arise (e.g., part–whole, micro–macro, or individual–society) and the connections among them. Third, take into account the time needed to explore when contradictory interests or processes each exert a separate influence on the problem. Fourth, introduce new concepts that either correct flaws in logic or provide a more encompassing perspective that dissolves the paradox. As discussed in Chapter 4, these four methods represent a classification system for undertaking multiple independent thought trials in developing conjectures for understanding anomalous situations.

Unfortunately, the implications of research are too often oversimplified and lean toward naïve simplicity. Schultz and Hatch (2005: 341) point out that management researchers 'often translate profound theoretical ideas and empirical findings into a few straightforward, conflict-free implications for practice,' in the mistaken belief that this is what practitioners want.' This downplaying of tensions and paradoxes risks presenting a story of organizational life that its managers and employees may not recognize. Schultz and Hatch (2005: 343) conclude that 'when discussing the implications of our findings, we should remain open to the paradoxes embedded in managerial practices.'

Finally, the existence of different interests among actors at a boundary makes clear that knowledge and power are concretely related. Carlile points out that

> ... even when actors have equal ability to use a common knowledge to effectively share and access each other's domain-specific knowledge, power is still being expressed.... When abilities to use the common knowledge are not equal or the common knowledge used does not have the capacity to represent a particular actor's knowledge and interests, mismatches arise.... Specialized knowledge is distributed across different domains and cannot always be equally represented at the same time. This temporal dimension of dependency means that the consequences of downstream knowledge generally have a harder time being represented earlier in the process, putting upstream knowledge in a politically stronger position relative to downstream knowledge. Given this, we should not assume the actors involved at a boundary occupy politically equal positions in representing their knowledge to each other. (Carlile 2004: 565)

Recognition that knowledge and power are closely related has led critical theorists and postmodern scholars to examine communication as a political process of expressing and suppressing different voices at the boundary. Power and meaning join together to distort voices. Even though they may be heard, they often echo the sentiment of the elite. Communications, therefore, reflect struggles between competing rather than univocal positions that are present in some latent or manifest form among actors at an ideological boundary (Putnam et al. 1996: 389). But knowledge without power is impotent. Powerful knowledge can be used for constructive and destructive ends. The ethos of moral and ethical communication is *sine qua non* and must never be forgotten.

THE NEED FOR MULTIPLE CONVERSATIONS

Managing knowledge at the pragmatic boundary requires multiple iterations. Addressing the consequences cannot be resolved with one try, but requires an iterative process of sharing and assessing knowledge, creating new agreements, and making changes where needed. The engaged scholarship process calls for repeated engagement of stakeholders in each activity of the research process: problem formulation, theory building, research design, and problem solving. 'As actors participate in each iterative stage, they get better at identifying what differences and dependencies are of consequence at the boundary; they improve at collectively developing more adequate common lexicon, meaning, and interests. Through this iterative capacity the invested and path-dependent nature of knowledge can be transformed' (Carlile 2004: 563). As people at the communication boundary scale the 'Tower of Babel' several times, they come down with a richer appreciation of one another's positions, assuming they respect each other and are willing to listen and learn. 'Without these essential characteristics, academics build castles and defend territories, and I think this is also true for some academics vis-à-vis practitioners' (Hatch, personal communication, February 9, 2006).

Conclusion

Researchers spend enormous resources and energy searching for and creating new knowledge. This is evident in the significant time and effort entailed in problem formulation, theory building, research design, and problem solving. Unfortunately, the products of this research are often not used to advance either science or practice. This chapter examined the problem solving phase of the engaged scholarship process, focusing on how research findings might be communicated and used more effectively by an intended audience. Whether undertaken for the purposes of description, explanation, evaluation, or intervention, extensive evidence shows that simply writing, publishing, and presenting a research report often does not result in its use by either scientists or practitioners. I argued that a deeper understanding of communicating knowledge across boundaries and a more engaged relationship between the researcher and his/her audience are needed if research findings are to have an impact in advancing science and practice.

I anchored this chapter in Carlile's (2004) framework of knowledge transfer, translation, and transformation, since it provides useful insights into how researchers might communicate their study findings at the knowledge boundaries with different audiences. The framework emphasizes that communication requires common knowledge of syntax, semantics, and pragmatics of language among people to understand each other's domain-specific knowledge. When the difference, dependence, and novelty of domain-specific knowledge between people increase, then progressively more complex processes of knowledge transfer, translation, and transformation are needed to communicate the meanings and potential uses of that knowledge. Carlile (2004) emphasizes that there is an additive character to these communication boundaries. That is, communicating at more complex boundaries still requires the capacities and the processes below them.

When the people at a knowledge boundary share the same common syntax for understanding their different and interdependent domain-specific knowledge, then it can be communicated using a conventional information processing view of knowledge transfer from a speaker to listeners through written and verbal reports. The major challenge of knowledge transfer is to craft a sufficiently rich message and medium to convey the novelty of the information from the speaker to the audience. For example, written reports, verbal presentations, and face-to-face interactions between the speaker and listeners represent three increasingly rich media for knowledge transfer. In addition, logos, pathos, and ethos represent three increasingly rich dimensions of a message.

Based on innovation adoption and diffusion research and rhetorical theory, five propositions were derived that provide useful guidelines for knowledge transfer.

1. Research findings are more likely to be adopted and diffused when they are perceived as having a relative advantage over the status quo, are compatible with current understandings of things, are simple to understand, and are explicit, observable, and can be tried out.
2. Research reports are more likely to be adopted when they engage and reflect the views of leading members of the adopting community.
3. Research reports are more likely to be adopted by a specific audience when they are presented in a rhetorically persuasive argument.
4. When crafting a research report you can increase the likelihood of influencing your intended audience with pathos, logos, and ethos justifications of research findings.
5. When crafting the message in a given report and over a series of reports, a rhetorical sequence that starts with pathos to grab a listener's emotional attention, moves to logos to provide rational explanations and evidence, and ends with ethos appeals to its moral legitimacy and social norms will have a rapid rate of initial adoption, a broad diffusion, and a slow abandonment (Green 2004).

Knowledge transfer, however, even when communicated in the richness of a rhetorical triangle, typically remains a one-way transmission of information from a sender to a receiver. The listener in knowledge transfer remains relatively silent, but is never inactive. Authors of research reports will not know this unless they engage in conversations with readers or listeners of a report. Then it becomes clear that listeners often have different interpretations and meanings of the novel information than the speaker intended. A research report is not treated as a social fact or as having a 'fixed' meaning. Rather, it is open to multiple and unlimited meanings, interpretations, and actions among participants (speakers and listeners) engaged in the text. Hence, when communicating research findings a research report should be viewed as a first—not the last—step for researchers to engage in conversations with potential users, and thereby gain a broader and deeper appreciation of the meanings of research findings.

When interpretive differences exist on the meanings of research findings, then a more complex semantic boundary of 'knowledge translation' must be crossed. At this boundary, speakers and listeners engage in conversations and discourse to mutually share, interpret, and construct their meanings of research findings. Speakers and listeners become co-authors in mutually constructing and making sense of their interactions. At the knowledge translation boundary, conversation is the essence and the product of research. Engaging in conversation and discourse with an audience requires researchers to adopt a hermeneutic 'participant view' rather than a 'God's Eye view' of research findings.

Several sources of interpretive differences between researchers and practitioners were discussed.

- Communications across cultural boundaries greatly influence expected patterns of communication. People socialized in individualistic and small power-distance cultures emphasize freedom and challenge, favor less centralized and autocratic leadership, and therefore, prefer a researcher to take a participant's viewpoint in discussing research findings. On the other hand, a God's Eye view may be more appropriate for communicating with people embedded in cultures of larger power distances and higher collectivism where there is a greater acceptance of inequalities and preferences for authoritarianism.
- Another source of interpretive difference between researchers and practitioners is between general statistical scientific findings and the specific individual context in which they may apply. Research findings are rarely self-evident to the practitioner but vary according to the context in which they are received and applied. Implementation of research findings requires a focus on local ideas, practices, and attitudes, and this suggests that the key is to engage in conversations with practitioners to interpret the meanings and potential uses of research.

- Scientists and practitioners are often interested in different kinds of research explanations. Scientists tend to emphasize 'trace explanations' that articulate the logical causes and evidence for the sequence of inferences that led to the theoretical conclusions, whereas practitioners are often willing to accept the conclusions as factual or true and may want strategic and deep explanations. 'Strategic explanations' place an action in context by revealing the problem-solving strategy implied by the research conclusions to perform a task. A 'deep explanation' addresses questions from the knowledge base of the listener, and not just the causes and consequences of research conclusions. Developing strategic and deep explanations typically require researchers to have face-to-face conversations with practitioners in order to develop empathy of each others' viewpoints and interpretations of the findings.
- Given the fact that scientific and practitioner audiences often have different pragmatic interests in understanding the meanings and uses of research, different research reports are often needed to communicate with scientific and practitioner audiences. But given the different meanings, interpretations, and uses of research findings, conversations with potential users of a study are a prerequisite to framing and summarizing learning experiences before writing these reports for each audience.

Knowledge transfer and translation may surface conflicting interests among parties. Crossing this even more complex pragmatic communication boundary requires parties to negotiate and politically transform their knowledge and interests from their own to a collective domain. As Carlile (2004) states, 'When different interests arise, developing an adequate common knowledge is a political process of negotiating and defining common interests.' I discussed several examples of the difficulties of negotiating and transforming research knowledge at the political boundary among academics and practitioners. Although social scientists tend to shy away from political discourse, developing such skills is clearly needed to communicate research knowledge at the political boundary. Based on a few personal experiences, several insights were discussed.

- The difficulties of negotiating and transforming conflicting interests among scholars and practitioners appear similar. When conflicting interests arise, both scholars and practitioners seem to engage in similar political struggles, where the knowledge that is 'at stake' for those who developed it in one domain may produce negative outcomes in another unless managed constructively.
- When conflicting interests arise, communication at the boundary entails a political process of negotiating and defining common interests. Sometimes agreements are only necessary on overarching working principles, including agreements among participants to disagree on operational details. In pluralistic situations heedful accommodations among participants

can provide constructive opportunities for learning by leveraging differences through arbitrage.

- Research evidence can facilitate political negotiation and collaboration across conflicting boundaries when the evidence is used to inform initiatives among functional managers. This occurs when corporate practitioners view research findings as neutral ground on which to recognize and negotiate their differences and enable action.
- Negotiating conflicting interpretations and applications of research knowledge entails risks for all parties at the boundary (i.e., both researchers and practitioners). No research findings or applications are known with complete certainty. Risk is inherent in all decisions to use—as well as not use—research findings for intervening in science and practice.
- Conflicting interests and paradoxes should be addressed in research reports. Too often researchers present their empirically rich findings 'into a few straightforward, conflict-free implications for practice, in the mistaken belief that this is what practitioners want.... When discussing the implications of our findings, we should remain open to the paradoxes embedded in managerial practices' (Schultz and Hatch 2005: 341).
- Conflicting interests make clear that knowledge and power are closely related. Knowledge without power is impotent. Powerful knowledge can be used for constructive and destructive ends. Moral and ethical communication is most important and should never be forgotten.

Finally, seldom can knowledge transfer, translation, and transformation be accomplished with only one communication among people across boundaries. Numerous interactions are required to share and interpret knowledge, create new meanings, and negotiate divergent interests. The engaged scholarship process provides a strategy to approximate this by repeated engagements of stakeholders in each activity of the research process: problem formulation, theory building, research design, and problem solving.

9 Practicing Engaged Scholarship

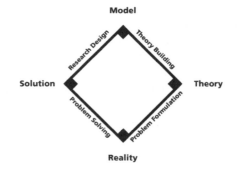

Connecting theory and practice is no simple trick; but when it occurs it can trigger dazzling insights.

(Lake Wobegon story)

When you have an opportunity to learn how someone in another group does what you do differently—go.

(Burt 2005: 245)

I begin this concluding chapter by telling a story[1] about engaged scholarship as viewed from a fictitious Lake Wobegon University. The story adopts the style of National Public Radio personality, Garrison Keillor from 'A Prairie Home Companion.' I hope to poke a little fun into our very serious subject and provide some insights into the ethos of practicing engaged scholarship. Following the story I discuss a number of alternative forms of engaged scholarship and the situations in which they tend to be practiced. I also discuss a number of practical considerations in engaging stakeholders in a given study.

A Story About Engaged Scholarship from Lake Wobegon

It's been a quiet year at Lake Wobegon University, where all the faculty think globally and act locally, the administrators act globally but think locally, and

[1] Earlier versions of this story were told in the Organization and Management Theory Division programs of the Academy of Management Conferences in Cincinnati, 1997, and New Orleans, 2004.

all the students become better than their faculty. That's because all the women are strong, the men are beautiful, and all the children are above average.

Lake Wobegon is located west of the Hudson and east of the Bay—maybe you have seen the map. Somewhere in that vast, uncharted territory called the Heartland. Unlike the hustling and bustling at Hudson and Bay Universities, it's been a quiet year at Wobegon.

Maybe it's the quiet here that helps people recognize that organizations are buzzing, blooming, and confusing. No one person or perspective can figure them out. This is hard to see when you are constantly pursuing one point of view. But you won't know that if you only talk to yourself. As Poggi (1965) said, 'A way of seeing is a way of not seeing.' You need to talk and listen to other people to understand their viewpoints, in order to figure out your own. Some academics fear that they may lose their distinctive competence by talking to practitioners. But they are mistaken. You identify and build your distinctiveness only by interacting with others.

Maybe Lake Wobegon's weather helps people understand this reality. This year it included record breaking cold, floods, and heat. Averages mean nothing; only outlying extremes are real. 'Sure is cold—ya, you betcha! It's the penalty we get for the nice sunny day last summer' (Fargo slang). There is nothing uncertain about nature's brute force. It makes reality undeniable. We don't need Karl Weick's sensemaking to figure that out. But we do need Karl's insights to make sense of our social world and its complex problems. This requires talking and listening to each other.

Extremes keep people inside to pass their time away by talking with one another. They talk and talk—brown bags, workshops, colloquia, hallways. All begin with 'How's the weather treating you?' 'Fine, it's a nice day, but we'll pay for it!'

They talk at home about work and at work about home. 'How is Timothy Smart's cold?' 'Oh, he's down under the weather a bit.' At the family supper table Prof. Hollander talks about the behavioral science course that he is teaching at the University. Mrs. Hollander asks their 7-year-old son, 'Do you know the meaning of behavioral science?' He retorts, 'Yup, I sure do! Behave or I'll give you science!'

He has a point. Out of the mouths of babes do we hear what we say, which is often not what we intend.

THERE'S A CONTROVERSY BREWING IN THE ACADEMY

At the annual meeting of the Academy of Management a speaker said that, 'Even a hermit in bleakest Antarctica must be aware of the disconnects between management theory and practice by now.' People here say, 'Do you think he means us? Can't say for sure. I've heard about it, so it must be true.

Ya, but it's a lot of to do about nothin'. There's more important things to worry about.'

Anyway, it's a squabble that started with a committee of academics exploring why research by faculty in business schools has had such little impact on practice, and what the Academy should do about it. Actually, the problem has been festering for a number of years and become the center of attention in special issues of several academic journals.[2] They report that academic research has become less useful for solving practical problems. Some say academic research is also not being used or cited to advance scientific knowledge. The gulf between science and practice seems to be widening.

Some say this gap represents a knowledge transfer problem. It is helpful and appropriate to view it this way when you have something to say. But Andrew Pettigrew tells us that knowledge transfer and dissemination is too late if the wrong questions have been asked. He says a deeper form of research that engages both academics and practitioners is needed to produce knowledge that is worthy of transfer to both science and practice.

ALL IS NOT PEACEFUL AND TRANQUIL AT LAKE WOBEGON UNIVERSITY EITHER

Like his cohorts aspiring to be doctoral candidates, Timothy Smart has been preparing for his PhD preliminary examinations—18 hours a day: morning, noon, and night. He is studying, cramming, and memorizing all those theories, all those studies. Organization and management theory is a buzzing, blooming, confusing world. Timothy Smart has been struggling to synthesize all of this into a 2×2 grid.

In frustration and despair, Timothy files a number of complaints accusing the faculty with everything that he thought was wrong with his education. He developed a list of 95 accusations that he nailed to the door of the Lutheran chapel. He created quite a raucous.

- You educated me terribly for this buzzing, blooming, confusing world!
- You trained me in the static linear model of variables, causal modeling, and experimental design. But organizations are dynamic, nonlinear, complex, and pluralistic. They cannot be explained with your unitary theories and linear methods.
- You forced me to read all those studies that explain no more than 2–10 percent of the variance in the real world. You didn't tell me the difference between statistical significance and practical significance.

---

[2] They include the *Academy of Management Journal* (2001), *British Academy of Management* (2001), *Academy of Management Executive* and *Administrative Science Quarterly* (2002), and other more specialized management journals.

- We learned a lot about organization and management theories and models, but very little about organizations and management. The classes were echo chambers between Contingency Theory, Resource Dependence Theory, Resource-Based Theory, Institutional Theory, Transactions Costs Theory, Agency Theory, Network Theory, Organizational Ecology Theory, and Complexity Theories.
- You exposed me to all these theories, but gave me no way to sift and winnow among them. How do I know which view is better or worse than another?

The Director of Graduate Studies talked to Timothy about his accusations. 'I'm sorry you feel that way. That's too bad. Maybe you should sleep on it. Go to bed. Rub some Vicks Vapor Rub on your chest. Put a scarf around your neck. And breathe deeply. I bet you'll feel better!'

CONFRONTING AND LEARNING FROM REALITY

Faculty at Lake Wobegon University debated with one another about Timothy's accusations. 'Well, what did you expect? Our school was a holding pen until students graduated. Now we have this new university–industry PhD training program, where our students get exposed to the real world. How are you going to keep them on the farm once they have seen Paris?'

Many of Timothy's accusations exposed major gaps between the theories that students cover in their PhD courses and the practices that they observe in their 'field' work. Connecting theory and practice is no simple trick; but when it occurs it can trigger dazzling insights.

In the university–industry program the PhD students, such as Timothy Smart, are given deep access to organizations to study problems and issues under the guidance of an executive sponsor and the mentorship of a faculty member. For example, Timothy Smart and two other PhD students were granted fellowships to study organizational integration in a recently merged healthcare system. In between their classes at the U., they go to the health care organization to sit in on regularly scheduled meetings of managers and professionals, conduct periodic interviews, surveys, and site visits with various organizational members and units.

Periodically, they also meet jointly with their executive sponsors Dr. Chell (in health care organization) and their faculty mentor, Prof. Hollander. They are asked, 'What are you learning? What problem are you studying?' Timothy answers, 'They don't have a single clear goal or strategy for directing change.' Prof. Hollander interrupts, 'No, that's a solution. What's the problem? What did you see?'

In a subsequent review session, Timothy reports, 'Well, I see tremendous strain, frustration, and lots of conflict between managers, physicians, and administrative staff. Executives are trying to corporatize medicine to create an efficient standardized system of health care. They are buying up clinics and merging hospitals and health plans to be competitive and increase market share. The clinicians report they are losing autonomy and control of their medical practice. They fear the drive for profit is at the expense of quality patient care. One physician questioned if the health care system is organizing for itself, against competitors, or for patients? He said, 'If we want to improve the health of the community, the enemy is disease, not other health care providers. An integrated system is a means, not an end to this lofty goal.'

Prof. Hollander comments, 'Now you are making progress. You are beginning to describe reality. What theories or models can help us explain this reality?' Timothy replies, 'Well, it's a pluralistic organization with physicians and managers subscribing to different ideologies, values, and models that are competing for attention and control of the organization. The different views seem equally legitimate and necessary for the long-run adaptability and survival of the healthcare system.'

Dr. Chell comments, 'Good, go on. How might this play out?' Timothy answers, 'This is contrary to almost all principles of management that rely on consensus. Such unity is not present here. The administrative and clinical groups are mutually dependent on each other for scarce resources and to serve patients. They need to interact and heedfully accommodate one another to create some kind of negotiated order. The managerial group seems to have greater power, and if it squelches the less powerful clinicians, you won't have a health care system—or you'll have a mediocre one at best.'

Prof. Hollander remarks, 'Very good, you have faced reality and it presented you with the crux of an important problem—*managing a pluralistic organization.* How might we design a pluralistic organization where competing models are tolerated, respected, and negotiated to achieve constructive ends for all parties? Focus your studies on this problem, for understanding it would be a significant novel advance to management theory and practice.'

Dr. Chell reflects on Prof. Hollander's remarks. 'You know, I have not thought of our problem this way. I feel a bit intimidated by your diagnosis, even though it may be correct. How do we hold our physician employees accountable when they reject our supervision? This is a crucial question that needs to be studied. Where and how might such a study lead? Perhaps we should form a study advisory committee of physicians, managers, and university people to guide your study.'

CONCLUSION

The current state of affairs between management theory and practice is much like this health system. Many of us are like Timothy Smart, struggling to make sense of the 'buzzing, blooming, confusing' worlds of practice seen in organ-izations and of theories being debated in academe. *Don't you think that if we ground our research questions in practice, and involve practitioners in problem formulation, theory building, research design, and problem solving that man-agement scholarship will flourish and the management profession will benefit?*

Well, that's the news from Lake Wobegon University, where all the women are strong, the men are beautiful, and the children are above average.

Summary of Engaged Scholarship Model

A central mission of scholars in professional schools is to conduct research that both advances a scientific discipline and enlightens the practice of a profession (Simon 1976). But the so-called gap between theory and practice indicates this mission remains an elusive ideal. As the Lake Wobegon story suggests, relating theory and practice is no simple trick; but when it happens it can trigger dazzling insights. It poses the important question of how scholars might design their research to address complex problems in the world. This book proposed a method of engaged scholarship for creating knowledge that advances understanding of complex problems or phenomena.

Engaged scholarship is a participative form of research for obtaining the different perspectives of key stakeholders (researchers, users, clients, sponsors, and practitioners) in producing knowledge about complex problems. By exploiting differences in the kinds of knowledge that scholars and other stakeholders from diverse backgrounds can bring forth on a problem, I argued that engaged scholarship can produce knowledge that is more penetrating and insightful than when scholars or practitioners work on the problems alone.

Past arguments for collaborative research have tended to be one-sided and focus on the relevance of academic research *for* practice. As the Lake Wobegon story conveys, I focused more attention in this book on the question of how scholarship that is engaged *with* (rather than *for*) practice can advance basic scientific knowledge? Engaged scholarship implies a fundamental shift in how scholars define their relationships with the communities in which they are located, including other disciplines in the university and practitioners in relevant professional domains. It emphasizes that research is not a solitary exercise; instead it is a collective achievement. Engagement means that scholars step outside of themselves to obtain and be informed by the interpretations of others about each step of the research process: problem formulation, theory building, research design, and problem solving.

Using a diamond model as illustrated in Figure 9.1, I argued that scholars can significantly increase the likelihood of advancing fundamental knowledge of a complex phenomenon by engaging people whose perspectives are relevant in each of these study activities:

- Problem formulation—situate, ground, diagnose, and infer the research problem by determining who, what, where, when, why, and how the problem exists up close and from afar. As discussed in Chapter 3, answering these journalist's questions requires meeting and talking with people who experience and know the problem, as well as reviewing the literature on the prevalence of the problem.
- Theory building—create, elaborate, and justify a theory by abductive, deductive, and inductive reasoning (see Chapter 4). Developing this theory and its plausible alternatives requires conversations with knowledge experts from the relevant disciplines and functions that have addressed the problem, as well as a review of relevant literature.
- Research design—develop a variance or process model for empirically examining the alternative theories. As noted in Chapters 6 and 7, doing this well typically requires getting advice from technical experts in research methodology and the people who can provide access to data, and of course, the respondents or informants of information.
- Problem solving—communicate, interpret, and apply the empirical findings on which alternative models better answer the research question about the problem. Chapter 8 argued that increases in the difference, dependence, and novelty of knowledge between people at a boundary require more complex forms of communication, starting with written reports and presentations for knowledge transfer, then conversations to interpret different meanings of the report, and then pragmatic and political negotiations to reconcile conflicting interests.

These activities can be performed in any sequence. In this book I followed a sequence customary to decision making or problem solving. However, there are many other possible starting-points and sequences. For example, some scholars may start with a theory and then search for a problematic situation that may be appropriate for applying and evaluating the theory. Other scholars may be methodologically inclined, and interested in finding problems and developing theories with their methodological tools (as was the case in early developments of social network analysis). These different starting motivations and orientations quickly meld together in the course of a study because the four activities are highly interdependent and are seldom completed in one pass. Multiple iterations and revisions are often needed throughout the duration of a study.

Maintaining balance in performing these tasks is important. Given finite resources for conducting a study, I recommend that scholars allocate their time and efforts about equally to problem exploration, theory building, research design and conduct, and problem solving activities. Spending too much time or effort on only one or two research activities often results in unbalanced or lop-sided results where some activities are 'over-engineered' while others are incomplete.

This suggestion of paying equal attention to all four research activities departs from that in many research methodology texts in the social sciences. They tend to focus on research design, and pay relatively little attention to the processes of problem formulation, theory building, and problem solving. In addition, while these texts provide good technical treatments of research designs, they largely ignore social processes of engaging stakeholders in problem formulation, theory building, research design, and problem solving (as illustrated in Figure 9.1). Social research is an intensely social process. Throughout the book I emphasized that all four research activities are equally important in conducting a study, and that each activity entails a different set of tasks that can be accomplished better by engaging relevant stakeholders rather than going it alone.

Chapters 3–8 discussed the considerations and tasks involved in problem formulation, theory building, research design, and problem solving. Less attention was given to the context factors listed on the top of Figure 9.1— research purpose, perspective, and complexity. They set the stage for determining the nature and extent of engagement of stakeholders in performing these activities. Engaged scholarship can have many alternative forms practiced in different contexts and settings. The Lake Wobegon story illustrates just one form of engaged scholarship. This chapter examines some alternative forms of engaged scholarship and the situations in which they tend to be

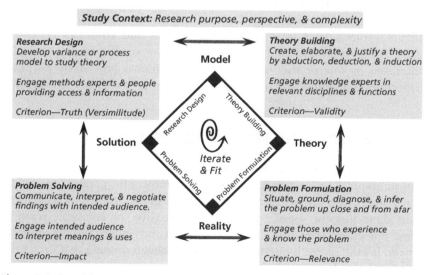

Figure 9.1. Practicing engaged scholarship

practiced. I also discuss a number of practical considerations for deciding what forms of engagement might be appropriate in a given study.

Forms of Engaged Scholarship

Engaged scholarship can be practiced in many different ways and for many different purposes. For example, researchers might engage stakeholders in order to: (1) obtain their perspectives and advice in conducting a basic social science study; (2) undertake a collaborative research project to co-produce knowledge on a question of mutual interest; (3) obtain their involvement in designing or evaluating a policy or program; or (4) intervene and implement a change to solve a client's problem. This section develops a typology of these four ways of practicing engaged scholarship. These different forms of engaged scholarship depend on the purpose, perspective, and complexity of the study being undertaken.

First, I discuss the study purpose and perspective that underlie the typology. The purpose of a study focuses on whether the research is being undertaken to describe, explain, evaluate, or intervene in a problem or question being investigated. Study perspective refers to the degree to which a researcher examines the problem domain as an external observer or an internal participant.

Variations in practicing the four types of engaged scholarship are influenced by the complexity of a study. Study complexity deals with the size and scope of a study and the number of stakeholders who may be affected by it. 'Big science' research programs that may involve many investigators in different projects, and from different disciplines and countries entail far greater engagement and coordination efforts than smaller studies typically undertaken by one or two researchers. I now discuss how study purpose, perspective, and complexity influence various forms of engaged scholarship.

RESEARCH PURPOSE: THE PROBLEM AND QUESTION

In street language, an underlying theme of this book is that *it's about the problem, stupid!* The less you know about the problem the greater the need to engage others who can instruct and ground you in the problem. Engagement is not done just for socially acceptable, persuasive, or enjoyable reasons; instead it is undertaken out of necessity to learn and understand the problem domain. It's the research question about the problem domain that drives the engaged scholarship process.

Problems may originate from any source—in the practical world of affairs, in a theoretical discipline, or in pursuit of an emancipatory social cause. As discussed in Chapter 3, all problems are theory-laden, and whether research is viewed as problem- or theory-driven depends on your viewpoint and the research activity being undertaken (i.e., problem formulation or theory building). Whether the problematic situation originates in theory, practice, or other domains, it defines the boundary conditions for undertaking engaged scholarship. In particular, decisions about how to conduct and who to involve in each step of the process should be guided by the research question about the problem being studied.

Social science studies tend to examine one or more of the following four kinds of research questions (Rescher 2000: 105):

- description (answering *what* and *how* questions about the characteristics of the problem domain and its processes of development);
- explanation (addressing *why* questions about the generating mechanisms, causes, or consequences of the problematic situation);
- design or evaluation (exploring *normative* questions about expectations for evaluating designs, policies, or programs for dealing with the problematic situation); and
- intervention or control (examining *clinical* questions about possible interventions for controlling or treating a problematic situation).

All of these questions are commonly examined in social research, and answers to each can make important contributions for advancing science and practice. As discussed in the next section, these questions imply different research objectives, forms of engaged scholarship, and evaluation criteria. Studies undertaken to describe or explain a problem or phenomenon tend to reflect basic research objectives, while questions of design, evaluation, and control tend to be applied and specific to a particular situation.

RESEARCH PERSPECTIVE

A research problem or question can be studied from a variety of perspectives ranging from an attached insider to a detached outsider. Evered and Louis (1981) contrast these modes of inquiry on a number of dimensions listed in Figure 9.2. This insider–outsider distinction was developed further by Sayer (1992) in terms of conducting research by intension or extension, and by Chandler and Torbert (2003) as whether the researcher speaks and practices in first, second, or third person voices. From the outside or extension, the researcher is characterized as being a detached, impartial onlooker who gathers data on many units in different contexts based on a priori theoretical

Dimension of Difference	MODE OF INQUIRY	
	From the Outside	**From the Inside**
Researcher's relationship to setting	Detachment, neutrality	←——→	'Being there,' immersion
Validation basis	Measurement and logic	←——→	Experiential
Researcher's role	Onlooker	←——→	Actor
Source of categories	A priori	←——→	Interactively emergent
Aim of inquiry	Universality and generalizability	←——→	Situational relevance
Type of knowledge acquired	Universal, nomothetic: theoria	←——→	Particular, idiographic: praxis
Nature of data and meaning	Factual, context free	←——→	Interpreted, contextually embedded

Figure 9.2. Differences between inquiry when taken from the inside and outside

Source: Evered, R. and Louis, M. R. (1981). 'Alternative Perspectives in the Organizational Sciences: "Inquiry from the inside" and "Inquiry from the outside,"' *Academy of Management Review*, 6(3): 389.

categories and measurement instruments in order to develop or test a general theory. In contrast, inquiry by intension, or from the inside, views the researcher as a participant immersed in the actions and experiences within the system being studied. By reflecting on experiences and interactions with other participants in the case, the inside researcher develops context-specific knowledge that can guide action in the immediate situation and provide input in developing hypotheses to guide further inquiry.

As this summary suggests, these two modes of inquiry produce different kinds of knowledge. Research from the outside generates what is typically called extensive scientific knowledge, whereas research from the inside is often called intensive practical knowledge (Sayer 1992). Evered and Louis (1981) discussed the complementary nature of knowledge gained from the inside and outside. For example, in terms of problem formulation discussed in Chapter 3, research from the inside provides a concrete grounding of the research problem in a particular situation, while research from the outside provides empirical evidence of the pervasiveness and boundary conditions of the problem. Both kinds of knowledge are needed to ground a research problem up close and from afar.

Many scholars have noted that linking the different kinds of knowledge produced by research from the inside and outside may be critical to bridging theory and practice (e.g., Lawler et al. 1985; Ragin 1987, 2000; Louis and Bartunek 1992; Sayer 1992; Adler et al. 2004). They have also discussed how research objectives and questions influence the research process. Figure 9.3 attempts to synthesize this literature by suggesting four alternative forms of

Research question/purpose

		To describe/explain	To design/control
Extension detached outside		Basic science with stakeholder advice	Policy/design science evaluation research for professional practice
Research perspective		1	3
		2	4
Intension attached inside		Co-produce knowledge with collaborators	Action/intervention research for a client

Figure 9.3. Alternative forms of engaged scholarship

engaged scholarship. These forms vary in terms of the research question and the researchers' perspective, as just discussed. Characteristics distinguishing the four forms of engaged scholarship are outlined in Table 9.1. These different forms of engaged scholarship are discussed below, followed by a consideration of factors influencing the relationships between researchers and stakeholders in different forms of engaged scholarship studies.

INFORMED BASIC RESEARCH

Informed research resembles a traditional form of social science where the academic researcher adopts a detached outsider perspective of the social system being examined, but solicits advice and feedback from key stakeholders and inside informants on each of the research activities as listed in Figure 9.1. The levels of this form of engagement may vary from simply talking informally with a few informants to conducting more formal review sessions with appropriate stakeholders on each step of the research process. Whatever the level of engagement, the roles of informants and stakeholders tend to be advisory only, and the researcher directs and controls all research activities including authoring the final report.

The Lake Wobegon story is based on a true university–industry PhD research training program that I coordinate with executives in a health care system undergoing change. It provides PhD students, like Timothy Smart, opportunities to access organizational participants and observe organizational activities to learn how to conduct field research in topics related to organizational change. In this program, the doctoral students have no

Table 9.1. Comparisons among forms of engaged scholarship

	Informed Basic Research	Collaborative Research	Design/Evaluation Research	Action/Intervention Research
Summary	Researcher conducts & controls study activities with advice of stakeholders	Research team composed of insiders and outsiders jointly share study activities to co-produce knowledge	Researcher develops and evaluates policy, design or program for profession or client	Researcher intervenes and implements a change to solve a client's problem
Research question	To describe/explain	To describe/explain	To design & evaluate	Clinical diagnosis and treatment
Relationship with or for stakeholders	Advisory	Collaborative	Exchange	Exchange
	With	With	For	For
Who controls process & outcomes	Researcher	Insider/Outsider Partners	Evaluation Researcher	Research Consultant
Researcher perspective	Detached/Outsider	Attached/Insider	Detached Evaluator	Immersed change agent
Examples	Traditional basic science informed by relevant stakeholders as in Figure 9.1.	University–Industry collaboratives Insider–Outsider research teams	Policy/design science Evidence-based practices Evaluation research	Action research Clinical research
Key references	This book	Louis & Bartunek 1992	Weiss 1998	Argyris et al. 1985
		Mohrman et al. 2001	Romme 2003	Lawler et al. 1985
		Pettigrew 2003	van Aken 2005	Adler et al. 2004

obligation to deliver research products to the host organization, but they are given access and advice in conducting their basic research. The researcher maintains authority and control over his/her study, but receives feedback and advice from organizational sponsors and university mentors. There is, of course, a tacit or informal understanding that the researcher will share findings with organizational sponsors.

You might ask why organizational professionals and executives want to participate in informed basic research? Since I don't know of research on this question, I can only rely on personal experiences. Based on my experience of receiving many rejections of invitations to organizational executives and professionals to participate in research, I would say that the majority do not have the time or interest to be engaged in informed basic research. However, almost all of the 'reflective' practitioners who have volunteered to participate in my research studies say they enjoyed it and the benefits of participation exceeded the costs. Once a relationship is established, practitioners tend to view me and my colleagues as friendly outsiders who facilitate a critical understanding of their situation. Reflective practitioners want to make sense of and learn from their experiences (Schon 1987). They seek opportunities to talk and reflect on their experiences with trusted outside researchers who they view as safe, impartial listeners and sounding boards for their ideas. This provides them a way to answer the Weickian question, 'How do I know what I mean until I hear what I say?' In addition, discussing basic science questions and topics with researchers represents a way for practitioners to remain current in a professional domain and to increase their absorptive capacity (Cohen and Levinthal 1990). Practitioners tend to appreciate the special expertise of academic researchers in bringing ideas from relevant theories and cases to the setting being studied, approaching ideas from the outside, reflecting ideas back to organizational participants, and providing opportunities for critical analysis and discussion. For example, in our longitudinal study of change in a healthcare system, the president of one organization told us she looks forward to our periodic interviews 'to receive therapy from my organizational shrink.'

Throughout Chapters 3–8, I referred to this informed kind of engaged scholarship because obtaining the advice of various stakeholders represents an important first step in studying a research problem from different viewpoints. Moreover, this book is written principally for doctoral students and junior faculty who are just launching their research careers. For a variety of pragmatic institutional reasons, they are generally expected to conduct studies that examine basic descriptive and explanatory research questions that advance the science more than the practice in a problem domain. As a budding scholar's career gets established and blossoms, then he/she is prepared to undertake more involved forms of engaged scholarship, as discussed in the sections below.

Many social scientists adopt this kind of informed research as a normal course of conducting their studies. To them this kind of informed basic research may represent nothing new. But as noted in Chapter 1, this kind of engaged basic research is often not reflected in research papers published in leading academic journals. These unengaged or disengaged studies typically reflect the following characteristics: (1) a research problem or question is posed but no evidence is presented that grounds the nature and prevalence of the problem, its boundary conditions, and why it merits investigation; (2) a single, theoretical model is proposed, but no consideration is given to plausible alternative models or the status quo approach for dealing with the research problem or question; (3) the research design relies on statistically analyzing questionnaire or secondary data files (such as PIMs, patent data, or census files) without the researcher talking to any informants or respondents in the field; and (4) results are presented on the statistical significance of relationships with little or no discussion of their practical significance and implications.

I encourage journal editors and reviewers to revise or reject research papers that reflect these characteristics of unengaged or disengaged scholarship.

Because such papers are not grounded in 'reality' nor informed by key stakeholders, they often result in making trivial advancements to science, and contribute to widening the gap between theory and practice. Anderson et al. (2001) characterize this kind of unengaged scholarship as 'puerile science' that is often low in both relevance and rigor. Simply talking with a few knowledgeable people about problem formulation, theory building, research design, and problem solving goes a long way to reducing these problems of disengaged scholarship. By stepping outside of themselves, researchers can gain a more informed perspective of their studies.

COLLABORATIVE RESEARCH

Collaborative research entails a greater sharing of power and activities among researchers and stakeholders than informed research. Collaborative research teams are typically composed of insiders and outsiders who jointly share in the activities listed in Figure 9.1 in order to co-produce basic knowledge that describes or explains a complex problem or issue being examined (Louis and Bartunek 1992). The division of labor is typically negotiated to take advantage of the complementary skills of different research team members. The balance of power or responsibility may shift back and forth among collaborators as demands for various perspectives and contacts are needed to perform the research activities. Because this collaborative form of research tends to focus on basic questions of mutual long-term interest to the partners, it has much less of an applied orientation than the design/evaluation or intervention forms of engaged scholarship. The motivations of individual parties to engage in collaborative research may vary. But as typically found in basic research and development projects undertaken in universities, corporations, and research institutes, there tends to be a strong shared curiosity in the problem among collaborators and a felt need for innovation and adaptation (Adler et al. 2004).

For example, in launching the Minnesota Innovation Research Program (see Van de Ven et al. 2000), we began by first forming an interdisciplinary academic research group of faculty from different university departments who were interested in studying innovation. After several meetings to develop shared interests in studying the process of innovation from concept to implementation in their natural field settings, the academic researchers then solicited managerial partners to collaborate with in conducting the study. This was done through a series of meetings with small groups of managers from various organizations that were launching innovations or new ventures in their organizations.

A 'snowball' sampling approach was used to invite managers and entrepreneurs to these meetings. It began by inviting practitioners that the academic investigators (particularly the senior faculty)[3] knew well based on prior engagements in research projects, executive education programs, consulting engagements, and participation in discussion groups. These managers, in turn, nominated and often personally invited their peers by encouraging them to attend subsequent meetings to explore interest in study participation.

In the meetings with innovation managers and entrepreneurs, we explored interests in collaborative research to study 'how and why innovations develop over time from concept to implementation.' Innovation managers shared their opinions of the research question, why it was important to them, and how it might be studied. The discussions made clear that the research question was interesting and important to study, that it had no immediate pay-off to practitioners or academics, but that academics and managers could each contribute useful ideas in studying the question. These meetings produced many useful ideas that subsequently guided the longitudinal research. A substantial proportion of innovation managers attending the meetings also expressed interest in participating in various ways as collaborators in the study or in providing access to conduct the research in their organizations.

From these meetings, I learned that at the time of designing a collaborative research project, prospective solutions to research questions are secondary in comparison with the importance of the research question that is being addressed. A good indicator of a big question is its self-evident capability to motivate the attention and enthusiasm of scholars and practitioners alike. Indeed, as Caswill and Shove (2000*b*: 221) state practitioners are 'often more attracted by new ideas and concepts than by empirical materials.'

Several good treatments and examples of collaborative research are available in the management literature (Lawler et al. 1985; Bartunek and Louis 1996; Rynes et al. 1999; Amabile et al. 2001; Anderson et al. 2001; Mohrman et al. 2001; Adler et al. 2004). Research teams in which one or more members are relative insiders to a setting and one or more members are relative outsiders have been argued to offer distinct advantages for integrating diverse perspectives on the problem or phenomenon being investigated (Van de Ven and Ferry 1980; Evered and Louis 1981; Louis and Bartunek 1992). While the composition of collaborative research teams varies with the topic and question, they typically consist of co-investigators from different disciplines and practices who meet repeatedly to design and conduct the study and interpret how its findings advance an understanding of the research problem or question (Bartunek and Louis 1996).

---

[3] Younger members of the research team, of course, had to rely on the network of contacts of senior colleagues since they did not have the experience and institutional relationships with practitioners in the managerial community. The important take-away from this observation is that junior scholars should not try to go it alone; take advantage of the relational network of senior colleagues in contacting and accessing practitioners and other stakeholders in a study.

The heart of this activity is a collective learning experience among collaborating partners. Through repeated meetings over an extended period of time, team members come to know and respect each other by sharing different but complementary perspectives on problems and topics of common interest. In addition, they can push one another to appreciate issues in ways that are richer and more penetrating than they understood before.[4]

Underlying this form of research is the proposition that collaborative research facilitates learning and enhances the likelihood of achieving the double hurdles of quality and relevance for scholars and practitioners (Hatchuel 2001; Pettigrew 2001). Anderson et al. (2001) and Hodgkinson et al. (2001) argue that stakeholder involvement in the research increases the impartiality of the research by incorporating the diverse perspectives of multiple stakeholders. Research collaborations that incorporate such diversity spur novelty and creativity through exposure to diverse assumptions, objectives, and ways of viewing phenomena (Rynes et al. 1999), and through the motivational effects of working on real-world problems (Lawler et al. 1985).

Various forms of collaboration can be structured into research teams as well as research review panels and advisory boards. This is a stated policy of university–industry research initiatives by the US National Science Foundation and National Institute of Health, as well the Advanced Institute of Management initiative in the UK that is funded by the two main British social research councils (ESRC/EPSRC). For example, I was involved in one such university–industry research consortium in which criteria for selecting proposals to be funded stipulated that members of each project team represent two or more university departments and at least one of the sponsoring companies. Teams of supported projects also agreed to make annual presentations of their progress and to adjust their work based on feedback from a review panel. The review panel for each project consisted of leading scholars in the project domain and practitioners from the companies.

The annual review consisted of a day-long site visit by the review panel. Typically each project team made a single presentation in the morning to an audience comprising its review panel, plus other interested members from the companies and the university community. In the afternoon the project team met with the review panel to discuss its feedback and suggestions. Following this meeting, the panel submitted a written report to the program's advisory board (consisting of university administration and company executives). Continued funding was contingent on a favorable response by the review panel and an overall evaluation of progress by the advisory board. The program led to a number of government-funded follow-up projects as well

---

[4] While researchers can learn much from data collected in a study, they can also learn much from knowledge that is already available among different members of a research team. This idea of knowledge arbitrage by learning from divergent perspectives is discussed later.

as several projects that were funded by individual companies. Personal communications with investigators who participated in this program revealed that it was one of the most productive learning experiences of their professional lives.

Several concerns about studying real-world problems in research collaborations have been expressed. These include the difficulties of meeting conventional scientific requirements of internal and external validity (Cook and Campbell 1979; Sackett and Mullen 1993). Practitioner involvement may compromise the independence and objectivity of the academic researcher (Beyer and Trice 1982; Hackman 1985; Grey 2001). Participating organizations may view the research findings as proprietary and not available for dissemination in the public domain (Lawler et al. 1985). These concerns (and others) represent risks inherent in any collaborative research venture (Rynes et al. 1999). Some of them originate in the way projects are designed and negotiated at the outset. Researchers with unclear objectives or little experience in collaborative research may unwittingly find themselves trapped in such difficulties because they did not carefully negotiate the initial terms and understandings of the research project with all participants. Hatchuel (2001) emphasizes that research collaborations require clear objectives and careful negotiation of the identities and roles of participants, the rules of engagement and disengagement, and the dissemination and use of study findings. A collaborative research project represents a joint venture, in which many of the principles for negotiating and managing strategic alliances and inter-organizational relationships apply (Galaskiewicz 1985; Ring and Van de Ven 1994; McEvily et al. 2003).

Amabile et al. (2001) note, however, that research projects tend to be collaborations among individuals or teams of different professions (academic disciplines and business functions) who are not all members of the same organization. They examined if and how the success of this 'cross-profession' collaboration is influenced by collaborative team, environment, and process characteristics. Based on a case study of their four-year TEAM (Team Events and Motivation) study, they found that creating a successful collaborative research team is difficult. They make five recommendations for designing an academic-practitioner research team: (1) carefully select academics and practitioners for diverse, complementary skills and backgrounds, intrinsic motivation in the problem being investigated, and a willingness to work with people of different cognitive styles and different professional cultures; (2) clarify commitments, roles, responsibilities, and expectations at the outset, and continually update them as they evolve; (3) establish regular, facilitated communication, especially if team members are not located in the same place; (4) develop ways for academics and practitioners to get to know and trust each other as people with possible cultural differences; and (5) occasionally set aside time for the team to reflect on itself and explicitly discuss task, process, and relationship conflict. These recommendations appear advisable for any heterogeneous working group (Hackman 1991).

Mohrman et al. (2001) empirically examined the perceived usefulness of research by practitioners in a context where researchers were not playing an action-oriented interventionist role. As anticipated by the discussion in Chapter 8, they found that practitioners in ten companies undergoing change viewed research results as useful when they were jointly interpreted with researchers and when practitioners had opportunities to self-design actions based on the research findings. Mohrman et al. (2001) conclude that 'perceived usefulness requires far more than simply doing research in relevant areas' (p. 369). Moreover, 'it would seem that researchers must do more than work collaboratively with organizational members to understand research findings. Perhaps they must become part of an organization's self-design activities if they wish to promote usefulness' (p. 370).

DESIGN/POLICY EVALUATION RESEARCH

A third form of engaged scholarship is research undertaken to examine normative questions dealing with the design and evaluation of policies, programs, or models for solving practical problems of a profession in question. Variously called 'design or policy science' or 'evaluation research,' this form of research goes beyond describing or explaining a social problem or issue (as discussed in the first two forms of engaged scholarship), but also seeks to obtain evidence-based knowledge of the efficacy or relative success of alternative solutions to applied problems.

In *The Sciences of the Artificial*, Simon (1996) discussed the fundamental differences between 'explanatory sciences'—studies as just discussed that attempt to describe, explain, predict social systems—and 'design sciences'—studies that create artificial knowledge of artifacts, policies, or programs for solving practical problems, as practiced in medicine or engineering. Design science 'is concerned with how things ought to be, with devising structures to attain goals' (Simon 1996: 133). The basic idea of design science involves developing and evaluating policies, programs, or artifacts that are being developed to address social problems—such as medical procedures (Glasgow et al. 2003), organizational designs (Dunbar and Starbuck 2006), or managerial practices (Romme and Endenburg 2006). These kinds of design studies focus on pragmatic research questions, such as 'Will it work?' and 'Does it perform better or worse than the status quo solution to a problem?' Romme (2003) and van Aken (2005) point out that the core mission of design science is to develop knowledge that can be used by professionals to design solutions to their field problems. 'Understanding the nature and causes of problems can be a great help in designing solutions. However, a design science does not limit itself to understanding, but also develops knowledge on the advantages and disadvantages of alternative solutions' (van Aken 2005: 22).

Evaluation research methods are typically used to assess the empirical usefulness of a policy or assess the impact of a program (Weiss 1998). Suchman (1967), one of the pioneers of evaluation research, defined it as 'the process of determining the value or amount of success of a policy or program in achieving a predetermined objective' (p. 28). In terms of the engaged scholarship model, evaluation research typically includes the steps of formulating the objective of a policy or program (problem formulation), identifying the values and criteria to use in measuring success (research design), determining and explaining the degree of success (theory building), and making recommendations for further program activity (problem solving). Suchman emphasizes that the methods used by evaluation researchers should adhere as closely as possible to applying accepted scientific methods. These research methods typically include mathematical simulation modeling, case studies, controlled experiments, and natural field experiments.

But Suchman (1967: 20) importantly adds that 'the same procedures that were used to discover knowledge are now being called upon to evaluate one's ability to apply this knowledge.' He points out that evaluation research and basic research are undertaken for different purposes. The primary objective of basic research is the discovery of knowledge using the conventional scientific methods to develop and test hypotheses. Usually no administrative action is contemplated or need follow. Evaluation research adds the additional challenge of addressing the potential utility of findings for improving a program or policy being evaluated given pragmatic political and administrative constraints. 'Only rarely can [an evaluation researcher] take consolation in the fact that "the operation was a success but the patient died"' (Suchman 1967: 21).

In recent years there is a trend to encourage professional providers to develop and implement 'evidence-based' models of practice in many fields, including medicine, mental health, social work, education, policing, management, and others (Denis and Langley 2002; Small and Uttal 2005; Rousseau 2006). Evidence-based practices are designs or interventions that have demonstrated effectiveness in rigorous research designs, across multiple studies, and in multiple settings. One of the first domains to institutionalize evidence-based practice is medicine with the adoption of randomized clinical trials (RCT) (Dopson et al. 2002). Typically undertaken to determine which of several drugs, devices, or treatments are safe and efficacious, the RCT is used by policy makers to justify practices that are undertaken at levels ranging from patient care, to the health delivery organization, and to the policies of government support (e.g., Medicare).

Most evaluation research studies, such as the RCT, leave unanswered the question of exactly how to treat an individual case with a specific problem (e.g., what to do with an individual patient). Even in the middle ground between theory and practice, achieving generality requires giving up the ability to develop knowledge for a specific context and instance of application (Guyatt et al. 1986; Marvel and Amodei 1992). This latter kind of knowledge comes from clinical experience of solving the particular problem at hand (as discussed in the next form of engaged scholarship).

The models or policies that form the basis of design science and evaluation research typically address types of problems or archetypes that are more general than the particular problems faced by a practitioner *in situ*, but are less aggregated or general than the problem domains often examined by scientists (Johnson et al. 1993; Dunn 1994; Hammond 1999). For example, they tend to focus on specific medical treatments for diabetes, bridge-building models for civil engineering, or alternative models for designing social programs or organizational structures.

When conducting these evaluation studies researchers typically take a distanced and outside perspective of the designs and policies being evaluated. Inquiry from the outside is necessary because evidence-based evaluations require comparisons of numerous cases, and because distance from any one case is required for evaluation findings to be viewed as impartial and legitimate. There are, however, important roles for engagement of stakeholders in the programs being evaluated. Principally, they focus on providing stakeholders opportunities to participate in evaluation study decisions that may affect them. In terms of the engaged scholarship model, these decisions include the purposes of the evaluation study (problem formulation), the criteria and models used to evaluate the program in question (research design), and how study findings will be analyzed, interpreted, and used (problem solving).

I learned first-hand of these challenges of engagement when designing and conducting organization assessment studies in the 1970s (Van de Ven and Ferry 1980). At the time, research methodology texts typically viewed an evaluation researcher as an outside expert who designed and conducted the evaluation in an objective and impartial way. But in practice, we learned that the interests and value judgments of many stakeholders need to be taken into account in making three key decisions: (1) Who decides what criteria should be used to evaluate an organization or program? (2) Whose conceptual framework should be used to guide the assessment? (3) How should the study be conducted to facilitate learning and use of evaluation study results among practitioners within the organizations being assessed?

As noted in Chapter 8, I believe an evaluation researcher has no unilateral right to impose his/her answers to these questions without informed consent of the people affected by these decisions. Any model or theory reflects multiple meanings and interests, some of which conflict with those of the users or the subjects. Hence, use of any theory or model should require negotiated consent of those assessed. In past research projects, involving representatives of managers and employees of the organizations being assessed in these questions entailed numerous discussions. But not only did I obtain consent, the process strengthened the evaluation design and resulted in requests to present and interpret study findings throughout the organizations (as discussed in Van de Ven and Ferry 1980).

ACTION/INTERVENTION RESEARCH

A fourth form of engaged scholarship, often called *action research*, takes a clinical intervention approach to diagnose and treat a problem of a specific client. The problem may be a medical condition of a patient, performance declines of an organization, or a strategic change initiative of an executive. As these examples suggest, two features distinguish action research from the other forms of engaged scholarship discussed before: (1) an applied clinical question or problem experienced by an individual client that is (2) addressed by engagement with and intervention in the client's setting.

Kurt Lewin (1945), a pioneer of action research, suggested a learning strategy of both engaging with and intervening in the client's social setting. The foundation of this learning process was client participation in problem solving using systematic methods of data collection, feedback, reflection, and action (Passmore 2001). Since Lewin's time, action research has evolved into a diverse family of clinical research strategies in many professional fields, such as business, education, human services, and a variety of social causes.

For example, Small and Uttal (2005) point out that feminist action research scholars in sociology, psychology, and family studies have used an array of action research methods to integrate knowledge and action to promote the political, social, and economic status of women. Social emancipation and empowerment agendas often use action research approaches to raise consciousness and equip individuals and community groups with knowledge that will help them gain mastery over their affairs and foster social change. In corporate research centers, a 'mode 2' form of action research for the production of knowledge has emerged as an alternative to the 'mode 1' form of university-based research (Gibbons et al. 1994). Common to these various forms of action research is engagement between researchers and clients for the purpose of learning how to address a problem or issue and simultaneously generating scientific knowledge (Lawler et al. 1985; Shani et al. 2004).

Action research projects tend to begin by diagnosing the particular problem or need of an individual client. To the extent possible, a researcher utilizes whatever knowledge is available from basic or design science, evidence-based practices, or clinical quality guidelines to understand the client's problem.

However, this knowledge may not apply or may require substantial adaptation to fit the ill-structured or context-specific nature of the client's problem. Moreover, action research projects often consist of N-of-1 studies, where systematic comparative evidence can only be gained through trial-and-error experiments over time. In this situation, action researchers have argued that the only way to understand a social system is to change it through deliberate intervention and diagnosis of responses to the intervention (e.g., Argyris et al. 1985; Schein 1987; Argyris and Schon 1996; Beer 2001). This interventionist approach typically requires intensive interaction, training, and consulting by the researcher with people in the client's setting.

Action researchers have also argued that to be useful, knowledge must be actionable. Argyris (2000) states that for knowledge to be actionable, the propositions should specify:

- The intended consequences;
- The behavioral or action sequences to produce the consequences;
- The causal relationship between the actions and the consequences; and
- The relevant governing values from which the action designs are derived (Argyris 2000: 425).

These criteria of useful actionable knowledge apply, of course, to addressing clinical questions of problem solving and control. To intervene in and control the problem of a client action researchers need causal conditional propositions of the form—if E conditions exist, do X to achieve Y, but be cautious of Z side effects. To implement such propositions, action researchers must often play the highly visible and proactive role of change agent in helping a client solve a problem.

Discussion

The four kinds of engaged scholarship just discussed represent different approaches for conducting social research. Each approach is aimed at addressing a different kind of research question (description, explanation, design, or control of a problematic situation). Sometimes advocates of a particular form of research make disparaging remarks about the irrelevance of other forms of research undertaken to examine different research questions. This is unfortunate. From my perspective, all four forms of engaged scholarship are legitimate and needed. Which is most appropriate depends on the research question and the perspective taken to examine the question. Pragmatically, the relevance of approaches and answers to research questions should be judged in terms of how well they address the intended question about the problematic situation (Dewey 1938).

The basic and applied research questions examined by the different forms of engaged scholarship are interdependent. Descriptions and explanations of problems often require careful and detached observations of a system's behavior in its natural condition. In contrast, questions of design, evaluation, and intervention often require more attached and direct interventions into the system being investigated. Moreover, since applied questions of design and intervention typically rely on knowing answers to basic questions of description and explanation, it is important to appreciate temporal interdependencies in the development of knowledge about these research questions. In general there is a circular relationship among these questions. Designs and interventions are based on correct descriptions and explanations of the processes and causal relations of the system being investigated. And when interventions or predictions don't work as planned, they require careful description and explanation.

In practice, there are many variations and overlaps (too numerous to discuss here) among the four forms of engaged scholarship presented above. Bartunek and Louis (1996) discuss a variety of insider/outsider team research designs that incorporate elements of collaborative and action research models. Bevan et al. (2006) have been using a design science approach that incorporates action research methods for undertaking a large scale planned change intervention in the British National Health Service. So also, Trullen and Bartunek (2006) examine overlaps between design science approaches with action research in studying OD (organizational development) intervention strategies. They point out that the design science approach of Romme (2003) incorporates action research methods for developing actionable knowledge proposed by Argyris (2000). Finally, one form of engaged scholarship may transition into another form in subsequent research projects. For example, Tushman et al. (2006) discuss how their initial informed basic science study in IBM transitioned after a few years into a collaborative research project as the researchers and practitioners came to know one another, shared common research questions and interests, and joined together to co-produce knowledge of planned organization change efforts.

Engagement is a common denominator in all these various forms of research. Engagement raises a number of challenges that are often not salient in traditional approaches to social research. These challenges include: (1) reconciling divergent viewpoints generated by engagement and triangulation; (2) negotiating the research relationship by establishing and building relationships with stakeholders; (3) being reflexive about the researcher's role in a study; and (4) spending time in field research sites. These challenges are now discussed. I frame this discussion from the perspective of the academic researcher, and suggest some practical strategies that might be useful to university-based scholars as they engage stakeholders in their research.

CHALLENGES OF ENGAGEMENT AND TRIANGULATION

A basic premise of engaged scholarship is that researchers can make more penetrating and insightful advances to science and practice by obtaining the perspectives of relevant stakeholders in problem formulation, theory building, research design, and problem solving than when they perform these research activities alone. The more ambiguous and complex the problem the greater the need for engaging others who can provide different perspectives for revealing critical dimensions of the nature, context, and implications of the problem domain. Engagement provides a way of triangulating on a research question.

Triangulation is the use of multiple methods and sources of information in a study. The concept of triangulation was introduced in the social sciences by Campbell and Fiske (1959) as a procedure for establishing the convergent and discriminant validity of measures through the application of a multitrait-multimethod matrix, and by Webb et al. (1966) who argued that the validity of propositions can be enhanced by using a variety of methods, including nonreactive measures. Denzin (1978) expanded the concept to include four types of triangulation through the use of multiple data sources, investigators, theoretical models, and methods for investigating social phenomena. Although the use of multiple methods and data sources are the most discussed types of triangulation, engaged scholarship emphasizes investigator triangulation by obtaining the perspectives of other investigators and stakeholders in the research process. These types of triangulation are complementary. For example, the perspectives from other investigators and stakeholders often include suggestions of what alternative models, methods, and data sources are most appropriate and feasible in a given study.

It is important to clarify, however, that triangulation through engaged scholarship is based on different assumptions and uses of triangulation than typically discussed. Mathison (1988) points out that arguments for triangulation are typically based on the assumption that the bias inherent in any particular source of investigator, data, model, or method will cancel out when used in conjunction with other sources, and that what is left is a reliable convergence upon the truth about what is investigated.

But in practice, the information obtained from triangulation may not converge; instead, it may be inconsistent or contradictory. Inconsistency occurs when different informants, methods, and data sources produce a range of perspectives or data that do not converge on a single proposition about the problem being investigated. Instead, the evidence presents alternative propositions containing different or opposing views of the social phenomenon being studied.

Given these different outcomes, Mathison raises the question of whether arguments for triangulation have confused validity with reliability. The evidence produced by alternative sources and methods might be different because of bias in data sources (reliability), or it may be that different methods and sources tap different dimensions or domains of knowing the phenomenon (validity). If we restrict ourselves to a reliability view of triangulation, we would report only the convergent findings on which all data sources and methods agree. 'By doing this, one would necessarily be unduly restrictive in making valid claims about social phenomena' (Mathison 1988: 16). Buchanan (2003: 18) states a more critical postmodern position—'The singular, coherent account which fails to expose conflicting views of the change process is deeply suspect.'

A metaphor from geometry may be helpful to distinguish valid from reliable representations of a phenomenon through a triangulation strategy. In geometry increasing numbers of dimensions are needed to represent (or plot all points) of more complex systems. For example, all points in a line can be represented completely in one dimension, all points in a square (or along two axes) requires two dimensions, all points in a cube or box require three dimensions, etc. The question is how many dimensions are needed to represent (or plot) the key features of a problem being investigated? To be considered valid, the dimensionality of the methods used should match the dimensionality of the phenomena observed. When unidimensional methods are used to study a multidimensional phenomenon the result will obviously be a myopic and only partially-valid representation of the phenomenon. Conversely, use of multidimensional methods to examine unidimensional phenomena will converge in a reliable way to the number of dimensions of the phenomenon observed. Valid measurement first requires establishing the dimensionality or complexity of the phenomena under investigation. Then one can examine the reliability (or convergence) of alternative methods in representing that complexity.

The dimensionality or complexity of a problem does not objectively exist 'out there' as this geometric metaphor implies. Instead, as discussed in Chapter 3, problems are theory-laden and reflect the social construction of observers. Dimensionality is a property of the models or theories used to represent a problem rather than the problem itself. A single observer (with a given mindset) tends to represent a problem in fewer dimensions than do multiple observers with different perspectives. If that is the case, engaging and triangulating the perspectives of various stakeholders increases the likelihood of surfacing more dimensions of a problem domain. Triangulation increases the richness (and complexity) of problem representation, which decreases the likelihood of myopic representations that other stakeholders may perceive as being biased and misdiagnosed views of the 'real-world' situation. When different stakeholders converge on the same dimensions of a problem, this reliability provides confidence in having a valid representation of the problem domain. But when the views of different stakeholders do not converge, this indicates that the dimensionality of a problem domain has not yet been mapped in a valid and reliable way. All one can conclude is that 'there is more to this problem domain than I envisioned.' This recognition should lead a researcher to search more deeply and broadly into the problem domain before proposing a theory or model for resolving it. Hence, it is important to note that the richness or quality of problem representation is a function of engaging and triangulating the perspectives of different stakeholders.

Mathison (1988) proposes a view of triangulation that is consistent with this notion of engaged scholarship. She says that 'the value of triangulation is not a technological solution to a data collection and analysis problem, it is as a technique which provides more and better evidence from which researchers can *construct meaningful propositions* about the social world. The value of triangulation lies in providing evidence such that the researcher can construct explanations of the social phenomena from which they arise' (Mathison 1988: 15, italics in the original).

An engaged scholar using different informants, sources, and methods to study a research question should not expect that the findings generated by those different methods will automatically come together to produce a convergent answer. The point of triangulation, Patton (1980) suggests is 'to study and understand when and why there are differences' (p. 331). Triangulation through engagement of diverse stakeholders provides different images for understanding a problem, thus increasing the 'potency' or validity of research explanations (Mathison 1988: 13).

So given different outcomes of triangulation, how might a researcher make sense of convergent, inconsistent, and contradictory evidence from different sources and methods?

It is often easier to construct meaningful explanations in cases where the evidence is convergent. For example, Azevedo (1997) advocates the use of multiple models for mapping a problem being investigated, and argues that knowledge that is reliable is invariant (or converges) across these models. Convergent explanations rely on similarities, consensus, and central tendencies in explaining a problem or issue under investigation. Convergent explanations tend to treat differences and inconsistencies as bias, errors, outliers, or noise.

More difficult (but often more insightful) explanations emerge when different data sources yield inconsistent or contradictory information. Arbitrage provides a strategy for developing holistic, integrative explanations based on different accounts of the same phenomenon. Friedman (2000: 24) points out that in academe and elsewhere, 'there is a deeply ingrained tendency to think in terms of highly segmented, narrow areas of expertise, which ignores the fact that the real world is not divided up into such neat little bits.' He argues that the way to see, understand, and explain complex problems in the world is to systematically connect the different dots, bits, and pieces of information through arbitrage—'assigning different weights to different perspectives at different times in different situations, but always understanding that it is the interaction of all of them together that is really the defining feature of the [system]...and thereby order the chaos' (Friedman 2000: 23–4). Arbitrage is a process that Wilson (1999) calls 'concilience,' integrating fragmented perspectives and bits of knowledge into a larger (gestalt) appreciation of the question being addressed. Arbitrage is a strategy of explaining differences by seeing the interdependencies and webs of entanglements between different and divergent dimensions of a problem, its boundaries, and context.

Finally, contradictory information from different sources may represent instances of conflicting values and interests among pluralistic stakeholders about the problem or issue being examined. Explanations of a problem domain should obviously reflect these contradictions when observed. Chapter 8 summarized four general methods for reasoning through paradoxes by either balancing between opposites, shifting levels of analysis, alternating positions over time, or introducing new concepts that dissolve the paradox (Poole and Van de Ven 1989). And, as discussed in Chapter 3, inconsistent and contradictory findings are often viewed as anomalies that trigger theory building through abductive reasoning.

In short, triangulation challenges the engaged scholar to be explicit, as much as possible, about the information obtained from engaging different stakeholders, models, methods, and data sources. Not only should the researcher report the triangulation procedures, but also the convergent, inconsistent, and contradictory information from which explanations about the research question are constructed. This explanation should rely on the data on hand. It also relies on a holistic understanding, obtained from engaging multiple stakeholders, of the problem itself, its history, the intentions of actors, and their evolving relationships in changing contexts. Mathison concludes that

It takes all of these levels to provide good explanations around the data collected through triangulation strategies....By explicating these three levels of information, the logic and plausibility of explanations are public and open to discussion—a minimal criterion for social science research. Without revealing this information, one would certainly be concerned about the quality of the data, plausibility, coherence, and accommodation of counter-factual evidence. (Mathison 1988: 16–17)

NEGOTIATING THE RESEARCH RELATIONSHIP

Negotiating a relationship with practitioners and other stakeholders and obtaining access to data sources are formidable challenges in launching any form of research. Most research questions represent novel and ambiguous ideas that are difficult to understand and are open to many interpretations and interests. Carlile's framework for managing knowledge across boundaries discussed in Chapter 8 applies equally well for communicating research questions and purposes between researchers and practitioners. A key implication of Carlile's model is that it requires many discussions to convey (transfer) the research message, interpret (translate) its many possible meanings, and negotiate (transform) differing interests into pragmatic uses that the parties find acceptable. Rarely does a single meeting (particularly if it is a 'cold call' among strangers) achieve sufficient common understandings and interests among parties to motivate their commitment to a research project. This communication process, however, is greatly facilitated when it occurs among friends or acquaintances who have worked together in the past. This implies that new or junior scholars to a research domain should not try to go it alone. As noted before, they should seek out and rely upon the social networks of senior colleagues to introduce, broker, and negotiate a research relationship with potential practitioners and stakeholders.

These negotiations should recognize that not all research relationships are alike. The different research questions examined with the four forms of engaged scholarship can be studied *with* and/or *for* practitioners and other stakeholders. Although this distinction is seldom made, it importantly influences the research relationship and the form of engagement. Research done *for* others (as in design/evaluation, and action research) typically implies an *exchange* relationship where research is undertaken in service of solving a problem of a client or user group. In an exchange relationship the purpose of engagement is to ensure that the interests and values of the client are reflected in the study. In contrast, research undertaken *with* others implies a *collaborative* relationship, as in the informed and collaborative forms of research. In a collaborative relationship the purpose of engagement is to obtain the different but complementary perspectives of collaborators for understanding the problem domain.

Being clear about the nature of the relationship between researchers and stakeholders is obviously important for clarifying the expectations and roles of all parties to a research project. Sometimes, however, researchers unwittingly negotiate studies both for and with other stakeholders without understanding their mixed and unintended consequences.

The interests of the researcher and consumer or client are often not the same and difficult to align. In an exchange relationship the client or consumer typically views the researcher as a consultant who is expected to solve his or her particular problem. Sometimes that researcher is less interested in the client's particular problem, but more interested in the general class of phenomena of which the particular problem is a part. In these cases the researcher may be willing to serve as a research consultant for the client in exchange for obtaining resources and data needed to pursue his/her own basic research agenda. In another case I know of a researcher who provides executive training to organizations in exchange for gaining access to these organizations to pursue his basic research agenda. In these cases the researcher is viewed as having the power of expert knowledge over the less powerful and dependent 'client, patient, user or subject,' but the latter's consent, access, and resources are needed to conduct social research.

Thus, we have a mixed motive tit-for-tat game situation that may result in win–lose or lose–lose situations for the researcher or the client, unless the exchange relationship is negotiated carefully and openly. In such exchange relationships engagement often represents an instrumental way to increase the likelihood that the research addresses the questions, problems, and interests of the client. Given divergent interests, it is not surprising that researchers fear involving clients in designing the research, for it may 'misdirect' or 'hijack' achieving the researcher's objectives. For example, Brief and Dukerich (1991), Grey (2001), and Kilduff and Kelemen (2001) argued that practitioner involvement in formulating research questions may steer the research in narrow, short-term, or particularistic directions. Such criticisms are premised on the researcher having an exchange relationship, rather than a collaborative relationship with stakeholders in a study. The divergent objectives, conflicting interests, and power asymmetries often produce instrumental and calculative consequences between researchers and clients. Ironically, this exchange relationship that underlies the action science model of Argyris et al. (1985) may unwittingly contribute to the very conditions of his Model 1 defensive behaviors and undiscussable issues that he abhors between action researchers and their clients.

Research undertaken *with* practitioners implies a collaborative relationship among equals whose differences are complementary in reaching a goal. The goal is to understand a problem or issue that is too complex for any party to study alone. Appreciating these individual limitations motivates some (certainly not all) researchers and practitioners to collaborate and learn with each other. In order to do this, the parties must come to know each other and negotiate their advisory or collaborative relationship— including how they will accommodate, adapt, and integrate their different perspectives on a problem or question being examined. Such a collaborative relationship is premised on a common desire to learn and to understand a complex problem or question that drives the engagement. Learning the nature of a question or phenomenon in ambiguous settings often entails numerous false starts and dead ends. Learning involves waste. We tend to forget how much paper was thrown away in order to learn how to write. Heedful accommodation to the diverse viewpoints of advisors and collaborators in a research project becomes a major challenge. When managed properly, diverse viewpoints can yield a richer gestalt of the question being investigated than the sensemaking of a single stakeholder (Morgan 1983; Weick 1995).

Engaging advisors and collaborators in a study does not necessarily imply that a researcher loses control of his/her study, but it does entail greater accountability to the stakeholders involved in a study. Engagement often raises false expectations that the suggestions and concerns expressed will be addressed. As noted before, engagement does not require consensus among stakeholders; much learning occurs through arbitrage by leveraging differences among stakeholders. Negotiating different and sometimes conflicting interests implies that creative conflict management skills are critical for engaged scholars. Without these skills, engagement may produce the ancient Tower of Babel, where intentions to build a tower to reach heaven were thwarted by the noisy and confusing language of the people.

BEING REFLEXIVE ABOUT THE RESEARCHER'S PERSPECTIVE

Entanglements with partisanship, politics, values, and ethics are inevitable in any form of engaged scholarship. That being the case, I argued that scholars should be reflexive by making clear whose perspectives and interests are served in a study. Adler and Jermier (2005) note that being reflexive remains an unpopular idea among many social scientists. They say,

Many still believe that all forms of partisanship should be purged from scientific research and theory development. They contend that politics should not enter into processes of knowledge creation, and many hold that it is inappropriate for scholars to engage actively in the application of knowledge. They believe that value-neutrality is the hallmark of proper scientific work, and that advocacy would undermine that objectivity. (Adler and Jermier 2005: 942)

Like many contemporary philosophers discussed in Chapter 2, Adler and Jermier (2005) challenge the possibility of value neutrality, for it would require scientists to 'do the God trick' or adopt a 'view from nowhere' (see Harding 2004).

That is, they require scholars to speak authoritatively and without bias, and to do so as if from no particular human position or social location. Standpoint theorists [in philosophy] contend that this is impossible. They argue that objectivity and understanding are better served if we [are] aware of, and make explicit, our epistemological and political baggage rather than deny we carry any (cf. Kinchloe & McLaren, 1994). Because there are no facts without theories, and because all theories are based on a standpoint that is shaped (at least in part) by political considerations, scholars should reflect on their underlying epistemological assumptions and develop an awareness of their standpoints. It also follows that we should consciously choose our standpoints and take responsibility for the impact (or lack of impact) of our scholarship on the world. (Adler and Jermier 2005: 942)

Reflexive research has two dimensions: careful interpretation and reflection. Interpretation implies that empirical data are subject to multiple meanings. As Chapter 2 discussed, most philosophers have rejected the metaphor of a simple mirror capturing the relationship between 'empirical facts' and research results (text). The second element, reflection, emphasizes the personality of the researcher, the relevant research community culture, and the problematic nature of language and narrative in the research context (Alvesson and Skoldberg 2000: 5–6).

In certain versions of postmodernism and post structuralism the emphasis is so firmly on one particular type of self-reflection that little energy is left over for anything else, such as empirical studies. It is often rhetorical or communicative aspects that attract attention, to the exclusion of everything else. Not only the critics but even several writers . . . are concerned about the risks of self-reflective isolationism, self-absorption, and impotent texts. (Alvesson and Skoldberg 2000: 246)

Reflexivity emphasizes the need to be sensitive to the viewpoints of others and whose interests are being served in a study. An internal focus is needed in order to process and reflect on your role as a researcher. But if carried to the extreme it can lead to a narrow inward turn of self-absorbing 'navel gazing.' Engaged scholarship emphasizes the need for an external 'reality check' on this internal reflection. It argues that you won't know your own assumptions and your own viewpoint until you also engage with others. An external orientation of engagement is also required to be reflexive.

Engaging stakeholders in a study also facilitates ethical research. Ethical research includes a well-known set of generalized principles and codes of ethics, such as governed by many university institutional review boards on the treatment of human subjects—provide informed consent, protect the privacy of individuals, avoid conflicts of interest and abuses in authority-dependency relationships, don't plagiarize, etc. Ethical research also requires context-specific intensive knowledge of the system being investigated in order to be sensitive to the range of human values embedded within a situation, and to reflect an awareness of the values of all stakeholders affected by a problem or issue being investigated (Dunham et al. 2006). Engagement does not assure ethical behavior on the part of the researcher. However, engagement is often a necessary prerequisite in order to identify these relevant interests and values of diverse stakeholders who are affected by, and have a stake in, a problem or issue being investigated.

Alvesson and Skoldberg (2000: 287) conclude that we should not get overwhelmed with the complexities of reflexive research. 'What is important is that the reflection is adapted to one's own personal abilities, the context of the problem being investigated, and to the perspectives of the stakeholders directly affected by the research project being undertaken.'

SPENDING TIME IN FIELD RESEARCH SITES

Time is critical for building relationships of trust, candor, and learning among researchers and practitioners (Mintzberg 1979; Pettigrew 2001). The importance of spending more time on site to build direct and personal relationships with organizational participants has been advocated to not only facilitate the implementation of research findings (Mintzberg 1979; Lawler et al. 1985), but also to increase the likelihood of making significant advances to a scholarly discipline (Daft 1984; Lawrence 1992; Weick 2001).

Empirical evidence for these claims is provided by Rynes et al. (1999), who examined 163 articles published in four leading management journals from 1993–95 and conducted a questionnaire survey of their authors. They found that the hours spent by academic researchers at organizational sites were significantly related to the implementation of research findings. Their explanation for this finding was that increased 'face time' increases affective trust of organizational members toward the researcher (e.g., Osborn and Hagedoorn 1997; Saxton 1997), and to keep the project salient in their minds. In addition, time spent on site is likely to bring the researcher closer to the phenomenon he or she is studying, as well as to increase the researcher's awareness of the ways in which organizational members are framing the topic or problem under investigation (Beyer 1997). Both of these types of insight are likely to increase the chances that the research process will lead to eventual implementation by organizational practitioners (Rynes et al. 1999: 873).

Moreover, Rynes et al. (1999) established a significant empirical relationship between research site time and scholarly contribution of the research. The factor most strongly associated with the impact of research (measured by paper citation rates) was the time spent by researchers at their research sites. One explanation is that it takes an extensive amount of direct and personal investigation to become acquainted with the dimensions and context of a phenomenon. Simon (1991), for example, argued that it takes ten years of dedicated work and attention to achieve world-class competence in a domain. While we might quibble with the amount of time it takes to achieve competence, the point is that one-time cross-sectional organizational studies only provide a single snapshot of an issue being investigated. Cross-sectional studies seldom provide researchers sufficient time and trials to become knowledgeable about their research topic.[5]

[5] I also think that too many scholars dilute their competencies by conducting an eclectic and unrelated series of cross-sectional studies in their careers.

Longitudinal research promotes deeper learning because it provides repeated trials for approximating and understanding a research question or topic. Becoming 'world class' is a path dependent process of pursuing a coherent theme of research questions from project to project over an extended period of time.

A basic, but often overlooked, fact of most academic research is that researchers are exposed to only the information that people in research sites are willing to share. Interviews in cross-sectional studies or initial interviews in longitudinal studies with research sites tend to be formal and shallow. Greater candor and penetration into the subject matter seldom occur until a sufficient number of interactions over time have occurred for participants to come to know and trust one another. Perhaps the 'one-minute manager' is an unfortunate social construction of the one-minute researcher.

One indication of comfort with a researcher is how practitioners treat you. For example, consider how a manager greeted me when I came to conduct the fourth yearly interview with him during my longitudinal field study of organizational change. When walking into his office he said, 'Normally I wear a coat and tie when outside visitors come. This morning I noticed that you were coming. So I decided not to wear a coat and tie.'

Candid information comes not only with familiarity and trust, but also with more knowledgeable and penetrating probes in responses to questions. A common self-assessment of field researchers is 'If I only knew then how the study findings turned out, I would have asked more probing questions.' Repeated interviews and meetings with practitioners in longitudinal research provide important opportunities to penetrate more deeply into the subject matter being investigated.

Longitudinal fieldwork has become a normal part of my everyday work. In addition to professorial teaching, writing, service, and administration, a normal work week includes about a day of field work in conducting site visits, interviews, observing meetings and events, and talking to people related to the organizational changes that are unfolding in real time. Trained initially in traditional approaches to studying variance theories, as Larry Mohr (1982) calls it, I have tended to launch my field studies with a specific research question and some general concepts and propositions that were derived from the literature. But as field observations began, I found it necessary in each case to alter some initial conceptions so they might better capture the process dynamics being observed. While frustrating at times, some of my greatest insights have come from field research, and they strongly influenced a growing appreciation of the dynamic processes of organizational change.

For example, while conducting a longitudinal study of the birth of child care organizations in Texas from 1972–80, I gained a new appreciation of organizational death. Organizational death is typically defined as the dissolution of the articles of incorporation of an organization in a government

Department of State. One child care organization I studied was the Mother Goose Learning center in Naccodoches, Texas. Mother Goose was experiencing financial difficulties and taken over by the Head Start center of the local Community Action Program. When I revisited the center shortly after the take over, I talked with the same center staff and held some of the same children in my arms that were enrolled in the Mother Goose center. But when I talked to the center's director, she emphatically stated 'Mother Goose is dead! We are now Head Start.'

Another new day care center that I studied was located in the Rio Grande Valley, and directed by a man named Pacco. He was an entrepreneur, who worked his heart out for the low-income people in the region. He obtained several federal grants to build low-income housing, child care centers, and healthcare clinics for low-income people in the region. He was not a very good bookkeeper, and commingled funds from various federal grants (HUD, Title XX, and others) that he got to support the diverse social service programs he was creating. The federal government indicted Pacco for commingling federal grants. He skipped town in 1977. I was fortunate to find him in a bar when I visited Dallas in 1979. He told me he was running a geriatric program in Fort Worth. After a few good beers, I asked him, 'How does it feel to be put out of business by the Feds?' I'll never forget his answer. He said, 'Look, I'm no different than a Northeast company that moved to the Southwest sunbelt and changed its product line.'

These two experiences leave me to believe that organizational births and deaths are not captured by government records; instead, they are social constructions. Experiences such as these lead me to suggest that letting go of initial conceptions and remaining open to new ideas and directions from field observations are important dispositions of engaged scholars. I recommend undertaking longitudinal field research, for it provides a rich laboratory for personal learning and development.

Conclusion

Engaged scholarship can be practiced in many different ways to address a variety of basic and applied research questions. This chapter examined four common ways. Informed basic science and collaborative research are two approaches that vary in levels of researcher control for studying basic questions of description, explanation, or prediction. Design and evaluation research is typically undertaken to examine applied questions dealing with the development and evaluation of designs, policies, and practices in a professional domain. Finally, clinical action research represents a family of approaches for diagnosing and intervening in problems of particular clients.

There are many variations of these four forms of engaged scholarship. A researcher should choose the specific form and level of engagement that fits his/her particular study.

Several considerations were discussed in making this choice. Briefly summarized, they include the following suggestions.

1. *The research problem and question.* It's the research question about the problem domain that drives the engaged scholarship process. The less you know about the problem, the greater the need to engage others who can instruct and ground you in the problem.

2. *Mode of inquiry.* Different modes of inquiry produce different kinds of knowledge: that conducted from a detached outside perspective generates what is typically called general scientific knowledge; that conducted from the inside produces practical knowledge in a particular context. These different kinds of knowledge can be linked and leveraged by engaging research team members and informants who reflect inside and outside perspectives of a problem being examined.

3. *Triangulation strategy.* The engagement of diverse investigators and stakeholders often produces suggestions of what alternative models, methods, and data sources are appropriate and feasible in a given study. The use of multiple investigators, models, methods, and data sources typically produce convergent, inconsistent, and contradictory information about the problem being investigated. These different outcomes expand traditional explanations of triangulation that focus on convergent central tendencies to include explanations of inconsistent findings through arbitrage and contradictory findings with methods for reasoning though paradoxical findings.

4. *Researcher–stakeholder relationships.* Whether the research is undertaken *with* or *for* stakeholders affects whether the researcher engages in a collaborative or exchange relationship with stakeholders, respectively. The two relationships are qualitatively different and entail unique challenges of engagement. To avoid the negative consequences of mixed motives and conflicts of interest, it is important for researchers to negotiate their relationships with stakeholders carefully and openly.

5. *Researcher's reflexive perspective.* Entanglements with partisanship, politics, values, and ethics are inevitable in any form of engaged scholarship. That being the case I argued that scholars should be reflexive by making clear whose perspectives and interests are served in a study. You can gain a better understanding and sensitivity of your own reflexive perspective by engaging with others rather than by taking an inward turn of self-absorption and reflection.

6. *Temporal duration of study.* Whether a cross-sectional or longitudinal study is undertaken depends on the research problem and question. But

it also depends on the levels of trust and mutual learning developed in prior engagements between the researchers and stakeholders. Because of the path-dependent nature of familiarity, trust, and candor in relationships, the time spent in field research sites is positively related to making higher quality knowledge contributions to science and practice.

7. *Limits of engagement.* Engagement does not necessarily imply that a researcher loses control of his/her study, but it does entail greater accountability to the stakeholders involved in a study. Engagement often raises false expectations that concerns expressed will be addressed. Engagement does not require consensus among stakeholders; much learning occurs through arbitrage by leveraging differences among stakeholders. Negotiating different and sometimes conflicting interests implies that creative conflict management skills are critical for engaged scholars. Without these skills, engagement may produce the ancient Tower of Babel, where intentions to build a tower to reach heaven were thwarted by the noisy and confusing language of the people.

8. *Study size and scope.* It is self-evident that 'big science' research programs involving many investigators in different projects and countries entail far greater engagement and coordination efforts than smaller studies typically undertaken by one or two researchers. They also tend to surface more political sensitivities, in terms of the number and degree of stakeholders who may be affected by a study and whose divergent interests may conflict. The greater the size and scope of a study, the greater the coordination costs of engagement. These costs can quickly outweigh the benefits of engaged research. Pettigrew (2003) provides a useful discussion of these issues. Engaging stakeholders (other researchers, users, and practitioners) in problem formulation, theory building, research design, and problem solving represents a more challenging way to conduct social research than the traditional approach of researchers going it alone. But the benefits far exceed the costs. By involving stakeholders in key steps of the research process, engaged scholarship provides a deeper understanding of the problem investigated than is obtained by traditional detached research.

In the final analysis the 'proof is in the pudding.' If my arguments are correct, then the researchers who adopt the engaged scholarship model of involving relevant stakeholders in problem formulation, theory building, research design, and problem solving should produce research findings that make more significant advancements both to science and to practice than the traditional approach of going it alone. As a result, research reports based on engaged scholarship should win-out in competitive reviews for research funding, publications in journals, presentations at professional conferences, and professional training and development programs over those based on unengaged or disengaged research. The cumulative record should result in career advancements and promotions for engaged scholars at disproportionately higher rates than disengaged scholars who go it alone in conducting their research. Time will tell.

Does the engaged scholarship model represent a 'one best way' of doing social research? I don't think a search for the 'holy grail' is feasible or desirable; I'm simply searching for a better way than the current status quo of creating knowledge for social science and practice. As discussed in the beginning of this book, there is a widespread belief that our current methods of research are not up to the task of understanding complex social phenomena. Research knowledge is often not used or adopted by either scientists or practitioners. Evidence for these unsatisfactory outcomes include criticisms of academic research in special issues of numerous journals and the few times published papers are cited as informing subsequent social science even five years after publication. I argued that the engaged scholarship model represents a better way of doing social research than the status quo of going it alone. Given the complexities of the social world and our limited individual capabilities, the lone investigator model of research is not doing the job. Instead, we need to think of engaged scholarship as a collective achievement. By interacting with others and developing and comparing plausible alternative models for understanding problems in the world, we are likely to gain a deeper, multifaceted appreciation of reality than any one perspective or person can create alone.

GLOSSARY TO PHILOSOPHY OF SCIENCE TERMS IN CHAPTER 2

Abduction/retroduction/retroductive reasoning: an inference to the best explanation. Its starts from a set of facts and infers the most likely hypothesis to explain the phenomenon.

Anti-essentialism (anti-essentialist): metaphysical doctrine that denies that objects have an essence or substance, which is a set of characteristics that are eternal and invariable.

Anti-foundationalism (anti-foundationalist): epistemological doctrine that denies the existence of self-justifying or self-evident first principles which guide or provide the foundation of scientific inquiry.

Age of Enlightenment/Enlightenment: period in European history between the seventeenth and eighteenth century which was characterized by a liberation from the theo-centric view of the world and replaced by an anthropocentric view that emphasized human reason as the sole source to understanding the world.

Analytic/synthetic statement: a statement is analytical if it is just true in virtue of the meaning of its constituent words. A statement is synthetic if neither it nor its denial is analytical (Boyd 1991: 4).

Axiomatic principles: primitive definitions or proposition whose truth is knowable prior to deduction or sense experience.

Cartesian dualism: Descartes construes the world as consisting of an external reality and human thought. Both reality and thought were viewed as independent of each other and thus the differentiation between the subject and the object or dualism.

Deduction: an inference to a conclusion from a finite sequence of axioms or premises considered to be true. Deduction is a system-relative concept whereby it only has meaning relative to a particular set of axioms or deductive rules.

Deductive rules (see Deduction).

Empiricism (empiricist): an epistemology that places primacy on experience as a source of human knowledge.

Epistemology: the study of nature and scope of knowledge or the theory of knowledge.

Falsification: the act of disproving a hypothesis or theory. Developed by Karl Popper.

Idealism (idealist): philosophical doctrine that views reality as mind-dependent or only mental entities are real.

Incommensurability: refers to the impossibility of comparing new/other scientific paradigms due to the differences in standards, methods, terms, world views. Thus asserting the theory-dependence of observation and denying scientific knowledge any type of objective/rational progression.

Induction: an inference to a generalization from its instances. The claim in the conclusion goes beyond the claims enumerated or stated in the premises or instances.

Instrumentalism (instrumentalist): philosophical doctrine that views concepts and theories as useful instruments for explaining or predicting phenomena.

Ontology: the study of the origin, nature, and constitution of reality.

Problem of induction: according to Reichenbach (1948) the problem of induction is the impossibility of arriving at one generalization from the enumeration of its observational instances.

Rationalism (rationalist): philosophical doctrine that privileges reason as a source of acquiring knowledge.

Referential value: refers to the existence of unobservable entities in the physical world which are represented using theoretical terms in science.

Semantic view of theory: theories consist of mathematical structures or models that are defined using mathematical language pertaining to their subject matter.

Syntactical view of theory: theories consist of axiomatic first-order logical relations among theoretical terms, and correspondence rules that give theoretical terms meaning based on their observational consequences.

Synthetic a priori: statements about reality which are acquired prior to experience.

Transcendental idealism (transcendental idealist): philosophical doctrine which holds that our mind contributes to our experience of things and subsequently we cannot know how things truly are.

Weltanschauung/paradigm: set of scientific and metaphysical principles which dictate the methods and standards by which theories are developed, confirmed, revised, and refuted.

□ BIBLIOGRAPHY

Abbott, A. (1984). 'Event Sequence and Event Duration: Colligation and Measurement,' *Historical Methods*, 17: 192–204.

—— (1988). 'Transcending General Linear Reality,' *Sociological Theory*, 6: 169–86.

—— (1990). 'A Primer on Sequence Methods,' *Organization Science*, 1(4): 375–92.

—— (1990). 'Conceptions of Time and Events in Social Science Methods: Causal and Narrative Approaches,' *Historical Methods*, 23: 140–50.

—— (1992). 'The Order of Professionalization,' *Work and Occupations*, 18: 355–84.

—— (2001). *Time Matters: On Theory and Method*. Chicago: University of Chicago Press.

—— (2004). *Methods of Discovery: Heuristics for the Social Sciences*. New York: W. W. Norton.

Abell, P. (1987). *The Syntax of Social Life: The Theory and Method of Comparative Narratives*. Oxford: Clarendon Press.

Abrahmson, E. and Rosenkopf, L. (1993). 'Institutional and Competitive Bandwagons: Using Mathematical Modeling as a Tool to Explore Innovation Diffusion,' *Academy of Management Review*, 18(3): 487–517.

Adler, P. and Jermier, J. (2005). 'Developing a Field with More Soul: Standpoint Theory and Public Policy Research for Management Scholars,' *Academy of Management Journal*, 48(6): 941–4.

—— and Kwon, S. W. (2005). *The 'Six West' Problem: Professionals and the Intraorganizational Diffusion of Innovations, with Particular Reference to Healthcare Organizations*. Working paper, University of Southern California, Los Angeles.

Adler, N., Shani, A. B., and Styhre, A. (eds.) (2004). *Collaborative Research in Organizations: Foundations for Learning, Change, and Theoretical Development*. Thousand Oaks, CA: Sage.

Agar, M. H. (1986). *Speaking of Ethnography*. Qualitative Research Methods Series, Vol. 2. Beverly Hills, CA: Sage.

Aldrich, H. E. (2001). 'Who Wants to be an Evolutionary Theorist: Remarks on the Occasion of the Year 2000 OMT Distinguished Scholarly Career Award Presentation,' *Journal of Management Inquiry*, 10(2): 115–27.

Allison, G. T. (1971). *Essence of Decision: Explaining the Cuban Missile Crisis*. Boston: Little, Brown, and Company.

Alvesson, M. (2003). 'Beyond Neo-Positivisms, Romanticists and Localists: A Reflective Approach to Research Interviews,' *Academy of Management Review*, 28(1): 13–33.

—— (2004). *Leveraging Mysteries and Breakdowns: Empirical Material as a Critical Dialogue Partner in Theory Development*. Working paper, Lund University, Sweden.

—— and Deetz, S. (1996). 'Critical Theory and Postmodernism Approaches to Organizational Studies,' in S. Clegg, C. Hardy, and W. Nord (eds.), *Handbook of Organizational Studies*. Thousand Oaks, CA: Sage, pp. 191–217.

—— and Skoldberg, K. (2000). *Reflexive Methodology: New Vistas for Qualitative Research*. London: Sage.

—— and Willmott, H. (1995). 'Strategic Management as Domination and Emancipation: From Planning and Process to Communication and Praxis,' in C. Stubbart and P. Shrivastava (eds.), *Advances in Strategic Management*, Vol. 11. Greenwich, CT: JAI Press.

Amabile, T., Patterson, C., Mueller, J. et al. (2001). 'Academic–Practitioner Collaboration in Management Research: A Case of Cross-Profession Collaboration,' *Academy of Management Journal*, 44: 418–35.

Anderson, N., Herriot, P., and Hodgkinson, G. P. (2001). 'The Practitioner–Research Divide in Industrial Work and Organizational (IWO) Psychology: Where We are Now, and Where do We Go from Here?' *Journal of Occupational and Organizational Psychology*, 74: 391–411.

Aram, J. D. and Salipante Jr., P. F. (2003). 'Bridging Scholarship in Management: Epistemological Reflections,' *British Journal of Management*, 14: 189–205.

Argyris, C. (2000). 'The Relevance of Actionable Knowledge for Breaking the Code,' in M. Beer and N. Nohria (eds.), *Breaking the Code of Change*. Boston: Harvard Business School Press, pp. 415–27.

—— and Schon, D. (1996). *Organizational Learning II: Theory, Method and Practice*. Reading, MA: Addison Wesley.

—— Putnam, R., and Smith, D. M. (1985). *Action Science: Concepts, Methods, and Skills for Research and Intervention*. San Francisco, CA: Jossey-Bass.

Aristotle (1941). *The Basic Words of Aristotle*, R. McKeon (ed.). New York: Random House.

—— (1955). 'The Nicomachean Ethics,' J. A. K. Thomson (Trans.), *The Ethics of Aristotle*. Baltimore, MD: Penguin Books.

Astley, W. G. and Van de Ven, A. H. (1983). 'Central Perspectives and Debates in Organization Theory,' *Administrative Science Quarterly*, 30: 497–513.

Axley, S. (1984). 'Managerial and Organizational Communication in Terms of the Conduit Metaphor,' *Academy of Management Review*, 9: 428–537.

Ayer, A. (1982). *Philosophy in the Twentieth Century*. New York: Random House.

Azevedo, J. (1997). *Mapping Reality: An Evolutionary Realist Methodology for the Natural and Social Sciences*. Albany, NY: State University of New York Press.

—— (2002). 'Updating Organizational Epistemology,' in J. Baum (ed.), *The Blackwell Companion to Organizations*. New York: Oxford University Press, pp. 715–32.

Bacharach, S. (1989). 'Organizational Theories: Some Criteria for Evaluation,' *Academy of Management Review*, 14(4): 496–515.

Bailey, J. R. (ed.) (2002). 'Refracting Reflection: Views from the Inside,' *Academy of Management Learning and Education*, 1(1): 77.

Bailey, K. D. (1982). *Methods of Social Research*, 2nd edn. New York: Free Press.

Baldridge, D. C., Floyd, S. W., and Markoczy, L. (2004). 'Are Managers from Mars and Academicians from Venus? Toward an Understanding of the Relationship Between Academic Quality and Practical Relevance,' *Strategic Management Journal*, 25: 1063–74.

Bales, R. F. and Strodtbeck, F. L. (1951). 'Phases in Group Problem-Solving,' *Journal of Abnormal and Social Psychology*, 46: 485–95.

Barley, S. R. (1990). 'Images of Imaging: Notes on Doing Longitudinal Fieldwork,' *Organization Science*, 1(3): 220–47.

Barnes, J. (ed.) (1995). *The Cambridge Companion to Aristotle*. Cambridge: Cambridge University Press.

Barnett, W. P. and Carroll, G. R. (1995). 'Modeling Internal Organizational Change,' *Annual Review of Sociology*, 21: 217–36.

Bartel, C. A. and Garud, R. (2003). 'Narrative Knowledge in Action: Adaptive Abduction as a Mechanism for Knowledge Creation and Exchange in Organizations,' in M. Esterby-Smith and M. Lyles (eds.), *Handbook of Organizational Learning and Knowledge*. Oxford: Blackwell, pp. 324–42.

Bartunek, J. M. and Louis, M. R. (1996). *Insider/Outsider Team Research*, Qualitative Research Methods Series, Vol. 40. Thousand Oaks, CA: Sage.

Bazerman, M. (1986). 'Biases,' in B. M. Staw (ed.), *Psychological Dimensions of Organizational Behavior*, 2nd edn. Engelwood Cliffs, NJ: Prentice Hall, pp. 199–223.

Beer, M. (2001). 'Why Management Research Findings are Unimplementable: An Action Science Perspective,' *Reflections*, 2(3): 58–65.

Berger, P. L. and Luckmann, T. (1966). *The Social Construction of Reality*. New York: Doubleday.

Bernstein, R. J. (1983). *Beyond Objectivism and Relativism: Science, Hermeneutics, and Praxis*. Philadelphia, PA: University of Pennsylvania Press.

Bevan, H., Robert, G., Bate, P., Maher, L., and Wells, J. (2007). 'Using a Design Approach to Assist Large-Scale Organizational Change: Ten High Impact Changes to Improve the National Health Service in England,' *Journal of Applied Behavioral Science*, forthcoming.

Beyer, J. M. (1997). 'Research Utilization: Bridging a Cultural Gap Between Communities,' *Journal of Management Inquiry*, 6: 17–22.

—— and Trice, H. M. (1982). 'The Utilization Process: A Conceptual Framework and Synthesis of Empirical Findings,' *Administrative Science Quarterly*, 27: 591–622.

Bhagat, R. S., Kedia, B. L., Harveston, P. D., and Triandis, H. C. (2002). 'Cultural Variations in the Cross-Border Transfer of Organizational Knowledge: An Integrative Framework,' *Academy of Management Review*, 27(2): 204–21.

Bhaskar, R. A. (1975). *A Realist Theory of Science*. Leeds: Leeds Books.

—— (1979). *The Possibility of Naturalism: A Philosophical Critique of the Contemporary Human Sciences*, 1st edn. Brighton: Harvester Press.

—— (1998a). 'General Introduction,' in M. Archer, R. Bhaskar, A. Collier, T. Lawson, and A. Norrie (eds.), *Critical Realism: Essential Readings*. New York: Routledge, Taylor and Francis Group, pp. ix–xxiv.

—— (1998b). 'Philosophy and Scientific Realism,' in M. Archer, R. Bhaskar, A. Collier, T. Lawson, and A. Norrie (eds.), *Critical Realism: Essential Readings*. New York: Routledge, Taylor and Francis Group, pp. 16–47.

—— (1998c). 'The Logic of Scientific Discovery,' in M. Archer, R. Bhaskar, A. Collier, T. Lawson, and A. Norrie (eds.), *Critical Realism: Essential Readings*. New York: Routledge, Taylor and Francis Group, pp. 48–104.

Blalock, H. M. (1969). *Theory Construction: From Verbal to Mathematical Formulations*. Englewood Cliffs, NJ: Prentice-Hall.

—— (1972). *Social Statistics*. New York: McGraw-Hill.

Blau, P. M. and Schoenherr, R. A. (1971). *The Structure of Organizations*. New York: Basic Books.

Bloor, D. (1976). *Knowledge and Social Imagery*. London: Routledge and Kegan Paul.

Blumberg, A. E. and Feigl, H. (1948). 'Logical Positivism,' *The Journal of Philosophy*, 28: 281–96.

Bouchard, Jr., T. (1976). 'Field Research Methods: Interviewing, Questionnaires, Participant Observation, Systematic Observation, Unobtrusive Measures,' in M. D. Dunnette (ed.), *Handbook of Industrial and Organizational Psychology*. Chicago: Rand McNally.

Boyd, R. (1991). *Confirmation, Semantics and the Interpretation of Scientific Theories*, in R. Boyd, P. Gasper, and J. D. Trout (eds.), *The Philosophy of Science*. Cambridge, MA: The MIT Press.

Boyer, E. L. (1990). *Scholarship Reconsidered: Priorities of the Professorate*. Princeton, NJ: Carnegie Foundation.

—— (1996). 'The Scholarship of Engagement,' *The Journal of Public Service and Outreach*, 1: 11–20.

Bransford, J. D. and Stein, B. S. (1993). *The Ideal Problem Solver: A Guide for Improving Thinking, Learning, and Creativity*, 2nd edn. New York: Freeman.

Brief, A. P. (2000). 'Still Servants of Power,' *Journal of Management Inquiry*, 9: 342–51.

—— and Dukerich, M. (1991). 'Theory in Organizational Behavior,' *Research in Organizational Behavior*, 13: 327–52.

Bringle, R. G. and Hatcher, J. A. (1996). 'Implementing Service Learning in Higher Education,' *Journal of Higher Education*, 67(2): 221–39.

Bromiley, P. (2004). *Behavioral Foundations of Strategic Management*. Oxford: Blackwell.

Bruner, J. (1973). 'Going Beyond the Information Given,' in J. M. Anglin (ed.), *Jerome S. Bruner: Beyond the Information Given*. New York: W. W. Norton, pp. 218–38.

—— (1986). *Actual Minds, Possible Worlds*. Cambridge, MA: Harvard University Press.

—— (1991*a*). *Acts of Meaning*. Cambridge, MA: Harvard University Press.

—— (1991*b*). 'The Narrative Construction of Reality,' *Critical Inquiry*, 18: 1–21.

—— (1996). *The Culture of Education*. Cambridge, MA: Harvard University Press.

Bryson, J. M. and Roering, W. D. (2000). 'Mobilizing Innovation Efforts: The Case of Government Strategic Planning,' in A. Van de Ven, H. Angle, and M. S. Poole (eds.), *Research on the Management of Innovation: The Minnesota Studies*. New York: Oxford University Press, pp. 583–610.

—— Ackermann, F., Eden, C., and Finn, C. B. (2004). *Visible Thinking: Unlocking Causal Mapping for Practical Business Results*. West Sussex: John Wiley & Sons Ltd.

Buchanan, D. A. (2003). 'Getting the Story Straight: Illusions and Delusions in the Organizational Change Process,' *Journal of Critical Postmodern Organization Science*, 2(4): 7–21.

Burns, T. and Stalker, G. M. (1961). *The Management of Innovation*. Oxford: Oxford University Press.

Burt, R. S. (1987). 'Social Contagion and Innovation: Cohesion versus Structural Equivalence,' *American Journal of Sociology*, 92: 1287–335.

—— (2005). *Brokerage and Closure: An Introduction to Social Capital*. New York: Oxford University Press.

Buyukdamgaci, G. (2003). 'Process of Organizational Problem Definition: How to Evaluate and How to Improve,' *Omega*, 31: 327–38.

Cahoone, L. (1996). *From Modernism to Postmodernism: An Anthology*, 1st edn. Cambridge, MA: Blackwell Publishers Inc.

Calleson, D., Kauper-Brown, J., and Seifer, S. D. (2004). *Community-Engaged Scholarship Toolkit: Community–Campus Partnership for Health*. Available at: http://depts.washington.edu/ccph/toolkit.html (accessed September 19, 2006).

Campbell, D. T. (1957). 'Factors Relevant to the Validity of Experiments in Social Settings,' *Psychological Bulletin*, 54: 297–312.

—— (1979). 'A Tribal Model of the Social System Vehicle Carrying Scientific Knowledge,' *Knowledge*, 2: 181–201.

—— (1988). *Methodology and Epistemology for Social Science: Selected Papers*, E. S. Overman (ed.). Chicago: University of Chicago Press.

—— (1989*a*). 'Being Mechanistic/Materialistic/Realistic about the Process of Knowing,' *Canadian Psychology*, 30: 184–5.

—— (1989*b*). 'Models of Language Learning and their Implications for Social Constructionist Analysis of Scientific Beliefs,' in S. Fuller, M. De Mey, T. Shinn, and S. Woolgar (eds.), *The Cognitive Turn: Sociological and Psychological Perspectives on Science*. Dordrecht: Kluwer, pp. 153–8.

—— (1990). 'Epistemological Roles for Selection Theory,' in N. Rescher (ed.), *Evolution, Cognition, Realism*. Lanham, MD: University Press of America, pp. 1–20.

—— (1991). 'Coherentist Empiricism, Hermeneutics, and the Commensurability of Paradigms,' *International Journal of Educational Research*, 15(6): 587–97.

—— (1993). 'Systematic Errors to be Expected of the Social Scientist on the Basis of a General Psychology of Cognitive Bias,' in P. D. Blanck (ed.), *Interpersonal Expectations: Theory, Research and Applications*. New York: Cambridge University Press, pp. 23–41.

—— (1995). 'The Postpositivist, Non-foundational, Hermeneutic Epistemology Exemplified in the Works of Donald W. Fiske,' in P. E. Shrout and S. T. Fiske (eds.), *Personality Research, Methods and Theory: A Festschrift Honoring Donald W. Fiske*. Hillsdale, NJ: Erlbaum, pp. 13–27.

—— and Fiske, D. W. (1959). 'Convergence and Discriminant Validation by the Multitrait-Multimethod Matrix,' *Psychological Bulletin*, 56(2): 81–105.

—— and Paller, B. T. (1989). 'Extending Evolutionary Epistemology to "Justifying" Scientific Beliefs (A Sociological Rapprochement With a Fallabilist Perceptual Foundationalism?),' in K. Hahlweg and C. A. Hooker (eds.), *Issues in Evolutionary Epistemology*. New York: State University of New York Press, pp. 231–57.

—— and Stanley, J. C. (1963). *Experimental and Quasi-Experimental Designs for Research*. Chicago: Rand McNally.

Campbell, J. (2002). 'Understanding Management Research: An Introduction to Epistemology (Book),' *Organization Studies*, 23(3): 479–81.

Carlile, P. R. (2002). 'A Pragmatic View of Knowledge and Boundaries: Boundary Objects in New Product Development,' *Organization Science*, 13: 442–55.

—— (2004). 'Transferring, Translating, and Transforming: An Integrative Framework for Managing Knowledge across Boundaries,' *Organization Science*, 15(5): 555–68.

—— and Christiansen, C. C. (2004). *The Cycle of Theory Building in Management Research*. Working paper, Harvard Business School, Boston, MA.

Cartwright, N. (1983). *How the Laws of Physics Lie*. Oxford: Oxford University Press.

—— (1999). *The Dappled World: A Study of the Boundaries of Science*. Cambridge: Cambridge University Press.

Caswill, C. and Shove, E. (2000*a*). 'Introducing Interactive Social Science,' *Science and Public Policy*, 27(3): 154–7.

—— —— (2000*b*). 'Postscript to Special Issue on Interactive Social Science,' *Science and Public Policy*, 27(3): 220–2.

Chalmers, A. F. (1999). *What is This Thing Called Science?* 3rd edn. Indianapolis, IN: Hackett Publishing Company, Inc.

Chandler, D. and Torbert B. (2003). 'Transforming Inquiry and Action: Interweaving 27 Flavors of Action Research,' *Action Research*, 1: 133–52.

Cialdini, R. B. (1993). *Influence: Science and Practice*, 3rd edn. New York: HarperCollins.

Clancey, W. J. (1985). 'Heuristic Classification,' *Artificial Intelligence*, 27: 289–350.

Cohen, W. M. and Levinthal, D. A. (1990). 'Absorptive Capacity: A New Perspective on Learning and Innovation,' *Administrative Science Quarterly*, 40(2): 227–51.

Cohen, M. D., March, J. G., and Olsen, J. P. (1972). 'A Garbage Can Model of Organizational Choice,' *Administrative Science Quarterly*, 17: 1–25.

Collier, A. (1994). *Critical Realism: An Introduction to Roy Bhaskar's Philosophy*. London: Verso.

Collins, R. (1998). *The Sociology of Philosophies: A Global Theory of Intellectual Change*. Cambridge, MA: Belknap Press of Harvard University Press.

Cook, T. D. and Campbell, D. T. (1979). *Quasi-Experimentation*. Boston: Houghton-Mifflin.

—— and Shadish, W. R. (1994). 'Social Experiments: Some Developments over the Past Fifteen Years,' *Annual Review of Psychology*, 45: 545–79.

—— Scott, D. N., and Brown, J. S. (1999). 'Bridging Epistemologies: The Generative Dance Between Organizational Knowledge and Organizational Knowing,' *Organization Science*, 10(4): 381–400.

Cronbach, L. J. (1982). *Designing Evaluations of Educational and Social Programs*. San Francisco: Jossey-Bass.

Crovitz, H. F. (1970). *Galton's Walk*. New York: Harper.

Cruichskank, J. (2002). 'Critical Realism and Critical Philosophy,' *Journal of Critical Realism*. London: The International Association for Critical Realism.

Cummings, T. G. and Jones, Y. (2004). 'Creating Actionable Knowledge,' conference theme for Academy of Management, New Orleans. Available at: http://meetings.aomonline.org/2004/theme.htm (accessed August 2004).

Cushman, E. (1999). 'Opinion: The Public Intellectual, Service Learning, and Activist Research,' *College English*, 61(3): 328–36.

Daft, R. L. (1983). 'Learning the Craft of Organizational Research,' *Academy of Management Review*, 89: 539–46.

—— (1984). 'Antecedents of Significant and Not-So-Significant Organizational Research,' in T. S. Bateman and G. R. Ferris (eds.), *Method and Analysis in Organizational Research*. Reston, VA: Prentice Hall.

—— and Lengel, R. H. (1984). 'Information Richness: A New Approach to Managerial Information Processing and Organizational Design,' in L. Cummings and B. M. Staw (eds.), *Research in Organizational Behavior*. Greenwich, CT: JAI Press, p. 6.

Dallmayr, F. (1987). 'The Discourse of Modernity: Hegel and Habermas,' *The Journal of Philosophy*, 84(11): 682–92.

Davis, M. (1971). 'That's Interesting!' *Philosophy of Social Sciences*, 1: 309–44.

—— (1986). 'That's Classic!' *Philosophy of Social Sciences*, 16: 285–301.

Dearborn, D. C. and Simon, H. A. (1958). 'Selective Perception: A Note on the Departmental Identification of Executives,' *Sociometry*, 21: 140–4.

Delbecq, A. L. and Van de Ven, A. H. (1971). 'A Group Process Model for Problem Identification and Program Planning,' *Journal of Applied Behavioral Science*, July/August, 7(4): 466–92.

—— —— and Gustafson, D. H. (1975). *Group Techniques for Program Planning: A Guide to Nominal Group and Delphi Processes.* Glenview, IL: Scott-Foresman.

Denis, J. L. and Langley, A. (2002). 'Introduction to the Forum,' *Health Care Management Review*, 27(3): 32–4.

Denzin, N. K. (1978). *The Research Act: A Theoretical Introduction to Sociological Methods.* New York: McGraw-Hill.

—— and Lincoln, Y. S. (eds.) (1994). *Handbook of Qualitative Research.* Thousand Oaks, CA: Sage Publications.

Deutsch, D. (1997). *The Fabric of Reality: The Science of Parallel Universes—And its Implications.* New York: Penguin Press.

Dewey, J. (1905). 'The Realism of Pragmatism,' *The Journal of Philosophy, Psychology and Scientific Methods*, 12(2): 324–7.

—— (1916). 'The Pragmatism of Peirce,' *The Journal of Philosophy*, 13(26): 709–15.

—— (1938). *Logic: The Theory of Inquiry.* New York: Holt.

Dimaggio, P. J. and Powell, W. (1983). 'The Iron Cage Revisited: Institutional Isomorphism and Collective Rationality in Organizational Fields,' *American Sociological Review*, 48: 147–61.

DiPadova-Stokes, L. N. (2005). 'Two Major Concerns About Service-Learning: What if We Don't Do It? And What if We Do?' *Academy of Management Learning and Education*, 4(3): 345–53.

Dooley, D., Fielding, J., and Levi, L. (1996). 'Health and Unemployment,' *Annual Review of Public Health*, 17: 449–65.

Dopson, S. (2005). 'The Diffusion of Medical Innovations: Can Figurational Sociology Contribute?' *Organization Studies*, 26: 1125–44.

—— FitzGerald, L., Ferlie, E., Gabbay, J., and Locock, L. (2002). 'No Magic Targets! Changing Clinical Practice to Become More Evidence Based,' *Health Care Management Review*, 27(3): 35–47.

Dougherty, D. (1992). 'Interpretive Barriers to Successful Product Innovation in Large Firms,' *Organization Science*, 3: 179–202.

—— (2002). 'Grounded Theory Research Methods,' in J. A. C. Baum (ed.), *Companion to Organizations.* Oxford: Blackwell Publishers, pp. 849–56.

Dubin, R. (1976). 'Theory Building in Applied Area,' in M. Dunnette (ed.), *Handbook of Industrial and Organizational Psychology.* Chicago: Rand McNally.

Duhem (1962). *The Aim and Structure of Physical Theory.* New York: Atheneum.

Dunbar, R. L. M. and Starbuck, W. H. (2006). 'Learning to Design Organizations and Learning from Designing Them,' *Organization Science*, 17(2): 171–8.

Dunham, L., McVea, J., and Freeman, R. E. (2006). 'Entrepreneurial Wisdom: Incorporating the Ethical and Strategic Dimensions of Entrepreneurial Decision-Making,' Conference on Entrepreneurship and Ethics, Carlson School of Management, Minneapolis, MN, April 2006.

Dunn, W. N. (1994). *Public Policy Analysis: An Introduction*, 2nd edn. Englewood Cliffs, NJ: Prentice Hall.

Dunnette, M. D. (1976). *Handbook of Industrial and Organizational Psychology.* Chicago: Rand McNally.

—— (1990). 'Blending the Science and Practice of Industrial and Organizational Psychology: Where are We and Where are We Going?' in M. D. Dunnette and L. M. Hough (eds.), *Handbook of Industrial and Organizational Psychology,* 2nd edn. Palo Alto, CA: Consulting Psychologists Press, Inc., pp. 1–27.

Eden, C., Jones, S., and Sims, D. (1983). *Messing About in Problems: An Informal Structured Approach to their Identification and Management.* Oxford: Pergamon Press.

Eisenberg, E. M. and Phillips, S. R. (1991). 'Miscommunication in Organizations,' in N. Coupland, H. Giles, and J. Wiemann (eds.), *Miscommunication and Problematic Talk.* Newbury Park, CA: Sage.

Eisenhardt, K. (1989). 'Building Theories from Case Study Research,' *Academy of Management Review,* 14: 532–50.

Elder, Jr., G. H., Caspi, A., and Burton, L. M. (1988). 'Adolescent Transitions in Developmental Perspective: Sociological and Historical Insights,' in M. R. Gunnar and A. Collins (eds.), *Minnesota Symposium on Child Psychology,* Vol. 21. Hillsdale, NJ: Erlbaum.

Engel, P. (2002). *Truth.* McGill: Queen's University Press.

Estabrooks, D. A. (1999). 'Mapping the Research Utilization Field in Nursing,' *Canadian Journal of Nursing Research,* 31(1): 53–72.

Evans, M. G. (1999). 'Donald T. Campbell's Methodological Contributions to Organization Science,' in J. A. C. Baum and B. McKelvey (eds.), *The Variations in Organization Science: In Honor of Donald T. Campbell.* Thousand Oaks, CA: Sage Publications, pp. 311–37.

Evered, R. and Louis, M. R. (1981). 'Alternative Perspectives in the Organizational Science: "Inquiry from the Inside" and "Inquiry from the Outside," ' *Academy of Management Review,* 6(3): 385–95.

Feigl, H. (1970). 'The "Orthodox" View of Theories: Remarks in Defense as well as Critique,' in M. Rudner and S. Winokur (eds.), *Minnesota Studies in the Philosophy of Science,* Vol. 4. Minneapolis, MN: University of Minnesota Press.

Feyerabend, P. K. (1962). *Explanation, Reduction, and Empiricism,* in H. Feigl and G. Maxwell (eds.), *Current Issues in the Philosophy of Science.* New York: Holt, Rinehart, and Winston, pp. 28–97.

—— (1975). *Against Method.* London: NLB.

Flavell, J. H. (1972). 'An Analysis of Cognitive-Developmental Sequences,' *Genetic Psychology Monographs,* 86: 279–350.

Flew, A. (1984). *A Dictionary of Philosophy.* New York: St. Martin's.

Folger, J. P., Hewes, D. E., and Poole, M. S. (1984). 'Coding Social Interaction,' in B. Dervin and M. Voight (eds.), *Progress in Communication Sciences,* Vol. 5. Norwood, NJ: Ablex, pp. 115–61.

Freeley, A. (1976). *Argumentation and Debate: Rational Decision Making,* 4th edn. Belmont, CA: Wadsworth.

—— (1996). *Argumentation and Debate,* 9th edn. Belmont, CA: Wadsworth/Thomson.

Friedman, R. L. (2000). *The Lexus and the Olive Tree,* newly updated and expanded edition. New York: Anchor Books, Random House.

Gadamer, H. G. (1975). *Truth and Method,* G. Barden and J. Cummings (eds.). London: Sheed & Ward (Original work published 1960).

Galaskiewicz, J. (1985). 'Interorganizational Relations,' *Annual Review of Sociology*, 11: 281–304.

Galtung, J. (1967). *Theory and Methods of Social Research.* New York: Columbia University Press.

Garfinkel, H., Lynch, M., and Livingston, E. (1981). 'The Work of a Discovering Science Construed with Materials From the Optically Discovered Pulsar,' *Philosophy of Science*, 11(2): 131–58.

Garud, R. and Van de Ven, A. H. (2000). 'Technological Innovation and Industry Emergence: The Case of Cochlear Implants,' in A. Van de Ven, H. Angle, and M. S. Poole (eds.), *Research on the Management of Innovation: The Minnesota Studies.* New York: Oxford University Press, pp. 489–532.

Gasche, R. (1988). 'Postmodernism and Rationality,' *The Journal of Philosophy*, 85(10): 528–38.

Gersick, C. J. G. (1991). 'Revolutionary Change Theories: A Multilevel Exploration of the Punctuated Equilibrium Paradigm,' *Academy of Management Review*, 16(1): 10–36.

—— (1994). 'Pacing Strategic Change: The Case of a New Venture,' *Academy of Management Journal*, 37(1): 9–45.

Getzels, J. W. and Csikszentmihalyi, M. (1975). 'From Problem Solving to Problem Finding,' in J. W. Getzels and I. A. Taylor (eds.), *Perspectives in Creativity.* Chicago: Aldine Publishing Co.

Ghiselli, E. E. (1973). 'The Validity of Aptitude Tests in Personnel Selection,' *Personnel Psychology*, 26: 461–77.

Gibbons, M., Limoges, C., Nowotny, H. et al. (1994). *The New Production of Knowledge: The Dynamics of Science and Research in Contemporary Societies.* London: Sage.

Gibson, C. B. and Zellmer-Bruhn, M. (2001). 'Metaphors and Meaning: An Intercultural Analysis of the Concept of Teamwork,' *Administrative Science Quarterly*, 46(2): 274–303.

Giddens, A. (1979). *Central Problems in Social Theory, Action, Structure, and Contradiction in Social Analysis.* Berkeley, CA: University of California Press.

Giere, R. N. (1984). *Understanding Scientific Reasoning*, 2nd edn. New York: Holt, Rinehart, and Winston.

—— (1988). *Explaining Science: A Cognitive Approach.* Chicago: University of Chicago Press.

—— (1997). *Understanding Scientific Reasoning*, 4th edn. New York: Harcourt Brace.

—— (1999). *Science Without Laws.* Chicago: University of Chicago Press.

Gioia, D. A. (2003). 'Give It Up! Reflections on the Interpreted World (A Commentary on Meckler and Baillie),' *Journal of Management Inquiry*, 12(3): 285–92.

Glaser, B. and Strauss, A. (1967). *The Discovery of Grounded Theory: Strategies for Qualitative Research.* Chicago: Aldine.

Glasgow, R. E., Davis, C. L., Funnell, M. M., and Beck, A. (2003). 'Implementing Practical Interventions to Support Chronic Illness Self-Management,' *Joint Commission Journal on Quality and Safety*, 29(11): 563–74.

Gluck, F. W., Kaufman, S. P., and Walleck, A. S. (1980). 'Strategic Management for Competitive Advantage,' *Harvard Business Review*, 58(4): 154–61.

Golden-Biddle, K., Locke, K., and Reay, T. (2002). 'Reconceptualizing Knowledge Transfer: Toward a Theory of Knowledge Movement as Communicative Process,' Working paper, University of Alberta, Canada.

Green, Jr., S. E. (2004). 'A Rhetorical Theory of Diffusion,' *Academy of Management Review*, 29(4): 653–69.

Greiner, L. (1972). 'Evolution and Revolution as Organizations Grow,' *Harvard Business Review,* July–August: 165–74.

Grey, C. (2001). 'Re-imagining Relevance: A Response to Starkey and Madan,' *British Journal of Management,* 12(Special Issue): S27–S32.

Guba, E. G. and Lincoln, Y. S. (1994). 'Competing Paradigms in Qualitative Research,' in N. K. Denzin and Y. S. Lincoln (eds.), *Handbook of Qualitative Research.* Thousand Oaks, CA: Sage, pp. 105–37.

Guilford, J. P. (1954). *Psychometric Methods,* 2nd edn. New York: McGraw-Hill.

Guyatt, G., Sackett, D., Taylor, W. et al. (1986). 'Determining Optimal Therapy Trials: Randomized Trials in Individual Patients,' *New England Journal of Medicine,* 314: 889–92.

Habermas, J. (1971). *Knowledge and Human Interests,* J. J. Shapiro (Trans.). Boston: Beacon Press.

—— (1979). *Communication and the Evolution of Society.* London: Heinemann.

—— (1984). *The Theory of Communication, Vol. 1: Reason and the Rationalization of Society.* London: Heinemann.

—— (1987). *The Theory of Communication, Vol. 2: Lifeworld and System: A Critique of Functionalist Reason.* Oxford: Polity Press.

—— (1990). *Moral Consciousness and Communicative Action.* Cambridge: Polity Press.

Hacking, I. (1983). *Representing and Intervening.* Cambridge: Cambridge University Press.

Hackman, J. R. (1985). 'Doing Research that Makes a Difference,' in E. E. Lawler (ed.), *Doing Research that is Useful for Theory and Practice.* New York: Lexington Books.

—— (ed.) (1991). *Groups that Work (and Those that Don't).* San Francisco: Jossey-Bass.

Hage, J. (1965). 'An Axiomatic Theory of Organizations,' *Administrative Science Quarterly,* 10: 289–320.

Hage, J. (1995). 'Formal Organization and Formalization Essays,' in N. Nicholson, R. Schuler, and A. Van de Ven (eds.), *Encyclopedic Dictionary of Organizational Behavior.* Oxford: Blackwell Publishers, p. 1182.

Hall, R. H. (1972). *Organizations, Structure, and Process.* Englewood Cliffs, NJ: Prentice-Hall.

Halpern, D. F. (1996). *Thought and Knowledge: An Introduction to Critical Thinking,* 3rd edn. Mahwah, NJ: Lawrence Erlbaum.

Hammond, K. (1999). *Human Judgment and Social Policy.* New York: Oxford University Press.

Hanson, N. R. (1958). *Patterns of Discovery: An Inquiry into the Conceptual Foundations of Science.* London: Cambridge University Press.

—— (1958). 'The Logic of Discovery,' *The Journal of Philosophy,* 55(25): 1073–89.

—— (1959). 'Is There a Logic of Scientific Discovery?' in H. Feigl and G. Marwell (eds.), *Current Issues in Philosophy of Science: Proceedings of Section L of the American Association for the Advancement of Science.* New York: Holt Rinehart & Winston.

—— (1969). *Perception and Discovery: An Introduction to Scientific Inquiry,* W. C. Humphreys (ed.). San Francisco, CA: Freeman, Cooper, and Company.

Harding, S. (2004). 'A Socially Relevant Philosophy of Science? Resources from Standpoint Theory's Controversiality,' *Hypatia,* 19(1): 25–47.

Harre, R. and Madden, E. A. (1975). *Causal Powers.* Totowa, NJ: Littlefield Adams.

Harvey, D. L. (2002). 'Agency and Community: A Critical Realist Paradigm,' *Journal for the Theory of Social Behavior,* 32(2): 163–94.

Hassard, J. (1994). 'Postmodern Organizational Analysis: Toward a Conceptual Framework,' *Journal of Management Studies*, 31(3): 303–24.

Hatchuel, A. (2001). 'The Two Pillars of New Management Research,' *British Journal of Management*, 12(Special Issue): S33–S40.

Heidegger, M. (1962). *Being and Time*, J. MacQuarrie and E. Robinson (Trans.). London: SMC Press (Original work published 1927).

Helson, H. (1964). 'Current Trends and Issues in Adaptation-Level Theory,' *American Psychologist*, 19: 23–68.

Henderson, J. (1967). 'From Introductory Lectures: Sociology 23, at Harvard University in the late 1930's,' *Journal of Applied Behavioral Sciences*, pp. 236–40.

Hendrickx, M. (1999). 'What can Management Researchers Learn from Donald Campbell, the Philosopher? An Exercise in Hermeneutics,' in J. A. C. Baum and B. McKelvey (eds.), *Variations in Organization Science: In Honor of Donald T. Campbell*. Thousand Oaks, CA: Sage Publications, pp. 339–82.

Hernes, G. (1989). 'The Logic of the Protestant Ethic,' *Rationality and Society*, 1(1): 123–62.

Hinings, C. R. and Greenwood, R. (eds.) (2002). 'ASQ forum: Disconnects and Consequences in Organization Theory,' *Administrative Science Quarterly*, 47(3): 411–21.

Hodgkinson, G. P. (ed.) (2001). 'Facing the Future: The Nature and Purpose of Management Research Reassessed,' *British Journal of Management*, 12(Special Issue): S1–S80.

—— Herriot, P., and Anderson, N. (2001). 'Re-aligning the Stakeholders in Management Research: Lessons from Industrial, Work and Organizational Psychology,' *British Journal of Management*, 12(Special Issue): S41–S48.

Hofstede, G. T. (1980). 'Motivation, Leadership, and Organization: Do American Theories Apply Abroad?' *Organizational Dynamics*, Summer: 42–63.

Hollway, W. (1984). 'Fitting Work: Psychological Assessment in Organizations,' in J. Henriques, W. Hollway, C. Urwin, C. Venn, and V. Walkerdine (eds.), *Changing the Subject*. New York: Methuen, pp. 26–59.

Holmes, M. E. (1997). 'Processes and Patterns of Hostage Negotiations,' in R. G. Rogan and M. R. Hammer (eds.), *Dynamic Processes of Hostage Negotiations: Theory, Research, and Practice*. Westwook, CT: Praeger, pp. 77–93.

Huber, G. and Van de Ven, A. H. (eds.) (1995). *Longitudinal Field Research Methods*. Thousand Oaks, CA: Sage.

Huff, A. S. (2000). 'Changes in Organizational Knowledge Production: 1999 Presidential Address,' *Academy of Management Review*, 25(2): 288–93.

—— (2002). 'Learning to be a Successful Writer,' in D. Partington (ed.), *Essential Skills for Management Research*. Thousand Oaks, CA: Sage, pp. 72–83.

Hutchins, E. (1983). 'Understanding Micronesian Navigation,' in D. Gentner and A. L. Stevens (eds.), *Mental Models*. Hillside, NJ: Lawrence Erlbaum Associates, pp. 191–225.

James, W. (1907). *Pragmatism*. New York: The American Library.

—— (1908). 'The Meaning of the Word "Truth," ' *Mind*, 17(67): 455–6.

Janis, I. L. and Mann, L. (1977). *Decision Making: A Psychological Analysis of Conflict, Choice, and Commitment*. New York: The Free Press.

Johnson, P. and Duberley, J. (2003). 'Reflexivity in Management Research,' *Journal of Management Studies*, 40(5): 1279–303.

—— —— (2000). *Understanding Management Research*. Thousand Oaks, CA: Sage.

—— Zualkernan, I. A., and Tukey, D. (1993). 'Types of Expertise: An Invariant of Problem Solving,' *International Journal Man-Machine Studies*, 39: 641–65.

Kahneman, D., Slovic, P., and Tversky, A. (eds.) (1982). *Judgment and Uncertainty: Heuristics and Biases*. New York: Cambridge University Press.

Kaplan, A. (1964). *The Conduct of Inquiry: Methodology for Behavior Science*. New York: Chandler Publishing Company.

Kemeny, J. G. (1959). *A Philosopher Looks at Science*. Princeton, NJ: Van Norstrand.

Kemp, S. and Holmwood, J. (2003). 'Realism, Regularity and Social Explanation,' *Journal for the Theory of Social Behavior*, 33(2): 165–87.

Kenworthy-U'Ren, A. (2005). 'Towards a Scholarship of Engagement: A Dialogue Between Andy Van de Ven and Edward Zlotkowski,' *Academy of Management Learning and Education*, 4(3): 355–62.

Kilduff, M. and Keleman, M. (2001). 'The Consolations of Organization Theory,' *British Journal of Management*, 12(Special Issue): S55–S59.

Kimberly, J. and Miles, R. (1980). *The Organizational Life Cycle*. San Francisco: Jossey-Bass.

Kinchloe, J. L. and McLaren, P. L. (1994). 'Rethinking Critical Theory and Qualitative Research,' in N. K. Denzin and Y. S. Lincoln (eds.), *Handbook of Qualitative Research*. Thousand Oaks, CA: Sage, pp. 138–57.

Kirk, R. E. (1995). *Experimental Design: Procedures for the Behavioral Science*, 3rd edn. Pacific Grove, CA: Brooks/Cole Publishing Co.

Klein, K. J. and Kozlowski, W. J. (2000). *Multilevel Theory, Research, and Methods in Organizations*. San Francisco: Jossey-Bass.

—— Tosi, H., and Cannella, A. A. (1999). 'Introduction to Special Topic Forum. Multilevel Theory Building: Benefits, Barriers, and New Developments,' *Academy of Management Review*, 24(2): 243–8.

Knorr-Cetina, K. and Amann, K. (1990). 'Image Dissection in Natural Scientific Inquiry,' *Science, Technology and Human Values*, 15(3): 259–83.

—— and Cicourel, A. (eds.) (1981). *Advances in Social Theory and Methodology: Towards an Integration of Micro and Macro Sociology*. London: Routledge & Kegan Paul.

Knudson, M. K. and Ruttan, V. W. (2000). 'The Management of Research and Development of a Biological Innovation,' in A. H. Van de Ven, H. Angle, and M. S. Poole, *Research on the Management of Innovation: The Minnesota Studies*. Oxford: Oxford University Press, pp. 465–88.

Kogan, N. and Wallach, M. A. (1967). 'Effects of Physical Separation of Group Members upon Group Risk-Taking,' *Human Relations*, 20(1): 41–9.

Kondrat, M. E. (1992). 'Reclaiming the Practical: Formal and Substantive Rationality in Social Work Practice,' *Social Service Review*, June: 237–55.

Kuhn, T. S. (1962). *The Structure of Scientific Revolutions*, 1st edn. Chicago: University of Chicago Press.

—— (1970). *The Structure of Scientific Revolutions*, 2nd edn. Chicago: University of Chicago Press.

Lachs, J. (1999). 'Peirce: Inquiry as Social Life,' in S. B. Rosenthal, C. R. Hausman, and D. R. Anderson (eds.), *Classical American Pragmatism: Its Contemporary Vitality*. Urbana, IL: University of Illinois Press, pp. 75–84.

Lakatos, I. (1978). *The Methodology of Scientific Research Programmes: Philosophical Papers,* Vol. 1. Cambridge: Cambridge University Press.

Langley, A. (1999). 'Strategies for Theorizing from Process Data,' *Academy of Management Review,* 24: 691–710.

—— and Truax, J. (1994). 'A Process Study of a New Technology Adoption in Smaller Manufacturing Firms,' *Journal of Management Studies,* 31: 619–52.

Latour, B. (1986). 'Visualization and Cognition: Thinking with Eyes and Hands,' *Knowledge and Society: Studies in the Sociology of Culture Past and Present,* Vol. 6. Greenwich, CT: JAI Press.

—— Woolgar, S. (1986). *Laboratory Life: The Construction of Scientific Facts,* 2nd edn. Princeton, NJ: Princeton.

Laudan, L. (1984). *Science and Values: The Aims of Science and their Role in Scientific Debate.* Berkeley, CA: University of California Press.

Lave, J. and Wenger, E. (1994). *Situated Learning: Legitimate Peripheral Participation.* Cambridge: Cambridge University Press.

Lawler III, E. E., Mohrman Jr., A. M., Mohrman, S. A. et al. (1985). *Doing Research that is Useful for Theory and Practice.* Lanham, MD: Lexington Books.

Lawrence, P. R. (1992). 'The Challenge of Problem-Oriented Research,' *Journal of Management Inquiry,* 1(2): 139–42.

Lazarsfeld, P. F. and Menzel, H. (1969). 'On the Relation Between Individual and Collective Properties,' in A. Etzioni (ed.), *A Sociological Reader in Complex Organizations,* 2nd edn. New York: Holt, Rinehart, and Winston.

Leplin, J. (ed.) (1984). *Scientific Realism.* Berkeley: University of California Press.

Levi-Strauss, C. (1966). 'The Science of the Concrete,' in C. Levi-Strauss (ed.), *The Savage Mind.* Chicago: University of Chicago Press, pp. 1–33.

Lewin, K. (1945). 'The Research Center for Group Dynamics at Massachusetts Institute of Technology,' *Sociometry,* 8: 126–35.

Lincoln, J. R., Hanada, M., and Mcbride, K. (1986). 'Organizational Structures in Japanese and U.S. Manufacturing,' *Administrative Science Quarterly,* 31(3): 338–64.

Lindblom, C. and Cohen, D. (1979). *Usable Knowledge: Social Science and Social Problem Solving.* New Haven, CT: Yale University Press.

Locke, K., Golden-Biddle, K., and Feldman, M. S. (2004). 'Imaginative Theorizing in Interpretive Organizational Research,' Academy of Management Best Conference Papers, Research Methods Division, B1.

Lorange, P. (1980). *Corporate Planning: An Executive Viewpoint.* Englewood Cliffs, NJ: Prentice Hall.

Lord, F. M. and Novick, M. R. (1968). *Statistical Theories of Mental Test Scores.* Reading, MA: Addison-Wesley.

Louis, M. R. and Bartunek, J. M. (1992). 'Insider/Outsider Research Teams: Collaboration Across Diverse Perspectives,' *Journal of Management Inquiry,* 1(2): 101–10.

Lovejoy, A. O. (1908). 'The Thirteen Pragmatisms,' *The Journal of Philosophy,* 5(1): 5–12.

Maier, N. R. F. (1970). *Problem Solving and Creativity in Individuals and Groups.* Monterey, CA: Brooks/Cole.

March, J. G. (2000). 'Citigroup's John Reed and Standford's James March on Management Research and Practice,' *Academy of Management Executive,* 14: 52–64.

—— and Simon, H. A. (1958). *Organizations*. New York: Wiley.

Markus, G. B., Howard, J. P. F., and King, D. C. (1993). 'Integrating Community Service and Classroom Instruction Enhances Learning: Results from an Experiment,' *Educational Evaluation and Policy Analysis*, 15(4): 410–19.

Martin, J. (1990). 'Deconstructing Organizational Taboos: The Suppression of Gender Conflict in Organizations,' *Organization Science*, 1(4): 339–59.

Marvel, M. K. and Amodei, N. (1992). 'Single-Subject Experimental Designs: A Practical Research Alternative for Practicing Physicians,' *Family Practice Research Journal*, 12(2): 109–21.

Mathison, S. (1988). 'Why Triangulate?' *Educational Researcher*, March: 13–17.

McEvily, B., Perrone, V., and Zaheer, A. (2003). 'Trust as an Organizing Principle,' *Organization Science*, 14: 91–103.

McGrath, J. E. (1988). 'Model-Centered Organization Science Epistemology,' in J. A. C. Baum (ed.), *The Blackwell Companion to Organizations*. Oxford: Blackwell Publishers, pp. 752–80.

—— and Tschan, F. (2004). 'Dynamics in Groups and Teams: Groups as Complex Action Systems,' in M. S. Poole and A. H. Van de Ven (eds.), *Handbook of Organizational Change and Innovation*. New York: Oxford University Press, pp. 50–72.

McKelvey, B. (1999). 'Toward a Campbellian Realist Organization Science,' in J. A. C. Baum and B. McKelvey (eds.), *Variations in Organization Science*. Thousand Oaks, CA: Sage Publications, pp. 382–411.

—— (2002*a*). 'Model-Centered Organization Science Epistemology,' in J. A. C. Baum (ed.), *The Blackwell Companion to Organizations*. Oxford: Blackwell, pp. 752–80.

—— (2002*b*). 'Appendix: Glossary of Epistemology Terms,' in J. A. C. Baum (ed.), *The Blackwell Companion to Organizations*. Oxford: Blackwell, pp. 889–98.

Meehl, P. E. (1995). 'Bootstraps Taxometrics: Solving the Classification Problem in Psychopathology,' *American Psychologist*, 50(4): 266–75.

Merton, R. K. (1968). *Social Theory and Social Structure*, enlarged edn. New York: Free Press.

—— (1973). *The Sociology of Science: Theoretical and Empirical Investigations*. Chicago: University of Chicago Press.

—— (1987). 'Three Fragments from a Sociologist's Notebooks: Establishing the Phenomenon, Specified Ignorance, and Strategic Research Materials,' *Annual Review of Sociology*, 13: 1–28.

Messinger, S. L. (1955). 'Organizational Transformation: A Case Study of a Declining Social Movement,' *American Sociological Review*, 30: 3–10.

Meyer, A. D. (1991). 'Visual Data in Organizational Research,' *Organization Science*, 2: 218–36.

Meyers, R. (1999). 'The Beginnings of Pragmatism: Peirce, Wright, James, Royce,' in R. Popkin (ed.), *The Columbia History of Western Philosophy*. New York: Columbia University Press, pp. 592–600.

Miles, M. B. and Huberman, A. M. (1994). *Qualitative Data Analysis: An Expanded Sourcebook*. Thousand Oaks, CA: Sage.

Miller, D. and Friesen, P. H. (1982). 'The Longitudinal Analysis of Organizations: A Methodological Perspective,' *Management Science*, 28: 1013–34.

Miller, G. A. (1956). 'The Magical Number Seven, Plus or Minus Two: Some Limits on our Capacity for Processing Information,' *Psychological Review*, 63: 81–97.

Mingers, J. (2004). 'Re-establishing the Real: Critical Realism and Information Systems Research,' in J. Mingers and L. Willcocks, *Social Theory and Philosophy for Information Systems*. New York: Wiley.

Mintzberg, H. (1979). 'An Emerging Strategy of "Direct" Research,' *Administrative Science Quarterly*, 24: 582–9.

—— (2005). 'Developing Theory About the Development of Theory,' in K. G. Smith and M. A. Hitt (eds.), *Great Minds in Management: The Process of Theory Development.* New York: Oxford University Press, pp. 355–72.

—— Raisinghani, D., and Theoret, A. (1976). 'The Structure of "Unstructured" Decision Processes,' *Administrative Science Quarterly*, 21(2): 246–75.

Misak, C. (2001). 'Peirce,' in W. H. Newton-Smith (ed.), *A Companion to the Philosophy of Science* Massachusetts: Blackwell Publishers pp. 335–9.

Mitroff, I. and Emshoff, J. (1979). 'On Strategic Assumption Making: A Dialectical Approach to Policy and Planning,' *Academy of Management Review*, 4(1): 1–12.

—— and Linstone, H. A. (1993). *The Unbounded Mind: Breaking the Chains of Traditional Business Thinking.* New York: Oxford University Press.

Mohr, L. (1982). *Explaining Organizational Behavior.* San Francisco: Jossey-Bass.

Mohrman, S., Gibson, C., and Mohrman, A. (2001). 'Doing Research that is Useful to Practice: A Model and Empirical Exploration,' *Academy of Management Journal*, 44: 357–75.

Morgan, G. (1983). 'Toward a More Reflective Social Science,' in G. Morgan (ed.), *Beyond Method.* Thousand Oaks, CA: Sage Publications.

Morgan, M. S. and Morrison, M. (ed.) (1999). *Models as Mediators: Perspectives on Natural and Social Science.* Cambridge: Cambridge University Press.

Morrison, M. and Morgan, M. S. (1999). 'Models as Mediating Instruments,' in M. S. Morgan and M. Morrison (eds.), *Models as Mediators: Perspectives on Natural and Social Science.* Cambridge: Cambridge University Press, pp. 10–37.

Mounce, H. O. (1997). *The Two Pragmatisms: From Peirce to Rorty.* London: Routledge.

Nagel, T. (1986). *The View from Nowhere.* New York: Oxford University Press.

Neter, J., Kutner, M. H., Wasserman, W., and Nachtscheim, C. J. (1996). *Applied Linear Statistical Models*, 4th edn. Columbus, OH: McGraw Hill.

Niiniluoto, I. (1980). 'Scientific Progress,' *Synthese*, 45: 427–64.

—— (1999). *Critical Scientific Realism.* New York: Oxford University Press.

Nonaka, I. (1994). 'A Dynamic Theory of Organizational Knowledge Creation,' *Organization Science*, 5(1): 14–37.

—— and Takeuchi, I. (1995). *The Knowledge-Creating Organization.* Oxford: Oxford Press.

Nutley, S., Walter, I., and Daviews, H. T. O. (2003). 'From Knowing to Doing: A Framework for Understanding the Evidence-into-Practice Agenda,' *Evaluation*, 9(2): 125–48.

Osborn, R. N. and Hagedoorn, J. (1997). 'The Institutionalization and Evolutionary Dynamics of Interorganizational Alliances and Networks,' *Academy of Management Journal*, 40: 261–78.

Osigweh, C. A. B. (1989). 'Concept Fallibility in Organization Science,' *Academy of Management Review*, 14(4): 579–94.

Paller, B. T. and Campbell, D. T. (1989). 'Maxwell and van Fraassen on Observability, Reality, and Justification,' in M. L. Maxwell and C. W. Savage (eds.), *Science, Mind, and Psychology: Essays in Honor of Grover Maxwell.* Lanham, MD: University Press of America, pp. 99–132.

Passmore, W.A. (2001). 'Action Research in the Workplace: The Socio-Technical, Perspective,' in P. Reason and H. Bradbury (eds.), *Handbook of Action Research: Participative Inquiry and Practice.* London: Sage, pp. 39–47.

Patton, M. Q. (1980). *Qualitative Evaluation Methods*. Beverly Hills: Sage.

Pedhazur, E. J. and Schmelkin, L. P. (1991). *Measurement, Design, and Analysis: An Integrated Approach*. Hillsdale, NJ: Lawrence Erlbaum Associates.

Peirce, C. S. (1955). *Philosophical Writings of Peirce*, J. Buchler (ed.). New York: Dover.

—— (1931–58). *Collected Works: 1931–1958*, in C. Hartshorne, P. Weiss, and A. Burkes (eds.). Cambridge, MA: Harvard University Press.

—— (1997). 'The Fixation of Belief,' in L. Menand (ed.), *Pragmatism: A Reader*. New York: Vintage Books, pp. 7–25. (Original work published 1878).

Peli, G. and Masuch, M. (1997). 'The Logic of Propagation Strategies: Axiomatizing a Fragment of Organizational Ecology in First-Order Logic,' *Organization Science*, 8: 310–31.

Pentland, B. (1999). 'Building Process Theory with Narrative: From Description to Explanation,' *Academy of Management Review*, 24: 711–24.

Pettigrew, A. (1985). *The Awakening Giant: Continuity and Change in ICI*. Oxford: Basil Blackwell.

—— (2001). 'Management Research After Modernism', *British Journal of Management*, 12 (Special Issue): S61–S70.

—— (2003). 'Co-Producing Knowledge and the Challenges of International Collaborative Research,' in A. M. Pettigrew, R. Whittington, L. Melin et al. (eds.), *Innovative Forms of Organizing*. Thousand Oaks, CA: Sage.

—— (2005). 'The Character and Significance of Management Research on the Public Services,' *Academy of Management Journal*, 48(6): 973–7.

Poggi, G. (1965). 'A Main Theme of Contemporary Sociological Analysis: Its Achievements and Limitations,' *British Journal of Sociology*, 16: 283–94.

Polanyi, M. (1962). *Personal Knowledge*. Chicago: University of Chicago Press.

Polkinghorne, D. E. (1988). *Narrative Knowing and the Human Sciences*. Albany, NY: SUNY Press.

Polya, G. (1957). *How to Solve It: A New Aspect of Mathematical Method*, 2nd edn. Garden City, NY: Doubleday.

Poole, M. S. (1983). 'Decision Development in Small Groups, III: A Multiple Sequence Model of Group Decision Development,' *Communication Monographs*, 50: 321–41.

—— Holmes, M. E. (1995). 'Decision Development in Computer-Assisted Group Decision Making,' *Human Communication Research*, 22: 90–127.

—— Roth, J. (1989). 'Decision Development in Small Groups V: Test of a Contingency Model,' *Human Communication Research*, 15(4): 549–89.

—— Van de Ven, A. H. (1989). 'Using Paradox to Build Management and Organization Theories,' *Academy of Management Review*, 15(3): 562–78.

—— Folger, J. P., and Hewes, D. E. (1987). 'Analyzing Interpersonal Interaction,' in M. E. Roloff and G. R. Miller (eds.), *Interpersonal Processes*. Beverly Hills: Sage.

—— Van de Ven, A. H., Dooley, K., and Holmes, M. (2000). *Organizational Change and Innovation Processes: Theory and Methods for Research*. New York: Oxford University Press.

Popkin, R. (1999). 'The French Enlightenment,' in R. Popkin (ed.), *The Columbia History of Western Philosophy*. New York: Columbia University Press, pp. 462–71.

Popper, K. (1959). *The Logic of Scientific Discovery*. New York: Harper Torchbooks.

—— (1972). *Objective Knowledge*. New York: Oxford University Press.

—— (1979). *Truth, Rationality, and the Growth of Scientific Knowledge*. Frankfurt: Klostermann.

Porter, L. W. (1958). 'Differential Self Perceptions of Management Personnel and Line Workers,' *Journal of Applied Psychology*, 42: 105–9.

Putnam, H. (1962). 'What Theories Are Not,' in E. Nagel, P. Suppes, and A. Tarski (eds.), *Logic, Methodology, and Philosophy of Science: Proceedings of the 1960 International Congress*. Stanford, CA: Stanford University Press, pp. 240–51.

—— (1981). *Reason, Truth and History*. Cambridge: Cambridge University Press.

—— (1993). *Renewing Philosophy*. Cambridge, MA: Harvard University Press.

—— Phillips, N., and Chapman, P. (1996). 'Metaphors of Communication and Organization,' in S. Clegg, C. Hardy, and W. Nord (eds.), *Handbook of Organization Studies*. Thousand Oaks, CA: Sage Publications, pp. 375–408.

Quine, W. V. (1951). 'Two Dogmas of Empiricism,' *Philosophical Review*, 60: 20–43.

Quinn, J. B. (1980). *Strategies for Change: Logical Incrementalism*. Homewood, IL: Irwin.

Quinn, R. E. and Cameron, K. S. (eds.) (1988). *Paradox and Transformation: Toward a Theory of Change in Organization and Management*. Cambridge, MA: Ballinger.

Ragin, C. C. (1987). *The Comparative Method: Moving Beyond Qualitative and Quantitative Strategies*. Berkeley, CA: University of California Press.

—— (2000). *Fuzzy-Set Social Science*. Chicago: University of Chicago Press.

Ramage, J. D. and Bean, J. C. (1995). *Writing Arguments: A Rhetoric with Readings*, 3rd edn. Boston: Allyn & Bacon.

Randall, Jr., J. H. (1960). *Aristotle*. New York: Columbia University Press.

Reichenbach, H. (1938). *Experience and Prediction*. Chicago: University of Chicago Press.

—— (1948). 'Rationalism and Empiricism: An Inquiry into the Roots of Philosophical Error,' *The Philosophical Review*, 57(4): 330–46.

—— (1963). *The Rise of Scientific Philosophy*. Los Angeles: University of California Press.

Rescher, M. (1987). *Scientific Realism: A Critical Reappraisal*. Dordrecht: D. Reidel Publishing Company.

—— (1996). *Process Metaphysics: An Introduction to Process Philosophy*. Albany, NY: State University of New York Press.

—— (2000). *Realistic Pragmatism: An Introduction to Pragmatic Philosophy*. Albany, NY: State University of New York Press.

—— (2003). *Nature and Understanding: The Metaphysics and Method of Science*. New York: Oxford University Press.

Riegel, K. F. (1969). 'History as a Nomothetic Science: Some Generalizations from Theories and Research in Developmental Psychology,' *Journal of Social Issues*, 25: 99–127.

Ring, P. S. and Van de Ven, A. H. (1994). 'Developmental Processes of Cooperative Interorganizational Relationships,' *Academy of Management Review*, 19(1): 90–118.

Roberts, J. M. (2001). 'Critical Realism and the Dialectic,' *British Journal of Sociology*, 52(4): 667–85.

Roberts, N. C. and King, P. J. (1996). *Transforming Public Policy: Dynamics of Policy Entrepreneurship and Innovation*. San Francisco: Jossey-Bass.

Rogers, E. M. (2003). *Diffusion of Innovations*, 5th edn. New York: Free Press.

Romme, A. G. L. (2003). 'Making a Difference: Organization as Design,' *Organization Science*, 14(5): 558–73.

—— Endenburg, G. (2006). 'Construction Principles and Design Rules in the Case of Circular Design,' *Organization Science*, 17(2): 287–97.

Rorty, R. (1961). 'Pragmatism, Categories, and Language,' *The Philosophical Review*, 70(2): 197–233.

—— (1979). *Philosophy and the Mirror of Nature*. Princeton, NJ: Princeton University Press.

—— (1980). 'Pragmatism, Relativism, and Irrationalism,' *Proceedings and Addresses of the American Philosophical Association*, 53(6): 717–38.

—— (1982). *Consequences of Pragmatism (Essays: 1972–1980)*. Minneapolis, MN: University of Minnesota Press.

Rosenblatt, P. D. (1981). 'Ethnographic Case Studies,' in M. B. Brewer and B. E. Collins (eds.), *Scientific Inquiry and Social Sciences*. San Francisco: Jossey-Bass.

Ross, D. (1949). *Aristotle*. London: Methuen.

Rousseau, D. M. (1985). 'Issues of Level in Organizational Research: Multi-Level and Cross-Level Perspectives,' in L. L. Cummings and B. Staw (eds.), *Research in Organizational Behavior*. Greenwich, CT: JAI Press, pp. 1–37.

—— (2006). 'Is There Such a Thing as "Evidence-Based Management"?' *Academy of Management Review*, 31(2): 256–69.

Russell, B. (1972). *A History of Western Philosophy*. New York: Simon and Schuster.

Ruttan, V. W. (2001). *Technology, Growth, and Development: An Induced Innovation Perspective*. Oxford: Oxford University Press.

Rynes, S. L., Bartunek, J. M., and Daft, R. L. (2001). 'Across the Great Divide: Knowledge Creation and Transfer Between Practitioners and Academics,' *Academy of Management Journal*, 44(2): 340–55.

—— Colbert, A. E., and Brown, K. G. (2002). 'HR Professionals' Beliefs about Effective Human Resource Practices: Correspondence Between Research and Practice,' *Human Resource Management*, 41(2): 149–74.

—— McNatt, D. B., and Bretz, R. D. (1999). 'Academic Research Inside Organizations: Inputs, Processes, and Outcomes,' *Personnel Psychology*, 52: 869–98.

Sackett, P. R. and Mullen, E. J. (1993). 'Beyond Formal Experimental Design: Towards an Expanded View of the Training Evaluation Process,' *Personnel Psychology*, 46: 613–28.

Sarasvathy, S. D. (2001). 'Causation and Effectuation: Toward a Theoretical Shift from Economic Inevitability to Entrepreneurial Contingency,' *Academy of Management Review*, 26(2): 243–63.

Saxton, T. (1997). 'The Effects of Partner and Relationship Characteristics on Alliance Outcomes,' *Academy of Management Journal*, 40: 443–62.

Sayer, A. (1992). *Method in Social Science: A Realist Approach*, 2nd edn. London: Routledge.

Schaie, K. W. (1965). 'A General Model for the Study of Developmental Problems,' *Psychological Bulletin*, 64: 92–107.

Schein, E. G. (1987). *The Clinical Perspective in Fieldwork*, Sage University Papers Series on Qualitative Research Methods, Vol. 5. Thousand Oaks, CA: Sage.

Schon, D. (1987). *Educating the Reflective Practitioner*. San Francisco: Jossey-Bass.

Schoonhoven, C. B., Eisenhardt, K. M., and Lyman, K. (1990). 'Speeding Products to Market: Waiting Time to First Product Introduction in New Firms,' *Administrative Science Quarterly*, 35(1): 177–207.

Schuh, G. E. (1984). *Revitalizing the Land Grant University*, Strategic Management Research Center, Discussion Paper # 36, University of Minnesota, Minneapolis, MN.

Schultt, R. K. (2004). *Investigating the Social World: The Process and Practice of Research*, 4th edn. Thousand Oaks, CA: Sage.

Schultz, F. C. (2001). 'Explaining the Link Between Strategic Decision Making and Organizational Performance,' unpublished doctoral dissertation, University of Minnesota Carlson School of Management, Minneapolis, MN.

Schultz, M. and Hatch, M. J. (2005). 'Building Theory from Practice,' *Strategic Organization*, 3(3): 337–48.

Schweiger, D. M., Sandberg, W. R., and Rechner, P. L. (1989). 'Experiential Effects of Dialectical Inquiry, Devil's Advocacy and Consensus Approaches to Strategic Decision Making,' *Academy of Management Journal*, 32(4): 745–73.

Scott, B. R. (1971). 'Stages of Corporate Development,' unpublished paper, Harvard Business School, Boston, MA.

Scott, W. R. (2003). *Organizations: Rational, Natural, and Open Systems*, 5th edn. Upper Saddle River, NJ: Prentice Hall.

Shadish, W. R., Cook, T. D., and Campbell, D. T. (2002). *Experimental and Quasi-Experimental Designs for Generalized Causal Inference*. Boston: Houghton Mifflin.

Shani, A. B., David, A., and Willson, C. (2004). 'Collaborative Research: Alternative Roadmaps,' in N. Adler, A. B. Shani, and A. Styhre (eds.), *Collaborative Research in Organizations: Foundations for Learning, Change, and Theoretical Development*. Thousand Oaks, CA: Sage Publications.

Shrivastava, P. (1986). 'Is Strategic Management Ideological?' *Journal of Management*, 12(3): 363–77.

Sim, S. (2001). 'Postmodernism and Philosophy,' in S. Sim (ed.), *The Routledge Companion to Postmodernism*, 2nd edn. New York: Routledge, Taylor and Francis Group, pp. 3–14.

Simon, H. A. (1973). 'The Structure of Ill Structured Problems,' *Artificial Intelligence*, 4: 191–201.

—— (1976). 'The Business School: A Problem in Organizational Design,' in H. A. Simon (ed.), *Administrative Behavior: A Study of Decision-Making Processes in Administrative Organization*. New York: Free Press, pp. 335–56.

—— (1991). 'Bounded Rationality and Organizational Learning,' *Organization Science*, 2(1): 125–35.

—— (1996). *Sciences of the Artificial*, 2nd edn. Cambridge, MA: MIT Press.

Singleton, Jr., R. A., Straits, B. C., and Straits, M. M. (1993). *Approaches to Social Research*, 2nd edn. New York: Oxford University Press.

—— Straits, B. C. (1999). *Approaches to Social Research*, 3rd edn. New York: Oxford University Press.

—— —— (2005). *Approaches to Social Research*, 4th edn. New York: Oxford University Press.

Small, S. A. and Uttal, L. (2005). 'Action-Oriented Research: Strategies for Engaged Scholarship,' *Journal of Marriage and Family*, 67: 936–48.

Smith, P. C., Kendall, L. M., and Hulin, C. L. (1969). *The Measurement of Satisfaction in Work and Retirement: A Strategy for the Study of Attitudes*. Chicago: Rand McNally.

Starbuck, W. H. (2005). *What the Numbers Mean*. Available at: http://www.stern.nyu.edu/~wstarbuc/whatmean.html (accessed July 25, 2006).

Starkey, K. and Madan, P. (2001). 'Bridging the Relevance Gap: Aligning Stakeholders in the Future of Management Research,' *British Journal of Management*, 12(Special Issue): S3–S26.

Staw, B. M., Sandelands, L. E., and Dutton, J. E. (1981). 'Threat-Rigidity Effects in Organizational Behavior: A Multi-Level Analysis,' *Administrative Science Quarterly*, 26: 510–24.

Steffy, B. and Grimes, A. (1992). 'Personnel/Organizational Psychology: A Critique of the Discipline,' in M. Alvesson and H. Willmott (eds.), *Critical Management Studies*. London: Sage.

Stinchcombe, A. (1965). 'Social Structure and Organizations,' in J. G. March (ed.), *Handbook of Organizations*. Chicago: Rand McNally, pp. 142–93.

—— (1968a). *Constructing Social Theories*. New York: Harcourt, Brace, and World.

—— (1968b). 'The Logic of Scientific Inference,' in A. Stinchcombe (ed.) *Constructing Social Theories*. New York: Harcourt, Brace, and World.

Strang, D. and Macy, M. (2000). 'In Search of Excellence: Fads, Success Stories and Adaptive Evolution,' *American Journal of Sociology*, 107(1): 147–82.

Strauss, A. L. (1987). *Qualitative Analysis for Social Scientists*. New York: Cambridge University Press.

Strauss, A. and Corbin, J. (1990). *Basics of Qualitative Research: Grounded Theory Procedures and Techniques*. Newbury Park, CA: Sage.

—— —— (1994). 'Grounded Theory,' in N. Denzin and Y. Lincoln (eds.), *Handbook of Qualitative Research*. Thousand Oaks, CA: Sage.

Suchman, E. A. (1967). *Evaluation Research: Principles and Practice in Public Service and Social Action Programs*. New York: Russell Sage Foundation.

—— (1971). 'Action for What? A Critique of Evaluative Research,' in R. O'Toole (ed.), *The Organization, Management, and Tactics of Social Research*. Cambridge, MA: Schenkman Publishing Company, Inc., pp. 97–130.

Suppe, F. (1977). *The Structure of Scientific Theories*, 2nd edn. Urbana, IL: University of Illinois Press.

—— (1989). *The Semantic Conception of Theories and Scientific Realism*. Urbana, IL: University of Illinois Press.

Thompson, J. D. (1956). 'On Building an Administrative Science,' *Administrative Science Quarterly*, 1: 102–11.

Thorngate, W. (1976). 'Possible Limits on a Science of Social Behavior,' in J. H. Strickland, F. E. Aboud, and K. J. Gergen (eds.), *Social Psychology in Transition*. New York: Plenum, pp. 121–39.

Toulmin, S. (1953). *The Philosophy of Science: An Introduction*. London: Hutchinson.

—— (1958). *The Uses of Argument*, 1st edn. Cambridge: Cambridge University Press.

—— (2003). *The Uses of Argument*, 5th edn. Cambridge: Cambridge University Press.

Tranfield, D. and Starkey, K. (1998). 'The Nature, Social Organization and Promotion of Management Research: Towards Policy,' *British Journal of Management*, 9: 341–53.

—— Denyer, D., and Smart, P. (2003). 'Towards a Methodology for Developing Evidence-Informed Management Knowledge by Means of Systematic Review,' *British Journal of Management*, 14(3): 207–22.

Trullen, J. and Bartunek, J. M. (2006). 'What a Design Approach Offers to Organization Development,' *Journal of Applied Behavioral Science*, forthcoming.

Tsoukas, H. (1989). 'The Validity of Idiographic Research Explanations,' *Academy of Management Review*, 14: 551–61.

Tsoukas, H. (2005). *Complex Knowledge: Studies in Organizational Epistemology.* Oxford: Oxford University Press.

Tuma, N. B. and Hannan, M. T. (1984). *Social Dynamics: Models and Methods.* San Diego, CA: Academic Press.

Tushman, M. and Romanelli, E. (1985). 'Organizational Evolution: A Metamorphosis Model of Convergence and Reorientation,' in B. Staw and L. Cummings (eds.), *Research in Organizational Behavior.* Greenwich, CT: JAI Press.

—— O'Reilly, C. A., Fenollosa, A., and Kleinbaum, A. M. (2007). 'Towards Relevance and Rigor: Executive Education as a Lever in Shaping Practice and Research,' *Academy of Management Learning & Education*, forthcoming.

Van Aken, J. E. (2005). 'Management Research as a Design Science: Articulating the Research Products of Mode 2 Knowledge Production in Management,' *British Journal of Management*, 16: 19–36.

Van de Ven, A. H. (1992). 'Suggestions for Studying Strategy Process: A Research Note,' *Strategic Management Journal*, 13(Summer): 169–88.

—— (2002). '2001 Presidential Address: Strategic Directions for the Academy of Management: This Academy is for You!' *Academy of Management Review*, 27(2): 171–84.

—— Delbecq, A. (1974). 'The Effectiveness of Nominal, Delphi, and Interacting Group Decision Making Processes,' *Academy of Management Journal*, 17(4): 605–21.

—— Ferry, D. L. (1980). *Measuring and Assessing Organizations.* New York: John Wiley & Sons.

—— Huber, G. P. (1990). 'Longitudinal Field Research Methods for Studying Processes of Organizational Change,' *Organization Science*, 1: 213–19.

—— Johnson, P. (2006). 'Knowledge for Science and Practice,' *Academy of Management Review*, 31(4): 802–21.

—— Polley, D. E. (1992). 'Learning While Innovating,' *Organization Science*, 3: 92–116.

—— Poole, M. S. (1995). 'Explaining Development and Change in Organizations,' *Academy of Management Review*, 20: 510–40.

—— —— (2005). 'Alternative Approaches for Studying Organization Change,' *Organization Studies* 26(9): 1377–400.

—— Schomaker, M. (2002). 'The Rhetoric of Evidence-Based Medicine,' *Health Care Management Review*, 27(3): 88–90.

—— Polley, D. E., Garud, R., and Venkataraman, S. (1999). *The Innovation Journey.* New York: Oxford University Press.

—— Angle, H. L., and Poole, M. S. (eds.) (2000). *Research on the Management of Innovation: The Minnesota Studies.* New York: Oxford University Press.

Van den Daele, L. D. (1969). 'Qualitative Models in Developmental Analysis,' *Developmental Psychology*, 1(4): 303–10.

—— (1974). 'Infrastructure and Transition in Developmental Analysis,' *Human Development*, 17: 1–23.

Van Maanen, J. (1995). *Representation in Ethnography.* Thousand Oaks, CA: Sage.

—— Barley, S. R. (1986). 'Occupational Communities: Culture and Control in Organizations,' in L. Cummings and B. Staw (eds.), *Research in Organizational Behavior.* Greenwich, CT: JAI Press, pp. 287–531.

Volkema, R. J. (1983). 'Problem Formulation in Planning and Design,' *Management Science*, 29(6): 639–52.

—— (1995). 'Creativity in MS/OR: Managing the Process of Formulating the Process of Formulating the Problem,' *Interfaces*, 25(3): 81–7.

Wacker, J. G. (2004). 'A Theory of Formal Conceptual Definitions: Developing Theory-Building Measurement Instruments,' *Journal of Operations Management*, 22(6): 629–50.

Wallace, W. A. (1983). *From a Realist Point of View: Essays on the Philosophy of Science*, 2nd edn. Lantham, MD: Catholic University Press of America.

Walster, W. and Cleary, T. A. (1970). 'Statistical Significance as a Decision Rule,' in E. Borgatta and G. Bohrnsteadt (eds.), *Sociological Methodology*. San Francisco: Jossey-Bass.

Walton, D. (2004). 'A New Dialectical Theory of Explanation,' *Philosophical Explorations*, 7(1): 71–89.

Wanberg, C. R., Glomb, T. M., Song, Z., and Rosol, S. (2005). 'Job-Search Persistence During Unemployment: A Ten Wave Longitudinal Study,' *Journal of Applied Psychology*, 90: 411–30.

Webb, E. J., Campbell, D. T., Schwartz, R. D., and Sechrest, L. 1966. *Unobtrusive Measures*. Chicago: Rand McNally.

Weick, K. E. (1979). *The Social Psychology of Organizing*, 2nd edn. Reading, MA: Addison-Wesley Publishing Co.

—— (1989). 'Theory Construction as Disciplined Imagination,' *Academy of Management Review*, 14(4): 516–31.

—— (1992). 'Agenda Setting in Organizational Behavior: A Theory-Focused Approach,' *Journal of Management Inquiry*, 1(3): 171–82.

—— (1995). *Sensemaking in Organizations*. Thousand Oaks, CA: Sage.

—— (1999). 'Theory Construction as Disciplined Reflexivity: Tradeoffs in the 90s,' *Academy of Management Review*, 24(4): 797–806.

—— (2001). 'Gapping the Relevance Bridge: Fashions Meet Fundamental in Management Research,' *British Journal of Management*, 12(Special Issue): S71–S75.

—— (2005). 'The Experience of Theorizing: Sensemaking as Topic and Resource,' in K. G. Smith and M. A. Hitt (eds.), *Great Minds in Management: The Process of Theory Development*. Oxford: Oxford University Press, pp. 394–413.

Weiss, C. H. (1998). *Evaluation: Methods of Studying Programs and Policies*, 2nd edn. Upper Saddle River, NJ: Prentice Hall.

Weston, A. (2000). *A Rulebook for Arguments*, 3rd edn. Indianapolis: Hackett Publishing Company.

Westphal, K. W. (1998). *Pragmatism, Reason, and Norms: A Realistic Assessment*. New York: Fordham University Press.

Wheelwright, B. (1962). *Metaphor and Reality*. Bloomington, IN: Indiana University Press.

Whetten, D. A. (1989). What Constitutes a Theoretical Contribution? *Academy of Management Review*, 14, 490–5.

—— (2002). 'Modeling-as-Theorizing: A Systematic Approach,' in D. Partington (ed.), *Essential Skills for Management Research*. Thousand Oaks, CA: Sage Publications.

Whitley, R. (1984). 'The Scientific Status of Management Research as a Practically-Oriented Social Science,' *Journal of Management Studies*, 21(4): 369–90.

Whitley, R. (2000). *The Intellectual and Social Organization of the Sciences*, 2nd edn. Oxford: Oxford University Press.

Whyte, W. F. (1984). *Learning from the Field: A Guide from Experience.* Beverly Hills, CA: Sage.

Willett, J. B. and Singer, J. D. (1991). 'How Long did it Take? Using Survival Analysis in Educational and Psychological Research,' in L. M. Collins and J. L. Horn (eds.), *Best Methods for the Analysis of Change.* Washington, DC: American Psychological Association, pp. 310–28.

Wilson, E. O. (1999). *Concilience.* New York: Prentice Hall.

Yin, R. K. (2003). *Case Study Research: Design and Methods*, 3rd edn. Thousand Oaks, CA: Sage.

Yu, J. (2006). 'One Size Does Not Fit All: Toward an Understanding of Local Adaptation of Organizational Practices in Cross-Boundary Practice Transfers,' unpublished doctoral dissertation proposal, University of Minnesota, Carlson School of Management, Minneapolis, MN.

Zaheer, S., Albert, S., and Zaheer, A. (1999). 'Time Scales and Organizational Theory,' *Academy of Management Review*, 24(4): 725–41.

Zald, M. N. (1995). 'Progress and Cumulation in the Human Sciences after the Fall,' *Sociological Forum*, 10(3): 455–79.

Zellmer-Bruhn, M. E. (2003). 'Interruptive Events and Team Knowledge Acquisition,' *Management Science*, 49(4): 514–28.

Zlotkowski, E. (ed.) (1997–2000). *AAHE's Series on Service-Learning in the Disciplines.* Washington, DC: American Association for Higher Education.

☐ INDEX

Lightning Source UK Ltd.
Milton Keynes UK
UKOW06f1003290315

248681UK00002B/2/P